A COMPLETE GUIDE

6TH EDITION

THE ADIRONDACK BOOK

Annie Stoltie and Elizabeth Folwell

The Countryman Press
Woodstock, Vermont

ISBN 978-1-58157-085-4

Cover photo of Mirror Lake, Lake Placid © Nancie Battaglia

Cover and interior photos by the author unless otherwise specified

Book design by Bodenweber Design

Composition by Opaque Design & Print Production

Maps by Mapping Specialists Ltd., Madison, WI, © The Countryman Press

Published by The Countryman Press, P.O. Box 748, Woodstock, Vermont 05091

Distributed by W. W. Norton & Company, Inc., 500 Fifth Avenue, New York, NY 10110

Manufactured in the United States of America

10 9 8 7 6 5 4 3 2 1

THE ADIRONDACK BOOK

THE NARROWS, LAKE GEORGE—THE QUEEN OF AMERICAN LAKES.
Delaware & Hudson Railroad.

Copyright, 1899, by H. C. Brown, 156 Fifth Avenue, N. Y.

View of the Narrows, Lake George, circa 1899, from a Delaware & Hudson Railroad brochure. Private collection

GREAT DESTINATIONS TRAVEL GUIDEBOOK SERIES

Recommended by *National Geographic Traveler* and *Travel + Leisure* magazines.

[A] CRISP AND CRITICAL APPROACH, FOR TRAVELERS WHO WANT TO LIVE LIKE LOCALS.
— *USA Today*

Great Destinations™ guidebooks are known for their comprehensive, critical coverage of regions of extraordinary cultural interest and natural beauty. The authors in this series are professional travel writers who have lived for many years in the regions they describe. Each title in this series is continuously updated with each printing to insure accurate and timely information. All the books contain more than one hundred photographs and maps.

Current titles available:

THE ADIRONDACK BOOK

ATLANTA

AUSTIN, SAN ANTONIO
& THE TEXAS HILL COUNTRY

THE BERKSHIRE BOOK

BERMUDA

BIG SUR, MONTEREY BAY
& GOLD COAST WINE COUNTRY

CAPE CANAVERAL, COCOA BEACH
& FLORIDA'S SPACE COAST

THE CHARLESTON, SAVANNAH
& COASTAL ISLANDS BOOK

THE CHESAPEAKE BAY BOOK

THE COAST OF MAINE BOOK

COLORADO'S CLASSIC MOUNTAIN TOWNS:
GREAT DESTINATIONS

THE FINGER LAKES BOOK

THE FOUR CORNERS REGION

GALVESTON, SOUTH PADRE ISLAND
& THE TEXAS GULF COAST

THE HAMPTONS BOOK

HONOLULU & OAHU:
GREAT DESTINATIONS HAWAII

THE HUDSON VALLEY BOOK

THE JERSEY SHORE: ATLANTIC CITY TO
CAPE MAY (INCLUDES THE WILDWOODS)

LAS VEGAS

LOS CABOS & BAJA CALIFORNIA SUR:
GREAT DESTINATIONS MEXICO

MICHIGAN'S UPPER PENINSULA

MONTREAL & QUEBEC CITY:
GREAT DESTINATIONS CANADA

THE NANTUCKET BOOK

THE NAPA & SONOMA BOOK

NORTH CAROLINA'S OUTER BANKS
& THE CRYSTAL COAST

PALM BEACH, MIAMI & THE FLORIDA KEYS

PHOENIX, SCOTTSDALE, SEDONA
& CENTRAL ARIZONA

PLAYA DEL CARMEN, TULUM & THE RIVIERA
MAYA: GREAT DESTINATIONS MEXICO

SALT LAKE CITY, PARK CITY, PROVO
& UTAH'S HIGH COUNTRY RESORTS

SAN DIEGO & TIJUANA

SAN JUAN, VIEQUES & CULEBRA:
GREAT DESTINATIONS PUERTO RICO

THE SANTA FE & TAOS BOOK

THE SARASOTA, SANIBEL ISLAND
& NAPLES BOOK

THE SEATTLE & VANCOUVER BOOK: INCLUDES
THE OLYMPIC PENINSULA, VICTORIA & MORE

THE SHENANDOAH VALLEY BOOK

TOURING EAST COAST WINE COUNTRY

WASHINGTON, D.C., AND NORTHERN VIRGINIA

YELLOWSTONE & GRAND TETON NATIONAL PARKS
AND JACKSON HOLE

YOSEMITE & THE SOUTHERN SIERRA NEVADA

If you are traveling to, moving to, residing in, or just interested in any (or all!) of these enchanting regions, a Great Destinations guidebook is a superior companion. Honest and painstakingly critical, full of information only a local can provide, Great Destinations guidebooks give you all the practical knowledge you need to enjoy the best of each region. Why not own them all?

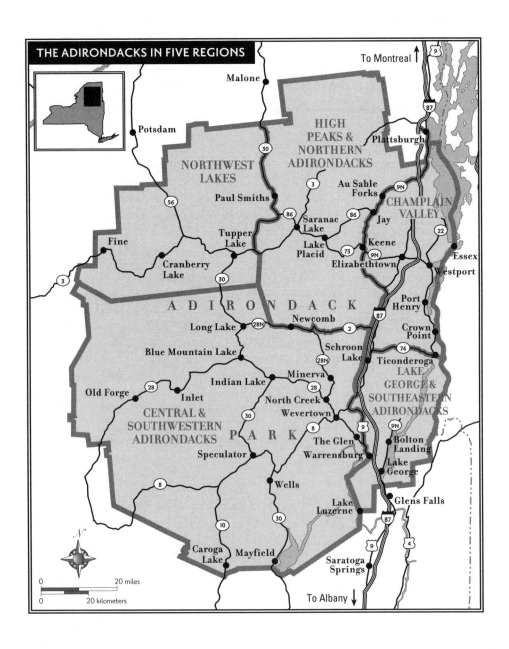

THE ADIRONDACKS IN FIVE REGIONS

To Montreal

Malone

Potsdam

HIGH PEAKS & NORTHERN ADIRONDACKS

Plattsburgh

NORTHWEST LAKES

Paul Smiths

Au Sable Forks

CHAMPLAIN VALLEY

Fine

Tupper Lake

Saranac Lake

Jay

Keene

Cranberry Lake

Lake Placid

Essex

Elizabethtown

Westport

A D I R O N D A C K

Port Henry

Long Lake

Newcomb

Crown Point

Blue Mountain Lake

Schroon Lake

Old Forge

Indian Lake

Minerva

Ticonderoga

Inlet

North Creek

LAKE GEORGE & SOUTHEASTERN ADIRONDACKS

CENTRAL & SOUTHWESTERN ADIRONDACKS

Wevertown

P A R K

The Glen

Bolton Landing

Speculator

Warrensburg

Lake George

Wells

Glens Falls

Lake Luzerne

Caroga Lake

Mayfield

Saratoga Springs

To Albany

0   20 miles

0   20 kilometers

Contents

7

RECREATION
A Land for All Seasons
211

8

SHOPPING
Woodsy Whimsy to Practical Gear
277

9

INFORMATION
Nuts, Bolts, and Free Advice
315

10

IF TIME IS SHORT
329

MAPS

ACKNOWLEDGMENTS

This book is really the offspring of Elizabeth "Betsy" Folwell. For more than three decades she's explored every pocket of this great park, all the while—fortunately for us—compiling her favorite dining hot spots, cross-country ski routes, tchotchke boutiques, spaces to see art, places to hear tunes or catch some zzzzs, appreciate a sunset, you name it. Betsy's extensive travels, meticulous notes, and indefatigable attention to detail led to the first edition of *The Adirondack Book*, in 1992, giving visitors endless insider info about this region. Today, completely updated and now with a chapter devoted to the park's gateway cities Saratoga Springs and Glens Falls, this book is still the next best thing to an audience with Betsy herself.

Since 2000 I've had the pleasure of working with Betsy at *Adirondack Life* magazine, and have been lucky enough to assist her on the fifth edition of *The Adirondack Book* and now this, the sixth edition. Her uncompromising editorial standards, patience, and good humor make Betsy an incredible mentor. She's a dear friend, too. I thank you, Betsy. Tom Warrington, Betsy's husband, also deserves a thank you for his input and understanding—I occupied an inordinate amount of Betsy's free time—consequently, Tom and Betsy time—with phone calls and lengthy e-mails.

Betsy and I are grateful to our Lake George connection, John Strong and Laura VonRosk; our Champlain Valley friends Michelle Maron and Libby Treadwell; High Peaks heroes Mike Gile and Nicole Crist; the Saranac Lake crew of Kelly Hofschneider, Ned Rauch, and Mary Thill; and Queensbury specialist Jane Mackintosh. A very special thank you goes to Amy Godine, of Saratoga Springs, whose discernable taste buds helped guide us in Chapter 3, and whose great knowledge and snappy writing makes Adirondack history fresh and exciting in Chapter 1. Thanks, too, to Angela Donnelly, at the Adirondack Museum, and Ted Comstock, of Saranac Lake, for their assistance with historic images. Kelly Kilgallon and Mark Bowie deserve our appreciation for their super photographs. And finally, enormous gratitude goes to my husband, Drew Sprague, for his patience and encouragement—all those meals out while I scribbled notes, times I asked him to stop the car so I could snap a photo, months and months of escorting me to concerts, plays, galleries, lectures, libraries, and community suppers. In Drew I have a loyal and enthusiastic companion—that goes for guidebook stuff and beyond.

—Annie Stoltie

INTRODUCTION

New York's Adirondack Park is a big park: bigger than Yellowstone and Yosemite put together and larger than any of the national parks in the lower 48. This park is better than national parks in many ways, too. You don't pay an entry fee when you cross the so-called Blue Line, the park's boundary; you don't need a permit to hike, climb a mountain, canoe, or explore the backcountry. People make this park their home and have lived here for many generations, giving this region a distinctive culture and offering an array of services to visitors.

The park has a year-round population of about 130,000 residents, and covers six million acres, about the size of the state of Vermont. Land owned by New York State—the Adirondack Forest Preserve—is about 2.5 million acres, and large landowners own another million acres and contribute significantly to the forested landscape and the local economy.

Through the years we've enjoyed visiting many different communities, exploring wild places, and learning about the region. Although the territory appears timeless, human endeavors change frequently. That's the impetus behind the sixth edition of *The Adirondack Book*—to supply information about new places and updates on classic spots. We hope that these pages encourage you to explore this great place.

—Annie Stoltie and Elizabeth Folwell

THE WAY THIS BOOK WORKS

To cover the Adirondack region, there are 10 chapters in this book—History, Transportation, Gateway Cities, Lodging, Culture, Restaurants and Food Purveyors, Recreation, Shopping, and Information—and many maps and indexes. Within each of these chapters, you'll find a subheading—"Fishing," for example—and under that topic is general information that's true for the whole park. Then specific services and businesses are grouped geographically by region: Lake George and Southeastern Adirondacks, Champlain Valley, High Peaks and Northern Adirondacks, Northwest Lakes, and Central and Southwestern Adirondacks. Towns are listed alphabetically in the regions. So, Bolton Landing may be the first town listed in the Lake George area, and pertinent businesses in that town will then be listed alphabetically. Other guidebooks group topics and subheads within separate chapters that represent each geographical area, but this approach would be a disservice to those visiting the Adirondacks. Here, it's not unusual to spend a day in multiple regions: perhaps you'll pass a morning at the Natural History Museum of the Adirondacks, in Tupper Lake, grab lunch in Lake Placid, spend the evening at the theater in Westport, then stay the night in Keene Valley.

Although the third chapter, "Gateway Cities," includes travel information on two places that are outside the Blue Line, Saratoga Springs and Glens Falls are fascinating destinations in themselves. Because these cities have long been the civilized gateways to the great woods to the north, they deserve a place in this book. In this chapter you'll find descriptions of lodgings, museums, restaurants, and recreational opportunities available in both towns.

Throughout the book, many of the entries have information blocks listing phone numbers, Web sites, addresses (although many Adirondack hamlets are so rural, all that's available is the name of a street or route), and so forth. We've checked these facts as close to the book's publication date as possible, but businesses do change hands and change policies. It's always a good idea to call ahead—a long-distance call is a whole lot cheaper than a tank of gas.

For the same reason, you won't find specific prices listed for restaurants, lodgings, greens fees, and so forth; we indicated a range of prices, which you'll find at the beginnings of the chapters or directly under the specific heading. Lodging prices are based on a per-room rate, double occupancy, during the high season, so that we had a consistent standard for comparison; off-season and mid-week rates are generally cheaper. Restaurant price ratings show the cost of one meal including appetizer, entrée, and dessert, but not cocktails, wine, tax, or tip.

	Lodging	Dining
Very Inexpensive	Under $40 per night, double occupancy	
Inexpensive	40–$70	Up to $15
Moderate	$70–$100	$15–$20
Expensive	$100–$200	$20–$35
Very Expensive	Over $200	Over $35

Credit Cards are abbreviated as follows:

AE—American Express	DC—Diner's Club
CB—Carte Blanche	MC—Master Card
D—Discover Card	V—Visa

1

HISTORY

The People's Park

Planning a trip to the Adirondacks in northern New York? Bring a road map, bring your bug spray, and by all means bring this book. But above all, bring your love of mystery and your capacity for wonder, for nothing is exactly as it seems here, and a taste for contradiction can only sweeten your encounter with a park bigger than the state of Vermont. How is it, for example, that more than half of this so-called park is in private hands? What kind of park is that? Lakes and rivers, cataracts, and rugged peaks you were expecting, but weed-capped cones of hundred-year-old iron ore tailings? Wyoming-worthy dude ranches and a hundred little towns? You keep reading in your pocket history book that Native Americans never really *lived* here—a "trackless wilderness" it was known as—yet here's another two-room town museum with a display case full of local arrowheads and beads. You keep hearing about these fabulous Adirondack Great Camps, rustic summer compounds as imperial and capacious, some of them, as European duchies, and one or two even open for a tour. But nobody prepared you for the moody rows of former company housing in Lyon Mountain or the kitschy miniature golf courses of Lake George. You thought these mountains, woods, and moonlit bogs were about as far from multiethnic city life as you could get, yet here, lost on a back road, is an Irishtown, and there a Spanish Settlement Road, and farther west, in Tupper Lake, a synagogue built by eastern European immigrant peddlers before World War I.

As for the seemingly unchanging forest, that also tells a more problematic story than what first meets the eye. It turns out that your favorite view of Edenic woods was once, and not so long ago, a veritable moonscape of slash and dust and ugly stumps; the gin-clear stream where you saw a moose standing up to its knobby knees was once turbid with the stinking liquor of tannery waste.

The Adirondack forest primeval? Not exactly. "Forever wild" is only one small version of what's in store. There is also—and no less dramatically—the forest recovered and the forest redeemed, the forest

Even a century ago, the elements of an Adirondack vacation were the same as today: fresh air, clear lakes, and wild mountains. Boating party on the Ausable lakes. Courtesy of Keene Valley Library

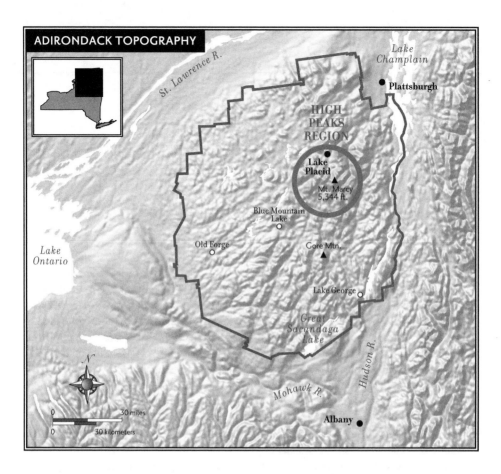

ADIRONDACK TOPOGRAPHY

industrial, and, sadly, the forest failing under the sour burden of acid rain. There is the Adirondacks of the solitary footpath lifting toward a rock-slick summit, and the rolling, easy Adirondacks that flanks the western shore of Lake Champlain, a mirror image of Vermont with its bosky apple orchards and tidy Yankee farmsteads. There is the watery, idyllic Adirondacks of the summer camp, and the Adirondacks of the boarded-over, passed-by village Main Street. Downstate politicians with a second home in Westport cherish one kind of Adirondacks. Sixth-generation Franco Americans juggling several backwoods jobs to keep afloat—maybe running a string of housekeeping cottages in the summer, doing a little wood chopping and some road work for the county—know and love another. Sometimes these Adirondacks intersect, but often they seem to belong to quite different, mutually uncomprehending worlds.

Of course, the region's greatest enduring mystery belongs to history. How did it come to pass that a vast swath of forest so relatively close to so many eastern cities was among the last in the lower 48 to gain the eye and expertise of the surveyor, cartographer, and lawmaker? Such marvelous proximity, and yet, for so long, so lightly valued and little known! So proudly venerable—yet so recent an addition to our pantheon of great parks! Like the proverbial girl next door who turns out to be a heart-stopping knockout, the Adirondack region has been, in terms of our appreciation of it, a very late bloomer. It took time for us to get wise to its rare beauty, time to learn to see and cherish the quiet treasure in our own backyard.

And maybe that's just as well, because the same forces that delayed a loving valuation of the region also stalled our rolling in and making an unholy hash of it (though the combined assault of extractive industries like mining, logging, and tanning took a hard toll). Start with the Native Americans, for whom the Champlain Valley corridor was long a borderland between hereditary enemies, the Iroquois and the Algonquin, or more particularly, the easternmost Iroquois tribe, the Mohawks, and from the other side of the lake, the Abenaki, westernmost of the wide-ranging Algonquins. Borderlands that double as sporadic war zones are no place to settle down, and permanent Native encampments were accordingly unknown. (Migratory visitations, on the other hand, have been going on for some 8,000 years, the summer-to-fall residency that accounts for those relics you'll keep seeing in the local village museum display case.)

The Adirondack region was not a draw for European settlers in the seventeenth and eighteenth centuries, when a distant, long-lived imperial conflict pitted the British Crown against the soldiers of New France in one bloody raid and skirmish after another, culminating, of course, in the French and Indian War. In the Champlain Valley, in particular, much more was at stake than a mere show of military muscle. Each nation was as hot to lay claim to this commercially strategic thoroughfare as it was keen to edge the other out. This key waterway (Lake Champlain and Lake George) was the conduit for the kind of abundant timber (including arrow-straight white pines that could mast a royal navy) that a wood-starved Europe hadn't seen for a century. It provided habitat and transport for enough furs to cloak all of gay Paris. Indeed, whosoever ruled these waters owned the markets that lined the royal purse. The upshot of this imperial conflict for the Adirondacks was inevitable. The eastern region on the west flank of Lake Champlain gained a reputation of, if not a full-blown war zone, at least a pretty darned dicey place to settle. And so, for the first two thirds or so of the eighteenth century, settlers stayed away.

Or mostly. In 1730, soldier-farmers from New France colonized a settlement on the west side of Lake Champlain where the banks are close as pincers. Fort Saint Frederic, at present-day Crown Point, thrived for another thirty years, time enough for the French pioneers to raise families; build a trading post, mill, and chapel; and befriend the traveling bands of Native Americans. But in 1758, hearing of the imminent approach of British troops under the tireless Lord Jeffrey Amherst, the French homemakers of the region's first European enclave destroyed their Adirondack Roanoke and fled to Canada, leaving the charred remains to be rebuilt and reinvented as His Majesty's massive fort, Crown Point.

The French and Indian War also gave American and British soldiers their first glimpse of this virgin wilderness, and some of them liked what they saw well enough to come back at the conflict's end. Bands of Quakers found the region, too, and gave Quaker names to several early settlements in the southern and eastern Adirondacks, among them, Wing's Falls, later called Glens Falls, the bustling mill town at the Adirondack's southeastern edge. Laboring under the delusion that the underpopulated Adirondack region might somehow escape the ever-growing tension between native-born Americans grown restive under British rule and those loyal to the Crown, the peaceable Quakers were in for a rude surprise. Once again, during the American Revolution and for some years after, the eastern Adirondack corridor between Montreal and Saratoga emerged as a bloody frontier warpath, and settlers hunkered down at their peril.

Among the ranks of the veterans who were nonetheless attracted to this dangerous frontier were many Scots, survivors of the Highlander regiments that fought with fabled valor at Lake George and Fort Ticonderoga. In the southern Adirondacks, Sir William

Johnson, the high-living Irish-born veteran and brilliant liaison between the Iroquois and the British Crown, bought himself a sweet chunk of real estate from the British-allied Mohawks and set about parlaying his riverside homestead into a wilderness fiefdom worthy of Joseph Conrad's Kurtz. (Proud local legends insist that the tireless Johnson sired 700 progeny, donned a kilt with his Scottish Highlander immigrant tenants, and reveled with the Mohawk braves who routinely camped and feasted on his baronial front lawns.) But the Johnson family was pro-British, and when William Johnson died and the patriotic fever of the Revolution took the Mohawk Valley by storm, his sons exiled

In 1609, Samuel de Champlain sailed down the lake that now bears his name. Near present-day Ticonderoga, his troops and their Algonquin guides overpowered the resident Iroquois, continuing the age-old enmity between the native groups.
Courtesy of Cornell University Library

themselves to Canada, their faithful Scottish tenants with them, and the old man's upstate kingdom was seized and broken up, never to be restored.

Johnson wasn't the only land baron to lose his hard-won Adirondack empire to the winds of revolution. The Scotsman Sir Philip Skene sowed his fertile corner of the Adirondacks near today's Whitehall (formerly Skenesborough) with sawmills, iron forges, settlers, and his own small crew of African American slaves. Sir William Gilliland, a Scots–Irish immigrant and, like Skene and Johnson, a veteran of His Majesty's Forces, set his dogged sights on the "howling wilderness" (his words) at the mouth of the Boquet River, near Willsboro (which he named for himself). Come the Revolution, the exiled Skene saw his shipyard seized, his slaves dispersed, and his pioneering iron forges used to fashion the cannonballs that stalled the British navy at the Battle of Valcour. Gilliland should have had better luck: He, at least, backed the winning party, even feeding 3,000 shell-shocked American soldiers in weary retreat from a disastrous foray into Canada. But patriot or not, Gilliland's grand feudal ambitions were ill suited to the democratic temper of his times. Benedict Arnold (of all people!) charged Gilliland with treason: Gilliland went to jail, lost his holdings and his farms to marauding Loyalists, landed in debtor's prison, and wound up freezing to death in the Adirondack woods, leaving a handful of Adirondack villages to honor his good work with Gilliland family names.

The ill-starred, quixotic sagas of these dreamy speculators have dominated the pages of most Adirondack histories. To the names of Johnson, Gilliland, and Skene, add Alexander Macomb, brief owner in 1791 of almost four million Adirondack acres; add the Rhode Island merchant John Brown, whose "tract" would encompass much of today's park before it reverted to New York State for taxes; add John Thurman, the New York City businessman who recruited Scottish pioneers to the region near the village that bears his name today. Little wonder we should still be fascinated: Their stories make such satisfying copy. The energetic Thurman: gored to death in his prime by a bull! The ever-hopeful Brown (who named his ghostly, never-settled townships things like Frugality, Sobriety, and Perseverance) lost his land agent, a son-in-law, to suicide, and his holdings to the state! The impecunious Macomb who wound up in debtors' prison, half mad!

More enduring, if less flamboyantly dramatic, was the experience of the nameless pioneers who discovered the region in the half century or so after the Revolution when a close-to-bankrupt New York State took over the crown lands of the northern wilderness and sold upstate parcels by the thousands. Only then did the region see anything like a real influx of settlers, many of them veterans of the Continental Army. In they poured from the worked-over, exhausted hill farms of New England, and it wasn't long—maybe a decade, maybe two—before sod huts and log shanties donned neat suits of locally milled clapboard, and every crossroads settlement could boast an inn, tavern, and makeshift church. Historians call it the Yankee Migration, and Puritan-descended Yankees these land-starved settlers mostly were. But there were Hessians, too, and bands of Scots–Irish from northern Ireland, and once again Quakers trickling northward from the Hudson Valley, and coming south after 1816, both French and Anglo Canadian homesteaders looking to make a fresh start after the quashing of the failed Canadian Rebellion.

Some came of their own accord, others in response to the propagandistic broadsides and handbills of land agents working for downstate speculators—speculators who had every reason to assume their settler-tenants would improve the value of their investment with each swing of the ax, even when they failed to pay rent or give over a portion of their crops. This time-honored colonial strategy had worked well enough elsewhere along the Eastern seaboard. What went wrong up here? Why did one Adirondack empire after another fail to prosper?

It is true that many of these so-called harpy land barons would not live on or anywhere near their tracts, and not a few tenant farmers chafed under the high-handed, semifeudal expectations of their absentee landlords. But far more demoralizing than a long-distance landlord was the daily, blunt, implacable resistance of the terrain. If it wasn't the bitter thinness of the Adirondack soil (a few lush river valleys aside), it was the length and harshness of the winters, the stinginess of the growing season, the roughness of the topography, or the dread ferocity of predators—wolves and panthers, bugs and bears. Nor was the situation eased by the absence of transportation routes that might have eased the settlers' transition from subsistence to a market economy. What did it profit them to grow the sweetest hops, the fattest turnips, the reddest apples in their township, if they lacked wagon route or railhead or boat landing to get their crops to market? To be sure, there were snug farming settlements in places as far-flung as Lake Placid and Lake Luzerne, but once other options were open (tourism, especially), agriculture as the prime force of the local economy quickly took a backseat.

The fact that the nineteenth-century Adirondack region was unvisited by marauding bands of horse-borne, painted Natives, or masked banditos, has made it hard for us to see it as a frontier territory every bit as dangerous and seemingly remote as the highlands of New Mexico or Arizona, but this is surely how it felt to the first lonely, forest-bound pioneers. As Adirondack cultural historian Philip Terrie has observed, "The only thing that distinguished the Adirondacks from western frontier regions was that exploitation of local riches—real or imaginary—did not involve the removal or slaughter of indigenous peoples."

Everybody knew the Adirondacks was no place for a farmer with any kind of means. Settlers moved there mostly when they couldn't afford better pickings elsewhere. But how many of these hopeful pioneers could guess at a glance that such fair-seeming country could make a poor man poorer still? Little wonder that so many from this first generation of Adirondack pioneers pushed on to greener pastures farther west when the Erie Canal opened for business in 1825, or hastened home to long-settled New England. At the same time, as the rough reality of Adirondack climate and topography eroded the Jeffersonian dreamscape of a thousand well-tended, self-sufficient little farms, another kind of vision cast its own enduring spell—the view of the Adirondack woodlands not as a hindrance to a farmer's fortune but as a fortune in itself, rich as Croesus in the two crops that are the bane of any farmer's existence: namely, tall trees and big rocks thickly seamed with iron ore.

It wasn't that these native crops weren't right there for the harvesting all along or that the colonists and the Native Americans before them were unmindful of them. But in 1700, what New Hampshire homesteader was thinking about the red spruce of the Adirondack interior? All the timber a colonist could hope for was right there in the back forty. It would take the depletion of the New England and southern New York forests to force a deeper move into northern New York, an advance that only quickened as innovations in the woods industries made it easier to get trees out. In the early 1800s, legislation that declared New York rivers public highways launched the great age of the Adirondack river drive. By mid-century fast-running Adirondack rivers—the Saranac, the Grasse, the Schroon, the Hudson—were sometimes so densely shingled over with floating logs a skilled river driver could hop from log to log for half a mile with nary a glimpse of the water roiling beneath.

By 1850 New York State led the nation in timber production. Tiny sawmills that once catered to the basic needs of pioneers now shipped and sledded their product north to Canada or south to Albany. The feudal land baron was supplanted by the capitalist lumber baron, and the homesteader once as game to burn a tree as look at it now added skilled logger or river driver to his resume. Every tree, it seemed, had its use: white pine and red spruce for ships' masts and house construction; hardwood for charcoal; hemlock for the bark whose tannin-rich liquor was essential in the curing of leather, a particularly vital Adirondack industry from 1860 to 1880. In the last two decades of the 19th century, the shift from rags to wood pulp in the papermaking industry brought a whole new world of trees into the loggers' line of fire. Pulp-grinding machinery didn't care how straight or true or old or long the wood it used. Cellulose fiber did the trick, and trees as skinny as 3 inches round were fair game.

As for that other bumper Adirondack crop, iron ore, it too owned a hearty appetite for vast stands of wood. Ore was so abundant in the northeastern Adirondacks you could see it plainly in the outcrops along Lake Champlain, and so famously pure, some of it, you could work it fresh from the seam. Better than 200 forges operated in the nineteenth-century Adirondacks, almost half of them along the iron-russet banks of two Adirondack rivers, the Ausable and the Saranac. Of the scores of remote hamlets that owed their founding to these charcoal-hungry forges, many are now ghost towns or little more than a cluster of leafy sinkholes in the woods, but in 1850, New York State led the nation in iron ore production. The lumber barons who had overtaken the "harpy land barons" were now joined in their pursuit of wood by mining magnates, whose prolific crews of woodchoppers and colliers (charcoal makers) kept their forges bright with burning charcoal. Thanks to those mining magnates, the Adirondack forest suffered its first scarifying clear-cut. Indeed, it was the mining industry, much more than lumbering, that did so much to load the quills of illustrators whose before-and-after engravings of the Adirondacks (virgin, then denuded) in magazines like Harper's and Frank Leslie's Illustrated Weekly, spurred an outraged readership to support the notion of an Adirondack forest preserve. Consider: It took two and a quarter cords of wood to make 100 bushels of charcoal, and up to 500 bushels of charcoal to generate a ton of Adirondack ore. The hills were alive with the sound of crashing hardwoods. Music to some ears, perhaps, but to others, an infernal racket.

As industrialization stepped up the demand for the extractive products of the northern

Adirondack rivers were declared highways so that logs could travel freely downstream to cities like Glens Falls and Lyons Falls. Courtesy of Ted Comstock, Saranac Lake

New York wilderness—tanbark, logs, pulpwood, ore—settlers found plenty of pick-up work to buttress the meager output from their hardscrabble farms. And a good thing, too: the flexible, seasonally responsive diversification of the Adirondack home economy—a potato farm in the summer, a logging gig in the winter, a little hauling, a little millwork, a job guiding city fishermen to favorite streams—was the key to survival, and this tradition, long honored by migratory bands of Native Americans, defines the Adirondack lifestyle even now.

But when local hands proved too few to meet the labor needs of fast-growing mining towns, tannery hamlets, and logging camps, another source of labor was introduced: immigrants and migratory workers. To an extent, different industries generated different ethnic enclaves. Irish immigrants, for example, were often drawn to tannery towns. French Canadians worked in the woods, Italians on the railroad tracks, Poles and Lithuanians in the mines. But no single ethnic group monopolized any single industry to the exclusion of any other. St. Regis Mohawk Indians worked on river drives and in Adirondack tanneries as well. In Lyon Mountain, Witherbee, or Mineville, eastern European miners worked cheek by jowl with Italians, Spaniards, Irish laborers, and African Americans; indeed, the first iron miners in the Adirondacks were the land baron Philip Skene's black slaves. The logging camp at Wanakena featured a Swedish sauna, and up near Chazy an encampment of Italian stonemasons built themselves a hive-shaped bread oven in the woods.

Because these rough-hewn, company-built settlements rose and dispersed with the success and decline of the industries that founded them, their story has excited little notice among Adirondack historians. If anything, the Adirondacks has enjoyed a certain nativist reputation as a demographic land apart, free and clear of "outsiders," the monolithic stronghold of the Yankee pioneer. But northern New York was never exempt from the demographic trends that salted so much of rural America with ethnic enclaves during the great age of industrialization. If a migratory lifestyle deprived many of these immigrant communities of a place in the written historical record, you can still trace the evidence of an ethnic presence in the tongue-twisting nomenclature of early headstones, the sunken remains of one-time railroad tracks, the French or Irish street names in Adirondack towns.

Old Rocks, New Mountains

The rocks beneath Adirondack peaks and valleys were formed from sediments laid down in shallow seas some 1.3 billion years ago. Though that sounds like a tranquil enough beginning, the intervening millennia between the Grenville period and modern times was a chaotic riot of rumpling, folding, shearing, compressing, cracking, and colliding. Himalayan-like peaks rose, then were beaten down by weather and wave; the land was then stretched and cloven as continents crashed into one another. The metamorphic rocks we walk on today, atop Mount Marcy or even along a southern Adirondack stream, were once buried 15 to 20 miles beneath the surface.

Today's mountain ranges, though, were ultimately shaped by the scraping action of a mile-thick glacier 10,000-plus years ago. This moving wall of ice took the jagged peaks down to their hardest bedrock, deposited sand as sinuous eskers, and left behind giant boulders—erratics—as calling cards. The Adirondack Mountains are rising still, reaching up at a rate of 2 to 3 centimeters a year, about the length of Lincoln's nose on a penny, thanks to a hot spot deep within the Earth.

From the high points of land, hundreds of rivers drain north into the St. Lawrence River, east to Lake Champlain, and south to the Hudson and Mohawk Valleys. Lakes often fill the ancient fault valleys, in diagonal lines between the mountains.

Previously jagged High Peaks were smoothed off by glacial ice thousands of years ago. Courtesy of Mark Bowie

Not every nineteenth-century Adirondack railroad spur bore carloads full of hemlock bark or iron ore, pulpwood, or massive logs. Some were built specially to ferry a special cargo *to* the woods: namely, the sightseers and "city sports" for whom, from 1870 to 1910 or so, a visit to the distant Adirondacks held all the exotic cachet of an African safari. The burgeoning resort scene was an inevitable extension of the "Grand Tour" of the North Country that already encompassed toney Saratoga Springs and elegant Lake George. And where railroad sleepers left off, stagecoaches and steamboats picked up—another source of seasonal employment for enterprising locals, some who would parlay modest stagecoach routes into backwoods transportation empires.

Ads, Dacks, and Adirondacks

The word *Adirondack* reportedly comes from an Iroquois word that means "they eat bark," an insult referring to the Algonquin's allegedly lousy woodcraft skills. That can't be proven, though (neither their ineptitude nor the etymology); using romantic Native-sounding words has long been a favorite pastime of mapmakers, writers, and even politicians. What can be defined are some North Country specifics:

The Adirondack Park: Established in 1892, it covers 6.1 million acres of public and private land in a shield shape that includes much of the northern third of New York State. It's the largest state park in the nation. It's not all wilderness: Everything within, from the summits of the highest peaks to the most remote bog to Main Street in Lake Placid, is in the park.

The Adirondack Forest Preserve: Established in 1885, this is about 42 percent of the Adirondack Park that is public land, and preserved as wilderness, wild forest, or primitive areas. It comprises many scattered parcels, not one contiguous unit, although some wilderness areas are vast enough to take days to cross on foot. In a nutshell, if you're on Forest Preserve land you're free to hike, hunt, fish, canoe, and do almost whatever else you want, although wilderness areas are off-limits to motorized vehicles (e.g., snowmobiles, ATVs, and motorboats). If you're not on public land, you're trespassing on somebody's property, unless you have permission to be there. Odd as it may seem to come across private land inside a state park, please respect it. If you want to go for a walk in the woods, look for trailheads with state Department of Environmental Conservation signs; they are on public land.

The Adirondack Mountains: The tallest summits—the celebrated High Peaks—occupy the northeast quarter of the Adirondack Park, but there are chains of mountains and scattered monadnocks throughout the region. They generally lie in parallel fault valleys, making a southwest to northeast diagonal across the park.

This new, bourgeois resort clientele expected rather different lodgings than the circuit riders and traveling peddlers who preceded them, and Adirondack hostelries made haste to adjust. The proverbial backcountry tavern with its rough pallets in the attic begat the North Country inn, which in turn begat the double-balconied hotel, with uniformed black waiters, Irish cooks, and ready stable of picturesque, authentically gruff Adirondack guides. More socially positioned visitors were lucky enough to

In the nineteenth century, steamboats delivered thousands of guests to lakefront hotels, from Blue Mountain Lake (pictured here) to Lake George and the Saranac lakes. Courtesy of Ted Comstock, Saranac Lake

enjoy an invitation to one of the Adirondack Great Camps, private compounds sometimes as built up as small towns. Here guests were plied with the bubbliest champagne, the mildest Cuban stogies, and the most delicious six-course feasts that the ruthlessly gotten gains of the Gilded Age could buy.

Wilderness no longer had to justify itself as a means to an agricultural or industrial end; it was increasingly an end in itself and it was held for spirit, soul, and body, especially those bodies in the early grip of tuberculosis. Lots of rest and good clean air—that pretty much summed up the homely prescription of Dr. Edward Livingston Trudeau, the great champion of the "Adirondack cure," and that's what a six-week stint in the screened-in porch of a Saranac Lake village cure cottage delivered. In this hill-bound hamlet, there were, in addition to Trudeau's well-known sanatorium, cure cottages for Lower East Side tenement girls, for Cuban aristocrats, for show business mavens, and for

Great Camp décor was often an eclectic mix of twigs, logs, bark, and stone—plus Japanese lanterns, Oriental rugs, and Indian baskets. Camp Cedars, interior, Forked Lake.
Courtesy of the Adirondack Museum, Blue Mountain Lake

Hungarian aesthetes. Robert Louis Stevenson did a turn at Saranac Lake. So did baseball star Christy Mathewson and the gangster "Legs" Diamond. You sat, you ate, you rested, you got bored out of your mind. But as often as not, you did get better. And if you didn't, your problem was you found the Adirondacks just too late to do you good.

What happened when the tourists and the travelers collided with the worked-over, roughed-up landscape of the Adirondack industrialist and his heavy-booted teams of loggers, tanners, river drivers, and mill workers? No matter how pristine the eventual destination, the view from the stagecoach or sleeper window almost certainly exposed the Adirondack adventurer to the occasional glimpse of clear-cut hillsides and tangled slash. Sometimes it seemed the more prolific the newly converted admirers of the region, the faster it was changing—and not for the better. Was it an accident that in the same year (1864) an anonymous editorial in *The New York Times* suggested that the Adirondack region be preserved as a "Central Park for the world" and George Perkins Marsh published his seminal book, *Man and Nature,* on the delicate relationship between a healthy forest and a secure watershed?

Cut too much, Marsh argued, and you set the scene for a tidal wave of muddy runoff and unleash the threat of flood and drought. Too much cutting can even make the climate change and diminish rainfall, which in turn would damage agricultural production. No more rain: no more farms, no more food—worst-case scenario, *no more people!* In New York State specifically, as surveyor Verplanck Colvin pointed out, a ravaged watershed in the north could mean lower water levels for the Hudson River and the Erie Canal—a disaster for commercial and transportation interests and for downstate politicians. A healthy watershed was also a safeguard against waterborne disease, a concern of no small moment to the epidemic-leery voters of metropolitan New York.

Although it would take a few more decades to gather steam enough to win the necessary political support, here was a perfectly utilitarian rationale for the founding of a preserve.

No early advocate ever argued for the Adirondack Park in aesthetic terms alone. It helped that the region was gorgeous, but it was health and public safety, not good looks and recreation, that won the day in 1885 with the creation of the Adirondack Forest Preserve, then comprising almost 700,000 acres scattered across eleven counties. Five years later the state began to consolidate its holdings with additional purchases, and the expectation was expressed that someday all the land within the penciled "Blue Line" that outlined the edges of this new park would comprise "One Grand, Unbroken Domain."

In 1892, the Adirondack Park was officially defined. Three years after that, a new state constitution declared these Forest Preserve lands should be "forever kept as wild forest lands." Private land could still be logged, but state land was off-limits, allowed to grow up and fall down without interference from humans. It was, notes the historian Philip Terrie, a provision that made the Adirondack Forest Preserve "one of the best protected landscapes in the world." And enacted not a day too soon: Late-nineteenth-century innovations in pulp making meant that virtually *all* the woods were fair game for the lumber magnates, and between 1890 and 1910, the very years the park was birthed, logging activity on privately held lands within the park actually peaked. Of course, the more frenetic the pace of logging, the faster the non-state-owned forest was depleted, and as shortages occurred, many lumber companies began to move their logging operations elsewhere, to tree-cloaked Quebec, for instance, or to the temperate South.

And what was moving in about this time, sputtering exhaust and spitting gravel and scaring horses half to death? Infernal combustion. Automobiles were rare enough in the Adirondack region in the early 1900s, but within a generation roads were snaking between passes. In their dusty wake followed not only carloads of vacationers but trailheads that met the roads and led hikers to remote summits; roadside auto courts, housekeeping cabins, and filling stations; and roadside attractions with music, dancing, and even dancing bears.

Presidents in Residence

Although we can't claim that George Washington slept here, the father of our country was certainly aware of the vital importance of fortifications at Ticonderoga and Crown Point along Lake Champlain's western shore. **Thomas Jefferson** and **James Madison** visited Lake George in 1791, on a summer reconnoiter to Vermont that doubled as a vacation; Jefferson, a seasoned world traveler, described the lake as one of the most beautiful he'd ever seen.

In 1817, **James Monroe** skirted the wild edge of what would become the Adirondack Park during a trip from Champlain to Sackets Harbor, on the St. Lawrence River. **Andrew Jackson**, who served in Congress from 1827–1829, was a close friend of Richard Keese II, after whom the village of Keeseville is named. Jackson ("Old Hickory") went north to see Keese, and in honor of the occasion, a hickory sapling was sought to plant in the front yard of the homestead. But no hickories could be found for miles around, so a bitter walnut was substituted. It thrived.

Chester A. Arthur stayed at Mart Moody's Mount Morris House, near Tupper Lake, in 1869, and slept on the floor like everyone else. When he was president, in 1881, Arthur named the guide and innkeeper postmaster of a new settlement named—surprisingly enough—Moody.

Grover Cleveland also knew Moody as a guide. While hunting near Big Wolf Pond, Cleveland reportedly said to him, "There's no wolves, here, darn it! But—there ain't a hundred pencils here, either, goin' every minute to take down everything I say." The president returned to the Adirondacks for his honeymoon, and also stayed at posh places like the Grand View, in Lake Placid, and the Saranac Inn.

President **Benjamin Harrison** visited his vice-presidential candidate Whitelaw Reid at Loon Lake during the 1892 campaign, and he whistle-stopped in Crown Point, Lyon Mountain, Bloomingdale, and Saranac Lake. Along the way, he was feted with band concerts and pageants and given gifts of iron ore and wildflower arrangements. In 1895, Harrison built a rustic log camp named Berkeley Lodge on Second Lake, near Old Forge.

William McKinley made a special trip here to John Brown's grave in 1897, but it was his assassination that led to one of the most exciting footnotes in Adirondack history. **Theodore Roosevelt**, who first came to the mountains as a teenager in 1871, was climbing Mount Marcy when news of McKinley's imminent demise was cabled north. A guide scrambled up the peak to tell T.R., who made it down in record time. Three relays of teams and wagons whisked him in the murk of night from the Tahawus Club to North Creek, and Roosevelt learned in the North Creek railroad station that he had become the twenty-sixth president on September 14, 1901.

Calvin Coolidge established a summer White House at White Pine Camp, on Osgood Pond, in 1926. This was at the height of Prohibition; silent Cal's place was a mere stone's throw away from Gabriels, a hotbed of bootleg activity.

Franklin D. Roosevelt was no stranger to the North Country. He officiated at the opening of the 1932 Winter Olympics, dedicated the Whiteface Veterans Memorial Highway in 1935, and celebrated the fifty-th anniversary of the Forest Preserve in Lake Placid that same year.

Bill Clinton's August 2000 visit to Lake Placid included golf and plenty of fresh air, but what locals remember is how a young woman flashed the commander-in-chief as he waited for a cone at Ben & Jerry's on Main Street.

George W. Bush came to Wilmington to promote his "Clear Skies" initiative in April 2002. Heavy snows, perhaps laden with noxious chemicals described in the initiative, forced the speeches from a beach on the Au Sable River to the lodge at Whiteface Mountain. Due to transportation screw-ups, several prominent Republicans never made it to the podium, stuck instead aboard an idling school bus at a police barricade.

Was it the end of the Adirondack Park or the beginning? Certainly the age of the automobile spelled the death of the Adirondacks' vaunted isolation and mystique. You didn't need to come for a season anymore. From the necklace of mid-size cities that outline the Adirondack region (Glens Falls, Plattsburgh, Ogdensburg, Watertown, Amsterdam, Gloversville, Massena, Malone), you could do it in a day! Or chug up from Albany or even Brooklyn for a nice long weekend: Pack the trunk with tent and camping gear, throw the kids in back under a blanket, check the oil, kick the tires—you're off. No two-week stay at one hotel; you could play connect-the-dots between lakeside campgrounds under the towering white pines, cook your own chow over an open fire instead of dealing with a stuck-up waiter in a uniform at some swank hotel. You didn't need to hire a guide; a good map and one of those new wood-canvas canoes could do you just as well.

Roads democratized the Adirondack experience as no paper legislation ever could, and with the ease of access, the reputation of the region as a recreational nirvana grew by leaps and bounds. Small towns reeling under the recent loss or exodus of the extractive industries rebounded with a plethora of services aimed squarely at the car-borne tourist: diners, supper clubs (maybe, during Prohibition, with a speakeasy in back), motels, and souvenir shops. (Step right up! Get your genuine Mohawk-made balsam pillows! Your German porcelain souvenir plaques! Your maple sugar candy and your Japanese paper flowers!) As the century wore on, those small town storefronts increasingly would include the recreational outfitter and the real estate office. Nothing like the completion of a superhighway, the "Northway," or Interstate 87, in 1967, to whet the appetite of city dwellers keen to build their Adirondack getaway.

Virgin Trees and Charismatic Megafauna

The Adirondack forest primeval—which survives today in scattered tracts of old growth in remote wilderness areas like the Five Ponds and West Canadas—varies according to elevation and soil. At the very tops of some mountains, only alpine shrubs and flowers grow, and below them are stunted trees known as the *krummholz*, which can be hundreds of years old yet only a few feet high. Lower down, thick spruce-fir forests grow; on steep, inaccessible slopes some patches have remained undisturbed for centuries. White pine and spruce take over at an elevation of 2,500 feet or so, with mixed hardwood forests—yellow birch, beech, sugar maple, plus eastern hemlock—covering miles and miles of the central Adirondacks. The understory in this woodland is the classic Adirondack landscape, with beautiful ferns and wildflowers like trillium, lady's slipper, and jack-in-the-pulpit.

Moose disappeared from the Adirondacks between 1870 and 1970, but have made a strong comeback. Road sign on NY 30. James Swedberg

White pine towering 150 feet tall and enormous spruce were the first to fall before the woodsman's ax. These logs were floated downstream to towns and sawmills as early as 1812, and following the Civil War, when paper-making technology made the great leap from rags to wood pulp, softwood forests were stripped bare. Hemlocks, too, had great commercial value; bark was a necessary ingredient in leather tanning, but the wood itself was left to rot where it fell. Many towns in the central and southern Adirondacks owe their existence to tanneries that processed South American hides into American shoe parts.

Early records show a wide variety of wildlife ranging through the different habitats of woods and waters. Elk lived in the St. Lawrence and Mohawk River Valleys as late as the 1820s, and moose were common throughout the lake country until about 1870. Mountain lions and wolves posed a serious threat to settlement, but generous bounties paid out by counties (in the mid-1800s, some locales paid more for bounties in a year than they spent on schools) decreased the numbers of predators considerably. Mountain lions are occasionally spotted today, although conservation officials deny any breeding population; questions linger about wolves. Did gray wolves ever really live in upstate New York, or are the smaller, reddish canines we call coyotes the historic Adirondack wolf?

Black bears have adapted remarkably well to life with humans; their numbers have been stable over this century. Other carnivores like fisher, pine marten, and bobcat are thriving in the forest. Lynx once were found in the High Peaks and other rugged countryside, preying on snowshoe hares, but disappeared due to hunting and habitat changes. Efforts to reintroduce the species in the 1980s have proven fruitless.

The big reintroduction success story is the beaver. For three centuries, well before maps and military expeditions, there was lively trade in beaver pelts, with furs shipped to Fort Orange (now Albany)

and Montreal. Beaver hair pressed into felt was used in fashionable hats, and demand soon exceeded the supply. By 1894 beavers were virtually extinct; in the early 1900s, they were reintroduced to the Old Forge area. By 1910 the animals had spread throughout the central Adirondacks, busily building dams and flooding woodlands. Today you can see evidence of their engineering on almost any Adirondack waterway.

In addition to the lakes, forests, and peaks, these beavers' efforts create habitat for the Adirondack bird population. Loons, revered for their haunting songs, inhabit many larger Adirondack lakes and ponds. With luck you may see an osprey, peregrine falcon, or bald eagle soaring on warm currents over a lakeshore or cliff. Hawks are fairly easy to spot; songbirds—especially warblers—are plentiful during warm weather; and at least ten varieties of ducks nest near the waterways of the park.

Indeed, so rapid was the proliferation of Adirondack second homes in the 1960s, and so potentially damaging was their impact on the landscape, that Governor Nelson Rockefeller appointed a commission that recommended a new agency just to oversee land use and development. Thus was spawned the controversial Adirondack Park Agency (APA) in 1974. Many are the local objections to the APA's unwieldy bureaucratic mandate (to guide development on public and private lands), but on one thing its critics can almost all wholeheartedly agree: the establishment more than a hundred years ago of the Adirondack Park was a miracle of timing, foresight, and good luck. It could not have happened any sooner, and it certainly could not have happened since. Love the park for its variety and beauty, and you won't be disappointed, but love it for its hidden history as well—the lost loggers, the vanished tannery towns, the boarded-over mine shafts, the stagecoaches, the peddlers, and the wedding cake hotels—and your love and understanding of it can only be enhanced.

—Amy Godine

2

TRANSPORTATION

Over the Rivers and through the Woods

On any road map of New York State, the Adirondack Park shows up as a green, shield-shaped polygon. Looking closer, you'll notice that the park boundary encloses much empty space, crossed by few highways and sparsely dotted with towns. This reflects the large portion of the park that's public land, and it doesn't mean that those spidery thin lines are bad roads. Major highways through the Adirondacks are well-maintained two-lane blacktop, the lifelines of the region. Come winter, platoons of snowplows and sand trucks keep the roads clear; two feet of snow causes far less trouble here than two inches, in say, Washington, D.C.

On that road map, you'll notice lots of blue rivers and lakes, the original travel corridors. By canoe or by snowshoe over the ice, Native Americans and the first Europeans followed these paths of least resistance. Although no single river provided passage through the entire rugged region, it was possible to travel from the southwest to northeast corners

A novelty in the early 1900s, the automobile proved to be the best way to navigate around the Adirondack Park. Courtesy of Saranac Lake Free Library, Adirondack Collection

via the Moose, Raquette, and Saranac River systems with but a few short "carries," the Adirondack word for portages. The importance of the rivers is underscored by the fact that in the early 1800s many streams were declared public highways for floating logs to downstream markets.

The first roads were hacked out of the forest to transport iron ore, charcoal, and other commodities between settlements. Later, some of these dirt tracks were paved with logs (known as corduroy roads), but they were not much more than wide, slightly less primitive trails. A stagecoach ride on one could be a bone-jarring, tooth-loosening experience, and a special passenger wagon, the "buckboard"—with a long springy board between the front and back wheels—evolved to make the best of terrible thoroughfares.

Even into the beginnings of the tourist era, waterways remained principal transportation routes, and most towns were built along a lake or river that allowed people to connect with the larger world. In response, specific vessels were developed: the guideboat—light, fast, and maneuverable, easy for one man to carry—with oars rather than paddles, marvelous for fishing and hunting on Adirondack ponds; and tiny steamboats, built to fit the small lakes of the interior.

The first widespread, modern, means of movement was the railroad. Originally built to haul out timber, the railroads quickly became a profitable, convenient way to haul in tourists. Beginning about 1900, a web of lines throughout the region offered several passenger trains a day speeding north from East Coast cities to destinations in the woods. One of the most popular targets, Blue Mountain Lake, could be reached by a remarkable trip that involved an overnight train ride from New York to Utica, transfer to a steamboat, change to the world's shortest standard-gauge railroad (less than a mile long), and a final leg on another steamboat for delivery to your hotel of choice.

By the 1920s, with the growing popularity of the automobile, roads were gradually improved until they surpassed the railroads, although such special offerings as ski trains enabled passenger service to struggle along until well after World War II. The late 1960s were a watershed time; the last passenger train serving the interior, the Adirondack Division of the New York Central (the Utica-to-Lake Placid line), rolled to a stop in 1965, and the Adirondack Northway, the only interstate highway in northeastern New York, was completed along the eastern edge of the park in 1967. This event seemed at once to ensure that the family car would be the way the vast majority of people would travel to the Adirondacks for years to come and to discourage the development of a public transportation system.

So, if you want to get around in the twenty-first-century Adirondacks, you'll need your own wheels. If you don't own a car, rent one before you get to the North Country. Even if you come here by some other means, once you arrive it can be difficult to do much without one. Public transportation is scarce and not always convenient.

The following information gives you the best routes for access to the Adirondacks and for getting around once you're here. We start with the most practical means of transportation—your car—and also provide details on bus, train, and air service. Routes that incorporate a Lake Champlain ferry crossing are also described. For car rentals within Saratoga, Glens Falls, and the Adirondacks, we suggest you contact the rental companies' Web sites or district offices.

BY CAR

Highways to Get You Here

Major highways can get you to the perimeter of the Adirondack Park from all points:
• *From New York City:* Take I-87 north. This is the New York State (or Thomas E. Dewey) Thruway, a toll road, to Albany (Exit 24); then it becomes the toll-free Adirondack Northway (I-87). Principal exits off the Northway for the interior are: 14 and 15 for Saratoga Springs, 18 for Glens Falls, 21 for Lake George (roughly four hours from metro New York), 23 for Warrensburg and the central Adirondacks, 28 for Schroon Lake and Ticonderoga (about five hours from New York), and 30 for Lake Placid, Saranac Lake, and the High Peaks.
• *From Philadelphia and South:* Take the Northeast Extension of the Pennsylvania Turnpike and then I-81 north to Syracuse. From Syracuse take I-90 east to entry points such as Utica and Amsterdam, or I-81 farther north and then east on NY 3 at Watertown to reach the northern areas. Either way, it's not as far as you might think—you can reach the southwest edge of the park in about six hours from Philadelphia. Or you can take I-88 from Binghamton to Schenectady, go east two exits on I-90 and head north on I-87 from Albany; see above, "From New York City." And there's always the Garden State Parkway to the New York Thruway, then proceed as above.
• *From Buffalo, Cleveland, and West:* Take I-90 east to Syracuse, then proceed as directed above ("From Philadelphia"). From Buffalo to the edge of the park north of Utica is a little more than four hours.
• *From Toronto and Detroit:* Take NY 401 toward Montreal. Three toll bridges cross the Saint Lawrence River. The one that provides the most direct access not only to the edge of the park but also to such interior locations as Lake Placid and Blue Mountain Lake leaps from Prescott (Highway 16 exit) to Ogdensburg; the toll in 2007 for a car is $2.75 U.S. one way. On the U.S. side, take NY 37 west a couple of miles to NY 68 south to Colton, and NY 56 into the park. From Toronto it's about five hours to the edge of the park and seven to the center. Travelers are required to present a passport or birth certificate at the border.
• *From Ottawa:* Take Highway 16 to the Prescott–Ogdensburg toll bridge and proceed as directed above ("From Toronto"). Allow two hours to the edge of the park, four to central points.
• *From Montreal:* Take Highway 15 south; this becomes I-87, the Adirondack Northway, at the border. Principal jumping-off exits for the interior are 38 (Plattsburgh), only an hour (plus customs wait, which can be lengthy) from the outskirts of Montreal; and 34 (Keeseville), twenty minutes south of Exit 38.
• *From Boston:* Take the Massachusetts Pike, I-90, to I-87, then head north and follow the directions given under "From New York," above, to get past Albany. Or, take I-93 north to I-89, to one of the Lake Champlain ferry crossings described below. Via Albany, the Adirondacks is about four hours from Boston; via the ferries it's closer to five, but the ferries are fun.

Highways to Get You Around Once You Get Here

North and South

Not surprisingly, four of the five north–south highways that traverse the Adirondacks do so in the narrow corridor between Lake Champlain and the mountains. This is where much of the region's population and many of its attractions are located, and it's also on a direct line between two concentrations of population: New York City and Montreal. These routes are:

• *NY 9N,* which rambles through lovely rolling countryside from Saratoga Springs northwest to Corinth and Lake Luzerne, then east to Lake George village, then up to Hague, and to Lake Champlain at Ticonderoga, where it meets:

• *NY 22,* which hugs Lake Champlain all the way from Whitehall up to Ticonderoga, where it joins 9N. The combined routes have expansive views of the lake on the east and farmland in the valley beneath the High Peaks on the west, passing through Crown Point and Port Henry. At Westport, NY 22 follows the lake valley north to Willsboro, while 9N heads west to Elizabethtown, over Spruce Hill and on to Keene. This historic route passes through Upper Jay, Jay, and Au Sable Forks, paralleling the Ausable River, and connects again with NY 22 at Keeseville.

• *US 9* begins in the park just north of Glens Falls and skirts Schroon Lake and the Schroon and Boquet Rivers, but its route has been mostly supplanted by:

• *I-87,* the Adirondack Northway, an honest-to-goodness interstate highway named "America's Most Scenic Highway" in 1966–1967.

• *NY 30,* the fifth north–south route, bisects the region from Gloversville via Speculator, Indian Lake, Blue Mountain Lake, Long Lake, Tupper Lake, and Paul Smiths to Malone. The remote and lightly populated western half of the region has no north–south highways.

East and West

Reflecting the reality that most travel in the Adirondacks always has been north–south, only three highways cross the entire region on the east–west axis, and two of them cover some of the same territory. These are:

• *NY 28,* which forms a semicircle from Warrensburg through North Creek, Indian Lake, Blue Mountain Lake, Inlet, Old Forge, and down to Utica.

• *NY 8,* which zigzags west from Hague, on Lake George, through Brant Lake, Chestertown, Johnsburg, Speculator, Lake Pleasant, Piseco, Hoffmeister, and southwest to Utica.

• *NY 3,* which crosses the northern part of the park from Plattsburgh, to Redford, Vermontville, Bloomingdale, Saranac Lake, Tupper Lake, Piercefield, Childwold, Cranberry Lake, Star Lake, and exits the Blue Line west to Watertown.

Additional Routes

Other shorter but scenic routes in the Adirondacks include:

• *Northeast on NY 73* from Underwood (Exit 30 of the Northway) to Lake Placid, which offers a 45-minute panorama of the High Peaks.

• *West on NY 86* from Jay, past the foot of Whiteface Mountain and through dramatic Wilmington Notch to Lake Placid, then on to Saranac Lake and Paul Smiths.

• *East on NY 374* from Chateaugay, past the Chateaugay Lakes and Lyon Mountain to Plattsburgh, which, in addition to views of the Adirondacks, provides a long-distance scan across Lake Champlain to the Green Mountains of Vermont as it drops down Dannemora Mountain.

• *Northwest on NY 28N* from North Creek on NY 28 to Long Lake. Be sure to stop at the roadside rest area at Newcomb, where a display identifies the High Peaks panorama to the north.

• *East on the "Number Four" Road* from Lowville, past Stillwater Reservoir and on to Big Moose and Eagle Bay, which is on NY 28. Rather than great views, this drive offers a

Adirondack Access

Blue Mountain Lake is central—it's 1½ to 2 hours to the edge of the park in every direction—so this location will serve as a reference point in determining about how long a drive to the Adirondacks will take:

City	Miles to Blue Lake Mountain	Approximate Time to Blue Mountain Lake
Albany	105	2 hrs
Binghamton	220	4 hrs
Boston (via Albany)	270	5½ hrs
Buffalo	280	5½ hrs
Burlington, VT	100	3 hrs (involves ferry)
Montreal	165	3½ hrs*
New York	260	5½ hrs
Ottawa	150	3½ hrs*
Philadelphia	390	8 hrs
Rochester	210	4½ hrs
Syracuse	140	3 hrs
Toronto	320	7 hrs*
Utica	90	2 hrs

*plus possible delays crossing border

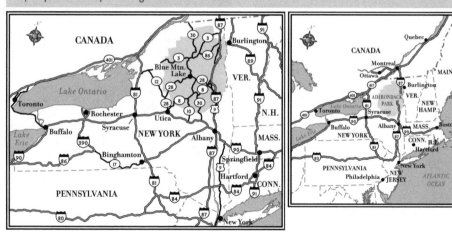

sense of the forest depths. About half of the 45 miles is gravel or graded dirt, and there are no services over the full distance.

The Adirondack North Country Association (ANCA) has created driving tours in and around the Adirondacks. These are arranged to hit scenic vistas, historic markers, craft shops, and so on. You can pick up a map of these routes at tourist centers and chambers of commerce, or contact ANCA at 518-891-6200 or www.adirondack.org.

BY BUS

Considering the size of the Adirondack region—you could fit Connecticut inside it—it's astonishing how little bus service exists. There's only one round trip a day that's of any use, and once you get off the bus you're dependent on traveling by foot or finding sparse taxi service and even sparser rental car possibilities. If you do plan to use bus service: **Greyhound Lines, Inc.** (1-800-858-8555; www.greyhound.com) and **Adirondack Trailways** (1-800-776-7548; www.trailwaysny.com), nowadays affiliated with one another, make stops in various locations in the park (stops at diners and shops remind you you're not in urban America anymore): Bolton Landing (Neuffers Deli), Keene Valley (Noon Mark Diner), Lake George (Lake George Hardware), Lake Placid (Olympic Authority), Paul Smiths, Ray Brook, Saranac Lake (Hotel Saranac), Schroon Lake (Mount Severance Country Store), and Warrensburg (Marco Polo Pasta). But these hubs come and go, and some are seasonal, so call ahead. Also, bus tickets can be purchased at these hubs. According to the Greyhound hotline at press time, there's no reason to reserve a seat—they're first come, first served. However, there's every reason to call ahead or visit your local terminal for the latest bus schedule since it changes season to season. In fall 2007 a one-way bus ticket from Port Authority, in Manhattan, to Lake Placid, was $67.

BY TRAIN

Amtrak

Amtrak (1-800-872-7245; www.amtrak .com) operates one train a day each way between New York City and Montreal. *The Adirondack* leaves each city in the morning and reaches its destination the same evening (schedules are different on Saturdays and Sundays). The train closely follows the west shore of Lake Champlain for the better part of 90 scenic miles. The New York departure is from Penn Station. It makes stops in Saratoga Springs, Fort Edward, and the Adirondacks— Ticonderoga, Port Henry, Westport, and Port Kent—but how to get around once you are deposited at these places can be prob-

Amtrak service to Westport and other towns parallels Lake Champlain, offering beautiful views of water, mountains, farms, and villages. James Swedberg

lematic. You may arrange, in advance, for shuttle service from the handsome Victorian depot in Westport to Lake Placid (or Elizabethtown or Keene) by calling **Ground Force One/Majestic Limousine** (518-523-0294), which makes a daily run between Westport and Lake Placid, or **Mountain Taxi** (518-962-2977), or **Rick's Taxi** (518-523-4741). Train travel may not be what it once was, but compared to buses and puddle-jumper airplanes, this remains the most relaxing, visually engaging way to get to the Adirondacks.

The trip is spectacular, involving tunnels, high trestles, rocky ledges 150 feet above the waters of Lake Champlain, and vistas of farm and forest, river, lake, and mountain that simply cannot be had any other way. The least expensive Fort Edward–Plattsburgh roundtrip fare was about $45 in 2007. One-way from Penn Station, in New York City, to Westport was about $55.

Amtrak's Empire Service leaves New York's Penn Station several times a day and stops in Albany–Rensselaer, Schenectady, and Utica, where you can arrange to rent a car by contacting **Hertz** (1-800-654-3131; www.hertz.com) or **Avis** (1-800-331-1212; www.avis.com). One train a day from Boston hooks up with this route at Albany–Rensselaer. Coming from the west, Empire Service originates in Buffalo; Chicago–Boston/New York and Toronto–New York Amtrak trains also ply this route.

An Amtrak passenger train offers trips from Utica to Thendara/Old Forge, allowing at least semiregular train service to the southwestern Adirondacks. Trains run primarily Wednesday through Saturday, June through October. The ride takes approximately 2 1/2 hours; an adult roundtrip fare in 2007 was about $34. Once you're in Old Forge, there's a shuttle bus to take you to the Enchanted Forest and shops on Main Street. This route is not in Amtrak's database, so contact Adirondack Scenic Railroad's office (315-369-6290 or 1-800-819-2291; www.adirondackrr.com) for schedule and fare information.

Tourist Trains

The **Adirondack Scenic Railroad (ASR)** operates a popular short line from its Thendara station (trains depart at 10 AM, 12:30 PM, and 2:45 PM) in spring through fall, with roundtrip runs south along the Moose River to Otter Lake, and north to Carter Station. Look for special events (simulated train robberies, historic tours) and unique travel opportunities (the ASR allows mountain bikers and canoeists—and their respective gear—to use the train as part of their explorations). Fares in 2007 were between $14–$26 for adults, depending on the trip. For fare and schedule information, call 315-369-6290 or visit www.adirondackrr.com.

The **Adirondack Railway Preservation Society**, the nonprofit outfit that operates the Adirondack Scenic, runs an excursion line on the 8 miles of track between Saranac Lake and Lake Placid. Permission to revitalize the entire rail corridor between Carter Station and Saranac Lake—which hasn't seen a train in almost forty years, and of which the Placid–Saranac line would be the first part—was granted by the state almost a decade ago. The project will take more time and money. Lots of time and money.

The **Upper Hudson River Railroad (UHRR)**, out of the North Creek depot, began service in 1999. As mentioned earlier, the station earned a place in history in September 1901 as the spot where Teddy Roosevelt, then vice president, learned that William McKinley had died in Buffalo, and that he was the next president of the United States. A museum in the North Creek station complex describes this event and showcases local history.

The UHRR runs 8.5 miles along the Hudson River to the beautifully restored Riverside Station in Riparius, where passengers can disembark for 30 minutes or so before the return trip. There is a gallery in the old station and a funky antiques shop across the street. The entire journey takes about 2 hours.

The 2007 fare was $16 per passenger, with discounts for seniors and children. Daily trips in July and August run at 10 AM and 2 PM from North Creek, with a reduced schedule from May through June and in September and October. Bicyclists can arrange to ride one way and pedal the other; an open car hauls canoes and kayaks so that paddlers can make an exciting whitewater run downstream and ride back to their cars. Kids go bonkers for the Thomas the Tank Engine. In 2007 the character train was on the tracks for two weekends in May and drew thousands of people. Also, inquire about excursions to Hadley and regional resorts, such as 1000 Acres Ranch, in Stony Creek. Call the UHRR at 518-251-5334 or visit www.uhrr.com to learn about fares and schedules.

Like the Adirondack Scenic, the Upper Hudson has big plans to connect with Saratoga Springs to the south. Real passenger service is still years off, but this is one line rail fans should watch for.

By Ferry

Ferries have crossed Lake Champlain between New York and Vermont for more than 200 years. Private collection

The only way to get to the Adirondacks from the east is to cross Lake Champlain, the largest freshwater lake in America after the Great Lakes. You can do that via the bridge at Port Henry, which has a nice view that lasts for about thirty seconds. Why not savor the journey and take one of the Lake Champlain ferries? The views last for up to an hour and you don't have to steer. Three of the four crossings are operated by Lake Champlain Transportation, the oldest continuously running inland navigation company in America (802-864-9804; www.ferries.com). Rates vary depending on type of vehicle, number and age of persons in it, and so forth; those shown were for car and one driver, one way, in 2007.

• *From Charlotte, Vermont, to Essex:* This may be the most scenic route, seeming to deliver you truly into the mountains. Crossing time is twenty minutes; trips run year-round, departing Charlotte starting at 6 AM or 7 AM, depending on the season. $9.

• *From Burlington, Vermont, to Port Kent:* This is almost as scenic, and delightful for its relaxing hour-long crossing of the widest part of the lake. Trips begin at 8 AM or 9 AM and run several times a day from mid-May through the beginning of October. Reservations made at least a day ahead are recommended. $16.50. (This is the only crossing where credit cards are accepted.)

• *From Grand Isle, Vermont, north of Burlington, to Plattsburgh:* A bit north of the Adirondacks, this route provides a decent if long-distance view of them. It operates twenty-four hours a day year-round, blasting through ice packs in even the coldest snaps, generally every twenty minutes (every forty minutes in the dead of night). Crossing time is twelve minutes. $9.

• *From Shoreham, Vermont, to Ticonderoga:* This crossing is a living museum. Following a route that's been in use since the British army arrived in the 1700s, it brings you to the foot of the promontory on which the restored fort reposes. This is one of the few cable-guided ferries left in America: The cable is attached at each landing and a tugboat provides power. Crossing time is six minutes; the one-way fare is about $8 per car, and trips run from 8 AM to 5:45 PM, from mid-May through late October, and from 8 AM to 6:45 PM July 1 through Labor Day. There's no set schedule; "We just go back and forth," says the captain. For more information: 802-897-7999.

Deer Crossing

Keep your eyes peeled for deer as you drive through the Adirondacks—not only to see them, which will be a pleasant memory of your trip, but also to avoid hitting them.

Deer are most active in the late afternoon and evening, and particularly just after sunset, when they're also hardest to see. They often travel in pairs or small groups; if one crosses the road ahead of you, others are likely to follow. They're especially mobile during fall, for several reasons: that's their breeding season; they have to travel more to find food at this time of year; and hunters disrupt their daily routines. In winter they seek out plowed roads since the going is easier. Around Old Forge, especially NY 28 and the South Shore Road, deer are as common as squirrels all year.

One more thing: The instinctive reaction of a deer caught by car headlights is to freeze, not to scramble out of the way. It's up to you to miss. Your best bet: Drive alertly, obey speed limits—and take those deer crossing, x miles signs seriously.

"Moose Crossing" signs have been installed across the park; they're not just a tourist gimmick but a real warning of a potential hazard. The moose population has grown steadily in the last 15 years, and sadly, car-moose encounters are becoming more common. During one month in 2007 there were four accidents involving moose in the Adirondacks. Pay special attention in the fall, when thousand-pound bulls can come crashing out of the forest directly into your lane, and at night, when your head-lights may shine under their bodies, without reflecting in their eyes.

BY AIR

Commercial Airports

In all this vast territory there's only one commercial airport: **Adirondack Regional Airport at Lake Clear** (518-891-4600), about 15 minutes from Saranac Lake and 30 from Lake Placid. In 2008 it will be served by the commuter line of a major carrier, which will offer daily service to and from Boston to connect travelers with national and international airline services and to and from Plattsburgh. Fares depend on the time of year, how far ahead you purchase your ticket, and so forth. In a random sampling, the nonrefundable price in winter 2008 for a flight from Boston to Saranac Lake was $215 roundtrip or $110 one way.

As these commuter airlines come and go, it's best to call first to make sure this one's still using Lake Clear. If you're calling another airport or a travel agent, ask about "Saranac Lake," not "Adirondack." Car rentals are available at the airport: **Hertz** (518-891-9044) or **Enterprise** (518-891-9216). **Lavigne's Taxi** (518-891-2444), **Rick's Taxi** (518-523-4741), and **Ground Force One/Majestic Limousine** (1-800-397-2602) also provide transportation to nearby towns. If you want to grab a bite to eat at the airport, Paula's Airport Café is open 7 AM to 2 PM.

Cities just outside the Adirondacks that offer air service are Albany, Syracuse, and Burlington, Vermont (amenities such as jets and a variety of rental cars), and Watertown and Plattsburgh (puddle-jumpers). The best source of up-to-date information about these options is your travel agent or travel Web sites such as www.kayak.com.

Private Airports

Private airports, ranging from a tarmac strip down to a patch of grass in the woods, can be found scattered about the Adirondacks, in places like Schroon Lake, Ticonderoga, and Westport. Consult a good navigational map. The most significant is on the outskirts of Lake Placid, with a 4,200-foot runway, public lounge, and other facilities: 518-523-2473. Another is at Piseco (518-548-3415). Better be prepared to be met at most of the others; taxi service and cars to rent are nowhere to be found in most cases, and it can be a hike to get to town. For the truly adventuresome, you can charter a seaplane to pick you up on the East River, at 23rd Street and Waterside Plaza, New York City; check under "Scenic Flights" in Chapter 7 for seaplane services.

Winter Driving

The Adirondack climate that dumps 10 or more feet of snow in an average winter may be great news for skiers and snowmobilers, but what about the road conditions, you might wonder. Throughout the Adirondack Park, the state and county highway departments have plenty of snowplows that toil night and day to keep roads clear. For several years, a "bare roads" policy has been in effect, meaning that sand and salt are applied liberally when roads may be slippery. Another plus for winter driving these days is the prevalence of four-wheel- and front-wheel-drive cars, which handle better on slick roads than the traditional rear-wheel-drive vehicles. (If you're coming to the wintry Adirondacks in a pickup truck, van, or passenger car with rear-wheel drive, try putting at least 150 pounds of weight—concrete blocks, sandbags, whatever—over your rear axle to help traction.)

The worst driving scenarios often occur at the beginning or end of winter, when temperatures hovering at the freezing point can cause a mixture of snow, rain, and sleet, with fog near lakes and low cold spots. Then it's best to consider your options: Can you wait out the storm at your lodgings, or are you prepared to rest at a remote pullout if conditions deteriorate? Every winter traveler's car should carry a sleeping bag, a small shovel, a snow scraper, extra windshield-washing fluid, a powerful flashlight, and some candy bars and bottled water, just in case you need to dig out of a snowbank or sit quietly beside the road for a few hours as the weather takes its course. Cell-phone owners beware: Coverage is spotty at best, so don't count on it.

3

Gateway Cities

Saratoga Springs and Glens Falls

Although neither Saratoga Springs nor Glens Falls is in the Adirondack Park, that fact is merely technical for people from downstate heading north on I-87. After the three-hour push out of metropolitan New York and up the Hudson Valley, the exit signs for Saratoga and Glens Falls are the starting gates that signal the home stretch, not to speak of the last chance for a double mocha latte or a month's supply of chèvre.

Saratoga Springs

Once in a blue moon the urge may overtake an Adirondacker to swap the warble of a loon for the strains of Yo-Yo Ma—and then it's off to Saratoga, which every summer serves up an arts and music calendar that leaves no day unfilled. This is the Adirondack region's favorite getaway, a retreat of high culture, fine dining, and matchless Victorian architecture. You can use Saratoga as a springboard to explore the North Country, or for its own hospitable, hedonistic self. Just peel off the Northway (I-87) at Exits 13, 14, or 15, and as fast as you can say, "I got the horse right here," you're there.

From the beginning, Saratoga—that's Mohawk for "Place of the Rapid Water"—has enjoyed a reputation as a bold exception to every imaginable rule. In the colonial era, when New York's wild country was a war zone for rival bands of Native Americans, Saratoga, home to scores of cherished therapeutic springs, was off-limits, an oasis of tranquility. Two centuries later, Prohibition-era gangsters honored a summer truce while ensconced in sumptuous Saratoga digs.

In the nineteenth century and through

Downtown Saratoga Springs, circa 1903, from a Delaware & Hudson Railroad brochure. Private collection

Take the waters at one of a dozen springs in downtown Saratoga, still bubbling after all these years. Bring your own cup. Courtesy of Kelly Kilgallon

the next, dingy, river-driven mill towns all around the Spa City rose and fell, while
Saratoga buffed its gleaming image as a world apart. Too self-impressed and naughty for
the staid decorum of the Hudson Valley to the south, too frivolous for the hard-featured,
rough-and-tumble Adirondacks to the north, the town played a vital role in both. Saratoga
was the first stop on the Grand Tour of the Northern Wilderness, which introduced Gilded
Age excursionists to the wonders of Ausable Chasm and Lake George. Halfway between
Manhattan and Montreal, here was founded the oldest running thoroughbred racetrack in
the country; here constructed the nation's biggest hotel, the Grand Union (halls that went
on for a mile and a half, carpets that stretched for seven acres). And here was built a perfect stunner of a casino that *The New York Times* called "the finest hell on earth."

Well, the grand piazzas have given way to street-side cafés, and Canfield Casino is now a
respectable historical museum, but you can still play the odds at the world's prettiest racetrack—or skip the horseplay completely. In the six-week "season" (which somehow seems
to get a little longer every year), Saratoga Springs is as good-times crazy as ever.

Nowadays, Saratoga's dozen-plus open-sided spring pavilions no longer draw dapper
men and wide-hatted women waiting for a dipper boy to dole out a dram. Hydrotherapy
fell from favor fifty years ago and with it the venerable tradition of the two- or three-week
"cure," an arduous regimen of porch sitting, park promenading, mud soaking, and ritual-
ized sipping of spring water reputed to be good for everything from eyestrain to arthritis.
But Saratogians swear by the stuff; pick up a map at the Urban Cultural Park on Broadway
and treat yourself to a walking tour of the downtown springs. Although the mud baths are
gone, you can still savor the romance of an old-time spa in the porcelain tubs at the
Roosevelt Baths and Spa (518-226-4663) in Saratoga Spa State Park and other sip-and-
soak options around town.

Broadway is a draw in its own right. Bracketed on the north by Victorian mansions and
the woodsy campus of Skidmore College, on the south by the Spa State Park, this is the
street that gives Saratoga Springs its architectural spine. The 1953 demolition of the landmark Grand Union Hotel was a wake-up call for preservation. Boarded-up Victorian storefronts and office buildings emerged from a deep sleep with smart new paint jobs and
market-savvy agenda. Ethnic restaurants joined the steak-and-spuds stand-bys. An infu-
sion of hip venues—a classy wine bar, an artisanal bakeshop, a gourmet food purveyor,
brewpubs, and a city arts center—revived half-dead facades. With the coming of many
chain stores, the Parisian-profile Broadway showed in Walker Evans's famous photograph
is gone, but it is still hands-down the sprightliest downtown around.

The people watching is fabulous, especially from the vantage of an espresso bar or outdoor bistro. On Broadway, you'll see high rollers in their summer whites, cigar-chomping
gamblers straight out of *The Sopranos,* Hispanic horse walkers, and frock-coated Chasids
from Brooklyn. Neon-headed skateboarders drift around in packs.

Then, when Broadway stales, stroll the side streets. Franklin Square, west of Broadway,
is crammed with architectural gems, some fixed-up, some in seedy disrepair. To
Broadway's east are Phila Street and Caroline Street, both chockablock with offbeat shops
and restaurants. On Phila is the modest entrance to the legendary **Caffè Lena** (518-583-
0022; www.caffelena.org; 47 Phila Street), the longest running coffeehouse in the country,
a funky upstairs 1960s throwback serving up good folk music most every night. Bob Dylan,
Dave Van Ronk, Arlo Guthrie, Greg Brown, Odetta, Rick Danko, and Emmylou Harris have
played here. Keep walking and you come to Circular Street, the heart of Saratoga's venerable Victorian district. Follow Circular to Union Avenue, lined with graceful homes, one

top-flight museum of horse racing, and the fabled thoroughbred track itself.

Saratoga Springs is ideally positioned for day trips. The Adirondack Park is as handy as the top third of Saratoga County, as distant as a 2.5-hour drive if you're aiming for the drama of the High Peaks. Five miles southwest on NY 50 brings you to Saratoga's spinster aunt, Ballston Spa, once as chic as Saratoga was unknown, today a laid-back village with a main street favored by antique dealers and artists. West on NY 9N takes you through the Adirondacks' piney borderlands. You can also find the Adirondacks by way of Corinth, birthplace of International Paper, and the nearby village, Lake Luzerne, cherished for a summer music colony and some nifty bite-size historical museums.

New England, or the feeling of it, finds you long before you reach Vermont in the spruced-up clapboard villages of Greenwich and Cambridge to Saratoga's east. This is farm country, rolling, open, early settled, a trove of early American architectural styles. Stop for the fresh-made cider donuts at **Saratoga Apple, Inc.** (518-695-3131; 1174 NY 29), mosey through drowsy Schuylerville, make a stop at **Old Saratoga Books** (518-695-5607; www.oldsaratogabooks.com; 94 Broad Street), and cross the Hudson River into Washington County. Hard by the county fairgrounds is the **Hand Melon Market** (518-692-7505; 533 Wilbur Avenue, Greenwich). Hand melon is a particularly tasty cantaloupe, and if you like it, you might try the homemade melon ice cream down the street at **The Ice Cream Man** (518-692-8382; www.the-ice-cream-man.com; 417 NY 29, Greenwich); however long the line, it's worth the wait. Cafés, shops, and a popular bistro with a fine arts gallery, **111** (518-692-8016; www.111mainstreet.net; 111 Main Street), anchor the meandering main street of pretty Greenwich. High in the hills is a terrific used bookstore, **The Owl Pen** (518-692-7039; 166 Riddle Road—and don't try finding it yourself, ask for directions), or, if you press on, the scenic **Batten Kill Railroad** (518-692-2160; 1 Elbow Street). The next stop, Cambridge, is home to art galleries, and **Hubbard Hall** (518-677-2495; 25 East Main Street), an old-time opera house where you can catch a fiddle contest or chamber music (this is where the talented Music from Salem players perform). The restored glorious old **Cambridge Hotel** (518-677-5626; www.cambridgehotel.com; 4 West Main Street) is the reputed birthplace of pie *à la mode*.

Although the mud baths are gone, you can still savor the romance of an old-time spa in the porcelain tubs at the Lincoln Bath House in Saratoga Spa State Park. Courtesy of Kelly Kilgallon

SARATOGA LODGINGS

Accommodations in Saratoga Springs range from bare bones to celestial, in keeping with the wildly diverse ways and means of summer throngs. Modest but serviceable motels line US 9 along the north and south exurbs of Saratoga Springs. Grander chains, with restaurants, conference centers, indoor pools, and parking—the **Hilton** (518-587-1500; www.hiltongardeninn.com; 125 South Broadway), **Saratoga Hotel and Conference Center** (518-584-4000; www.thesaratogahotel.com; 534 Broadway), and **Holiday Inn** (518-584-4550; 232 Broadway)—anchor both ends of Broadway, with one plain-but-honest hometown standby, the **Saratoga Downtowner Motel** (518-584-6160; www.saratogadowntowner.com; 413 Broadway), pinning down the middle. The trade gravitates to the boutique hotels and B&Bs, for which Saratoga is renowned.

Whatever the class or quality of lodging, from a Depression-era housekeeping cottage to a palatial suite at the **Batcheller Mansion Inn** (518-584-7012; www.batchellermansioninn.com; 20 Circular Street), one rule abides for all—when the track is open, rates go up. Waaaaayyyy up.

Very Inexpensive: Under $40 per night, double occupancy
Inexpensive: $40–$70
Moderate: $70–$100
Expensive: $100–$200
Very Expensive: Over $200

SARATOGA SPRINGS

Adelphi Hotel
Owner: Sheila Parkert
518-587-4688
www.adelphihotel.com
365 Broadway
Open: May through October
Price: Expensive to Very Expensive
Credit Cards: MC, V
Handicap Access: Yes
Restrictions: No pets

Once the haunt of gangster types, now a favorite of the New York City Ballet, the Adelphi is the undisputed jewel in the crown of Saratoga's elite hotels. Flanking Broadway at Caroline, it is the only surviving grand hotel from the Gilded Age, still boasting the original second-story piazza above the handsome entrance. Rooms are small but uniquely atmospheric; ask for one with a Broadway view. Late at night, the lobby and moonlit patio are great places to order a drink and a dessert and lounge under hand-painted wallpaper on a Mae West fainting couch, ogling the celebrities.

The Adelphi Hotel is the last of Saratoga's grand old hotels on Broadway. James Swedberg

Batcheller Mansion Inn
Owner: Bruce Levinsky
518-584-7012 or 1-800-616-7012
www.batchellermansioninn.com
20 Circular Street
Price: Expensive to Very Expensive
Credit Cards: AE, MC, V
Handicap Access: No
Restrictions: No children under 14; no pets

If you're a fan of Victorian Gothic design, your stay at the luxurious Batcheller Mansion Inn with its stunning mansard roof, clamshell arches, and dome-capped minaret, will make you think you went to historic conservation heaven. Named the Inn of the Month in *Country Inns* magazine, this over-the-top B&B was the first residence in the United States to be patented (the minaret was inspired by the original owner's appointment as magistrate to Cairo under President Ulysses Grant). Rooms range from simply elegant to outright decadent, with canopy beds, double Jacuzzis, billiard tables, and, in the library, a 48-inch TV, should Saratoga's nightlife fail to divert.

Saratoga Arms
Innkeepers: Noel and Kathleen Smith
518-584-1775
www.saratogaarms.com
497 Broadway
Price: Expensive to Very Expensive
Credit Cards: AE, D, DC, MC, V
Handicap Access: Yes
Restrictions: No children under 12; no pets

If the Adelphi is a giddy debutante, the sixteen-room Saratoga Arms is the oh-so-suave bachelor—quiet, eminently tasteful, scrupulously private, and set up with every boutique treat (bathrobe, iron, Wi-Fi, and hair dryer in each room, and, according to the *London Financial Times*, "the best coffee this side of the Hudson River").

Meticulously restored down to the antique wicker on the porch, this concierge hotel on the north end of Broadway is a get-away within a getaway, and only a stone's throw from the heart of downtown.

Union Avenue, the elegant thoroughfare that runs from the artists' retreat Yaddo past the thoroughbred racetrack to Congress Park, is Saratoga's gold coast for upscale bed and breakfasts. Here are some of the better known, each commanding its own faithful clientele:

Six Sisters Bed And Breakfast
Innkeepers: Kate Benton and Steve Ramirez
518-583-1173
www.sixsistersbandb.com
149 Union Avenue
Price: Moderate to Expensive
Credit Cards: AE, MC, V
Handicap Access: No
Restrictions: No children under 8; no pets

Cheery vibes, designer coffee, hearty breakfasts, and expert insider advice (co-owner Benton is a third-generation Saratogian) keep the patrons coming back. This Victorian favorite, with quirky gingerbread fretwork, is only a short stroll from the track. Particularly popular is a hotel-and-spa package deal with the Crystal Spa.

Union Gables
Innkeepers: Kelley Hamik and Thomas Van Gelder
518-584-1558
www.uniongables.com
55 Union Avenue
Price: Expensive to Very Expensive
Credit Cards: AE, MC, V
Handicap Access: No

In 1992, this grand Queen Anne—stalwart designed by R. Newton Brezee underwent a massive restoration and emerged a sparkling kid-friendly B&B with all the trimmings: hot tub, exercise room, bikes for guests, and a refrigerator in every lavish room. While some are themed (the Adirondack-style room, for instance, features branches for curtain rods), most hew faithfully to Saratoga's high Victorian style. There are ten rooms, each with a distinct "personality," and two guest rooms in an adjacent carriage house.

Westchester House
Innkeepers: Bob and Stephanie Melvin
1-800-581-7613
www.westchesterhousebandb.com
102 Lincoln Avenue
Price: Expensive to Very Expensive
Credit Cards: AE, CB, D, DC, MC, V
Handicap Access: No
Restrictions: Children welcome on a "limited basis"; no pets

A puckishly offbeat pastel paint job, seven rooms, lovely grounds, and the Melvins' keen knowledge of the local scene keep regulars returning to this impeccably managed, longtime Victorian B&B. Only blocks from Union Avenue in a city neighborhood called Five Points, centrally located between the track and the Saratoga Performing Arts Center.

CORINTH

The Agape Farm
Owners: Fred and Sigrid Koch
518-654-7777
4839 NY 9N
Price: Moderate to Expensive
Credit Cards: D, MC, V
Handicap Access: No
Restrictions: No pets

Children are not only put up with but are positively welcome at this homey B&B some fifteen minutes northwest of Saratoga on rural NY 9N. A mile south of the Adirondack mill village of Corinth, the Agape Farm offers thirty-three bosky acres of woods and fields, a stream full of trout, and a barn packed with goats, geese, and chickens. You can pound away at the piano, unwind on the wraparound porch, and help farmer Fred gather eggs for breakfast.

SCHUYLERVILLE

Bacon Hill Inn
Innkeepers: Tim and Katie Cartwright
518-695-3693
www.baconhillinn.com
359 Wall Street Road
Price: Expensive to Very Expensive
Credit Cards: D, MC, V
Handicap Access: No
Restrictions: Well-behaved children welcome; no pets

A New York State senator and farmer built this Italianate farmhouse in 1862. Impeccably restored, the Bacon Hill Inn is one of several farmhouse-style bed & breakfasts in the vicinity of Saratoga Springs, just a ten-minute drive east from the racetrack. The innkeepers can whip up a dinner party for guests (with notice), and in-house massages are available from co-owner Katie Cartwright, a licensed massage therapist. A billiard room downstairs invites a friendly game.

SARATOGA RESTAURANTS & FOOD PURVEYORS

Saratoga Springs has always been a city with an outsized appetite. High-roller Diamond Jim Brady could pack away four dozen oysters, six lobsters, a whopping steak, and a dozen crabs at a sitting. You can still chow your way through a brace of country or Victorian-themed steak-and-salad joints, or find yourself an all-you-can-eat Chinese or Mexican buffet.

But you can also eat well. Very well. And spend a lot of money doing it—which Saratogians and a lot of other northern New Yorkers are evidently prepared to do. But humbler spots abound as well, down-home diners and night-owl getaways, ethnic takeout joints, and pizza parlors galore.

Restaurant pricing follows this range for entrée, appetizer, and dessert:

Inexpensive: Up to $15
Moderate: $15–20
Expensive: $20–$35
Very Expensive: Over $35

Credit Cards:
Credit cards are abbreviated as follows:

AE: American Express   DC: Diners Club
CB: Carte Blanche   MC: MasterCard
D: Discover   V: Visa

Beekman Street Bistro

518-581-1816
www.thebeekmanstreetbistro.com
62 Beekman Street
Open: Daily
Cuisine: American
Serving: D
Price: Expensive to Very Expensive
Credit Cards: AE, MC, V
Reservations: Yes
Handicap Access: Yes

This stylish hot spot in the new vaunted Art District takes advantage of Saratoga Springs's proximity to farm country. When owner Tim Meaney and chef Dan Spitz started this place in 2005 (though Meaney is now the solo proprietor) the idea was to operate using the freshest local products available. That formula, along with great wine and creative dishes that evolve with regional harvests, has turned Beekman Street Bistro into one of the most popular restaurants in the Spa City.

Diners appreciate reading on the menu just where the ingredients for their meal comes from, places like Flying Pigs, Brookside, Lewis Wait, New Minglewood, and Three Cornersfield Farms. Dishes range from Niman Ranch grilled flank steak with wild mushrooms and arugula to porcini-dusted roasted chicken with Kilpatrick Farms string beans and lemon sage butter. Slow food never tasted so good.

Chez Sophie Bistro

518-583-3538
www.chezsophie.com
Saratoga Hotel, 534 Broadway
Open: Daily
Cuisine: French
Serving: B, L, D
Price: Very Expensive
Credit Cards: AE, CB, DC, MC, V
Reservations: Recommended
Handicap Access: Yes
Remarks: Weeknights feature a Pink Plate Special

When Robert Redford filmed *The Horse Whisperer*—the story goes—he virtually camped out at this second-generation family-run Saratoga institution back when it was in an old diner south of town; new digs are in the Saratoga Hotel. The food, a streamlined classic haute cuisine, is flat-out wonderful, with dishes like rabbit braised in Sylvaner with *fazzoletti di seta,* bison steak with red-wine reduction, and grilled escolar with a tropical fruit vinaigrette. Chef and co-owner Paul Parker and his talented sous chef Mark Graham, a terrific wine list (the restaurant's cellar features 400 French wines), and seasoned wait staff bring faithful crowds. Parker and his wife, Cheryl Clark, scrupulously pursue the freshest of the fresh at a bevy of local venison, trout, and free-range poultry farms and farmers' markets. The pacing is stately but not poky, and for the budget-minded, the weeknight Pink Plate Special is a steal.

Chianti II Ristorante

518-580-0025
www.chiantiristorante.com
208 South Broadway
Open: Daily
Cuisine: Italian
Serving: D
Price: Expensive to Very Expensive
Credit Cards: AE, MC, V

Reservations: No
Handicap Access: Yes

The Roman cuisine at a former Long John Silver's is as exuberant as the ochre-heavy, mural-rich decor. Line chefs behind the wrought-iron counter work with the confidence and speed of street magicians, and the golden-voiced owner-maître d' might treat you to his favorite aria or the latest disco-techno hit from Milan. A nice range of pasta selections, rich risottos, and grilled meats fills the menu, with nightly specials. Good red wine, too, and lots of it. No pretense here, just lots of fun.

Dine

518-587-9463
www.dinesaratoga.com
26 Henry Street
Open: Year-round, call for days and hours
Cuisine: Global comfort food
Serving: D
Price: Expensive
Credit Cards: AE, D, MC, V
Reservations: Recommended
Handicap Access: Yes

Ensconced in, of all places, a former Freihofer's bread outlet, this brash eatery earns a mention for the sheer chutzpah of Chef Stevie Knopf's off-the-wall specials (oyster wasabi shooters, pheasant pie, chocolate tamarind ice cream, roast elk) and for the cool L.A.-style slickness of the decor. The menu—a little French, a little Italian, a little all-American—seems to change with the rapidity of a roulette wheel, depending on what lights Knopf's fire. A wide-ranging taster's menu is available at the romantically sequestered Chef's Table, a Moroccan-style gentleman's pantry.

Hattie's

518-584-4790
www.hattiesrestaurant.com
45 Phila Street
Open: Daily
Cuisine: Soul food
Serving: L, D
Price: Moderate to Expensive
Credit Cards: AE, D, MC, V
Reservations: No
Handicap Access: Yes

A new spin on soul food is served up at Hattie's, a local landmark for generations.

Courtesy of Hattie's; photograph by Heather Bohm-Tallman

Owners Jasper and Beth Alexander are determined to maintain Hattie Mosley's beloved legacy of solid Southern and New Orleans-style soul food at this Depression-vintage downtown icon. On hot nights grab a table in the patio out back. You can't lose with the tried-and-true deep-fried chicken, pork chops, mac and cheese (with andouille sausage or chicken), or shrimp. If you're feeling like a break from convention, Jasper's ever-changing specials like Creole jambalaya and smothered pork chops are a welcome touch. For Food Network fans, in 2007 Jasper beat out Southwestern-cuisine phenom Bobby Flay in the televised competition, *Throwdown with Bobby Flay*.

The Ripe Tomato, An American Grill
518-581-1530
www.ripetomato.com
2721 US 9, Malta
Open: Daily
Cuisine: Italian/American
Serving: L, D
Price: Moderate
Credit Cards: AE, MC, V
Reservations: Recommended
Handicap Access: Yes

The theme is more or less Italian but just about everything shows up on the ambitious menu of this hearty, old-school supper club south of town. Patrons rave about the Yankee pot roast and the roast pork. Children can't lose with the million and one pasta entries. "How Mom cooked it" is the mantra; portions are more than generous, and the price is better than right.

Springwater Bistro
518-584-6440
www.springwaterbistro.com
139 Union Avenue
Open: Daily
Cuisine: Fusion
Serving: D
Price: Expensive to Very Expensive

Credit Cards: AE, D, DC, MC, V
Reservations: Recommended
Handicap Access: Yes

This place has been a beloved Saratoga eatery for almost a decade now, since rotisserie star David Bruce Britton and trend-savvy restaurateur Richard Rodriguez bailed out of Bolton Landing's esteemed Trillium at the Sagamore and commandeered the kitchen on tony Union Avenue. Unexpected Asian and Mediterranean high notes mix it up with a range of regional American favorites such as spit-roasted rabbit and osso bucco. Super-fresh fish is a strong suit here. Most ingredients come from local farms, so every night the menu changes, based on what's available. If you're watching your pennies, come Monday for the American Tapas Menu (prices range from $4 to $9). Even the wait here is a pleasure, thanks to the fireplace flanked with cozy chairs.

The Wine Bar
518-584-8777
www.thewinebarofsaratoga.com
417 Broadway
Open: Tuesday through Saturday, 4 PM
    —midnight; open Sunday in summer
Cuisine: Tapas
Serving: D
Price: Expensive to Very Expensive
Credit Cards: AE, D, DC, MC, V
Reservations: Recommended for parties of
    four or more
Handicap Access: Yes; call ahead, elevator
    in rear

Executive Chef John Ireland, who previously ran the kitchen at the Ritz Carlton in D.C., has helped transform this former wine bar and tapas hangout to an establishment with a full, creative menu—light plates, entrees, gourmet cheeses, and homemade desserts—served on two floors and, in summer, on the patio. The bar itself is still an elegant spot with live piano music and an endless wine list, but do venture to the dining room for

Ireland's rack of lamb with artichoke lemon fritter, grape tomatoes, and arugula, or his scallops with cauliflower puree, and fig, yogurt, and balsamic reduction. And ask about the Wine Bar's overnight suite for a luxury getaway.

BREAKFAST, LUNCH, UNUSUAL FARE, AND LATE-NIGHT GETAWAYS AND DIVES

For a quick and easy morning fix, a poppy-seed bagel with a lox and cream cheese schmeer at **Uncommon Grounds Coffee & Tea** (518-581-0656; 402 Broadway) is a winner every time. Many other spreads, toppings, and bagel flavors are available as well.

Early-rising city workers pack no-nonsense **Compton's** (518-584-9632; 459 Broadway) for the swiftest and most reliable four-square breakfast on Broadway. Another town favorite, the cozy **Country Corner Café** (518-583-7889; 25 Church Street; or 518-584-8300; 165 High Rock Avenue) draw a Skidmore crowd with their Green Mountain coffee, berry pancakes, and orange juice in jelly jars.

The menu at the refurbished **Saratoga Family Restaurant** (518-584-4044; 153 South Broadway, in front of the Greyhound bus terminal) is enormous, and breakfasts are as filling as they are affordable. Fancier fare such as German apple pancakes, designer omelets, fresh-squeezed orange juice, and quiches may be savored at the upscale, often crowded **Beverly's** (518-583-2755; 47 Phila Street).

If you're visiting during the race season, **breakfast at the track** (518-584-6200) is a longstanding tradition. Get there early because clubhouse tables fill up fast, starting at 7 AM. Or bring your own basket with juice and muffins and climb the bleachers to a long view. A free tram ride takes you to the barns.

Good, solid, fail-safe lunches are available at all of the above, but if you're after something more original, try **Ravenous** (518-581-0560; www.ravenouscrepes.com; 21 Phila Street) for spicy crêpes and crisp *pommes frite;* **Maestro's** (518-580-0312; 371 Broadway) for rich creamy pastas; or a local favorite, **Sperry's** (518-584-9618; 30 1/2 Caroline Street), for bistro fare—broiled cod, steak *au poivre*—as reliable as Big Ben. **Scallions,** too, has quality lunches of high-end California bistro fare with décor to match (518-584-0192; 44 Lake Avenue), and **Lime** (518-584-4315; www.limesaratoga.com; 7 Caroline Street) offers super service and Caribbean-flavored meals—try the lime chili and island beef kabobs. The elegant **Mouzon House** (518-226-0014; 1 York Street) makes mostly Creole-infused cuisine—never overdone cajuny, just delicious. The wine list is nice, and High Rock Park is just a stroll away.

There's also the upscale pizzeria **Bruno's**, complete with jukebox and wood-fired pizza (518-583-3333; 237 Union Avenue), or **Nunzio's** (518-584-3840; 119 Clinton Street, site of the former Pink Store), which will make gluten-free pizza pies. **Gotchya's Trattoria** features homemade pasta and portraits of mobster thugs on its walls (518-584-5772; www.gotchyas.com; 68 Beekman Street), and **Circus Café** (518-583-1106; www.circus cafe.com; 392 Broadway) has the nicest staff in town and is a good place to take the kids. In summer head to **PJ's** for barbecue and shoofly pie (518-583-7427; www.pjsbarbq.com; South Broadway).

A wide range of delicious take-out fare may be found at neighborhood joints like **Spring Street Deli & Pizzeria** (518-584-0994; 132 Spring Street) and **Pepper's Market & Deli** (518-584-3430; 173 Lake Avenue). For a family-run Italian deli, go to **Roma Foods** (518-587-6004; 222 Washington Street).

FOOD PURVEYORS

So you've got a cooler, you've got a picnic blanket. Where's the view and what's for lunch? Well, there are long, wide vistas of the Hudson from the **Saratoga National Historical Park** (518-664-9821) off NY 32 and NY 4, the site of bloody American Revolution battles. In Schuylerville, the **Fort Hardy Visitors Center** (518-695-4159) on the Hudson offers tables, toilets, grills, and a beach to launch a canoe. A 1911 power-house flanks the picnic area at Lock 5 on the **Champlain Canal**, where boaters can put in (518-695-3919). Go north on I-87 to Exit 17, backtrack south to **Moreau Lake State Park** (518-793-0511), where great trails and a good small beach await you. Back in town, the public lawn, and rose garden at **Yaddo** (518-584-0746; www.yaddo.org), a famous art colony, are a lovely place to picnic—if you can manage to ignore I-87 roaring just behind the wall of white pines.

As for that picnic, Saratoga's food purveyors and takeout places will not disappoint. But let's start with coffee. This city even has an espresso bar in the library. You can't get more hard-core than that.

Coffee

Saratoga Coffee Traders (518-584-5600; www.saratogacoffeetraders.com; 447 Broadway). The perfect combination: aromatic all-organic fair-trade coffee, retro candy, a light Mediterranean menu, and ice cream from The Ice Cream Man, of Greenwich. This is a nice, quiet place to stop for a light meal. Or have your food delivered with a handful of sweets and some of SCT's Giving Bean coffee (for every pound brewed and sold the shop will donate proceeds to a local community center).

Uncommon Grounds Coffee and Tea (518-581-0656; 402 Broadway). Fresh flowers on the tables, a new art show on the walls each month, giant burlap bags of beans, an obliga-tory rack of magazines and newspapers, a coffee roaster as big as a phone booth, and toothsome bagels—this hometown favorite still draws loyal throngs despite many new pre-tenders to the throne. If there's a line, hang in there. It chugs along fast enough. Hard-hustling Skidmore students man the espresso bar. Featured soups change every day.

Virgil's House (518-587-2949; 86 Henry Street). This joint has an old-school aura: no cell phones or laptops allowed, but lots of board games. If you need a place to get away from it all, sip your joe in the smushy chairs, play chess or Twister, listen to the Victrola, and flip through the old *Life* magazines from the 1960s.

Natural Foods

Four Seasons Natural Foods Store and Café (518-584-4670; www.fourseasonsnaturalfoods.com; 33 Phila Street). Load up on organic chips, exotic fruit pops, fruit leather, and kefir, or head through the packed store to the dining area, brack-eted on one side by an all-vegetarian, fresh-made-daily, surprisingly diverse buffet. The soups are creamless, rich, and hearty; the salads fresh, the entrées heavy on tofu, root veg-etables, and grains. Great baba ghanoush, foccacia, and rice pudding—and you can pack everything to go.

Saratoga Farmers' Market (518-587-0766; www.saratogafarmersmarket.org; in sum-mer: High Rock Park on High Rock Avenue, behind the City Center; in winter: Salvation Army building, 27 Woodlawn Avenue). Follow the lines of cars to the place to see and be seen every Saturday summer morning: The ever-expanding Saratoga Farmers' Market is always bursting with vendors. Cut flowers, hanging flower baskets, organic eggs, rare perennials, lamb sausage, free-range poultry, mesclun, fresh fava beans, beefalo soup bones, heirloom tomatoes, sweet corn, beeswax candles, raspberry jam, homemade soap, varietal melons, weird-looking squash, an apple for every palate, recipe, and plate.

Specialty Foods and Bake Shops

The Bread Basket Bakery (518-587-4233; www.saratogabreadbasket.com; 65 Spring Street). Regulars line up here for muffins, scones, and bear claws and a great array of sandwich breads. The irresistible cinnamon swirl makes brilliant toast, and one thick slice of the potato bread or the virtuous seven grain will keep you fueled and good to go for days. Homemade soups are a hit. Cozy tables overlook Congress Park.

Mrs. London's Bakery and Cafe (518-581-1652; www.mrslondons.com; 464 Broadway). The real deal here: nothing but Valrhona chocolate, Pluga butter, the purest of biodynamic grains. The prices are not for the faint-hearted, but hard-core pastry lovers won't care. You won't find a better double-berry charlotte, cherry clafouti, or Ricard-flavored Gâteau Basque north of New York City, and the hot chocolate is divine. Michael and Wendy London are the wizards behind the curtain here—and their sense of atmosphere is every bit as sophisticated as their pastry. Decor is high-end French-inflected Jacksonian America, and if the chandeliers look like something off the set for the movie *Amistad*, well, they are.

Putnam Market Place (518-587-3663; www.putnammarket.com; 435 Broadway). As close to Zabar's as Saratoga will ever get, this zealously upmarket gourmet emporium offers smartly prepared food to go (great albacore tuna salad, thick rounds of pink beef tenderloin, cold poached salmon), ridiculously outsized sandwiches, a terrific cheese board, and a bold miscellany of cold fruit drinks and teas. There are several small tables toward the rear and café-style tables outside. Come August, the place is mobbed. Cooking classes are offered onsite.

Roma Importing Company (518-587-6004; 222 Washington Street). Hand-cut Italian subs (try the lean cappicola), pillowy fresh mozzarella, and good olives keep locals coming to Roma's, a family institution. The breathless efficiency and wisecracking bonhomie of the staff make shopping fun and easy. Don't neglect the bountiful shelves of exotic condiments from all over the world.

NIGHTLIFE

Rumor has it that the dim-lit, moody, forty-seat jazz-scored **9 Maple Avenue** (518-583-2582; www.9mapleavenue.com) has the largest selection of single-malt scotch in New York State and a martini menu longer than your arm. **The Wine Bar** (518-584-8777; www.thewinebarofsaratoga.com; 417 Broadway) earns high marks for the courage and ambition of its list as well (for starters, fifty wines by the glass), and a waiter can help you match your tapas to your selection. **The Parting Glass** (518-583-1916; www.partingglasspub.com; 40–42 Lake Avenue) is for the Guinness-loving dart-and-penny-whistle crowd and acoustic music fans, and live jazz is the draw at the atmospheric **One Caroline Street Bistro** (518-587-2026; www.onecaroline.com). Here, the bar is always busy, and the waiters bearing plates of hearty Italian food move with skill between the close-set tables. And don't miss a nightcap and a dessert on the patio of the **Adelphi Hotel** (518-587-4688; www.adelphihotel.com; 365 Broadway).

SARATOGA CULTURE

Arts & Historical Centers

If you like your history but museum captions make your eyes water, head to the **Saratoga Springs Heritage Area Visitor Center** (518-587-3241; www.saratogaspringsvisitorscenter.com; 297 Broadway) across from Congress Park. A minigallery laden with photos of the Spa City in its heyday, the exhibit is very nearly bereft of text. Built in the Beaux-Arts style in 1915 as a trolley station, the "VC" is the best place to load up on news of current events and walking tour brochures on Saratoga's historic districts, one of which includes a tour of its elegant old springs. Of the three Depression-era spa complexes developed by Governor Franklin D. Roosevelt, only the Lincoln Bath still brings the old-time fizz. The Spa Park itself is as serene and restorative as ever, even if day guests know it less for its constellation of mineral springs than for a lovely eighteen-hole championship golf course, a posh hotel (the Gideon Putnam), and a great open-sided concert arena, the Saratoga Performing Arts Center, set like a moonstone in a grove of pines. The local volunteers are well informed and helpful; the location is as central as it gets.

Catercorner to the "VC" at the corner of Broadway and Spring is a building that resembles nothing more than the old city library, which it was. Today it houses the handsome **Saratoga County Arts Council at The Arts Center** (518-584-4132; www.saratoga-arts.org; 320 Broadway), home to a flourishing arts council; a theater space where the **Saratoga Film Forum** shows great indie flicks on Thursday and Friday nights at 8 (518-584-FILM; www.saratogafilmforum.org for listings); and a roomy art gallery whose monthly exhibitions range from equine art to the hippest of video installations (opening nights are a blast).

A mere two blocks away is the **Saratoga Springs Public Library** (518-584-7860; www.sspl.org; 49 Henry Street)—as big as a city hall with a nice restaurant and espresso bar, a superb little-used bookstore, a massive DVD collection, an always-booked community room—and, oh yeah, books and books and books.

Exhibitions about social history in Saratoga County are featured at the **Saratoga County Historical Society at Brookside** (518-885-4000; www.brooksidemuseum.org; 6 Charlton Street, Ballston Spa)—call it Brookside, for short. In a modest Georgian clapboard building thought to be the oldest hotel in the nation are a handful of galleries and snappily named exhibitions on subjects as homely and diverse as baseball ("Batter Up!"), county schools ("Go to the Head of the Class!"), and Saratoga tourism ("Be Our Guest!"). Ballston Spa is also home to the **National Bottle Museum** (518-885-7589; www.nationalbottlemuseum.org; 76 Milton Avenue) in an old downtown commercial building. Arrayed here are thousands of hand-blown bottles, the tools that made them, and the stories of the eighteenth- and nineteenth-century settlements that manufactured New York's glassware for generations. The Bottle Museum also features a diorama of an 1880s glass furnace and hosts an annual antique bottle show in Saratoga Springs. And for those looking for a quirky stop, go to the **Iron Man Museum** (518-695-5497; www.oldsaratogatradingpost.org; 40 Spring Street), in Schuylerville, to see a collection of vintage washing machines, old-school coal clothes irons, doorstops, and all sorts of oddities, some even for sale.

Museums

Children's Museum at Saratoga
518-584-5540
www.childrensmuseumatsaratoga.org
69 Caroline Street
Open: Year-round
Admission: $5 general admission; children under 1 free
Handicap Access: Yes

This determinedly hands-on children's museum will work your youngsters, ages seven and under, into a frenzy. A gaily colored mock-up of a generalized downtown offers stations to play postal worker, storekeeper, short-order cook, and firefighter (slide down the pole, pull on the boots, climb on the fire truck, and you're off); small-town life never looked as lively as it does here. Another floor features stations for making and hopping through giant bubbles, climbing into a tree house, suiting up in old-time clothes from "The Attic," and learning how to make music by breaking up electronic beams in a mini-bandstand. Kids love serving up orders in the 1950s diner and practicing their hammering skills in the construction zone.

The Historical Society of Saratoga Springs
518-584-6920
www.saratogahistory.org
Canfield Casino, Congress Park
Open: Year-round
Admission: $5 adults, $4 seniors and students
Handicap Access: Yes

A calm oasis in the middle of busy Congress Park, the city-managed Canfield Casino boasts a top-floor Victorian house museum, a permanent and in-depth exhibition on the history of Saratoga Springs, a revolving gallery (often focusing on some offbeat aspect of local history), and the architectural landmark, the casino itself. Although it was Richard Canfield who added the Beaux-Arts dining room, the gardens, and the Tiffany window when he bought the place in 1895, the real star of the Italianate structure is the scrappy spirit of prizefighter and Troy politico John Morrissey, who established it as a gaming club in 1870 and who, more than anyone, put Saratoga on the map. Gambling was outlawed when the casino fell into the hands of the city in 1911, and the building was overtaken by springs sippers and tea parties. But you can admire the old chips, roulette wheel, and cards in the "High Stakes Room" and even rent the glorious grand old place for a wedding party or a bash.

National Museum of Dance
518-584-2225
www.dancemuseum.org
99 South Broadway at the Saratoga Spa State Park
Open: Late May through mid-October, Tuesday through Sunday, 10–5
Admission: $6.50 adults; $5 students and seniors; $3 children
Handicap Access: Yes

Occupying the former Washington Bath House, an Arts and Crafts–style structure built in 1918, the National Museum of Dance—overseen by the Saratoga Performing Arts Center and located in the Saratoga Spa State Park—is the only museum in the country devoted expressly to American professional dance. A recent exhibition celebrated the work of black dancers and choreographers, while a permanent Hall of Fame honors the abiding genius of Fred Astaire, Bill "Bojangles" Robinson, Ted Shawn, Martha Graham, Alvin Ailey, Jerome Robbins, and Trisha Brown, plus a hundred others. The interactive kids' Discovery Room allows future dancers to try on costumes and perform on a miniature stage. This is a lovely place for a break between your afternoon chamber music concert at the Little Theater and your next symphony at the Saratoga Performing Arts Center.

Saratoga's National Museum of Dance is the only museum in the country devoted expressly to American professional dance. Courtesy of Kelly Kilgallon

National Museum of Racing and Hall of Fame
518-584-0400
www.racingmuseum.org
191 Union Avenue
Open: Year-round
Admission: $7 adults; $5 seniors and students; members and children under 5 free
Handicap Access: Prior notice required

When your luck flags at the track and celebrity spotting loses its allure, stroll down Union Avenue to the sleekly reconditioned National Museum of Racing. You don't have to love or even like horse racing to be seduced by the interactive exhibits, the life-size starting gate with hidden soundtrack (hoofbeats drumming, the crowd roaring), the gorgeous jockeys' silks, gleaming trophies, first-rate equine art collection, and the Racing Hall of Fame. There's a little gift shop, too.

New York State Military Museum

518-581-5100
61 Lake Avenue
Open: Year-round, Tuesday through Saturday, 10–4; Sunday, noon–4
Admission: Free
Handicap Access: Yes

Given its place in military history, Saratoga is a fine place for a military museum. This one, located in a nineteenth-century armory, houses the records and stories of New York State's military forces and veterans. Some 10,000 artifacts from the Revolutionary War to World War II to contemporary conflicts have a permanent home here, everything from uniforms to weapons to flags (there are more than a thousand state battle flags in this collection, more than half from the Civil War).

Soldiers' experiences are captured in the Veterans Research Center, the museum's 2,000-volume library, which has endless photographs (more than 2,300 images from the Civil War), scrapbooks, maps, and letters. The research center is open Tuesday through Friday, 10 AM–4 PM, although appointments are recommended.

Saratoge Automobile Museum

518-587-1935
www.saratogaautomuseum.org
110 Avenue of the Pines at Saratoga Spa State Park
Open: Year-round
Admission: $7 adults, $5 seniors, $3.50 6–16 years old; children under 5 free
Handicap Access: Yes

Vintage car buffs and youthful gearheads alike are thronging to the colorful installations at the Saratoga Automobile Museum, in an old bottling plant in Spa Park. Courtesy of the Saratoga Automobile Museum

Thrills, chills, and spills! In the handsome old bottling plant in the heart of the Spa Park is a flashy automobile museum. Vintage car buffs and youthful gearheads alike are thronging to the colorful installations. The permanent exhibition "East of Detroit" features the automobile industry in New York State, another hall explores the world of racing, and a third, "Sprockets to Rockets," fires up the kids. A recent exhibit, "Barn Finds," showcased gorgeous vehicles (such as a Cobra 427) that sat in backyards and outbuildings undisturbed for, in some cases, decades. The cars displayed at the museum change constantly. In summer, lawn shows bring hot rods, famous motorcycles (one ridden by Audrey Hepburn, another owned by Elvis), and all sorts of international models to the museum.

The Frances Young Tang Teaching Museum and Art Gallery
518-580-8080
www.skidmore.edu/tang
815 North Broadway
Open: Year-round
Admission: Free
Handicap Access: Yes

A touch of edginess in Saratoga (and high time, too), the Tang art museum at Skidmore College can look like a giant foundering ship or a streamlined Incan monument or . . . heck, you name it—everybody else has. Exhibitions, which are always changing, are provocatively interdisciplinary and designed to make you think. Past shows have focused on museum display and racism, the "Tumultuous Fifties" as captured by photographs from *The New York Times* Photo Archives, Rube Goldberg cartoons, and photographs of ritual adornment and spirituality of masquerade in West Africa. The UpBeat on the Roof—yup, on the roof—summer evening music series is very cool.

Music & Performing Arts

Saratoga Performing Arts Center
518-587-9330
www.spac.org
Saratoga Spa State Park, Hall of Springs
108 Avenue of the Pines
Open: June through September
Admission: Ticket prices vary
Handicap Access: Yes

SPAC is the summer home of the New York City Ballet, the Philadelphia Orchestra, the Saratoga Chamber Music Festival, and Freihofer's Jazz Festival; the **Homemade Theater** (518-587-4427; www.homemadetheater.org) and Lake George Opera Festival sojourn in Spa Little Theater, also in Spa Park. On the packed schedule, the opera and ballet go first (more or less through July). When Philly claims the stage you might expect to see the likes of Yo-Yo Ma, Sarah Chang, Kathleen Battle, and Joshua Bell. SPAC is touted for its outdoor sound, so if you'd sooner watch the stars than Maestro Charles Dutoit's back, buy a lawn ticket and bring a blanket to the big grassy slope in front of the amphitheater, along with binoculars and bug spray. In August, pop and rock events, such as performances by the Allman Brothers, Fall Out Boy, Lucinda Williams, Bruce Springsteen, and John Mayer fill the place.

SPAC and other venues around town host dynamite annual events. Some of the best include the Saratoga Food & Wine Festival; the many free readings from the Writers Institute at Skidmore College (regular guests include novelist Russell Banks and Poet Laureate Robert Pinsky); the big-ticket Travers Stakes in late August (dress sharp, bet big, lose nice); the Saratoga Native American Festival; and the Nutcracker Tea Party.

Saratoga Recreation

A few years back, die-hard historic preservationists protested the introduction of an Ilion carousel in Frederick Law Olmsted's historic Congress Park. Now that it's installed, complaints are few. The carousel runs weekend afternoons from late spring into fall—rides cost just $.50—and it's a stunner. So, for that matter, is Congress Park, famous with the stroller set for its ducks, ponds, and pretty fountains.

The **Saratoga Spa State Park** (518-584-2535; www.saratogaspastatepark.org; US 9) on the outskirts of town makes a big splash with the youngsters for its two vintage outdoor pools: the big shallow Peerless is pretty much for children only. A tree-shaded, somewhat unkempt but still hugely popular wading pool in the **East Side Recreation Field** on Lake Avenue (NY 29) keeps the toddlers cool in summer, and there are jungle gyms and sand boxes and swings for all (518-587-3550).

The **Bog Meadow Brook Nature Trail,** 3 miles from downtown, is a level, easy hike (518-587-5554). Another way to get some exercise: bring a bike and sample Saratoga's growing tangle of bike loops.

Family-friendly events include Sunday evening bandstand concerts in Congress Park and tailgate picnics at the **Saratoga Polo Grounds** (518-584-8108; www.saratogapolo.com; Bloomfield Road). Around the middle of July the **Saratoga County Fair** (518-885-9701; www.saratogacountyfair.org) comes to Ballston Spa. The fairgrounds in Greenwich, 15 miles to the east, host the more expressly agricultural and better-known **Washington County Fair** (518-692-2464; www.washingtoncountyfair.com) in late August—tractor pulls and pig races, a midway, and barns full of livestock.

A great family movie option is the old-time **Malta Drive-In Theater** (518-587-6077; www.maltadrivein.com) just south of town on US 9. And last but by no means least, in summer there is the **horse track** (518-584-6200; www.saratogaracetrack.com; 267 Union Avenue). As far as children go, forget the races—it's the paddock that brings the news. Small wiry men in giant polka dots! Huge horses, swishy tails! How excellent is this!

Saratoga Shopping
Some locals lament the invasion of the chains like **Eddie Bauer** (518-581-8001; 338 Broadway) and **Banana Republic** (518-226-0909; Congress Park Centre), but independent stalwarts like **Symmetry** (518-584-5090; www.symmetrygallery.com; 348 Broadway), peddling art glass, and **G. Willikers's** (518-587-2143; 461 Broadway) upmarket toys hold firm, along with **Gallery 100** (518-580-0818; www.gallery100.net; 462 Broadway), which exhibits a variety of fine art. Bibliophiles will lose themselves in the labyrinthine antiquarian bookshop, the **Lyrical Ballad** (518-584-8779; 7 Phila Street), and appreciate exotic pieces at **deJonghe** jewelry (518-587-6422; www.djoriginals.com; 470 Broadway). Also, on Saratoga's west side, check out the **Candy Company** (518-580-0499; www.saratogacandy.com; 5 Washington Street), all sorts of artistic endeavors at **Beekman Street Artists Co-op** (518-583-0086; www.saratogaartists.com; 79 Beekman Street), paintings with horse and jazz themes at **Crimson Gallery** (518-587-8190; www.artedelfumo.com; 73 Beekman Street), and snazzy designer handbags at **Mimosa** (518-583-1163; 70 Beekman Street).

Browsing Broadway is a must. G. Willikers, one of the shops along this stretch, sells upmarket toys.
Courtesy of Kelly Kilgallon

Big-box retailers galore—**Target**, **Lowes**, **Kohl's**, and **Home Depot**—can be found just east of town on NY 50.

GLENS FALLS

If Saratoga Springs is the Emerald City, where many a cabin-fevered Adirondacker likes to steal away for a big night on the town, Glens Falls, the self-styled "Gateway to the Adirondacks" in southeastern Warren County, is Kansas. The Falls is as down to earth as Saratoga is razzle-dazzle.

Glens Falls was named "Hometown U.S.A." by the editors of *Look* magazine in 1944 and 19 years later voted America's "most typical town" by Swedish National Television. The little city is a true child of the Adirondacks, a hard-working, four-square mill town.

Woods and rivers and mother lodes of lime and marble put this place on the map. Economically, Glens Falls looks north; that's where many of its residents hail from, that's where many of them go to work. It even smells like the north, that sweet-and-sour whiff of wood pulp. In Glens Falls speech, the hard, evenly paced cadence may be a legacy of French Canada; Saratoga's accent blows north from New York City, with hints of Brooklyn and undertones of New Jersey.

Saratoga may own bragging rights to the "Turning Point of the American Revolution" (a distinction, it must be noted, claimed by several other towns with famous battlefields), but when it comes to really regional history, the story of the Adirondacks, surely Glens Falls commands center stage. Quakers founded the settlement in 1763, built a sawmill, ran a tavern, lost their shirts, and saw their homes go up in smoke during the Revolutionary War, their pacifism provoking the suspicion of Tory and patriot alike. After the revolution the settlement bounced back, buoyed by an influx of pioneers from New England and Warren County's emerging lumber industry and bolstered by the adoption of the fast-running Schroon and Hudson Rivers as highways for the log drives. Glens Falls earned a century of industrial fame and quiet fortune thanks to logging and papermaking. The Hudson, which winds through Glens Falls from west to east, gave rise as well to a smoky necklace of long-lived mills and factories—lime kilns, canal boat operators, foundries, cement mills, collar factories, railroad spurs, and, looming over all, the pulp and paper mills whose chimney-borne emissions give the city a fragrance all its own.

Finch, Pruyn & Company, for nearly 150 years the major employer in town as well as a major Adirondack landowner, drove the local economy, philanthropy and even recreation, through its 160,000 acres of woodland. Sale of the paper mill and land in 2007 has left many wondering about the fate of the mill, but at press time, the pulp grinders are still going and book paper is being made. The Hudson River in Glens Falls remains the city's industrial heart. But it isn't really a company town—the city was also home to an impressive number of insurance companies, the largest of which, Glens Falls Insurance, built the blocky downtown edifice that is Glens Falls's skyscraper and has a helpful way of looming into view and getting you oriented when you're on the verge of getting lost. (The building is now general rental office space—Glens Falls Insurance itself is gone.)

The city is far from all business. One of the finest little art museums in New York flourishes here on the high banks of the Hudson, and several other museums, too. The **Hyde Collection Art Museum** (518-792-1761; www.hydecollection.org) was the inspired notion of Charlotte Pruyn, daughter of lumber magnate Samuel Pruyn, and Charlotte's art-loving husband, Louis Fiske Hyde. Mentored by the savvy likes of Bernard Berenson, the world-traveling, fast-learning Hydes amassed an art collection that continues to delight visitors for its diversity and taste. Here, in the Hydes' former home (an Italian Renaissance—Revival mansion overlooking the mill that made the family fortune) are paintings by Rembrandt, Degas, Seurat, Rubens, El Greco, and Botticelli, as well as American masters Eakins, Hassam, Ryder, and Whistler. In 1952, eighteen years after her husband's death, Charlotte Hyde bequeathed the art collection to Glens Falls. The museum opened in 1963, adding a stylish wing for temporary exhibitions in 1989 and undergoing a massive restoration and expansion project, completed in 2004—testament to the civic spirit and philanthropic imperative that defined the hometown, small city capitalist in a more unashamedly paternalistic age.

On the other side of town is another monument to the civic fealty of the local bourgeoisie: the former home of merchants, the DeLong family, now the **Chapman Historical Museum** (518-793-2826; www.chapmanmuseum.org). Part classic nineteenth-century house museum, the Chapman also offers a temporary exhibition gallery and space dedicated strictly to the work of the Adirondacks' best-known late-nineteenth-century photographer, Seneca Ray Stoddard (1843–1917). In the mid- and late-nineteenth century, the Adirondack region attracted hordes of painters and photographers. No shutterbug could match the range and detail of Stoddard's vision of this changing landscape with its log drives and rough-hewn towns on the one hand, its posh lakeside resorts and scenery-seeking swells on the other. Scrutinize Stoddard's photographs at the Chapman and you come away with a fair idea of the industrial and cultural currents that helped sweep Glens Falls into its age of prosperity and growth.

Today, Glens Falls's center is finally getting the respect it deserves. Old storefronts have been revitalized as toy stores, bookshops, a coffee roaster, gift galleries, and interesting restaurants. A rotary at the downtown five-point intersection was finished in 2007, along with brand-new sidewalks, making a pedestrian-friendly destination. The former Woolworth's is now home to the Adirondack Theatre Festival as well as a huge, beautiful shop featuring New York wines.

The Adirondack Theatre Festival presents original productions, cabarets, and solo performances in a former Woolworth's building in downtown Glens Falls. Scene from a comedy, Behave Yourself.
Courtesy of the Adirondack Theatre Festival

GLENS FALLS LODGING

Because it is not itself a tourist destination, Glens Falls doesn't offer many cozy bed & breakfasts. Motels abound off Exit 19 on I-87 at Aviation Mall and along US 9 heading north and south out of Glens Falls, where chains like **Econo Lodge** (518-793-3700; 543 Aviation Road) and **Ramada Inn Glens Falls** (518-793-7701; 1 Abby Lane, Queensbury) are available. A new hotel in Queensbury, **Six Flags Great Escape Lodge & Indoor Waterpark** (1-888-708-2684; 89 Six Flags Drive), means family fun year-round.

Inside the city proper, lodging choices winnow down to a fine few, each offering comfortable rooms at sensible rates that—along with Saratoga room rates—shoot up in the "high season" of August.

Glens Falls Inn

Innkeeper: Armanda Squadrilli
646-824-8379
www.glensfallsinn.com
25 Sherman Avenue
Open: Year-round
Price: Expensive–Very Expensive
Credit Cards: AE, D, MC, V
Handicap Access: Yes

Brass beds and nice quilts are among the
scrupulously period features that characterize this sunny bed & breakfast in a one-
hundred-plus-year-old Victorian home.
The inn offers five rooms with private bath,
Internet access, AC, cable, and queen beds,
plus the Top of the Inn, a roomy apartment
suite.

The Manor Inn

Innkeepers: Denise and Ron Lavoie
518-793-2699
www.themanorinn.net
514 Glen Street
Price: Moderate to Expensive
Credit Cards: MC, V
Handicap Access: No
Restrictions: No pets

This 1920s bed & breakfast in a leafy neighborhood full of historic homes offers five
guest bedrooms with AC and Internet
access. As if the fireplace in the parlor and
the period antiques weren't sufficiently
enticing, the Manor Inn also serves a full
breakfast by candlelight—surely an
Adirondack first.

The Queensbury Hotel

518-792-1121
www.queensburyhotel.com
88 Ridge Street
Price: Expensive
Credit Cards: AE, D, MC, V
Handicap Access: Yes
Restrictions: No pets

The belle of the ball—if there were a ball, if

the ballroom that once pulsed to the beat of
Benny Goodman and Guy Lombardo hadn't
changed to a reception room years ago—is
surely the historic Queensbury, a 125-room
full-service hotel in the heart of town, the
darling of conventioneers and visiting
politicos and stars. Ronald Reagan stayed at
the Queensbury, as well as Bobby Kennedy,
ZZ Top, Ozzy Osborne, Bob Dylan, and
Phish. The Who also stayed here, in splendid anonymity, working out the kinks of a
North American tour.

In 1924, a hundred local businessmen,
bolstered by substantial start-up gifts from
Finch, Pruyn and Glens Falls Insurance,
joined forces to get a hotel built in the heart
of their beloved boomtown. More than
eight decades later the Queensbury remains
a fine place to stay, handy to downtown with
requisite shop and lounge, pool and Jacuzzi,
restaurant, salon, and exercise room.

GLENS FALLS RESTAURANTS & FOOD PURVEYORS

132 Glen Bistro

518-743-9138
www.132glenbistro.com
132 Glen Street
Open: Daily
Serving: L, D
Cuisine: Upscale, creative bistro
Price: Moderate to Expensive
Credit Cards: MC, V
Reservations: Yes
Handicap Access: Yes

This small, noisy, busy storefront—hip, colorful, and adorned with historic photographs—brings you into downtown and
serves up wholesome fare. You'll find one of
your favorite comfort foods on the limited
menu. Chef-owner Kevin M. Bethel skips
the appetizers, since he wants you to enjoy
his ample entrées, which come with a soup
or salad. He willingly creates lighter por-

tions if that's your desire. Six of fifteen entrées reflect his delight in seafood—the salmon and tuna dishes are terrific. Bethel's homemade salad dressings are inspired, and Cuban sandwiches are really something special. You just can't go wrong here.

Do leave room for dessert. A small handwritten dessert menu sits beneath the glass on most tables. The key lime pie is yellow (a good sign), creamy, and tangy. Carrot cake and ice creams appeal, also. In this beer-or-wine-only bistro, the lover of robust brews is in for a treat. Cooper's Cave beers, conceived and brewed locally (by a Bethel brother), are served. If you'd like to eat this creative comfort food in the comfort of your own home, order a meal to go.

Fiddleheads

518-793-5789
21 Ridge Street
Open: Daily
Serving: L, D
Cuisine: Gourmet—Continental & American
Price: Expensive to Very Expensive
Credit Cards: AE, D, MC, V
Reservations: Yes
Handicap Access: Yes

Located downtown only half a block off the main drag (Glen Street), this quiet, upscale restaurant offers the best and most satisfyingly innovative food around. On the limited but thoughtful menu you may be tempted by a favorite or "must-try" selection, created here rather than some portion-control warehouse. The appetizers—although common in name—are delightful. The smoked salmon arrives with two sauces, both delicious, one piped from a pastry bag and served as a mound of ripples. Beautiful to the eyes, nose, and palate. Soups are superb. More crab than cake is found in Fiddleheads's signature entrée, Maryland crab cakes. Other main plates range from fresh seafood to rack of lamb, and desserts

are a treat. Bill Brown Jr, the chef-owner, sends you home satisfied and relaxed. Then it's off to a hockey game, a show at the theatre festival, or some time on the couch.

Heidelberg Inn

518-792-5556
www.heidelberginn.net
352 Quaker Road, Queensbury
Open: Daily
Cuisine: German and American
Serving: L, D
Price: Moderate to Expensive
Credit Cards: AE, D, MC, V
Reservations: No
Handicap Access: No

Quaker Road traffic can make you crazy and stressed. Step through the doors of this modest, family-run establishment and you immediately feel welcome. The inviting German atmosphere of this single-roomed restaurant is reinforced by the large and small nutcrackers that stand at attention on the sills of the diamond-paned windows and on every shelf. Deli sandwiches, salads, omelets, a quiche, a homemade soup, and appetizers and fish platters broaden the lunch menu from specialty sandwiches with German names, unusual club sandwiches (the Munich Club is outstanding), wursts, and Heidel-burgers. Dinner entrées include sauerbraten, jager schnitzel, and weiner schnitzel. Each is tasty but not exactly as your Tante Brunhilde made them—but better. The full service bar can provide a hearty German beer. Save room for dessert, which are all made here, straightforward, very good, and huge. This immensely popular restaurant doesn't take reservations, so if eating earlier or later suits you, you'll sit right down.

Jake's Round-Up

518-761-0015
www.jakesroundup.com
23 Main Street, South Glens Falls

Open: Daily
Cuisine: Southwestern Tex-Mex, Good Old
  Comfort Food
Serving: L, D
Price: Moderate to Expensive
Credit Cards: AE, MC, V
Reservations: Recommended
Handicap Access: Yes, from the parking lot

Frenetic and friendly. Sit in one of many
connected rooms, at a table covered with
vinyl cowhide. Chile pepper lights, vintage
booths, saddles, cowboy art, café tables,
and ropes provide a festive Western
ambiance.

This could be the North Country's only
source for chicken-fried steak. Meals come
with spicy miniature loaves of cornbread.
As much care goes into the excellent sides
(baked beans, mashed potatoes, cole slaw,
and sweet potato fries) as the main courses.
Pot roast is a succulent bargain. Beef or
pork ribs are brushed with house barbecue
sauce, not too sticky or cloying, a good
blend of flavors. Mexican dishes are very
good, with the combo burrito grande at the
top of the list.

Children are very welcome and will
enjoy this quirky eatery. The coin-operated
horse and boat inside but out-of-the-way
as well as the nearby pinball machine can
keep them occupied while parents linger
over a beer or coffee.

Massie's Restaurant

518-792-3383
69 Main, South Glens Falls
Open: Daily
Cuisine: Italian, American
Serving: L, D
Price: Moderate to Expensive
Credit Cards: MC, V
Reservations: Yes
Handicap Access: Yes, from the parking lot;
  restroom available but difficult

South Glens Falls is a blue-collar town, and
Massie's is a robust family dining experience.

Garlic toast, a relish dish from grandma's
table, ice-cream scoops of butter and pâté, a
choice of two soups (the minestrone is
unusually tasty), and a salad arrive well before
your chosen entrée. Appetizers are unnecessary unless you have a true hankering.

Your ample main course will leave you
groaning if not carrying some away. The veal
dishes are tender, and the signature brasciola
is delicious. Pasta is neither mushy nor hard
but done to perfection. If Italian dishes are
not to your taste, there are steaks, prime ribs,
and club sandwiches.

Three or four of the desserts are made by
the restaurant and are good . . . if you still
have room. Cappucino, espresso, and ordinary coffees are available to finish a boisterous evening.

Siam Thai Sushi

518-792-6111
196 Glen Street
Open: Daily
Cuisine: Thai
Serving: L, D
Price: Moderate to Expensive
Credit Cards: AE, D, MC, V
Reservations: Yes
Handicap Access: Yes

Locals rave about this place, and say that
after just one meal here, it becomes a
favorite stop. The curry dishes are delicious, the pad Thai a house special, and the
sushi a fine treat for a place so far from the
Big Apple. Also, the Thai iced tea is terrific.
Service with a smile—the staff is quiet and
capable—brings folks back, too.

Siam Thai is in an old storefront with
impossibly high ceilings stapled with
stamped tin. The space is airy and bright,
with exposed brick walls and wood floors.

QUICK BITES & SPECIALTY FOODS

Poopie's? Dirty John's? These beloved places reflect the owners' nicknames and not failed hygiene. The nickname thing is part and parcel of Glens Falls's mill town roots—where lunch counters are like Cheers, without beers.

It's A Wrap (518-743-0920; 242 Quaker Road, Queensbury) offers a variety of wrap and bagel sandwiches. It's near Lowe's if you're exhausted and hungry after home shopping. **High Peaks Java** (518-798-9088; www.highpeaksjava.com; 153 Maple Street, Glens Falls) is the place to go for organic coffee. **Cool Beans** (518-743-1367; 2 S. Western Avenue, Glens Falls; or 518-798-8398; 270 Quaker Road, Queensbury) also has casual lunches, serving up half sandwiches and soups. Top off lunch with ice cream or a frosty one at **Cooper's Cave Ale Company** (518-792-0007; www.cooperscaveale.com; 2 Sagamore Street, Glens Falls)—the root beer is excellent. Find more suds at **Davidson Brothers Restaurant & Brewery** (518-743-9026; www.davidsonbrothers.com; 184 Glen Street, Glens Falls) in a historic exposed-brick building with a courtyard for outdoor dining. Onion rings on a stick are the perfect accompaniment to a cold beer.

East Wok (518-745-5975; 175 Broad Street, Glens Falls) has excellent Chinese takeout. **Gourmet Café** (518-761-0864; www.downtowngourmet.com; 185 Glen Street, Glens Falls) has soups, salads, sandwiches—served on Rock Hill bread—ample options for vegetarians, and an outdoor café. If you're looking for dinner, the café's Friday and Saturday pasta nights are very popular, and the kitchen is happy to prepare meals to go. **Jack's Bistro** (518-798-1797; 730 Upper Glen Street, Queensbury) has fantastic contemporary American dishes. Although it's tucked behind an anonymous strip mall, like a modern speakeasy, it's lovely inside—hip without being self-conscious. Swing by **Gambles** (518-793-5384; 920 US 9, Queensbury) for cookies and cakes.

For another bagel sandwich and soup option there's **Lox of Bagels & Moor** (518-793-8681; 89 1/2 Main Street, Queensbury). Or check out **New Way Lunch** (518-792-9803; 54 South Street, Glens Falls; or 518-761-3356; 731 Glen Street, Queensbury), famous for its Dirty John's hot dogs with meat sauce.

Peter's Diner (518-792-9772; 36 South Street, Glens Falls), a real locals' hangout, serves basic diner fare. **Poopie DiManno's Lunch Inc.** (518-792-6155; 54 Lawrence Street, Glens Falls) has the best breakfasts. Since World War II, it's been run by the DiManno family. Expect huge portions, scrumptious slabs of ham, and attitude at no charge—listen and watch from the counter. The cheeseburgers are always drippy and good. Don't wait for your server to deliver your check—you're expected to go up to the cash register and settle your tab. **Rock Hill Bakehouse** restaurant (518-615-0777; www.rockhillbakehouse.com; restaurant: 19 Exchange Street, Glens Falls; and 518-743-1627; bakery: 1338 US 9, South Glens Falls), a sunny spot with bistro tables near the hospital, serves lunch: smoked turkey and cranberry sandwiches with cheese, Black forest ham, roast beef, all on signature Rockhill breads. The chowders, minestrone, and beef barley soups are worth trying, too, plus good coffee and sweets. The other location is strictly a bakery, offering jalapeno cheddar bread, sun-dried tomato bread, baguettes, sourdough, farm bread, real artisan breads, plus biscotti, scones, and rock cakes (really plump cookies). **Samantha's Café & Catering** (518-792-5839; www.samanthascatering.com; 11 Broad Street, Glens Falls), in a cool industrial-looking space with funky furniture, brightly painted ductwork, and exposed brick, makes great homemade soup and sandwiches served on thick multigrain or the house specialty—burlap bread.

The Silo Country Store (518-798-1900; 537 Aviation Road, Queensbury) is an atmospheric place—poke around the old barn for sandwiches, soups, and salads. **Steve's Place** (518-793-5855; 194 Broad Street, Glens Falls) is a twenty-four-hour diner. And **Sutton's Market Place** (518-798-1188; www.suttonsmarketplace.com; US 9, Queensbury) has croissant sandwiches and excellent choices for ladies who lunch. Get a dose of tunes with your martini or meal at **Wallabee's Jazz Bar** (518-792-8282; www.wallabeesjazzbar.com; 190 Glen Street, Glens Falls).

GLENS FALLS CULTURE

Cinema

Between the seven-screen multiplex at Hoyt's **Aviation Mall Cinema 7** (518-793-3332) in Queensbury and Hoyt's **Route 9 Cinema 5** (518-793-5233), a mile south of Six Flags The Great Escape amusement park, Glens Falls suffers from no shortage of first-run options. Moviegoers after a less commercial, more edgy style pack the free movies Tuesday night at **Crandall Public Library** (518-792-6508; www.crandalllibrary.org; 251 Glen Street, Glens Falls), or go to **Aimie's Dinner & Movie** (518-792-8181; www.aimesdinnerandmovie.com; 190–194 Glen Street, Glens Falls). The food is good, the setting great, and the whole package works well. In warm months visit the **Glen Drive In Theater** (518-792-0023; www.glendriveintheater.com; US 9, one mile south of The Great Escape), where moviegoers have been watching big-screen flicks since 1958.

Galleries, Libraries & Museums

Chapman Historical Museum
518-793-2826
www.chapmanmuseum.org
348 Glen Street, Glens Falls
Open: Year-round; closed Monday
Admission: Free; guided tours $2 per person
Handicap Access: Yes

The Victorian portion of the Chapman Historical Museum is decked out in the kind of period furniture that reflects the taste of former occupants, the DeLongs. A newer section offers a roomy three-part gallery featuring the work of famed Adirondack photographer Seneca Ray Stoddard and provocative exhibitions about local history. Lectures, holiday events, school programs, and other activities keep the place bustling all year.

Crandall Public Library
518-792-6508
www.crandalllibrary.org
251 Glen Street, Glens Falls
Open: Year-round, daily; gallery is open during main library hours
Handicap Access: Yes

The library is a true anchor for downtown, with excellent book, DVDs, and periodical selections; a helpful staff; and a full roster of events, from film to lectures. Folklorist Todd DeGarmo curates exhibitions in a vest-pocket gallery at Crandall. Sample exhibits have explored the drawings of Navajo children, the photographs of Alan Lomax, and crafts of the Colonial era.

At the museum the **Center for Folklife, History and Cultural Programs** (518-792-3360), an archival resource for regional historians, is open Monday through Saturday, and also hosts great readings, workshops, and performances.

Hyde Collection Art Museum
518-792-1761
www.hydecollection.org
161 Warren Street, Glens Falls
Open: Year-round; Tuesday through Saturdays, 10–5; Sunday, noon–5
Admission: Free
Handicap Access: Yes

The Hyde Collection Art Museum is the city's pride and joy. It features a fine collection of old and modern masters—works by Rembrandt, Homer, da Vinci, Degas, Eakins, Rubens, van Gogh—in the Hydes' lovingly furnished and newly restored 1912 Italian palazzo home and its adjoining arts complex. Recent temporary exhibitions include "The Last of the Mohicans," Volumes I and II—a first edition of James Fenimore Cooper's American literary classic on view; "European Works on Paper," including Picassos from the museum's permanent collection; and "Luminist Horizons: The Art and Collection of James A. Suydam." The museum's Helen Froehlich Auditorium hosts lectures and performances; studios and classrooms provide space for art workshops for adults and children; and the gift shop, incidentally, is as eclectic and appealing as any store in town.

The Hyde is also backdrop for the de Blasiis series—chamber music that includes such groups as the Biava String Quartet, with performances inside the house in an enclosed patio with soaring windows and tile floors.

Lower Adirondack Regional Arts Council (LARAC)
518-798-1144
www.larac.org
7 Lapham Place, Glens Falls
Open: Year-round

Adirondack artisans and artists are featured in the gallery of this clearinghouse for regional arts organization and a promoter of numberless community arts events. A summer must-see is LARAC's huge craft fair in the city park by Crandall Library.

The Shirt Factory
518-793-9309 or 518-824-1290
Lawrence and Cooper Streets, Glens Falls
Open: Year-round

Nearly three dozen artists and shopkeepers have zapped new life into a former clothing manufacturing facility. The historic four-story brick structure's renovated, light-filled studios are leased by watercolorists, printmakers, sculptors, and potters, and an upscale gallery fills the first floor. The place also houses retail spaces such as **SensibiliTeas** (tea salon and gift shop), **Adirondack Quilts** (fabric, quilting supplies, and sewing products), and **Elements of Art** (supplies). **Lemon Tree Yoga & Healings Studio** and the **Acupuncture Studio** are also based here. Unfortunately, there's no one Web site listing all the events at the factory, though you can imagine it's a hotbed of activity, so call about open houses, exhibits, or swing by to check out the scene. Some Shirt Factory artists participate in the Glens Falls **Third Thursday Art Walks** (April–October; www.thirdthursday.org).

The Visual Arts Gallery at Adirondack Community College

518-743-2328
640 Bay Road, The Dearlove Building, Queensbury
Open: Year-round; Monday through Thursdays; call for times
Admission: Free

Lively, enthusiastic opening nights are one happy hallmark of this roomy college gallery, which showcases the work of up-and-coming artists from the region.

Music & Theater

Adirondack Theatre Festival

518-798-7479
www.atfestival.org
Charles R. Wood Theater, 207 Glen Street, Glens Falls
Open: Summer; occasional winter shows in other venues

The Adirondack Theatre Festival was launched in 1995. Founders of the company were involved with the original production of the Broadway hit *Rent,* and bring real sophistication to their shows, performed in a theater that was converted from an old Woolworth department store (see listing below). The season begins in June, with five or six shows, children's workshops, and new play readings. Summer 2007's big hit was *Tick...Tick...Boom!,* an autobiographical musical by Pulitzer Prize–winning composer Jonathan Larson.

Charles R. Wood Theater

518-798-9663
www.woodtheater.org
207 Glen Street, Glens Falls
Open: Year-round

This new theater in downtown Glens Falls has 30,000 square feet of space for performances, rehearsals, meetings, receptions—you name it. The place's namesake, the late Charles R. Wood, was the founder of Storytown, now The Great Escape, and a driving force in funding community-based projects and organizations—he played a heavy hand in shaping an old Woolworth's into this modern theater. You'll see it all here: the Adirondack Theater Festival in summer, and an assortment of acts, troupes, and galas throughout the rest of the year. Recent events include plays by Pendragon and Glens Falls Community Theater; an evening of sea shanties, folk tunes, and Irish drinking songs; a performance of *The Nutcracker* by the Adirondack Ballet; and a jazz ensemble concert.

Glens Falls Community Theatre
518-792-1740
www.gfcommunitytheatre.org
P.O. Box 687, Glens Falls
Open: Year-round

Think *Waiting for Guffman:* The old-fashioned family-friendly Glens Falls Community Theatre serves up hearty rations of drawing-room mysteries, vintage dramas, musicals, and revues—community-supported and community-staffed all the way. Recent productions were *Our Town* and *The Pajama Game.*

Glens Falls Symphony Orchestra
518-792-1348
www.fgso.org
7 Lapham Place, Glens Falls
Open: Year-round

A repertoire that ranges from Bach's *St. Matthew's Passion* to commissioned pieces by the resident composer at Union College hints at the confidence and skill of this small city orchestra. A high-school chorus augments offerings during the holiday season, and every Fourth of July, the orchestra gives a free performance at City Park; fireworks follow.

The symphony plays at a variety of venues in the area, including the First Presbyterian Church and Christ Church United Methodist, in Glens Falls; and Queensbury High School, Hudson Falls High School, and Maple Street Middle School, in Saratoga Springs.

Seasonal Events & Festivals
See also "Recreation and Family Fun" for more information. *The Chronicle*, Glens Falls's free newspaper, is a good place to check for regional events (518-792-1126; www.readthechronicle.com).

LARAC Arts Festival (518-798-1144; www.larac.org) in City Park, whose 200-plus booths draw upwards of 25,000 in June.

The Adirondack Drum Corps Competition (518-747-4342; www.adirondackdrums .com) comes to the East Field Stadium Complex in July; bagpipe lovers, make a note.

Adirondack Balloon Festival (518-761-6366; www.adirondackballoonfest.org), a famed four-day hot-air balloon event in mid-September, attracts folks from all over the world. This is a big draw and if you aim to catch it up close and personal, make your way to the Warren County Airport by dawn's early light and no later.

Taste of the North Country (518-745-7076), a downtown food fair that drawsforty-plus restaurateurs of every description to City Park in September, is a nosher's delight.

Pumpkin Festival (518-638-6301) is an autumn fiesta of pumpkin carving, pony rides, music, food, and other kids' activities, in October.

The Chronicle Book Fair (518-792-1126; Queensbury Hotel, 88 Ridge Street, Glens Falls) is a gathering of dozens of authors, publishers, and members of nonprofit groups who sign books, discuss writing, and offer various workshops and kids' activities.

Adirondack Stampede Charity Rodeo at the **Glens Falls Civic Center** (518-798-0202)—and a wild and wooly night it is, happily evocative of the long-gone heyday of Warren County's once thriving rodeo and dude ranch scene in nearby Lake Luzerne—heats up chilly November. This is a Professional Rodeo Cowboys Association—sanctioned event.

GLENS FALLS RECREATION & FAMILY FUN

The excellent **Glens Falls Family YMCA** (518-793-3878; www.glensfallsymca.org; 600 Glen Street) and the adjacent Crandall Park, with its running trails, tennis courts, and pond, offer plenty of recreational options. Or runners, dog walkers, and bicyclists can get a blast of fresh air, New York–engineering history, and a seven-mile workout on a graded path that runs the length of the **Feeder Canal Park** (518-792-5363), from the feeder dam 2 miles southwest of Glens Falls to five massive combines in Fort Edward. In 1822, a canal was dug from the Hudson River to "feed" the Champlain Canal some miles off. The surviving locks at the Five Combines Historic Lock Area in Fort Edward are the only ones in New York State that date from the time of the Erie Canal. Kayakers and canoeists can put in at small launch areas at either end of the canal—it's a mellow, easy ride for little kids. No swimming there, but try the pool at **Haviland's Cove Beach** on the Hudson River at East Field Park (518-761-3819), as well, of course, as the hard-used beach itself. Diving sales, rentals, instruction, and boat charters are available through **Morin's Dive Center** (518-761-0533; www.morinsdivecenters.com; 20 Warren Street, Glens Falls). **Adirondack Rowing** (518-745-7699; www.adirondackrowing.com; 46 Meadow Lane, Queensbury) sells all kinds of modern shells and offers lessons.

The Feeder Canal Park also marks the southern tip of a 12-mile Warren County Bikeway that traces a scenic stretch of the old Delaware & Hudson line to fetch up in Lake George's Battlefield Park. Bikers should figure on a one- to two-hour ride each way. **Rick's Bike Shop** (518-793-8986; www.ricksbikeshop.com; 368 Ridge Road, Queensbury) offers a great selection of sports equipment and information, catering to road cyclists, backcountry bikers, and even winter bikers who install spikes on their tires.

For scenic flights, if you want to float on air, call **Adirondack Balloon Flights** (518-793-6342; www.adkballoonflights.com).

Typical of perhaps a half dozen Adirondack towns, Glens Falls has a ski slope of its own: **West Mountain Ski Center** (518-793-6606; www.skiwestmountain.com; 59 West Mountain Road). It's small, family-operated, mere minutes from downtown, and with more than twenty trails there's a slope for every skier and snowboarder's speed and style. Another just source of civic pride are the **Crandall Park International Ski Trails** (518-761-3813): 7 groomed kilometers of wooded trails lighted for night skiing and free to all, right within the city's limits. **Fall Line Ski Shop** (518-793-3203; www.falllineskishop.com; 366 Quaker Road, Queensbury) rents and sells downhill and cross-country skis. The **Inside Edge** (518-793-5676; www.insideedgeskiandbike.com; 624 Upper Glen Street, Queensbury) offers downhill and cross-country ski sales and rentals; it's the best local source for racing supplies.

There are plenty of golf courses in Glens Falls and the surrounding area, including the **Glens Falls Country Club** (518-792-1186; www.glensfallscountryclub.com; 211 Round Pond Road, Queensbury), **Sunnyside Par 3 Golf Course** (518-792-0148; 168 Sunnyside Road, Glens Falls), and **Bay Meadows Golf Club** (518-792-1650; 31 Cronin Road, Queensbury), to name a few.

For more family fun, Glens Falls is within a few minutes' drive of many outdoor amusement parks and roadside attractions. The best-known and most popular is **Six Flags The Great Escape & Splashwater Kingdom** (518-792-3500; www.sixflags.com/greatEscape), in Queensbury—more than a hundred rides strong, it is the biggest fun park of its kind in northern New York State. It's open spring through fall, but if you're looking for year-round fun, check out the new adjoining **Six Flags Great Escape Lodge and Indoor Water Park**

(888-708-2684; www.sixflagsgreatecapelodge.com), a great place for you and the kids to chase away the winter blahs. For information on the galaxy of theme parks, miniature-golf courses, wax museums, and waterslides in nearby Lake George, see Chapter 7.

Glens Falls Shopping

For basic fare (food and clothing, furniture, housewares, and office supplies), local folks head for the malls, following the out-migration of department stores and specialty shops some years ago. But antique hounds might want to sample **200 Glen Antique Marketplace** (518-792-0323; 200 Glen Street, Glens Falls) or **Glenwood Manor Antiques** (518-798-4747; 60 Glenwood Avenue, Queensbury).

Both the Hyde Collection Art Museum and the Chapman Historical Museum feature first-rate gift shops. **Red Fox Books** (518-793-5352; www.redfoxbookstore.com; 28 Ridge Street, Glens Falls) has an excellent selection of titles, and hosts regular readings and signings by regional writers. A fun kids' and parents' shop, **Dog Ate My Homework** (518-792-0133; 206 Glen Street, Glens Falls) sells children's books and furniture and all sorts of imaginative gifts. Fine home furnishings, luxury bed and bath linens, and other designer gifts can be found at **Sterling & Company** (518-745-6808; www.shopsterlingandco.com; 203 Glen Street, Glens Falls). Crafts and upscale gifts are a big draw at a local favorite, **Sutton's Market Place** (518-798-1188; www.suttonsmarketplace.com), just north of town on US 9 in Queensbury before The Great Escape (you can score a tasty lunch or breakfast there as well). Sutton's is a sprawling complex with a nice gourmet shop, quality note cards and wrapping papers, gifts, and interesting women's clothing that you will not find at the mall. Look here for natural linens and cottons in hip styles, plus jewelry. Off the same parking lot is a furniture store, with gorgeous leather couches, and chairs, some twig pieces, rugs, bookshelves, and accessories for town or country homes. The Toy Cottage at Sutton's is another popular standby. For more Adirondack-style products many people browse the aisles at **The Silo** (518-798-1900; 537 Aviation Road), at Exit 19.

The ladies' shops and menswear stores have mostly migrated away from downtown. **Aviation Mall** (518-793-8818; www.shopaviationmall.com; 578 Aviation Road, Queensbury), also off Exit 19, has T.J. Maxx, the Bon-Ton, Sears, J.C. Penney, Target, and other shops. But the big shopping experience is toward Lake George, at the **"Million Dollar Half Mile"** (The Factory Outlets of Lake George; www.factoryoutletsoflakegeorge.com), with eighty-plus brand-name factory outlet stores such as Ralph Lauren, Jones New York, Timberland, Coach, Orvis, Levi's, and Eddie Bauer. Traffic can be snarly, but snag a good spot and walk from plaza to plaza, then park on the other side of the road and do likewise.

Visitor Information

For more information about town and around, contact the **Adirondack Regional Chamber of Commerce** (518-798-1761; www.adirondackchamber.org); for Saratoga Springs, call the city's **Visitor Center** (518-587-3241; www.saratogaspringsvisitorcenter.com).

4

LODGING

Rustic, Classic, and Basic

Travelers to the eastern Adirondacks in the early 1800s were welcomed at inns and taverns, although accommodations occasionally fell short of expectations: A visitor to the Pavilion, a hotel near Ticonderoga, described the place in 1855 as "noisy and ill-conducted. . . . The food is bad, the cooking worse, the rooms are small, the bedsteads large, and you have your choice between a feather-bed and one made of corn-husks, with now and then a corn-cob thrown in by way of variety."

After the Civil War, and the publication of *Adventures in the Wilderness* by William H. H. Murray, the entire Adirondack region—from the High Peaks to the lake country—became popular as a tourist destination. The demand for lodging—luxurious lodging that could compare with hotels in Newport or Saratoga Springs—grew, and huge hotels multiplied on lakeshores from Blue Mountain Lake to Westport, Bolton Landing to Lake Placid. Lake George's Fort

Lodging in the Adirondacks ranges from rustic cabins to decadent luxury resorts. Courtesy of the Whiteface Lodge

William Henry Hotel had scores of rooms and tiers of piazzas; the Mansion House, in Elizabethtown, boasted rooms for 200 guests; Paul Smith's St. Regis House was described as "first class in every respect, and patronized by the very best class of people in the country."

Those vast hotels succumbed to fire and/or the changing tastes of the traveling public. The Adirondacks in the late nineteenth century was an exclusive place, a destination that was difficult to reach, and with the advent of modern steamship travel, the spas of Europe

Miller's Saranac Lake House was a favorite with the hunting and fishing crowd. Private collection

became accessible to the wealthy. At the same time, the middle class was increasing in numbers, automobiles were becoming affordable, and ordinary people started taking vacations. They eschewed stodgy old hotels and headed for tent campgrounds, resorts, and roadside cabins.

Resorts of the 1920s combined planned activities like dances, waterfront contests, and games for kids with amenities such as common dining rooms and private cabins. The housekeeping-cottage colonies—groups of buildings without a central dining facility—took that notion of privacy a step further, and became popular because families could prepare all their meals. Motels, designed for people who just wanted a clean place to rest overnight, were built on the edges of many towns.

The 1980 Winter Olympics in Lake Placid led economic planners to worry that not enough rooms would be available for the legions of spectators. Many homeowners took the plunge into accommodating guests, and one Olympic legacy is many freshly converted bed & breakfasts. B&Bs continue to thrive as owners of historic properties in the Champlain Valley and the central Adirondacks began taking in guests.

A word here differentiating the various lodging terms: Generally, in New York, a bed & breakfast is defined as a place that holds ten or fewer guests. Breakfast is served and the owner usually lives on the premises. An inn is larger, often serves dinner or lunch as well as breakfast, and has to comply with state codes for public safety and food service. Then there is the bed-&-breakfast inn, which is a place that's bigger than a B&B, is regularly inspected by the state, and offers the morning meal in the price of a night's stay. As long as we're on the subject of definitions, a housekeeping cabin includes a kitchen or kitchenette, so guests can cook meals.

Nowadays the variety of Adirondack lodgings covers the full spectrum: There are country lodges that offer hearty meals and access to hiking or cross-country skiing; vast old hotels filled with antiques; lakeside resorts with a full roster of activities; housekeeping cottages nestled by the beach; and motels. For many visitors, the classic Adirondack vacation is a week on the lake in the same housekeeping cottage that they enjoyed as a child. Some families come back the same week every year, and for that reason, many of the nicest places are booked years in advance. If you want to try a housekeeping cabin and have flexibility in your vacation time, consider May through June or September through October.

Listed in this chapter you'll find a whole range of accommodations. Our criteria for selection was to seek out places with a special approach—an individual personality—that offer comfort, cleanliness, and hospitality. For some listings, the setting is a primary consideration; in others, it's wonderful architecture; some sites offer first-class amenities and services; in still others, it's the hosts and hostesses that set the place apart. With this kind of intuitive categorization, you'll find positive notes on a few modest, inexpensive places that succeed at what they're trying to do, just as you'll find perhaps briefer mention of the highly acclaimed spots. Above all, we try to offer a range of prices and options.

At the end of the chapter, you'll find a listing of motels, simple cabins, and private campgrounds. There are many, many more places to stay in the Adirondacks than you'll read about in this book (if we catalogued all the places in Lake George village alone that would fill this entire chapter); phone numbers and Web sites for tourist information offices can be found in Chapter 9. To learn about various lodgings online, click on the Adirondack Bed & Breakfast Association's site, www.adirondackbb.com, or search for the particular town or region you plan to visit.

ADIRONDACK LODGING NOTES

Rates

Some cottages and resorts are available only by the week during July and August, and this is indicated in the "Minimum Stay" section of the information box. Extrapolate the per-night, double-occupancy rate by seven, and you should get an idea of what a week's visit costs. It's possible for a single woman to stay at Wiawaka Holiday House, on Lake George, for $300 per week, just as a couple can spend upward of $2,000 for a single night at The Point, on Upper Saranac Lake.

Rates quoted are for per-room, double occupancy during the prime tourist season, which in most cases is July and August. Some places that are open year-round charge more during January through March because of increased heating costs. You can usually expect lower rates for midweek stays, off-season rentals, or package deals; it's definitely worthwhile to ask. At places described as bed & breakfasts, you can expect that breakfast is included in the price of your room; many resorts and inns offer full or modified American meal plans.

Some places add 10 percent or 15 percent gratuity to the bill, and motel and hotel rooms are subject to New York's 7 percent sales tax. Also, Essex County, which includes Lake Placid and much of the Champlain Valley, enacted a 3 percent bed tax. The rates that are listed here don't include these additional charges.

Very Inexpensive: Under $40 per night, double occupancy
Inexpensive: $40–$70
Moderate: $70–$100
Expensive: $100–$200
Very Expensive: Over $200

Minimum Stay

Many of the resorts and housekeeping cabins rent units by the week only in the summer, with guests arriving and leaving on a Saturday or Sunday. In the winter, some accommodations ask for a two-night minimum stay to make it worthwhile to turn up the heat in the cabin. Midweek in the off-season many places will happily welcome overnight guests; if no minimum stay is specified, you can assume that one night is fine.

Deposit/Cancellation

Reservation arrangements vary greatly from place to place. Some resorts and cottages that rent by the week ask for a 50 percent deposit; some winter-season places have a "no-snow" cancellation policy so that guests don't get stuck if the weather fails to cooperate. A handful of bed & breakfasts ask for full payment of one night's stay fourteen days in advance.

Private Rentals and Reservation Services

Most real-estate agents handle private seasonal rentals. These places might be anything from backwoods camps to new condominiums to lovely old houses with private lakefront, boats, and all the up-to-date creature comforts. "Mt. Marcy Marketplace" classifieds, found in the bimonthly *Adirondack Life* magazine (518-946-2191; www.adirondacklife.com; P.O. Box 410, Jay, NY 12941), can be a terrific source for vacation rentals. On the Web, check out www.adirondackbyowner.com. Securing private accommodations takes considerable planning, but can be ideal if you're traveling with pets or have a large family in tow. Some private campgrounds are described in this chapter, but a list of the Department of Environmental Conservation campgrounds in the Adirondack Park is in Chapter 7.

Credit Cards

Credit cards are abbreviated as follows:

AE: American Express   DC: Diners Club
CB: Carte Blanche   MC: MasterCard
D: Discover   V: Visa

LODGING IN THE ADIRONDACKS

Lake George and Southeastern Adirondacks

BOLTON LANDING

Boathouse Bed & Breakfast

Owners: Patti and Joe Silipigno
518-644-2554
www.boathousebb.com
44 Sagamore Road
Open: February through October
Price: Very Expensive
Credit Cards: AE, MC, V
Handicap Access: No
Minimum Stay: Two nights; three nights on
   holiday weekends
Remarks: No children; no pets; Wi-Fi

This extravagant boathouse was once the summer digs of Gold Cup–winning speedboat racer George Reis. It offers an absolutely perfect backdrop for a relaxing getaway on Lake George, no matter what season. There are four rooms and a suite, which has an enclosed sunporch, in the main house, all with Jacuzzi tubs, mini fridges, and either queen or king beds. The separate carriage house offers two suites, both with lake views, king-size beds, and gas fireplaces. Guests can swim the lake, park their boat in the available slips, soak in the hot tub on the dock, and have free access

For some, the quintessential lodging remains the Adirondack lean-to and the best bed one made from balsam boughs. Courtesy of Ted Comstock, Saranac Lake

to the fitness center and indoor pool at the nearby Sagamore. Included in the price are family-style three-course hot breakfasts.

Hilltop Cottage Bed & Breakfast

Owners: Anita and Charlie Richards
518-644-2492
www.hilltopcottage.com
4825 Lake Shore Drive
Open: May through October
Price: Moderate to Expensive
Credit Cards: None
Handicap Access: No
Remarks: No pets; no smoking

The Bolton Landing to Lake George Road was known as "Millionaires' Row," and Hilltop Cottage belonged to a caretaker for one of the grand estates. It's directly across the street from the Marcella Sembrich Opera Museum, a museum honoring the Romanian-born diva.

The clapboard cottage has two guest rooms upstairs; one can accommodate a family, the other just a couple. There's also a guest cabin on the property that sleeps two; it has an efficiency kitchen, heat, and TV. Anita, a former German teacher, and Charlie, a retired guidance counselor, bought the eleven-room house in 1985 and opened it as a B&B three years later. Hilltop Cottage is a friendly, homey place, and after a breakfast of German apple pancakes on the screen porch, you can walk over to Bolton's tennis courts and lakefront parks.

The Sagamore

Managing Director: David Boyd
518-644-9400
www.thesagamore.com
110 Sagamore Road
Open: Year-round
Price: Expensive to Very Expensive
Credit Cards: AE, DC, MC, V
Handicap Access: Several units; elevators in
   hotel
Remarks: Two gourmet restaurants, pub,

dinner cruise; spa; fitness center; tennis courts; conference facilities; children welcome; no pets; Wi-Fi

For more than a century there's been a Sagamore hotel overlooking Lake George. Completed in 1883, the grand lodge has survived two fires and weathered the Depression, but gradually declined during the 1970s. In 1983 the island property was bought by a real-estate developer who launched extensive renovations. Today the Sagamore is the pride of the community and winner of numerous awards for excellence in serving the traveling public.

The elegantly appointed public areas include a conservatory with lake views, six restaurants—everything from fine dining to tapas to pub fare—a spa, and a gift shop. Guests have 350 deluxe units to choose from, including suites, hotel bedrooms, lakeside lodges, and executive retreats with lofts. The list of Sagamore amenities is impressive: a huge indoor pool and fitness center; miniature golf; an indoor tennis-and-racquetball facility; an indoor rock-climbing wall; outdoor tennis courts; playground; a beautiful sandy beach; docks for guests' boats; and a Donald Ross–designed championship golf course 2 miles away.

The Sagamore is a popular spot for conferences and weddings, offering excellent facilities for large and small groups. There's no need to leave the kids at home if one or both parents are attending meetings: The social department has plenty of supervised activities for children.

The Sagamore is on an island in Lake George, and boasts gourmet dining, championship golf, a full-service spa, and lovely accommodations. Courtesy of the Sagamore

CHESTERTOWN

The Chester Inn

Innkeepers: Bruce and Suzanne Robbins
518-494-4148
www.thechesterinn.com
6347 Main Street
Open: Year-round
Price: Expensive
Credit Cards: MC, V
Handicap Access: No
Remarks: No pets; children 12 and older
welcome; Wi-Fi

One of Chestertown's beautiful homes listed on the National Register of Historic Places, this Greek Revival inn dates back to 1837. Beyond the grand hall, with its mahogany railings and grain-painted woodwork, there are four lovely second-floor guest rooms with private baths, including the Victorian Suite, which has its own sitting room and bath with a deep, old-fashioned tub. Downstairs is a common room with a TV/VCR and plenty of books. Guests are welcome to explore the thirteen-acre property, which has gardens, a horse barn, smokehouse, and an early cemetery; during Chestertown's bicentennial celebration in 1999, archeologists explored the property and found the inn's ancient privy to be a treasure trove of artifacts.

Nondrivers take note: Chestertown is a regular stop on the Adirondack Trailways bus line, and this inn is just a block from the station. It's also next door to the Main Street Ice Cream Parlor or a short walk to a movie at the Carol Theatre.

The Fern Lodge

Innkeepers: Sharon and Greg Taylor
518-494-7238
www.thefernlodge.com
46 Fiddlehead Bay Road
Open: Year-round
Price: Very Expensive
Credit Cards: AE, MC, V
Handicap Access: No
Remarks: No pets; Wi-Fi; porches over-
looking lake

Looking for an over-the-top spot to get away from it all? The Taylors, former owners of Friends Lake Inn, have worked their magic to create yet another fine establishment that offers guests the ultimate in luxury. Every room at Fern Lodge, on Friends Lake, has king-size beds, massive stone fireplaces, lake or mountain views, mini refrigerators for chilling wine or cheese boards, spacious baths with steam showers, Jacuzzi tubs, and elegantly rustic décor.

Ramble, cross-country ski, or snowshoe the Taylors' surrounding seventy acres, stroke their kayaks out on the lake, or hang around the lodge, where you can read in the impressive great room, shoot pool, watch movies in the private theater, relax in the sauna, get fit in the exercise room (where equipment is modern and varied), or browse the fine wine cellar for the perfect vintage. Enjoy an evening boat tour with historic narrative and wine; in the morning linger over an extraordinary multicourse breakfast with homemade breads and pastries.

Do check out photographs of the Fern Lodge on its Web site—this place will blow you away.

Friends Lake Inn

Innkeepers: John and Trudy Phillips
518-494-4751
www.friendslake.com
963 Friends Lake Road
Open: Year-round
Price: Very Expensive (price includes
breakfast and dinner for two guests)
Credit Cards: AE, MC, V
Handicap Access: Yes
Minimum Stay: Two nights on weekends
during peak season; three nights over
New Year's
Remarks: Outdoor hot tub; cross-country-
ski trails; mountain-bike rentals; guide

The new Fern Lodge, in Chestertown, is an over-the-top spot for a lakeside Adirondack getaway. In addition to impressive accommodations, there are seventy surrounding acres to explore, plus a private movie theater, wine cellar, and evening boat tours on Friends Lake. Courtesy of The Fern Lodge; photograph by Randall Perry Photography

service for outdoor treks; gourmet restaurant; extensive wine list and wine cellar.

For most of its 140-or-so-year history, the Friends Lake Inn has been a hostelry of one kind or another, although its first tenants, the tannery workers, would marvel to see people rather than cowhides soaking in the enormous wooden hot tub outdoors. The Phillips offer guests seventeen comfortable rooms and small suites—either "traditional-" or "Adirondack-style"—all with private baths, some with steam showers and whirlpool tubs, fireplaces, private entrances and balconies, and views of Friends Lake.

Truly an inn for all seasons, guests can enjoy cross-country skiing or snowshoeing on 32 kilometers of groomed trails here in the winter; fishing in the spring; swimming and mountain biking in the summer; hiking in the fall. From time to time, there are wine-, Scotch-, or beer-tasting dinners and other themed events. Small business conferences are easily accommodated. There's no need to travel far for dinner—the restaurant on the first floor is delightful (see Chapter 5). Inquire about seasonal packages, everything from massage, fall foliage, adventure trek, ski, or romantic getaways.

Landon Hill Bed & Breakfast

Owners: Judy and Carl Johnson
518-494-2599
www.bedbreakfast.net
10 Landon Hill Road
Open: Year-round
Price: Expensive
Credit Cards: MC, V
Handicap Access: Yes
Minimum Stay: Two nights on weekends
Remarks: Children welcome; no pets; no
   smoking; Wi-Fi

This lovely Victorian home set among rolling hills on a country lane is peaceful and comfortable. A beautiful oak spiral staircase leads you to the four tastefully decorated guest rooms upstairs (all with private baths), and downstairs are a handicap-accessible guest room and bath. Before the sit-down breakfast, have coffee and homemade muffins by the woodstove; then, after stoking up on quiche and fresh fruit, explore the Johnsons' eighty-nine acres, or head for Chestertown's historic district or the nearby Schroon River for fishing and canoeing. Guests can unwind in the outdoor hot tub. Landon Hill is just a mile from I-87, the Northway, so it's a convenient jumping-off spot for further adventures.

DIAMOND POINT

Canoe Island Lodge

Owners: Thomas and Carla Busch Burhoe
518-668-5592
www.canoeislandlodge.com
3820 Lakeshore Drive
Open: Mid-May through mid-October
Price: Expensive
Credit Cards: None
Minimum Stay: weekly summer; three
   nights (off season)
Handicap Access: Yes
Remarks: Private island; sand beach; sailboats, rowboat and windsurfers; tennis;
   children welcome; no pets; Wi-Fi

In 1943, Bill Busch financed the down payment on Canoe Island with a couple hundred bushels of buckwheat, and in June 1946 he welcomed the first guests to his lodge. The twenty-one-acre, twenty-five-building complex now offers all kinds of family vacation options from quaint log cabins to modern suites and private chalets. There are clay tennis courts, a sandy beach on Lake George, hiking trails, and numerous boats to sail. Perhaps the best part of a stay here, though, is the chance to enjoy the lodge's very own three-acre island, about three quarters of a mile offshore. Shuttle boats take guests to the island where they can swim, snorkel, fish, sunbathe, and explore a beautiful, undeveloped part of the lake.

The Burhoes take great pride in offering hearty European-style meals with homegrown vegetables, homemade breads and pastries, and treasured old-country recipes. On Thursday, there is an island picnic and on Saturday, a lavish buffet; dances, movies, and children's programs are also on tap, although there's no pressure to join in.

The lodge accommodates 175 people at peak capacity. In spring and fall, rates include breakfast, lunch, and dinner.

HAGUE

The Locust Inn

Innkeepers: Carolyn and David Dunn
518-543-6934
www.locustinn.com
NY 9N & 8
Open: Year-round
Price: Expensive
Credit Cards: None
Minimum stay: Two nights during summer
Handicap Access: One room
Remarks: Beach, boat ramp; no pets or young children

A graceful homestead built in 1865, the Locust Inn has operated as a bed & breakfast for more than two decades. It's packed with antiques and art, and conveniently next to the town beach and boat ramp on Lake George.

The three attractively appointed guest suites—all with lake views—have queen beds, private baths, sitting areas, and TVs. The third-floor suite, under the eaves—which can sleep four and has a sitting room, kitchen, and private bath—is charming. The carriage house is a separate cottage open in summer, located on Hague Brook.

Ruah Bed & Breakfast

Owners: Judy and Peter Foster
518-543-8816
www.ruahbb.com
9221 Lakeshore Drive
Open: May through January
Price: Expensive
Credit Cards: AE, D, MC, V
Handicap Access: No
Remarks: Hiking trails; fireplace; balconies; children under 12 by special arrangement; no pets; all rooms are air-conditioned

Such an appealing place naturally has amusing legends: This stone mansion was designed by Stanford White; part of the estate was won in a poker game; the Lake George monster—the biggest hoax ever seen in northern New York—was created in the studio of the original owner, artist Harry Watrous. Bing Crosby and Jack Dempsey slept here. Stay at Ruah and you'll have your own stories to tell—about visiting a lovely inn overlooking a beautiful lake.

The four guest chambers are upstairs and have private baths. The Queen of the Lakes is outstanding, quite spacious, with access to the balcony and views from every window. The Watrous Suite is a separate wing with two adjoining bedrooms and balconies. Common areas downstairs include

Guests at Ruah can enjoy breakfast from the glassed-in porch overlooking Lake George.

James Swedberg

a vast living room with a fieldstone fireplace and an antique grand piano, a cozy library, and an elegant dining room. To give you an idea of the scale of this inn, the veranda stretches across the front of the house and measures about 80 feet long.

Trout House Village Resort

Owners: The Patchett Family
518-543-6088 or 1-800-368-6088
www.trouthouse.com
9117 Lakeshore Drive
Open: Year-round
Price: Moderate to Expensive
Credit Cards: AE, D, MC, V
Minimum Stay: Two nights on weekends; holiday weekends have a three-night minimum
Handicap Access: No
Remarks: Boats and bikes for guests; 400-foot sandy beach; fireplaces; cable TV with HBO; children welcome; no pets except in off-season

One of the few four-season resorts on the quiet northern portion of Lake George, Trout House is a handsomely maintained complex of log cabins and chalets. Many of the cabins have fireplaces, decks, and complete kitchen facilities; there are numerous suites and rooms in the main lodge, all with private baths. There are canoes, rowboats, sailboats, kayaks, bikes, and even a nine-hole putting green for guests. Trout House is a short distance from historic sites such as Fort Ticonderoga and Crown Point, while the Ticonderoga Country Club—a challenging eighteen-hole course—is just up the road.

By January, the atmosphere changes from that of an active resort to a quiet country inn, perfect for cold-weather getaways. Cross-country skiers and snowshoers can venture out from the front or back doors to explore miles of countryside.

LAKE GEORGE

Alpine Village

Owners: Lil and Ernest Ippisch
518-668-2193
3054 Lakeshore Drive
Open: May 2 through October 31
Price: Moderate to Expensive
Credit Cards: D, MC, V
Minimum Stay: Three nights
Handicap Access: No
Remarks: Private beach; pool; children welcome; no pets

The sitting room of the main lodge is an Adirondack gem, and log cabins of all sizes, from the spacious main lodge to cute duplex cottages with fireplaces, characterize this lakeside resort. The grounds are nicely landscaped, leading down to a private beach; other amenities include rowboats and canoes, a recreation room, pool, and limited dock space for visitors' boats. In summer, Alpine Village's "breakfast restaurant," in a dining room overlooking the lake, is open seven days a week.

Dunham's Bay Resort

Owners: Alan and Andrea Goldstein
518-656-9242
www.dunhamsbay.com
2999 NY 9L
Open: Year-round
Price: Moderate to Expensive
Credit Cards: AE, D, MC, V
Minimum Stay: Three nights on summer weekends
Handicap Access: No
Remarks: Sandy beach; tennis courts; indoor heated pool; play area; restaurant; children welcome; no pets; Wi-Fi

The centerpiece of this stylish resort on the less-developed side of Lake George is a massive stone lodge built by a well-to-do Glens Falls dentist in 1911. New owners have completely revamped this place into a welcoming resort that can cater to individual guests or large groups (this is a super spot for conferences, weddings, or other private parties). There's a sports bar in the basement, with football specials and live entertainment and karaoke, and the new **Destinations** restaurant is on-site and open year-round, seven days a week, offering Sunday brunch, light fare all day, and dinner entrees from 5 on.

The resort's accommodations range from twenty-one two-bed, two-bath cottages, each with kitchenette, flat-screen TV, and sleeper sofas (they can accommodate up to six people), to twenty renovated hotel suites, either rooms with standard queen-size beds, rooms with king-beds, or multiple bedroom suites.

Fort William Henry Resort & Conference Center

Manager: Sam Luciano
518-668-3081 or 1-800-234-0267
www.fortwilliamhenry.com
48 Canada Street
Open: Year-round
Price: Moderate to Expensive
Credit Cards: AE, D, DC, MC, V
Handicap Access: Yes
Remarks: Restaurants; pool; children welcome; no pets; Wi-Fi

For almost a century and a half there's been a hotel named Fort William Henry on this bluff overlooking Lake George. The current version is a modern complex with 198 rooms, an indoor pool, and eighteen acres of manicured grounds. The resort has four restaurants, open seasonally, including the **White Lion**, which, according to the resort, offers "the best damn breakfast with a view." Interesting package options are available, such as a two-night bicycle adventure that includes breakfast, dinner, bike rentals, and a trail map, or a golfer's getaway. Note also that rates for Labor Day through late June are less than half price compared with the summer season.

Right next door is the **Fort William Henry Museum** (www.fwhmuseum.com), portraying French and Indian War history on the site of the original fort: Cannons boom, muskets blaze, and uniformed soldiers go through their drills. If contemporary amusements are more to your taste, there's miniature golf and the Million Dollar Beach a short walk away.

Lake George Bed & Breakfast

Innkeepers: Marilyn and Mike Holmes
518-668-5477
www.lakegeorgebb.com
47 Montcalm Street
Open: Year-round
Price: Moderate to Expensive
Credit Cards: DC, MC, V
Handicap Access: No
Remarks: No smoking; no pets; no young children; Wi-Fi

Finding an inn with character—rather than generic motel décor—is a challenge in the heart of Lake George. The village has scores of motor inns cheek by jowl, but not many other options. This big, lovely home, offering eight rooms with private baths, is set away from Canada Street, but not so far you can't stroll on down for an ice-cream cone or a concert in the park. The Million Dollar Beach is five or ten minutes from the inn. Guests are offered a full hot breakfast.

Rockledge on the Lake

Owner: Salim Amersi
518-668-5348
www.rockledgeonthelake.com
3072 Lake Shore Drive
Open: June 2 through mid-September
Price: Inexpensive to Expensive
Credit Cards: MC, V
Handicap Access: No
Remarks: 540 feet of lakefront; sandy beach; pool; children welcome; no pets

The original "Rockledge," a three-story mansion built in 1886, stands guard under the pines on this fourteen-acre lakefront property. Although the historic house isn't open to guests, the building's gracious presence adds a special touch to this otherwise thoroughly modern resort.

Rockledge offers one- or two-bedroom housekeeping cottages, and very affordable motel rooms. Cottages are generally available by the week only. There's an outdoor pool, a sandy beach, and room for badminton, volleyball, and shuffleboard.

Wiawaka Holiday House
518-668-9690; off-season 518-203-3101
www.wiawaka.org
3778 NY 9L
Open: Early June through mid-September
Price: Inexpensive; price is determined on
    a sliding fee scale (rate includes three
    meals a day)
Credit Cards: MC, V
Handicap Access: Yes
Remarks: Private beach with 1,500 feet of
    lakefront; primarily for women; no chil-
    dren or pets

Founded in 1903 as a place where working women could take inexpensive vacations, Wiawaka, which means "The Great Spirit of Women," offers clean, simple accommodations in three pretty Victorian cottages, a rustic dormitory reputedly designed by Stanford White, and a motel. Set on sixty unspoiled acres on the east side of Lake George, the place is remarkably peaceful.

Vacationing at the nonprofit Wiawaka is a bit like staying at a YWCA camp: There are no phones or TVs; guests are expected to make their own beds and sweep out their rooms; swimming, boating, and horseshoe pitching are part of the fun, as are Monday night movies. Three meals a day are included in the room rate; taking a room without meals is not permitted. In 1990 the first male guests were welcomed here (before that, they had to stay elsewhere in Lake George). Kids are not allowed (guests must be over 18).

Wiawaka is a recipient of grant funding from the New York State Council on the Arts and Poets and Writers. Numerous workshops, lectures, and conferences are offered during the season that cover topics such as writing, painting, yoga, quilting, Tai Chi, and knitting.

LAKE LUZERNE

The Lamplight Inn Bed & Breakfast
Owners: Linda and Gene Merlino
518-696-5294 or 1-800-262-4668
www.lamplightinn.com
231 Lake Avenue
Open: Year-round
Price: Moderate to Expensive
 Credit Cards: AE, MC, V
Minimum Stay: Two nights on weekends; in
    summer three nights
Handicap Access: One room
Remarks: Fireplaces; no pets; children 12
    and older welcome

Built in the 1890s as the bachelor "cottage" for a wealthy lumberman, the Lamplight Inn has been painstakingly refurbished by Gene and Linda Merlino. The public room has rich chestnut wainscoting; beamed ceilings; two fireplaces; Oriental rugs; lace curtains; and lots of antiques. The spacious, sunny dining room, although a recent addition, is entirely in keeping with the Victorian style.

An ornate keyhole staircase leads upstairs to the eight guest chambers (all with private baths, some with Jacuzzis), and five of the rooms have gas-burning fireplaces. The furniture and décor are different and delightful in each room: For example, one has a coffered ceiling, skylight, and a high-back old-fashioned oak bedstead; another has a queen-size canopied bed. The handsome Carriage House has five suites, all with queen-size beds and gas-burning fireplaces, phones, cable TV, and air conditioning. The

Brookside Guest House contains two lovely suites with fireplaces, TVs, and phones. Breakfast, included in the room rate, is fresh fruit and sweet breads or cake, home-made granola, omelets, and daily specials like apple crêpes or Belgian waffles.

The Lamplight Inn is surrounded by ten acres for walking. It's close to the Saratoga Racetrack and tends to be full in August. November through April room rates are offered at special savings, with packages for leaf-peepers, holiday shoppers, cross-country and downhill skiers, and couples hoping for a romantic break during dreary mud season.

PARADOX

Lake Paradox Club
Owner: Helen Wildman
518-532-7734
www.lakeparadoxclub.com
River Road
Open: Year-round (only three houses remain open after mid-October)
Price: Moderate
Credit Cards: None
Minimum Stay: One week for houses July through August
Handicap Access: No
Remarks: Children welcome; pets accommodated with prior arrangements for cabins; private sand beach; boats; massages available in summer

Helen Wildman's family has owned hundreds of acres on the western end of Paradox Lake for more than a century; eight of the twelve lakefront rental houses were built by her grandfather. These places are big—four to six bedrooms—and have full kitchens, old-fashioned stone fireplaces, and screen porches. There's nice swimming at the club's private beach, canoes and rowboats for exploring pretty Paradox Lake, plus tennis, horseshoes, hiking trails, and a baseball field. Guests can rent kayaks,

canoes, an outboard for fishing, or a Sunfish for sailing. Helen says, "Many of our tenants return regularly, year after year, but there's always room for newcomers, especially if your vacation plans are flexible."

In spring and fall, weekly rental rates are about half the fees charged in July and August. Three of the houses are winterized, great for ice fishermen and cross-country skiers who'd like to explore nearby Pharaoh Lake Wilderness Area.

SCHROON LAKE

Schroon Lake Bed & Breakfast
Innkeepers: Jane and Jack Baumgarten
518-532-7042
www.schroonbb.com
1525 US 9
Open: Year-round
Price: Moderate to Expensive
Credit Cards: AE, MC, V
Minimum Stay: Two nights on summer weekends and holidays
Handicap Access: Yes
Remarks: Fireplace; no smoking; no pets; children 12 and older welcome; Wi-Fi

Only minutes off the Northway (I-87) is this lovely country inn with five attractive guest rooms (one of which is in an adjacent Adirondack-style cottage), all with sparkling private baths and most with fireplaces and private sitting areas. The living room has a stone fireplace, shelves of books and magazines, DVDs, and comfortable sofas for curling up with the novel of your choice. Guest quarters have polished hardwood floors, Oriental rugs, fine antiques, and thick terrycloth robes in the closet.

Silver Spruce Inn
Innkeepers: Phyllis and Cliff Rogers
518-532-7031
www.silverspruce.com
2005 US 9
Open: Year-round

Price: Moderate
Credit Cards: D, MC, V
Minimum Stay: Two nights on weekends;
   inquire
Handicap Access: Yes
Remarks: Fireplaces; no pets; inquire about
   children

This historic home is a true gem. Encompassing more than 8,000 square feet and containing twenty-eight rooms, the place manages to be luxurious and unpretentious, rustic and elegant, at the same time. At present there are three guest rooms with queen beds and two large suites with king-size beds and fireplaces; all accommodations have wonderful oversize bathrooms with deep porcelain tubs that date back to the days when the building belonged to the owners of a major plumbing-supply company. Silver Spruce is an ideal setting for friends traveling together or a small corporate retreat.

The adjacent carriage house provides two more suites with king-size beds, fireplaces, and Jacuzzis. Both suites have refrigerators and microwaves, and are handicap accessible.

The lovely great room spans the entire width of the building, with plenty of couches and chairs, a piano, and an electric organ clustered by a huge fireplace. Running the length of the building is a spacious sunporch with wicker furniture. In the basement is a surprise, a cozy tavern that dates back to Prohibition days, complete with bookshelves that hide stashes of liquor and a back bar that once graced the Waldorf Astoria Hotel, in New York City.

Word of Life Inn & Conference Center
Manager: Mike Bush
518-532-7114
www.wol.org
210 Registration Way
Open: Year-round
Price: Moderate to Expensive (price

includes breakfast and dinner)
Credit Cards: D, MC, V
Handicap Access: Yes
Remarks: Indoor pool; children welcome;
   Christian atmosphere; recreational
   facilities; summer camps for youth

A full-service Christian resort, the Word of Life Inn offers all kinds of accommodations, from chalets and rustic lakeside cabins to executive and honeymoon suites. There's a complete roster of activities, concerts and inspirational speakers, plus tennis, heated indoor pool, saunas, boating, hiking, and special events. Beside the inn, which is just south of Schroon Lake village, there's a family campground farther down the lake with sites for tents, travel trailers, and motor homes (some sites have electrical, water, and sewer hook-ups), plus housekeeping cabins.

SILVER BAY

Northern Lake George Resort
Owners: The Martucci Family
518-543-6528
www.northernlakegeorge.com
8074 Lakeshore Drive (P.O. Box 2677)
Open: Year-round
Price: Moderate to Expensive
Credit Cards: MC, V
Handicap Access: Some accommodations
Remarks: Sandy beach; 400 feet of lakefront; free rowboats and canoes; hiking
   trails nearby; children welcome; dive
   shop; no pets; Wi-Fi; all rooms air-conditioned

Opened as the Hotel Uncas in 1896, the Northern Lake George Resort bills itself as the last of the lake's original hotels still open to the public. The main lodge has been changed significantly over the years, although the third floor with dormer windows was removed in the 1950s, and balconies and porches were added. The great room maintains the appeal of an old

Adirondack lodge with its stone fireplace and polished wood floors.

Guests can select from rooms on the second floor with private balconies providing views of the lake; winterized lakeside villas with fireplaces, kitchens, cable TV, and decks; or motel rooms. There's a cocktail lounge and restaurant on the premises, open from late June through early September or by arrangement.

The depths of Lake George hold numerous wrecks from French and Indian War *bateaux* to sidewheel steamboats. The Northern Lake George Resort has a full-service dive shop offering tank fills and supplies; dive charters to underwater historic sites can be arranged. Call for group adventure packages.

Silver Bay YMCA of The Adirondacks
Executive Director: Marty Fink
518-543-8833
www.silverbay.org
87 Silver Bay Road
Open: Year-round
Price: Moderate to Expensive
Credit Cards: MC, V
Handicap Access: Yes
Remarks: Full conference facilities;
    planned activities; waterfront

With nearly a square mile of picturesque property on Lake George and sixty-plus buildings, Silver Bay YMCA is an awesome complex. Many of the graceful Victorian structures harken back to the turn of the 19th century, yet meals and amenities are thoroughly modern. The list of activities is almost endless, from swimming and fishing to crafts and aerobics classes. Hiking and cross-country ski trails weave among the hillsides. The ice-cream store and craft shop are open year-round.

Accommodations run the full range from Spartan double rooms in old-time lodges to comfortable cabins; it's possible to stay here without being part of a conference or joining the association; daily full membership fees are $18.

Silver Bay can accommodate weddings, family reunions, and other private parties.

WARRENSBURG

Allyn's Butterfly Inn
Innkeepers: Al and Lynn Smith
518-623-9390
www.alynnsbutterflyinn.com
69 NY 28
Open: Year-round
Price: Expensive
Credit Cards: MC, V
Minimum Stay: Two nights July through
    August
Handicap Access: Yes
Remarks: No pets; no children under 10; air
    conditioning; Wi-Fi

Formerly known as The House on the Hill, the Smiths have run this grand old place since 1999. Public areas are elegantly appointed, and the huge wraparound porch invites lingering on a summer day to watch the real butterflies visiting the garden.

All five guest chambers are named after native butterflies, have private baths, coffee makers, and small refrigerators; three have Jacuzzis and fireplaces. A full gourmet breakfast is served daily at 8:30. Inquire about special packages, including fall foliage specials and murder mystery events.

Country Road Lodge B&B
Innkeepers: Sandi and Steve Parisi
518-623-2207
www.countryroadlodge.com
115 Hickory Hill Road
Open: Year-round
Price: Moderate
Credit Cards: None
Handicap Access: No
Remarks: Hiking and ski trails; no pets;
    children 10 and older welcome; Wi-Fi

In 1974, Steve Parisi began transforming an

old farmhouse on the banks of the Hudson River into a year-round bed & breakfast that's a haven for cross-country skiers. Country Road Lodge is decidedly off the beaten path, well suited to bird watchers, hikers, and others who want to explore the secluded forty-acre property and adjacent state lands.

There are four comfortable guest rooms with private baths. Winter weekend packages include meals (full country breakfast of choice off a menu, trail lunch, and dinner on weekends), plus après-ski treats. There's no TV at Country Road Lodge, but plenty of books, magazines, board games, and a panoramic view of the Hudson River and Sugarloaf Mountain.

The Merrill Magee House

Owners: Chris Brown, John Brown, Stuart
    Smith, and Connie Maxam
518-623-2449
www.merrillmageehouse.com
3 Hudson Street
Open: Year-round
Price: Expensive
Credit Cards: AE, MC, V
Minimum Stay: Two nights on holidays and
    weekends
Handicap Access: Yes
Remarks: Restaurant; tavern; Wi-Fi

A quartet of new owners purchased this lovely Greek Revival house in the center of town in 2006. The oldest part of the original house is now the tavern and reception rooms; the back portion of the restaurant, circa 1812, actually came from another homestead some miles away. Merrill Magee House is listed on the National Register of Historic Places.

The Peletiah Richards Guest House, behind the inn, combines twenty-first-century conveniences, like private baths, with nineteenth-century décor; each room has its own fireplace, brass or four-poster bed, and handmade quilt. These rooms are named after herbs, and "Parsley" is wheelchair accessible.

Merrill Magee's grounds are beautifully landscaped, with flower gardens and shady nooks. In the summer, you can sit on the porch and listen to evening concerts in the bandshell on the other side of the white picket fence. Special events include an annual Beaujolais Nouveau celebration in the fall; conferences and meetings and weddings are cheerfully accommodated.

Ridin' Hy Ranch

Managers: Andy and Susan Beadnell
518-494-2742
www.ridinhy.com
64 Ridin Hy Ranch Road
Open: Year-round, except closed December
    1 through 26
Price: Moderate (includes three meals a day)
Credit Cards: AE, D, MC, V
Minimum Stay: Two nights on weekends,
    but inquire ahead
Handicap Access: Yes
Remarks: Horseback riding; indoor pool;
    children welcome; no pets

Western-style dude ranches were once abundant in the southeastern Adirondacks, but many have closed in the last couple of decades. Ridin' Hy, an 800-acre complex on Sherman Lake, continues to prosper, offering everything from a private intermediate-level downhill ski area to rodeos. There are 50 miles of trails for snowmobiling, cross-country skiing, or horseback riding. In warmer weather, guests can swim, row, or water-ski on Sherman Lake, and fish in Burnt Pond or the Schroon River.

The centerpiece of the ranch is an enormous log cabin that contains a cocktail lounge, living room, game room, and dining room. Accommodations include chalets, lodge rooms, and motel units, all finished with natural wood. Midweek and off-season packages are available.

Seasons B&B
Owner: Eileen Frasier
518-623-3832
www.seasons-bandb.com
3822 Main Street
Open: Year-round
Price: Moderate to Expensive
Credit Cards: AE, MC, V
Minimum Stay: Two nights on holidays and
    summer weekends
Handicap Access: No
Remarks: Fireplace; children 12 and older
    welcome; no pets; no smoking; Wi-Fi;
    air conditioning and cable in all rooms

James Fenimore Cooper was a guest at
Peletiah Richards's house when he was
researching *The Last of the Mohicans.* In those
days, the home was among the grandest in
town, and later in the nineteenth century
this place became more elaborate still, with
the addition of an Italianate tower, a long
veranda, and a bay window. Details inside
the Seasons, formerly the Donegal Manor,
are lovely: There's an ornate fireplace in the
parlor, a beautiful coffered wood ceiling
above the staircase, and antiques throughout.

There are four guest rooms upstairs, two
with private baths and two that share a bath.
A section of the house that dates from 1820
has been renovated into a handsome suite
with a corner fireplace in the living room,
queen-size bed, and spacious bathroom
with double whirlpool with separate shower.
Guests are treated to a fine, full breakfast.

Eileen recently opened an upscale con-
signment shop in the barn behind the B&B.
Browse the furniture, artwork, rugs, and
other items.

Champlain Valley

ELIZABETHTOWN

Old Mill Bed & Breakfast
Owners: Beki Maurello-Pushee and Bruce

Pushee
518-873-2294
www.adirondackinns.com/oldmill
136 River Street
Open: Year-round
Price: Moderate to Expensive
Credit Cards: AE, MC, V
Handicap Access: No
Remarks: No pets; children welcome

In the 1930s and '40s this lovely property—
bounded on two sides by the Boquet River—
was an art school led by landscape painter
Wayman Adams. Now it's a lovely bed and
breakfast packed with antiques, Oriental
rugs, paintings, and sculpture. Four guest
rooms (all with private baths) are in the
main house.

Breakfast, served 7:30 to 8:30, is a highlight here. On sunny, warm mornings it's
served on the enclosed patio that has a
fountain as its centerpiece, and the rest of
the time the feast is presented in the formal
dining room. Muffins, juice, poached pears
with cream, or baked grapefruit with honey
are the starters, followed by bourbon
French toast, lemon soufflé pancakes, or
quiche with fresh tomatoes.

Stoneleigh Bed & Breakfast
Owners: Rosemary Remington
518-873-2669
www.stoneleighbedandbreakfast.com
18 Stoneleigh Way
Open: May through November
Price: Moderate
Credit Cards: AE, D, MC, V
Handicap Access: No
Remarks: Fireplace; children and pets wel-
    come

Architects copied designs by H. H.
Richardson, a Boston-based architect, to
build this imposing Germanic-looking castle for local judge Francis Smith in 1886.
The house, with babbling Barton Brook in
front, has a fine library, as befits a country
judge, and several porches and balconies

under the tree-shaded, secluded grounds.
There's also a TV room for guests.
Downstairs, there's a suite with private
bath; upstairs, four spacious rooms share a
bath and a half. A separate carriage house
with private bath is also available.

ESSEX

Cupola House
Manager: Donna Lou Sonnett
518-963-7494
www.thecupolahouse.com
2278 Main Street
Open: Year-round
Price: Expensive
Credit Cards: MC, V
Minimum Stay: Two nights on weekends
Handicap Access: No
Remarks: Boat slips; no smoking; children
   and pets welcome; Wi-Fi; art workshops
   and outdoor excursions

A prim and proper Greek Revival with wonderful two-story porches, Cupola House has
two handsome apartments decorated with
antiques and Adirondack furniture that are
just a quick walk up from the Essex Marina.
Both have complete kitchens and full baths
and access to the upstairs porch. The south
apartment nicely accommodates two couples or a family; the north apartment has
one bedroom but can accommodate more
than one couple. A lakeside cottage accommodates two to six people. Guests have
access to kayaks, a canoe, and bicycles.

Cupola House is two blocks from the ferry
to Vermont and conveniently close to all of
Essex's shops and restaurants. With prior
notice, Donna will deliver guests from the
Westport train station to the Cupola House.

The Essex Inn
Owners: Trish and John Walker
518-963-8821
www.theessexinn.com
2297 Main Street

Open: Year-round
Price: Moderate
Credit Cards: AE, MC, V
Handicap Access: Two downstairs suites

Stretching along Main Street with two tiers
of porches is this carefully restored inn. The
building is surprisingly narrow—just one
room and the hallway wide—with a café,
courtyard, and dining room, plus four spacious guest rooms downstairs, one of which
is pet-friendly. Upstairs there are three
bedrooms, plus two more suites: One
includes a bedroom, bath, while the other
has two bedrooms, a sitting room, and bath.

The hotel is full of antiques, plus handsome period engravings and photographs.
A small gift shop, the **Happy Cat**, is inside
the inn; the restaurant is open for lunch
and dinner—in warm weather you can eat
outside.

The Stonehouse
Innkeeper: Sylvia Hobbs
518-963-7713
3 Church Street
Open: Memorial Day through Columbus
   Day
Price: Expensive
Credit Cards: None
Minimum Stay: Two nights on weekends
Handicap Access: No
Remarks: Fireplaces

Step into this 1826 Georgian stone house
and you feel as if you've entered a classic
English country house. Tall windows suf-
fuse dappled light into the living spaces;
private gardens ring the property. Two
suites with private baths and two rooms
with a shared bath occupy the second floor;
renovations to the top floor transformed
the space into an exceptional 20' x 30' room
with exposed beams and stone walls, and
French doors that open onto a rooftop deck
with a sweeping view of Lake Champlain.
An adjacent guest cottage with two bedrooms, two baths, and a kitchen sleeps six.

Breakfast could be categorized as first-rate continental, with fresh baked goods from Montreal, seasonal fruits, and gourmet coffee and tea. Note that the Stonehouse is located across the street from one of Essex's historic churches and is available for receptions and private gatherings.

PORT HENRY

The King's Inn
Innkeepers: Kevin and Michele Flanagan
518-546-7633
42 Hummingbird Way
Open: Year-round
Price: Moderate
Credit Cards: AE, D, MC, V
Handicap Access: No
Remarks: Pub serving dinner; fireplaces; pets accepted with restrictions

Slowly but surely downtown Port Henry is refurbishing neglected buildings from the town's heyday as an iron-mining center. One bright spot is the restored King's Inn, an 1893 mansion on a hill overlooking the lake. There are six nice rooms upstairs, all with private baths. Three have working fireplaces; two have views of the lake. The best room in the house has a big sitting area with two east-facing windows, and a great big bathroom with a deep porcelain tub.

Port Henry's shops, historic sites, and waterfront are within walking distance. There's no need to walk very far for a good meal, though: The restaurant on the first floor is fine, and you can enjoy a cocktail while sitting in an antique wicker chair on the wraparound porch.

The innkeepers welcome private parties and banquets.

WESTPORT

All Tucked Inn
Innkeepers: Bill and Kathleen Wilson
518-962-4400
www.alltuckedinn.com
6455 Main Street
Open: Year-round
Price: Moderate to Expensive
Credit Cards: None
Handicap Access: No

A grand old Dutch Colonial home, All Tucked Inn occupies a prominent spot on Westport's Main Street. There are nine lovely rooms, all with private baths; five rooms have views of Lake Champlain. A suite on the first floor has its own porch and fireplace. From the inn, you can walk to the Westport Yacht Club, the marina, tennis courts, and even the eighteen-hole golf course.

Guests can walk to Lake Champlain, tennis courts, or an eighteen-hole golf course from All Tucked Inn.
James Swedberg

The Inn on the Library Lawn
Innkeepers: Alexandra and Anthony Wheeler
518-962-8666
www.theinnonthelibrarylawn.com
1234 Stevenson Road
Open: Year-round
Price: Moderate to Expensive
Credit Cards: AE, MC, V
Minimum Stay: Two nights on weekends in July and August
Handicap Access: No
Remarks: Children 16 and older welcome; no pets; Wi-Fi

As you might imagine given the name, this charming little hotel—which dates back to 1875—is situated just across from Westport's wonderful old library. Extensive renovations have created peaceful, refined public areas and 10 comfortable rooms with private baths. A small bookstore with a sitting room and fireplace welcomes visitors downstairs. The on-site **Inn Café**, which is open year-round, offers a fine breakfast and lunch.

The Westport Hotel

Innkeepers: Wayne and Wendy Deswert
518-962-4501
www.thewestporthotel.com
6691 Main Street
Open: Year-round
Price: Moderate
Credit Cards: AE, D, MC, V
Handicap Access: No
Remarks: Restaurant; no pets

When the railroad came to Westport in 1876, Albert Gates opened his hotel on the other side of the tracks. Ever since, the spacious clapboard building has been operated as an inn. Guests can now choose from eight rooms decorated with antiques and hand-stenciled walls; most have private baths. In warm weather, use the breezy wraparound porch for watching the world go by on NY 9N or enjoying a meal from the hotel's **Gyphon's Nest** restaurant.

People who are traveling without a car should note that there's daily Amtrak service to Westport, and many of the town's charms, from the Essex County Fair and Depot Theatre to the lakefront, are nearby.

High Peaks and Northern Adirondacks

ELK LAKE

Elk Lake Lodge

Managers: Cammy and Michael Sheridan
518-532-7616
www.elklakelodge.com
1106 Elk Lake Road
Open: Early April through mid-October
Price: Expensive; includes all meals
Credit Cards: None
Minimum Stay: Two nights
Handicap Access: No
Remarks: Two private lakes; 40 miles of private mountain hiking trails; canoes and rowboats for guests; fishing; children welcome; no pets

In a nutshell, Elk Lake Lodge is the quintessential Adirondack lodge. Set on a breathtaking private lake ringed by the High Peaks, in the midst of a 12,000-acre preserve, the place offers everything an outdoorsperson could ask for: great fishing, unlimited wilderness hiking, and canoeing on an island-studded lake that's off limits to motorboats. Of course, if just hanging out, listening to the loons, and admiring the view are your kinds of recreation, this place has that in spades.

There are six rooms in the turn-of-the-century lodge, all with twin beds and private baths. Around the lakeshore there are seven cottages, ranging from Little Tom, a cozy spot under the trees for two, to Emerson Lodge, which sleeps up to twelve. Several of the cabins are equipped with kitchens and fireplaces or have decks overlooking the lake; all are nicely decorated.

At Elk Lake Lodge, you can hike, canoe, fish for brook trout, or simply kick back at this quintessential Adirondack retreat. James Swedberg

The price of a stay at Elk Lake includes all meals, which are served in the dining room where huge picture windows reveal the mountains and lake.

JAY

The Book and Blanket
Innkeepers: Kathy Recchia and Fred Balzac
518-946-8323
www.bookandblanket.com
12914 NY 9N
Open: Year-round
Price: Moderate
Credit Cards: AE
Minimum Stay: Two nights on holiday
   weekends
Handicap Access: No
Remarks: Children welcome; no pets

Rooms in this restored Greek Revival home are named for authors: The Jack London chamber has a north-woods ambiance, queen-size bed, and private bath with a whirlpool tub; the Jane Austen room has a queen-size bed and a quiet nook for reading; the F. Scott Fitzgerald room has a double bed and shares a bath. All of the rooms—upstairs and down—have lots of books, and guests are encouraged to browse and borrow at will. Or they can relax by the fire in the living room and watch a classic film.

KEENE

Bark Eater Inn
Owner: Joe-Pete Wilson
518-576-2221
www.barkeater.com
Alstead Hill Road
Open: Year-round
Price: Moderate to Expensive
Credit Cards: AE, D, MC, V
Minimum Stay: Two nights on holiday
   weekends; four nights during Christmas
   and New Years
Handicap Access: No
Remarks: Cross-country skiing; horseback riding; polo games; children welcome; special packages

More than 150 years ago, the stagecoach carrying travelers from Lake Champlain to Lake Placid stopped overnight here; since the 1940s, members of the Wilson family have taken in guests. The main part of this country inn is a beautiful farmhouse with two stone fireplaces and wide-board floors. There are seven rooms upstairs that share baths, plus four rooms in the carriage house with private baths. The log cottage has two three-bedroom suites and two guest rooms with private baths. High Country, another log cabin, is the perfect honeymoon suite with its queen-size bed, in-floor heat, gas fireplace, private deck, and whirlpool tub. Breakfast is served family-style in the dining room.

   Guests come to the Bark Eater not just for the marvelous views of the High Peaks, but for horseback riding, hiking, and cross-country skiing. The lodge has dozens of well-mannered English and Western mounts and many miles of woodland trails. Polo games are held in a nearby field on summer Sunday afternoons. In winter the bridle trails become groomed ski trails; Bark Eater's 20 kilometers connect with the Jackrabbit system, so you could ski for days and never cover the same territory.

KEENE VALLEY

Keene Valley Lodge
Innkeepers: George and Laurie Daniels
518-576-2003
www.keenevalleylodge.com
1834 NY 73
Open: Year-round
Price: Moderate
Credit Cards: AE, D, MC, V
Minimum Stay: Two nights on summer
   weekends
Handicap Access: No
Remarks: Fireplace; children welcome; no
   pets; Wi-Fi

From 1929 to 1949 this big Italianate home was known as Beede Cottage; now it's a cozy inn with all the modern comforts in nine guest rooms. On the first floor, there's a suite with queen-size bed, full bath, and its own entrance; a highlight upstairs is the room with queen-size bed, big picture windows framing mountain views (in wintertime after the leaves have fallen), and a private bath. Most of the second-floor rooms have private baths and king-size beds. All are furnished with antiques and hand-stitched quilts. A full breakfast buffet is included in the rate.

Mountain Meadows Bed & Breakfst
Hosts: Cricket and Patricia Quinn
518-576-4771
1756 NY 73
Open: Year-round
Price: Moderate
Credit Cards: None
Handicap Access: No
Remarks: Children welcome; pets permitted with special arrangements

The East Branch of the Ausable River curls through this property and the pointy peak of Noonmark Mountain looms to the west. Mountain Meadows is a haven for hikers, cross-country skiers, and rock climbers; Pat Quinn will help you plan an outing.

The bed & breakfast is actually two comfortable Adirondack-style houses that share a sunny deck. The bedroom wing has three large rooms with king-size beds that convert to twins and that share two baths. There's another chamber with private bath and a southern exposure.

Trail's End Inn
Innkeepers: Dave Griffiths and Susan Lindteigen
518-576-9860 or 1-800-281-9860
www.trailsendinn.com
62 Trail's End Way
Open: Year-round

Price: Moderate
Credit Cards: AE, D, MC, V
Handicap Access: No
Remarks: Fireplaces, hiking trails, children welcome; pets allowed in some rooms; Wi-Fi

A gambrel-roofed house with eyebrow windows on a quiet road, Trail's End calls itself a hikers' lodge, implying that the accommodations aren't so fancy that you need to worry about blow-drying your hair before you come to breakfast. Downstairs, the lodge has a large comfortable living room with a fireplace and DVD plus a winterized sunporch full of toys and games for kids.

Guest rooms upstairs include Catamount, which has a corner fireplace, a private porch, and full bath; Marcy Suite, a two-room suite with king-size bed, TV, bath, and futons on a sleeping porch; and Gothics, with a fireplace, king-size bed, and whirlpool tub. There are four double rooms that share baths, plus a two-bedroom cottage with complete kitchen, TV, and washer/dryer that accommodates up to six guests and even a pet. At times, hiking clubs or family groups take over the entire place, which can hold about forty comfortably. Meals can be arranged for large groups.

You don't need a car to enjoy Trail's End and vicinity. The bus stops every day at the Noon Mark Diner, a five-minute walk away, and from the inn, there's easy access to Roostercomb and other peaks. Note that Dave and Susan also rent fully equipped, renovated vacation houses along the Ausable River in Keene.

LAKE PLACID

Adirondack Loj
Manager: Janet Morgan
518-523-3441
www.adk.org
1002 Adirondak Loj Road
Open: Year-round

Price: Inexpensive to Expensive
Credit Cards: MC, V
Handicap Access: Yes; no men's handicap-
    accessible restroom; accessible trail
    around Heart Lake
Remarks: Hiking; outdoor workshops; tent
    campground; backcountry cabins; High
    Peaks Information Center

With its sweeping panorama of Mount
Marcy and Indian Pass, the drive in to
Adirondak Loj sets you up for a visit to the
Adirondack Mountain Club's (ADK) wilderness retreat. On Heart Lake in the midst of
the High Peaks, the 1920s-era lodge is a
rustic, comfortable place. In the living
room, you can rock in an Old Hickory chair
in front of the vast stone fireplace and
choose from the shelves practically any
book that's ever been written on the
Adirondacks. Breakfast—the wake-up bell
rings bright and early—is served buffet
style, as is dinner, at picnic tables in an
adjoining room. Bag lunches are available,
and plain, home-cooked dinners are served
when the lodge is busy.

There are four private rooms, four
bunkrooms, and a huge co-ed loft. The
bunkrooms, which have four built-in log
beds, are snug and cozy, like cabins on a
ship; the loft can be a hard place to get a
good night's sleep if there are any snorers
in the crowd. The management refers to the
bathrooms as "semi-private," but they're
really similar to facilities in a college dorm.
You don't need to be a member of ADK to
stay at the Loj, but you must make advance
reservations.

On Heart Lake are two cabins that
accommodate four to 16 people during the
fall, winter, and spring. For the intrepid
traveler, ADK has three excellent backcountry cabins that are accessible by foot—all are
a 3.5-mile hike in from Keene Valley: Johns
Brook Lodge, which is open Memorial Day
through Columbus Day (in July and August
you can get two hot meals and bag lunches

here); and Grace Camp and Camp Peggy
O'Brien, which are open year-round and
have tiers of bunks, gas lights, and propane
heat; they're excellent bases for hiking,
snowshoe, or ski weekends.

The Interlaken Inn

Owner: Mary Neary
518-523-3180
www.theinterlakeninn.com
15 Interlaken Avenue, around the corner
    from Mirror Lake Inn
Open: Year-round, except for April
Price: Expensive to Very Expensive
Credit Cards: AE, D, MC, V
Handicap Access: No
Remarks: Fireplace; fine restaurant and bar

Walnut-paneled walls, tin ceilings, a polished garnet fireplace, a winding staircase,
and antiques make the Interlaken a true
oasis. Built in 1912 by one of the founders
of the Bank of Lake Placid, the secluded
spot has been operated as an inn for most
of its existence. There are seven lovely
guest rooms, two suites and a carriage
house, most with queen-size beds, all with
private baths—some with Jacuzzis or a clawfoot tub.

Downstairs, the dining room is elegant
yet casual. Off the living room is the cozy
bar, where there's a pub menu and an
extensive wine list. The restaurant is one of
the best in town. (See Chapter 5.)

The inn makes an elegant backdrop for
small weddings and other gatherings.

Lake Placid Lodge

Manager: Megan Yates
518-523-2700
www.lakeplacidlodge.com
Whiteface Inn Road
Open: Year-round
Price: Very Expensive
Credit Cards: AE, MC, V
Handicap Access: Yes; elevator in main
    lodge; one cabin

Remarks: Boats and bikes for guests; fireplaces in rooms; well-behaved dogs and children welcome

First, a geography lesson: The village of Lake Placid is on tiny Mirror Lake; the lake named Placid is slightly west of downtown and it's a big body of water with a trio of islands and gorgeous views. Only a few lodgings are located on the secluded western shore of Lake Placid.

Originally built as a summer home at the turn of the last century, Mae and Teddy Frankel opened the place as a hotel in 1946, and for nearly forty years ran it with a personal touch. Christie and David Garrett bought the Lodge in 1993 and transformed it into a stunningly beautiful resort that compared favorably to The Point, the Garretts' world-class hotel on Upper Saranac Lake.

Sadly, the Lake Placid Lodge burned to the ground in 2005, but a new—even more marvelous—building is in the works, to be opened in 2008.

Also on the property: luxury cabins, a postage-stamp-size sandy beach, and canoes, sailboards, pedal boats, and bicycles on hand for guests. The beautiful, challenging Whiteface Inn golf course is an easy walk from the Lodge.

Mirror Lake Inn Resort & Spa

Owner: Edwin Weibrecht
518-523-2544
www.mirrorlakeinn.com
77 Mirror Lake Drive
Open: Year-round
Price: Very Expensive
Credit Cards: AE, D, MC, V
Handicap Access: Yes
Remarks: Spa/salon; tennis; heated indoor/outdoor pools; sauna; whirlpool; ice skating; tennis; restaurant; pub; conference facilities; children welcome; Wi-Fi

On a hillside overlooking Mirror Lake, this delightful resort hotel in the heart of town has an array of amenities and services. The spa offers everything from mud wraps and honey-almond exfoliation treatments to massage therapy, plus all kinds of exercise classes led by professionals. If your interest is relaxing, improving your skin, or launching a healthier lifestyle, there's someone on the staff who can help.

The inn has five lodging buildings—three across the street from Mirror Lake and the other two by a small, private beach. Some rooms have mountain or lakeside views and fireplaces; suites are also available to accommodate families. The Colonial House Ultimate Suites are sensational. These brand-new rooms are decorated with fine furniture, Oriental rugs, and have cathedral ceilings, enormous living quarters, marble tubs, and are directly on Mirror Lake.

All rooms include plush robes, hair dryers, DVD players, refrigerators, and magnifying makeup mirrors; they're all upscale and quite lovely.

The inn has a nice new restaurant (see Chapter 5), a cozy pub, and various nooks and crannies for guests to relax in. The inn is an exceptional facility for conferences, with plenty of attractive meeting rooms for large or small groups. Packages are available for early-season downhill skiing, midweek visits, romantic getaways, and golf.

Paradox Lodge

Innkeepers: Nan and Moses (Red) LaFountaine
518-523-9078
www.paradoxlodge.com
2169 Saranac Avenue
Open: Year-round, except for April and November
Price: Expensive to Very Expensive
Credit Cards: MC, V
Handicap Access: No
Remarks: Dinner by reservations; children age 13 and older; no pets; access to Paradox Bay of Lake Placid; three kayaks

and one canoe available; all rooms air-conditioned; Wi-Fi

In 1999, a century after Paradox Lodge was built, the property reopened as a cozy inn. Although the place has been scrubbed, rewired, replumbed, painted, and decorated with an eclectic mix of antiques and art (clearly the LaFountaines have a sense of humor combined with a knack for finding cool stuff), the house's underlying character—wainscoting, window trim, angles, and windows—is handsomely intact. Four rooms, all with private baths, are upstairs. The Treetop Suite is quite nice, with lots of windows and a sitting room, clawfoot tub, and queen-size bed. The new Cedar Lodge has four elegantly rustic upscale rooms, each with king-size bed, Jacuzzi tub, deck, gas fireplace, robes, and stocked refrigerator.

A living room with gas fireplace for guests is downstairs, along with two dining rooms that seat twenty people. The cuisine, prepared by Chef Red is creative and fantastic, featuring fresh seafood, poussin, and prime beef with whatever's in season for fruits, vegetables, and herbs. If you stay at Paradox Lodge, don't miss the opportunity to eat here, too.

South Meadow Farm Lodge & Maple Sugarworks

Owners: Nancy and Tony Corwin
518-523-9369 or 1-800-523-9369
www.southmeadow.com or www.maplesug arworks.com
67 Sugarworks Way
Open: Year-round
Price: Expensive
Credit Cards: AE, D, MC, V
Minimum Stay: Two nights for weekends and holidays; inquire
Handicap Access: No
Remarks: Cross-country-ski trails; fireplace; family-style breakfast; working maple sugarhouse; children welcome; no pets; Wi-Fi

Near Mount Van Hoevenberg's cross-country ski and biathlon facilities is a small family

Whether it's fine dining or luxury lodging, Mirror Lake Inn Resort & Spa does everything right.
Courtesy of Mirror Lake Inn Resort & Spa

farm that operates as a homey bed & breakfast. The lodge property contains ski trails that are part of the fifty-kilometer Olympic complex and is close to hiking trails up Cascade and Pitchoff Mountains, making this an ideal spot for outdoorspeople.

Accommodations include seven rooms, six with private baths. The lodge's living room is handsome and centers around a massive fireplace. Breakfast is included in the nightly rate; trail lunches are available. This is a great spot for weddings and private parties.

Van Hoevenberg Lodge and Cabins

Owner: Wayne Failing
518-523-9572
www.adklodging.com
4529 Cascade Road
Open: Year-round
Price: Moderate
Credit Cards: AE, MC, V
Minimum Stay: Two nights
Handicap Access: No
Remarks: Guide service; hiking trails; sauna; children welcome; pets allowed; kitchens and baths in all cabins

Eight cabins and four guest rooms in the lodge would make accommodations appealing in any Adirondack setting, but the great attraction here is the proximity to excellent cross-country skiing, hiking, and mountain biking. The cabins and lodge are next to the 50 kilometers of groomed tracks at the Olympic cross-country complex and connects with the Cascade Ski-Touring Center and Jackrabbit Trails. You can head into the High Peaks Wilderness Area without parking your car at a trailhead and afterward enjoy an invigorating wood-fired sauna.

A bonus: Wayne is a fantastic and respected New York State–licensed guide, who will take you on the rafting trip, hiking trek, or fishing or hunting adventure of your life.

The Whiteface Lodge

Manager: Olivier Bottois
1-800-903-4045
www.thewhitefacelodge.com
7 Whiteface Inn Lake
Open: Year-round
Price: Very Expensive
Credit Cards: AE, D, MC, V
Handicap Access: Yes
Remarks: Fine restaurant and bar; spa; skating rink; indoor and outdoor pools; bowling alley; Wi-Fi

Since this luxury resort opened in 2005 it has appeared in all sorts of travel magazines, including *Conde Nast Traveler.* Although it isn't located on waterfront or at the base of a mountain, there are nice views and the lodge itself is over-the-top in Adirondack-style detail and décor. The lodge has the feel of an elegant nineteenth-century Adirondack Great Camp, but with all the comforts of the modern world. It's also an extraordinary place for families with kids, with so many amenities and activities "on campus." Evening s'mores gatherings are a hit.

The Whiteface Lodge operates as a resort hotel and private residence club—folks can buy full and partial ownership. Rooms are spacious and incredible—nothing has been overlooked here—and the resort includes a state-of-the-art spa, an outdoor boating club on Lake Placid, indoor and outdoor swimming pools, an outdoor skating rink, movie theater, bowling alley, boccie and tennis courts, and a separate facility with massive porch and banquet hall that makes a perfect backdrop for wedding receptions or other gatherings.

Diners rave about the elegant on-site **Steak and Stinger** restaurant—perfect for a romantic meal or special occasion. Dinner attire is recommended, as are reservations. Guests may sign up for private cooking classes.

NEWCOMB

Aunt Polly's Bed & Breakfast
Owners: Maggie and Doug Alitz
518-582-2260
www.auntpollysbb.com
5795 NY 28N
Open: Year-round
Price: Moderate to Expensive
Credit Cards: MC, V
Handicap Access: No
Remarks: Hiking trails; dinners available
    by prior arrangement; horses and sta-
    bles on premises; horse and wagon rides

Before the Civil War, Polly Bissell took in
travelers at her home on the edge of the High
Peaks, and in 1995, Maggie and Doug Alitz
opened the doors once again. Their house is
lovely, packed with eclectic antiques; four
nice guest rooms share two modern baths.

There's also a new four-bedroom cottage
with a bath and a half and a large deck.

The seventy-acre property includes hiking and cross-country ski trails that lead back
to a quiet pond, and recreational opportunities abound in and around Newcomb. You can
take the ten-mile trek into Santanoni
Preserve on foot, bikes, skis, or by horse-
drawn wagon, head off to climb in the High
Peaks, or tour the Visitor Interpretive Center.
The wagon to Santanoni can be booked here;
the teams of Belgians belong to the Alitzes.

SARANAC LAKE

Ampersand Bay Resort and Boat Club
Hosts: Ira and Kathryn Holland
518-891-3001
www.ampersandbay.com
31 Bayside Drive

The brand-new Whiteface Lodge, in Lake Placid, is a hit with families. Rooms are spacious and plush, and activities are endless. Courtesy of the Whiteface Lodge

Open: Year-round
Price: Expensive
Credit Cards: AE, D, MC, V
Minimum Stay: One week during summer
   for suites and cottages
Handicap Access: No
Remarks: Private beach; watercraft rentals;
   boat launch; children welcome; no pets

A short distance from downtown Saranac
Lake, but directly on beautiful Lower
Saranac Lake, Ampersand Bay has numerous accommodations: cedar log cabins and
lakeview cottages and suites. All have
kitchens and Adirondack-style décor; some
include screened-in porches and fireplaces.
If you're traveling with your own boat, you
can handily launch and dock here. The
Hollands' forty-acre retreat includes a private sandy beach and canoe, pontoon boat,
kayak, and rowboat rentals, so guests can
explore the many state-owned islands in the
lake. From Lower Saranac you can travel
through the locks to Middle Saranac Lake,
or Oseetah, Kiwassa, and Lake Flower.

Fogarty's Bed & Breakfast
Owners: Emily and Jack Fogarty
518-891-3755 or 1-800-525-3755
www.adirondacks.com/fogarty
74 Kiwassa Road
Open: Year-round
Price: Moderate
Credit Cards: None
Handicap Access: No
Remarks: Boat dock for guests; swimming;
   children welcome; no pets; Wi-Fi

Built in 1910 as a cure cottage for tuberculosis patients, this attractive home overlooking Lake Flower has handsome woodwork,
leaded-glass windows, wonderful porches,
and five bedrooms sharing three baths.
Although Fogarty's is a quick walk from
Saranac Lake's business district and restaurants, it's in a peaceful neighborhood and
even has a dock on the lake for swimmers
and boaters. Winter guests note that cross-

country skiing at Dewey Mountain is about a
mile away, and in early February, when the
winter carnival is in full swing, you can look
over to the fabulous ice palace on the opposite shore of the lake. One point to keep in
mind about Fogarty's: Because the house is
set on a steep hillside, you've got to climb a
lot of steps (seventy-three to be exact, says
Emily) to get to the entrance.

Harbor Hill Inn & Cottages
Hosts: Denise and Wayne Bujold
518-891-2784
www.adirondackvacations.com
1 Harbor Hill Lane
Open: Year-round
Price: Moderate to Expensive
Credit Cards: MC, V
Handicap Access: No
Remarks: Sandy beach; fireplaces; boats for
   guests; dockage; children welcome;
   catering and private masseuse available

A cluster of cabins on Lake Flower, Harbor
Hill provides waterfront activity within a res-
idential neighborhood. On a July or August
Friday night, guests sitting on the docks can
enjoy the outdoor concerts from across the
water, or they can canoe over to the bandshell. In the winter, they can ice skate
(weather permitting) from the front door.
   Seven winterized housekeeping cabins
have fireplaces and some include outdoor
hot tubs; cabins range in size from one to
three bedrooms, and all have picture windows and decks overlooking the water.
There are also homes and suites that can be
rented. There's a private beach for swimming (though you can see the traffic across
the lake and passersby can see you, too);
dock space for visiting motorboats; fishing
and pontoon boat rentals; and rowboats,
pedal boats, bikes, and canoes for guests.

The Hotel Saranac
518-891-2200 or 1-800-937-0211
www.hotelsaranac.com

100 Main Street
Open: Year-round
Price: Moderate to Expensive
Credit Cards: AE, DC, MC, V
Handicap Access: Yes
Remarks: Restaurant; cocktail lounge; elevators; children and pets welcome; Wi-Fi

For more than six decades, this landmark downtown hotel is where hospitality-management students of Paul Smith's College received on-the-job training. But private owners recently took over this Saranac Lake institution, so changes are still in effect. There are eighty-nine air-conditioned rooms, all with private baths. The second-floor grand hall, with beautiful painted wood beams, a grand piano, fireplace, and potted plants, is elegantly welcoming and true to architect William Scopes's vision of how a fine hotel should look. **A. P. Smith's Restaurant**, named after the famed North Country hotelier Paul Smith, is open from breakfast to dinner, while the **Boathouse Tavern**—a congenial pub—serves light meals as well. On the ground floor is a large gift shop featuring quality crafts.

Tour groups or conferences are accommodated and Canadian money is accepted at par. Travelers wishing to see the Adirondacks via public transportation should note that the Adirondack Trailways/Greyhound bus stops here, and it's quite easy to see Saranac Lake on foot and take a cab to Lake Placid.

The Porcupine

518-891-5160
www.theporcupine.com
350 Park Avenue
Open: Year-round
Price: Expensive to Very Expensive
Credit Cards: D, MC, V
Minimum Stay: Two nights on summer weekends
Handicap Access: No
Remarks: Fireplaces; porches

Architect William Coulter built this massive six-gabled, gambrel-roofed house for Thomas Bailey Aldrich, *Atlantic Monthly* editor, author of *The Story of a Bad Boy*, and friend of Mark Twain. The name "Porcupine" isn't some cute modern affectation: The place acquired that title in the early 1900s because "it had so many good points and because it was occupied by a quill driver"—the quill driver being author Aldrich. He brought his wife and sons to Saranac Lake not on some vacation whim but because one of his twin sons had tuberculosis, and the family hoped that the fresh mountain air and good doctors at nearby Trudeau Sanatorium could cure him. Sadly, the young man died.

A decade ago another, happier, chapter unfolded for this grand home. With some furniture wax, window cleaner, plenty of elbow grease, and lots of enthusiasm, the place opened as a bed & breakfast. Downstairs is a comfortable, large living room with fireplace, as well as a billiards room, wine bar, and there are antiques scattered artfully throughout.

Five guest rooms—quite spacious and nicely separate from each other—are on the second floor, up the beautiful Jacobean-style staircase. All have private baths; most have glassed-in "cure porches," an architectural element dating back to the days when TB patients were made to sleep in unheated rooms, swaddled in blankets. Charles's Room, at the top of the stairs, has a working fireplace, a comfortable sitting area, and a porch with wicker chairs overlooking the garden. The Mohawk Suite, also with a fireplace, has a king-size rustic-frame bed. The Saranac Suite is quite large, with a big cure porch, and has two double beds.

Breakfast is served in a big, bright dining area. An outdoor hot tub allows for soaking and relaxing in all weather.

UPPER JAY

Wellscroft Lodge Bed & Breakfast

Innkeepers: Linda and Randolph Stanley
518-946-2547
www.wellscroftlodge.com
66 Wellscroft Way
Open: Year-round
Price: Expensive to Very expensive
Credit Cards: AE, D, MC, V
Handicap Access: No
Remarks: Full breakfast, feather beds, inset
  porches and gazebo; no children under
  14; no pets

Rescued from a near-total derelict state, this Arts and Crafts mansion is an unexpected beauty in sleepy Upper Jay. The Stanleys have spent years bringing the property back to its original splendor through attention to minute details as well as eyes on the big picture. William Morris wallpaper imported from England, gleaming oak beams, classic lighting fixtures, rugs, fabrics, and furniture add up to a decidedly unrustic, but Adirondack, experience. Each of the seven guest rooms has a large private bath, and many rooms have fireplaces or window seats with views. The house is huge—some 12,000 square feet on the first and second floors. There's a formal living room, a cozy bar, a billiard room, dining room, plus porches overlooking the Ausable River Valley.

Wellscroft Lodge, in Upper Jay, is a Tudor Revival Great Camp. James Swedberg

Wellscroft is convenient to skiing at Whiteface Mountain, trout fishing on the West Branch of the Ausable, hiking in the High Peaks, yet secluded.

WILMINGTON

Willkommen Hof B&B

Owners: Heike and Bert Yost
518-946-SNOW or 1-800-541-9119
www.willkommenhof.com
5367 NY 86
Open: Year-round, except April 15 through
  May 15; October 15 through November 15
Price: Moderate to Expensive
Credit Cards: MC, V
Handicap Access: No
Remarks: Traditional German meals available; sauna; hot tub; children and pets
  welcome; ski packages; Wi-Fi

A European-style guesthouse within a one-minute walk of the Ausable River's spectacular flume, Willkommen Hof has three rooms with private baths, a three-room suite, and three rooms that share baths, to house a maximum of 24 guests. Full breakfasts and after-ski treats are included in the room rate; hearty dinners may be arranged.

World-famous trout waters are nearby, as are numerous state-marked trails for cross-country skiing and hiking. (The Yosts can suggest trips off the beaten path on foot or by bike, or book Bert, a licensed guide, for an outdoor excursion.) Willkommen Hof is popular with Whiteface Mountain downhill skiers because it's just minutes away from the slopes. After all that exertion, guests can wind down in either the outdoor hot tub or indoor sauna.

Northwest Lakes

LAKE CLEAR

Hohmeyer's Lake Clear Lodge

Innkeepers: Cathy and Ernest Hohmeyer
518-891-1489
www.lodgeonlakeclear.com
6319 NY 30
Open: Year-round
Price: Moderate to Expensive
Credit Cards: MC, V
Minimum Stay: Two nights in chalets and
   lakeside vacation rentals; two nights on
   holiday weekends
Handicap Access: No
Remarks: Fireplaces; restaurant; children
   welcome; pets allowed in chalets and
   vacation rentals (deposit required)

The Hohmeyers have made the Lake Clear
Lodge highly acclaimed for home-style
German cuisine, and overnight guests have
enjoyed the family's gracious hospitality for
more than four decades. On twenty-five
secluded lakeshore acres, accommodations
here combine modern conveniences with
Old World charm.

Four guest rooms in the 1886 lodge each
have a private bath; three winterized
chalets with fireplaces offer woodsy privacy; and three lakeside cottages can
accommodate larger groups—perfect for
weddings or retreats.

Guests may use canoes, rowboats, a picnic area, and beach; and Cathy is happy to
arrange mountain-bike rentals, guide service, or overnight canoe trips for visitors.
The lodge also offers packages ranging from
wellness weekends to romantic getaways.

PAUL SMITHS

Northbrook Lodge

518-327-3379
www.northbrooklodge.com
White Pine Road
Open: Mid-June through mid-September

Price: Expensive
Credit Cards: None
Minimum Stay: Three nights
Handicap Access: No
Remarks: Fireplaces; lakefront; sandy
   beach; children welcome; no pets

Set on a pine-shaded peninsula on Osgood
Lake, Northbrook Lodge was constructed as
a millionaire's retreat in the 1920s by the
same builder as the magnificent Adirondack Great Camp, Topridge, a few miles
away.

Sixteen rooms for guests are in appealing cottages connected by covered walkways
and porches; all have private baths, refrigerators, and separate entrances; three have
fireplaces.

Breakfast and dinner are included in the
room rate, and meals—made completely
from scratch—are served in the dining hall.
The boathouse has a bar/lounge with a classic Brunswick Balke billiard table; canoes
and rowboats are available for guests at no
extra charge.

White Pine Camp

Manager: Lynn Witte
518-327-3030
www.whitepinecamp.com
White Pine Road
Open: Year-round
Price: Expensive
Credit Cards: AE, D, MC, V
Minimum Stay: One week in July and
   August; two nights in spring and fall
Handicap Access: No
Remarks: Historic site; fireplaces; children
   welcome; pets on a limited basis

Imagine a week spent at a real Great Camp,
once the summer White House of President
Coolidge. Four of the cabins along Osgood
Lake are available to guests by the week in
July and August and for shorter visits in
spring and fall; a couple of units will be
available for winter rentals as well. All thir-
teen cabins—furnished with an eclectic

assortment of rustic and Mission-style antiques—have porches, kitchens, separate bedrooms that accommodate two to eight people, and some either fieldstone fire-places or woodstoves. Guests can use the beach, boathouse, Japanese teahouse, cro-quet lawn, bowling alley, canoes, rowboats, and kayaks, and enjoy the extensive grove of wild rhododendrons that covers the hillside.

White Pine Camp also operates as a his-toric site; Adirondack Architectural Heritage offers tours on Saturdays in July and August.

SARANAC

Sunday Pond Bed & Breakfast
Owners: Lesley and Dick Lyon
518-891-1531
www.sundaypond.com
5544 NY 30
Open: Year-round

A short walk from White Pine Camp's cabins is the lovely Japanese teahouse. Elizabeth Folwell

Price: Moderate
Credit Cards: AE, D, MC, V
Handicap Access: No
Remarks: Guide service available; children welcome

Say you're a paddler or hiker and you want to explore the St. Regis Canoe Area with its dozens of lakes and ponds, but you hate the thought of camping out. Look no further: Sunday Pond is set where you can start all those adventures right from the front door.

The Lyons' home—one of a very few in this corner of the park—is quite nice, with a long porch, skylights, a fireplace, and a big family room. Guests can choose from three rooms or spacious sleeping loft, all with private baths. Breakfasts are ample and healthy; hearty trail lunches and dinners (including curried chicken breast, London broil, baked shrimp with herb stuffing, and vegetarian pasta dishes) are available to guests by request.

TUPPER LAKE

Three Pillars
Owners: Honor and Neil Shofi
518-359-3093; winter: 914-948-1650
www.tupperlakeinfo.com/threepillars.htm
1361 NY 30
Open: Mid-June through mid-September
Price: Moderate
Credit Cards: None
Minimum Stay: One week in summer; three days in fall
Handicap Access: No
Remarks: Private beach; lakefront; children welcome; no pets

With about a quarter mile of shoreline on Big Tupper Lake, the secluded cabins at Three Pillars have a great view. The location, close to Bog River Falls, is one of the best you'll find on this large lake.

There are three pine-paneled, comfort-ably furnished housekeeping cottages with complete kitchens, fireplaces, and screen porches, plus a three-bedroom apartment above the boathouse that gives the wonderful sensation of being right on the water. There's a nice sandy beach and a long dock for guests' boats. Ask about where to find the walleyes.

UPPER SARANAC LAKE

The Point
Owners: The Garrett Group
518-891-5674 or 1-800-255-3530
www.thepointresort.com
P.O. Box 1327
Open: Year-round, except April (though schedule changes year to year)
Price: Very Expensive
Credit Cards: AE, MC, V
Minimum Stay: Two nights on weekends; three nights on holidays
Handicap Access: No
Remarks: Great Camp; gourmet meals; boats for guests; member Relais et Châteaux; no children under 18

William Avery Rockefeller built a drop-dead gorgeous Great Camp named Wonundra on an Upper Saranac Lake peninsula in the 1930s, and if you've read any recent articles about the Adirondacks, chances are you've seen The Point, that Rockefeller place that's now a Relais et Châteaux property. A roundup of comments from the press gives you a glimpse of what's so special here: "Absolutely, but absolutely, lovely, a place in which everything you see is total perfection," wrote Rene Lecler in *The 300 Best Hotels in the World*. "A private estate that sweeps all honors as the most enchanting lakefront sanctuary of its kind in America," stated *The Hideaway Report*. "It's rather like those European castles where one can arrange to spend a week as the guest of the duke and duchess," commented the *Yale University Alumni Magazine*; "The Point: the wilderness at its most luxurious," summarized *Vogue*.

The eleven rooms, in four different buildings, each have vast beds, lake views, and fireplaces, and are filled with an astutely planned mixture of antiques, Adirondack furniture, Oriental rugs, old prints, and stuffed beasts. The Boathouse is a gem, with its own private dining alcove and wrap-around balcony, but all the rooms are divine.

In the main lodge, the great hall measures 30 by 50 feet; fireplaces of astonishing proportions blaze away. The atmosphere here is that of a truly elegant house party, with black tie suggested for dinner on Wednesday and Saturday nights. The food warrants that treatment, too, with menus deftly combining native bounty, fine herbs, exquisite seafood, and imported ingredients in an imaginative kaleidoscope of flavors. The wine list is unsurpassed, and the bar is always open.

All this elegance and hedonism comes at a price, with one night for a couple at The Point costing more than a week for two at the Hedges or Elk Lake Lodge. But *Forbes* magazine summed it up well: "There are no telephones, no newspapers, and no menu choice. You partake of what is prepared each day and sit down to dine at the appointed hour. If you don't like the hosts, the food, the guests or the digs, tough luck . . . [yet] for those in search of sybaritic creature comforts, there is only one destination—The Point."

Don't expect to be able to drive in for just a look at the place. No signs mark the way to The Point, and only registered guests get the secret directions.

Central and Southwestern Adirondacks

BENSON

Lapland Lake Cross-Country Ski & Vacation Center
Owners: Ann and Olavi Hirvonen
518-863-4974 or 1-800-453-SNOW
www.laplandlake.com
139 Lapland Lake Road, Northville

Open: Year-round
Price: Moderate
Credit Cards: AE, D, MC, V
Handicap Access: No
Remarks: Cross-country-ski trails; sauna,
   ski-rental shop; ski lessons; snack bar;
   live reindeer; children welcome; no pets

Just when you think that you got the directions wrong to this rather remote spot, you see road signs in . . . Finnish? Quickly, the view opens up to a ski shop and a bunch of neat little cottages. With 50 kilometers of trails, this cross-country-ski center offers lots of amenities, plus plenty of snow.

Summertime is lovely at Lapland Lake, too. There's a small spring-fed lake on the 300-acre property where guests can swim, canoe, and fish. Trails here connect with state-owned hiking trails; you can pick up the Northville–Lake Placid Trail less than a mile away.

Ten housekeeping cottages range in size from two to four bedrooms, and are called *tupas,* which means "cabin" in Finnish. They're spotless and comfortable; most have woodstoves or screen porches. The biggest place, Lapin Tupa, is the original farmhouse. It has a dining room with a view of the pond, a big eat-in kitchen, four bedrooms, and two full baths.

Trailhead Lodge

Owner: John Washburn
518-863-2198
www.adirontreks.com
206 Washburn Road
Open: Year-round
Price: Inexpensive to Moderate
Credit Cards: None
Minimum Stay: Two nights winter weekends; three nights holiday weekends
Handicap Access: No
Remarks: Fireplace; children 6 and older
   welcome

John Washburn's grandfather took in hunters and fishermen here more than a

century ago and guided them to the big ones. Nowadays you can do much the same thing in a bit more comfort at Trailhead Lodge. On the outside, the building looks like a typical farmhouse; inside, the walls are finished off with pine boards and Adirondack décor—snowshoes, pack baskets, and such. There are five guest rooms; a delicious country breakfast is included with the price of lodging.

John, a licensed Adirondack guide, is very knowledgeable about the woods and wildlife; he leads map-and-compass and other workshops for groups. By the roaring fire on a chill night, you might coax him to recite Robert Service poems or tall tales.

BIG MOOSE LAKE

Big Moose Inn

Innkeeper: Robert Hankey
315-357-2042
www.bigmooseinn.com
1510 Big Moose Road
Open: Year-round, except April, November
Price: Moderate; meal plan available
Credit Cards: AE, D, MC, V
Handicap Access: No
Remarks: Canoes and kayaks; restaurant;
   snowmobile trails; lakefront; children
   welcome; no pets; Wi-Fi; massage

Mud season is about the only time you can't enjoy Big Moose Inn. In late spring, you can canoe and fish on Big Moose Lake; summertime you can hike around Pigeon Lake Wilderness Area or visit nearby towns like Inlet and Old Forge; in the fall you can see beautiful foliage or hunt; when the snows arrive, there's snowmobiling or cross-country skiing practically right to the front door.

There are sixteen guest rooms to choose from, all with TVs and DVD players. Most chambers have a nice view of the lake; one has a fireplace, king-size bed, and Jacuzzi tub. Big Moose Inn's restaurant is one of the best in the neighborhood. (See Chapter 5.)

Covewood Lodge

Owners: Major and Diane Bowes
315-357-3041
www.covewoodlodge.com
120 Covewood Lodge Road
Open: May through October
Price: Moderate to Expensive
Credit Cards: None
Handicap Access: Yes
Remarks: Sandy beach; lakefront; water-
    skiing; cross-country-ski trails; children
    welcome; kids program; no pets; Wi-Fi

One of the all-time great woodsy Adirondack retreats, Covewood was built as a hotel
back in the days when guests stayed all
summer long. Along the shoreline and in
the trees are eighteen housekeeping cabins,
available in summer. There's a big rustic
lodge, built in 1924 by well-known Big
Moose Laker Earl Covey, with a stone fireplace for guests to enjoy after they've
explored the wild woods nearby.

    Guided bird-watching tours are avail-
able; Covewood offers sailboat, kayak,
canoe, or motorboat rentals. There's also a
popular kids' program operated by two
counselors who provide daily activities for
youngsters. The lodge and surroundings
provide a fine, woodsy spot for a wedding.

The Waldheim

Owners: Nancy Martin Pratt
315-357-2353
www.thewaldheim.com
502 Martin Road
Open: Mid-June through Columbus Day
Price: Expensive (includes three meals)
Credit Cards: None
Handicap Access: One cabin
Remarks: Sandy beach; boats for guests;
    children welcome; rustic buildings;
    fireplaces; Wi-Fi

The Waldheim was built in 1904 by E. J.
Martin from trees cut on the property, and
there's a wonderful old-time feel to the
place. ("No phone, no TV, no clocks," says

Nancy Pratt, the third generation of her
family to run The Waldheim.) Many of the
fifteen cabins are made of vertical half logs
and some have twig-work railings on the
porches. The places are aptly named "Cozy,"
"Comfort," "Heart's Content," and each one
has a fireplace. Rates include three full
meals a day, which are served in a gracious
dining room furnished with antiques.

    When the cottages open (and if the deer
stay away), lovely wild azaleas bloom along
the pathways. Guests can hike, canoe,
swim, and fish; arrangements can be made
to have a seaplane pick you up at the dock
for a scenic flight. There are no planned
activities except the weekly camp picnic, a
moveable feast taken to a remote part of the
lake by boat. The 300-acre property is
adjacent to state land so the location is
secluded indeed.

BLUE MOUNTAIN LAKE

Curry's Cottages

Owners: Mike and Bob Curry
518-352-7355
NY 28
Open: May through October
Price: Moderate
Credit Cards: None
Minimum Stay: One week in July through
    August; weekends May through June,
    September
Handicap Access: No
Remarks: Boat launch; children welcome

These charming barn-red housekeeping
cottages are a familiar sight to Blue
Mountain Lake visitors; photographs of the
chorus line of white Adirondack chairs
along the beach have appeared in numerous
national magazines. Three generations of
Currys have operated the cottages, and Bob,
the current Curry, is always at work making
improvements.

    Eight cottages accommodate couples to
families of six; four cottages are on the water,

four are on the edge of the woods across the road. The beach at Curry's is a favorite with families; it's safe and shallow for kids.

The Hedges

Owner: Pat Benton
518-352-7325
www.thehedges.com
1 Hedges Road on Blue Mountain Lake
Open: Late May through mid-October
Price: Expensive to Very Expensive (meal plans included)
Credit Cards: None
Handicap Access: Three cottages
Remarks: Private sandy beach; boats and bikes for guests; tennis; meals; children welcome; kids' program; no pets; Wi-Fi

Colonel Hiram Duryea, a Civil War veteran and millionaire industrialist, began building the Hedges in 1880. The main house, with four wonderful guest rooms all with private baths, has an unusual mansard roof line that sweeps onto a wraparound porch. The lovely Stone Lodge, built about 1890, has a two-bedroom suite with fireplace on the first floor, and six rooms with private baths upstairs. Antiques and beautiful woodwork are found throughout these two lodges.

There are nine one- to three-bedroom sleeping cabins along the lakeshore (and several more nearby). All accommodations are offered with modified American plan; picnic lunches are available at a small charge. Guests have use of canoes, kayaks, rowboats, a clay tennis court, and the library; the Birch Room, a museum-quality gem of rustic detail, is worth a visit.

Meals are served in the dining room lodge, another appealing old building, which has stamped-tin walls and ceilings and a stone fireplace. The food is quite good, and some reservations for nonguests are available with at least one-day notice.

Blue Mountain Lake is a very beautiful, quiet lake; the Hedges is in a particularly lovely, private spot. Generations of families have returned since the hotel opened in the 1920s.

Hemlock Hall

Owners: Susan and Paul Provost
518-352-7706
www.hemlockhall.com
Maple Lodge Road
Open: Mid-October through mid-May
Price: Moderate to Expensive (meal plan included)
Credit Cards: None
Minimum Stay: Three nights in summer; as available spring and fall
Handicap Access: No
Remarks: Private beach; boats for guests; meals; children welcome; no pets; no alcohol served on the premises

On Maple Lodge Road, a mile off the state highway, is another stunning Adirondack hostelry. Hemlock Hall was carefully restored by Eleanor and Monty Webb in the 1950s, and their hard work still shows. The woodwork in the main lodge—a complicated pattern of wainscoting on the walls and ceilings—still gleams, and there are numerous antiques throughout. The stone fireplace has hearths on two sides, opening onto part of the living room and a wing of the dining room. There's even a fireplace in an upstairs hallway.

There are twenty-three rooms for guests, in the lodge with shared baths, motel units, and two- or three-bedroom cottages. The tower suite in the main lodge has its own screen porch and charming window seats; several of the lodge rooms have lake views; you can even rent the top floor of the boathouse. Breakfast and dinner are included in the room charges.

The dining room serves wholesome, plentiful food in a family-style arrangement. There's one entrée offered each evening, with chicken and biscuits on Wednesday a great favorite. (Nonguests can dine with prior reservations.) Folks are seated at different tables each night so they get to mingle with the other visitors; alcoholic beverages, which might make all this mingling a bit easier, are not permitted in the dining room.

LaPrairie's Lakefront Cottages
Owners: Ernie and Kim LaPrairie
518-352-7323
The Steamboat Landing, 144 Main Street
Open: May through October
Price: Moderate to Expensive
Credit Cards: None
Minimum Stay: One week in July and
    August
Handicap Access: No
Remarks: No pets; waterfront; fireplaces

Sometimes it's hard to grasp where the "town" of Blue Mountain Lake lies. There's a gas station at the intersection of NY 28, 28N, and 30, and when you head west toward Old Forge you find the firehouse, post office, and Adirondack Lakes Center for the Arts. LaPrairie's Lakefront Cottages, a cluster of historic buildings and house-keeping cabins, are in the heart of the hamlet, yet with plenty of water's edge to enjoy and a ring of ridges where the sun sets.

Steamboat Landing, the main structure, is three stories tall, built at the turn of the twentieth century to house the *Tuscarora*, a huge boat that delivered guests to hotels around the lake. But for more than fifty years the place has served tourists in another way, through lodging and shops. Now, with nicely renovated housekeeping cottages flanking the Steamboat Landing and apartments in the main boat shelter and outbuildings, this place offers plenty for families and others: kitchens, fireplaces, cable TV, braided wool rugs and handmade quilts, plus beach, dock for fishing and canoes or kayaks to rent at Blue Mountain Outfitters.

Prospect Point Cottages
Owners: The Ostreicher Family
518-352-7378
www.prospectpt.com
NY 28
Open: Year-round
Price: Moderate to Expensive
Credit Cards: AE, D, MC, V
Minimum Stay: One week July through
    August; three nights spring and fall
Handicap Access: Wheelchair ramps on
    some cabins; one fully equipped handi-
    cap unit
Remarks: Private sandy beach; children
    welcome; library/game building for
    large gatherings; no pets

This beautiful peninsula on Blue Mountain Lake was once the site of the mammoth one-hundred-room Prospect House, the first hotel in the world to have electricity. (Never mind that technology went only so far; guests trudged off to outhouses when nature called.) Now a dozen two-bedroom housekeeping cottages occupy the point; they line the curving shore. Five cottages are winterized, with fireplaces and picture windows. If you were turned off by the way this property looked a few years ago, try again. Some cabins have skylights, screened-in porches, TVs, and phones.

The view of Blue Mountain is simply magnificent. From Prospect Point, which is close to town but off the highway, it's an easy walk to the arts center for a concert, the boat livery for a tour of the chain of lakes, or the post office to mail those pic-ture postcards saying "Wish you were here."

INDIAN LAKE/SABAEL

1870 Bed & Breakfast
Host: Bill Zullo
518-648-5377
www.bandb.bizland.com
36 West Main Street
Open: Year-round

Price: Moderate
Credit Cards: None
Handicap Access: No
Remarks: Fireplace; children welcome; no
   pets; Wi-Fi

Guestbooks from decades ago capture the flavor of this place: "Our stay here was wonderful as usual. In the past sixteen years, nothing has changed," commented one visitor thirty years ago. You'll still find real braided rugs on the floors, tatted spreads on the antique beds, ruffled curtains in the windows, family pictures dating back to the 1890s on the walls, and a homey, quiet atmosphere.

There is one bedroom on the first floor, and four nice rooms upstairs. The living room has comfortable Grandma's-house-type furniture, a fireplace, cable TV, plus shelves of board games and puzzles. From the shady front porch, you can look out over the perennial garden, and farther back on the old farm, there's a big raspberry and blackberry patch that's open for grazing. Tennis courts (at the school) are kitty-corner.

Binder's Cabins

Owner: Melanie Stiffel
518-648-5500
NY 28
Open: Year-round
Price: Inexpensive
Credit Cards: AE, D, MC, V
Handicap Access: Yes
Remarks: Children welcome; lake access;
   pets welcome

When you enter the hamlet of Indian Lake from the east, one of the first places that comes into view is Binder's cluster of well-kept cabins on NY 28 across from Lake Adirondack. In the summer, the border of bright red dahlias in the front yard might catch your eye.

The seven cabins sleep up to five people, and are fully outfitted with kitchen equipment, linens, towels, and so on. There are screen porches on all the cottages, making them particularly enjoyable during bug season. These cabins have been a mainstay of local lodging for fifty years, popular with rafters, anglers, hikers, hunters, boaters, and cross-country skiers. Rowboats and canoes for exploring the nearby lake are provided.

Camp Driftwood

Owners: Jon and Brenda Voorhees
518-648-5111
www.goodcabins.com
199 Sabael Road
Open: Year-round
Price: Moderate
Credit Cards: None
Minimum Stay: One week July through
   August
Handicap Access: No
Remarks: Private beach; boats for guests;
   well-behaved pets welcome; boats and
   firewood provided; Wi-Fi

Indian Lake is about 13 miles long, with numerous bays and publicly owned islands to explore, and Camp Driftwood is a good base from which to plan day trips or simply to relax. Jon and Brenda Voorhees rent ten housekeeping cabins along the shore and tucked back in the woods. Maple Cabin is an old lodge, with three bedrooms, a fireplace (and backup heat), screen porch, and deck; Birch also has three bedrooms, and you can practically roll out of bed in the morning for a dip in the lake. All cottages have full kitchens and woodstoves for cool mornings, plus outdoor fireplaces for barbecues. Three cabins are winterized. Guests need to bring bed linens and towels.

There's a sandy beach for wading, a float for advanced swimmers, canoes, kayaks, a sailboat, and rowboats for guests, and genuine hospitality from the Voorhees family. This is the kind of place where families settle in for two weeks or more and pretend they're at home.

Timberlock

Owner: Holly and Bruce Catlin
518-648-5494, winter: 802-457-1621
www.timberlock.com
NY 30 on Indian Lake
Open: Mid-June through mid-September
Price: Expensive (full American meal plan
  included)
Credit Cards: None
Minimum Stay: Three nights
Handicap Access: No
Remarks: Private beach; boats; horseback
  riding; tennis; children welcome; no
  pets; Wi-Fi

Timberlock welcomed its first guests in
1898. Not much has changed since those
days: The common buildings and the
guests' log cabins are still equipped with
gaslights and woodstoves. The atmosphere
here is rustic, relaxed, peaceful, yet the
resort offers a surprising variety of activities and amenities.

There are two Hartru tennis courts and
two clay courts; gentle horses for guided
trail rides; an excellent sandy beach;
numerous boats to sail, paddle, or row on
Indian Lake; and trails on the property for
hiking and birding. If you'd prefer to discover the Adirondacks on your own, the
Catlins have assembled a thick book outlining car trips, picnic spots, mountain
climbs, museums, and other sites to
explore.

"Timberlock is not for everyone," says
owner Bruce Catlin. "We are not a luxury
place and have not paved away the wildlife."
There are sixteen "family cottages," which
have full baths, screen porches, and lake
views, plus some small cabins without
baths. Rates include three hearty meals a
day and use of all the facilities and activities
except horseback riding. There are no
neighbors within miles of Timberlock, and
your wake-up call in the morning may well
be a loon's yodel from the lake.

The Crosswinds

Owner: Jan and Bill Burwell
315-357-4500
76 NY 28 (P.O. Box 326)
Open: End of June through September
Price: Moderate
Credit Cards: None
Minimum Stay: One week July through
  August; overnights welcome in off-sea-
  son
Handicap Access: No
Remarks: Private beach; children welcome;
  no pets

Located right on Fourth Lake are the
Crosswinds cabins, five attractive two-bedroom housekeeping units. All the places
have completely equipped, knotty-pine-
paneled kitchens; guests need to supply
their own linens and towels. There's a 200-
foot private sandy beach, and a large dock
for boats (small extra charge for dock
space). It's a short walk from the
Crosswinds to downtown Inlet, which has a
movie theater, restaurants, tennis courts,
outfitters, liquor store, and shops.

Holl's Inn

Innkeeper: Rosemary Holl
315-357-2941; winter: 315-733-2748
www.hollsinn.com
56 South Shore Road
Open: July and August
Price: Moderate to Expensive
Credit Cards: None
Minimum Stay: Two nights
Handicap Access: twenty-five rooms have
  ramps
Remarks: Private beach; restaurant and
  bar; library

Rosemary Holl says, "The way we were is
the way we still are!" This spacious resort—
150 beautiful acres on Fourth Lake—dates
back to the 1920s, and the Holl family has
been in charge since 1935. The buildings

and grounds are meticulously maintained and quite secluded.

There are fifteen rooms with private baths in the original hotel building; large rooms in the lakefront Annex; and more rooms still in the housekeeping cottages and Alpine House. Guests get three hearty meals a day in the dining room, which is also open to the public with advance reservations. The Tyrolean Bar is charming, done up in Dresden blue, yellow, and red, with cozy booths and hand-decorated plates commemorating all the honeymooners who have stayed at Holl's over the years. After all that food and drink, there are plenty of ways to work off the extra calories: swimming, tennis, rowing, or canoeing.

Parquet House
315-794-8076
162 NY 28
Open: Year-round
Price: Expensive
Credit Cards: AE, D, MC, V
Handicap Access: No
Remarks: Close proximity to beach and
    shopping; fireplace

New owners took over this funny little hotel in 2004 and transformed it into a super retreat, set amid the splendors of downtown Inlet. There are nine bedrooms, five and a half baths, a kitchen, and a common area with granite fireplace. The public

Inlet's Parquet Hotel was a happening place in the 1940s. Recently restored as the Parquet House, it again welcomes guests. Private collection

beach, playground, and tennis courts are a two-minute walk away; also close by: the Tamarack Café and Movie House, shopping, and miles of groomed snowmobile and cross-country-ski trails.

Rocky Point Townhomes
315-357-3751
www.rockypointproperties.com
NY 28
Open: Year-round
Price: Expensive to Very Expensive
Credit Cards: MC, V
Minimum Stay: One week July and August
Handicap Access: No
Remarks: Docks for guests' boats; children
    and pets welcome

The original Rocky Point, an enormous old lodge, was razed to make room for two-story lakeside three-bedroom town houses. Each one is nicely appointed and has a fireplace, three full baths, and cable TV/DVD; kitchens have microwaves, dishwashers, and washer/dryers (linens not included in rates). The beach is excellent, nearly a quarter-mile long, but if the water's too chilly there's an indoor pool and spa. Three tennis courts and private docks for boats and fishing are on the property, and two eighteen-hole golf courses are within a five-minute drive.

The Woods Inn
Innkeepers: Jay Latterman and Joedda
    McClain
315-357-5300
www.thewoodsinn.com
148 NY 28
Open: Year-round
Price: Expensive
Credit Cards: D, MC, V
Handicap Access: Yes
Remarks: Restaurant and tavern; full-moon
    night hikes; classes and workshops; Wi-Fi

This sweeping resort was built by Fred Hess in 1894 and four years later purchased by

Philo Wood, who renamed it The Wood Hotel. Much has changed in more than a century, but thanks to a recent massive restoration by Jay Latterman and Joedda McClain, this place, which was ready to topple to the ground, has been saved, and is now operating as the grand inn it once was.

Guests can choose between twenty rooms in the inn, all with private baths, some with balconies, Jacuzzis, and mountain and lake views; two nearby cottages, both with kitchens; or several Adirondack Guide Tents, throwbacks to nineteenth- and early-twentieth-century luxury platform tents. The tents are beautifully furnished and have electric lights and woodstoves. The adjacent bathhouse is heated and offers a double shower for two.

Breakfast is included in the cost of a night's stay. A restaurant serving a varied menu and plenty of comfort food is open to the public (see Chapter 5); the **Laughing Loons Tavern** is a cozy place for a cocktail.

This is a dreamy place for a wedding, even in winter. Ask Joedda about the functions she's hosted.

LONG LAKE

Adirondack Hotel

Owner: Carol Young
518-624-4700
www.adirondackhotel.com
1245 Main Street
Open: Year-round
Price: Moderate
Credit Cards: AE, MC, V
Handicap Access: No
Remarks: Bar and restaurants; fireplace; gift shop; no smoking; no pets; Wi-Fi

There's been a lodge at this spot overlooking Long Lake since before the Civil War, and portions of the current Adirondack Hotel date to the 1870s. On the first floor are the **Victorian Dining Room**, **Lake Street Café**, rustic taproom, and a gift

shop; the lobby has a cool turned-spindle cashier's booth. Taxidermy specimens (full-size black bear, giant moose head, and a goodly assortment of Adirondack mammals) add to the old-time feel.

Nineteen guest rooms plus an apartment are on the second and third floors. Many have been renovated and have modern bathrooms, but some rooms share baths.

Green Harbor Motel & Cottages

Owners: Ellen and Ken Schaeffer
518-624-4133
www.greenharbormotel.com
NY 30
Open: May 15 through October 15
Price: Moderate
Credit Cards: None
Minimum Stay: One week in July and August
Handicap Access: No
Remarks: Beach; boat docks; gift shop; no pets

Nine housekeeping cottages and a small motel are set on a private sandy beach at Green Harbor; cabins have cable TV and decks or porches with views of the water—some have air-conditioning. Winter visitors can stay in three bed and breakfast rooms in the main house and venture out on Long Lake's miles of cross-country-ski or snowmobile trails. There's a game room with ping-pong table, library, and large color TV.

MINERVA

Morningside Camps and Cottages

Owners: David and Randi LaBar
518-251-2694 or 1-866-210-2694
www.morningsidecamps.com
NY 30
Open: Mid-May through mid-October
Price: Moderate to Expensive
Credit Cards: D, MC, V
Minimum Stay: One week in summer; two

nights spring and fall
Handicap Access: No
Remarks: Private beach; children welcome;
    no pets; coin laundry

Set on eighty acres of land accessible by a
private road, Morningside Camps offers
waterfront seclusion on Minerva Lake.
There are fifteen camps—a combo of handsome log cabins and chalets, all of which
have complete kitchens, bathrooms, stone
fireplace or woodstove, and decks or screen
porches. The property has a private beach,
a play area with a tree house, a tennis court,
docks for canoes and rowboats, and hiking
trails through the woods that lead you to the
general store, the town beach, or around
the shoreline. Each cabin is given the
option of a canoe, rowboat, or kayak to
explore Minerva Lake.

Understandably, there's a waiting list for
the cabins in July and August, but places are
available before the Fourth of July and after
Labor Day. Don't be afraid to ask.

NORTH CREEK

Goose Pond Inn
Innkeepers: Beverly and Jim Englert
518-251-3434 or 1-800-806-2601
www.goosepondinn.com
196 Main Street
Open: Year-round
Price: Moderate to Expensive
Credit Cards: None
Handicap Access: No
Remarks: Fireplace; wood-fired sauna;
    children 10 and older welcome; mid-
    week ski packages; no pets

A beautifully restored Victorian home set
back on a shady lawn off Main Street, Goose
Pond Inn has four lovely bedrooms, each
with its own bath. Antiques, old prints, and
amusing details are found throughout. Jim
cooks up superb breakfasts, such as
brandied French toast with sautéed apples,
crêpes with rhubarb sauce, or Belgian waf-

fles with flambéed bananas. From the inn,
it's a five-minute drive to downhill skiing at
Gore Mountain or to any of the whitewater
rafting headquarters for trips down the
Hudson Gorge. If adventure isn't your thing,
you can walk to Tannery Pond Community
Center for a concert, play, or art exhibit.

NORTH RIVER

Garnet Hill Lodge
Owners: Mary and Joe Fahy
518-251-2444
www.garnet-hill.com
Thirteenth Lake Road
Open: Year-round
Price: Expensive
Credit Cards: AE, D, MC, V
Handicap Access: Yes
Remarks: Cross-country-ski trails; ski
    shop; restaurant; Irish pub; fireplaces;
    private lakefront; maple syrup opera-
    tion; children welcome; some pet-
    friendly units; Wi-Fi

Cross-country skiers flock to Garnet Hill:
There are some 35 miles of groomed trails,
a full ski shop, and reliable snow cover. But
you don't have to ski to enjoy this country
inn. You can mountain bike or hike on the
trails, plan a trip into Siamese Ponds
Wilderness Area, or watch the days pass in
a beautiful setting from a comfortable chair
near Thirteenth Lake.

The Log House, built in 1936, has sixteen upstairs guest rooms, all with private
baths. Downstairs is the **Log House
Restaurant** and **Miners Pub** (see Chapter
5), a game room, and a massive fireplace
made of local garnet. The Tea House has
four luxurious rooms, with king-size beds
and whirlpool baths, and its own living
room; the Birches has five family-size
rooms, each with private bath and a large
common room.

Garnet Hill visitors can swim at the private beach, play tennis on the resort's courts,

and use canoes, rowboats, and sailboats for exploring motorless Thirteenth Lake.

NORTHVILLE

Inn at the Bridge

Owners: Linda Bruno
518-863-2240
www.innatthebridge.com
641 Bridge Street
Open: Year-round
Price: Moderate
Credit Cards: AE, D, MC, V
Handicap Access: One room
Remarks: Fireplace; lakefront; well-
    behaved children welcome; no pets

A grand Queen Anne–style mansion with porches, gables, and a tower, the Inn at the Bridge is a handsome place. All six bedrooms are furnished with Victorian antiques and have new private baths. There's a lovely fireplace in the parlor, which also has comfortable couches, television, and books galore. Breakfast includes an assortment of homemade breads, muffins, bagels, fruit, and so forth; the inn serves dinner on weekends and by prior arrangement for parties of four or more. (Some diners cruise over in their boats.) There's a gazebo on the lawn overlooking Great Sacandaga Lake, docks for guests, and visitors can stroll through town to the Adirondack Country Store and other interesting shops along Main Street.

OLD FORGE/THENDARA

Van Auken's Inne

Innkeepers: The Marks Family
315-369-3033
www.vanaukensinne.com
108 Forge Street
Open: Year-round
Price: Moderate to Expensive
Credit Cards: MC, V
Minimum Stay: Two nights on weekends in
    high season

Handicap Access: No
Remarks: Restaurant and bar; children
    welcome; no pets

This grand old hotel was a year old when the Adirondack branch of the New York Central made its first stop in Thendara station in 1892. Since then, the trains have come and gone (and are back again for scenic excursions from Thendara), while Van Auken's has remained a constant presence across the way.

The second floor—where twenty bedrooms used to share two baths—has been made into twelve nice guest rooms, each with private bath. Original details and antique furniture have been incorporated into these modern accommodations, and some rooms open onto the huge second-floor veranda. The public areas downstairs, like the taproom and the lobby, have polished wood floors, stamped-tin ceilings, and other elegant touches. The restaurant is open for lunch and dinner.

PISECO

Irondequoit Inn

518-548-5500 or 1-888-497-0350
www.irondequoitinn.com
Old Piseco Road
Open: Year-round, except April and
    mid–November through December 26
Price: Moderate to Expensive
Credit Cards: MC, V
Handicap Access: One cabin
Remarks: Private beach; private island; tent
    campsites; tennis court; canoes, kayaks,
    and fishing boats to rent; children wel-
    come; no pets; no smoking

The Irondequoit Inn was founded in 1892 by a group of upstate New York businessmen as an outdoor getaway. Now the property covers 650 acres and spans nearly two miles of shoreline on Piseco Lake. From the front porches of the two main buildings, you can look down the lawns to see Oxbow, Rogers, and Piseco Mountains. There's even a private undeveloped island in the lake that guests can canoe to for picnics, swimming, or sleeping out under the stars. Visitors have described a stay here as like summer camp for families.

There are nine rooms, which share three baths; one-bedroom efficiencies; and housekeeping cabins. There's also a campground by the lake (hot showers and flush toilets are available).

Room rates for the main lodge include full breakfast. Dinners—family-style fare— are available to guests and the public by reservation.

SPECULATOR

Alpine Meadow Chalets
Owners: Chari and Chuck Smith
518-548-5615
1 Old Indian Lake Road
Open: Year-round
Price: Moderate
Credit Cards: No
Minimum Stay: Inquire
Handicap Access: No

Off the state highway between Speculator and Indian Lake are a cluster of pleasant, winterized one- and two-bedroom chalets. They feature all the comforts of home: grills, picnic tables, microwaves, TVs, and have easy access to snowmobile trails, Lake Pleasant's waterfront, and the shops, restaurants, and activities found in "Sparkle City," as some call downtown Speculator.

Bearhurst Lakeside Cottages
Owners: Helen and Dick Armstrong
518-548-6427
www.bearhurst.com
South Shore Road
Open: June through September
Price: Moderate to Expensive
Credit Cards: None
Minimum Stay: One week July through
    August; two nights June, September
Handicap Access: No

Remarks: Private lakefront; dockage for guests' boats; children welcome; no pets; no Jet-Skis

Most folks associate Great Camps with Raquette or the St. Regis Lakes, but in other parts of the park there are some smaller estates that are of equal architectural interest. One of these is Bearhurst, which was built in 1894 by Herman Meyrowitz (fashionable optical shops in Paris, Geneva, and Milan still carry his name), and it occupies a quarter mile of shoreline on Lake Pleasant.

Guests stay in five of the original outbuildings, including the icehouse, pumphouse, summer kitchen, and boathouse, all of which have been converted into delightful modern accommodations while still maintaining historical charm. The living rooms in each have fireplaces, and the fully outfitted kitchens have dishwashers.

The centerpiece of the property is the main lodge, a stunning log building with

A rustic gazebo looks out over Lake Pleasant at Bearhurst. Elizabeth Folwell

lovely leaded-glass windows and gracious porches; the stonework is intricate, with spiral stone staircases leading down from the front porch. One second-floor fireplace has an inset oval leaded-glass window. The Armstrongs live in the main lodge, but guests can certainly enjoy the building from the outside.

There's a private beach, dock space for guests' boats, and a pretty, rustic gazebo for watching the sunset over the lake. If you visit in June, the grounds are covered with pinksters, the graceful wild azaleas.

STILLWATER RESERVOIR

The Norridgewock III

Manager: Pat Thompson
315-376-6200
www.beaverriver.com
150 Norridgewock Lake Road
Open: Year-round
Price: Moderate to Expensive
Credit Cards: AE, D, MC, V
Minimum Stay: Two days in cabins
Handicap Access: No
Remarks: Remote location; water taxi; chil-
    dren welcome; no pets

Beaver River is a settlement on Stillwater Reservoir that's way off the beaten path—you can't drive here, although you can hike, cross-country ski, snowmobile, or canoe nine miles to reach the cottages and motel rooms at the Norridgewock. (The place accommodates up to forty people.) The Thompson family, who has run this unique lodge for three generations, also operates a water taxi that will pick up and deliver

guests. It also offers a wilderness cruise on Stillwater every day except Wednesdays from July 4 through Labor Day, and on weekends through Columbus Day.

The place is self-sufficient, generating its own power. The tavern has a full menu and there's a gift shop, too.

Stillwater

Owners: Marian and Joe Romano
315-376-6470
www.stillwateradirondacks.com
2591 Stillwater Road
Open: Year-round, except April
Price: Moderate
Credit Cards: AE, D, MC, V
Minimum Stay: Two nights in winter
Handicap Access: No
Remarks: Boat launch; restaurant; children
    welcome; no pets; air-conditioning in
    units in summer; high-speed Internet
    access

Stillwater Reservoir, which is several miles back from the main highways via a winding gravel road, has 117 miles of shoreline, forty-five islands, and thousands of acres of public land for you to discover. There are more loons here than any other lake in the Adirondacks, and the fishing's not too bad, either. Stillwater is understandably popular with snowmobilers because the snow cover is excellent and several trail systems are accessible from the property. On the western end of the lake is the Romano's hotel/restaurant complex, the only accommodations that you can drive to on the reservoir. There are seven winterized motel rooms, plus a good restaurant and a friendly bar.

MOTELS AND CAMPGROUNDS

For a list of state-owned public campgrounds, see "Camping" in Chapter 7.

LAKE GEORGE AND SOUTHEASTERN ADIRONDACKS

For a complete list of accommodations in the Lake George–Chestertown–Warrensburg area, contact **Warren County Tourism Department** (1-800-95VISIT; www.visitlake george.com; 1340 US 9, Lake George). A sampling of motel and campground accommodations is listed below.

Bolton Landing

Adirondack Park Motel (518-644-9800; www.adirondackparkmotel.com; 5680 Lakeshore Drive). Price: Moderate. Pleasant, family-run motel with single and double rooms, efficiencies, two-bedroom cottages, and a five-bedroom house on Lake George. Playground; pool; private beach. Open: Memorial Day through Columbus Day.

   Melody Manor (518-644-9750; www.melodymanor.com; 4610 Lakeshore Drive). Price: Moderate to Expensive. forty rooms. Private beach; pool; boats; tennis; restaurant serving breakfast and dinner on premises; no pets. Open: May through October 30.

Diamond Point

Chelka Lodge on Lake George (518-668-4677; www.chelkalodge.com; 4204 Lakeshore Drive). Price: Moderate. Nice motel and efficiency units; private sand beach; free breakfast served; new beds, carpeting, bathrooms, TVs, and refrigerators. Open: May through October.

Lake George

Balsam Motel (518-668-3865; www.balsammotel.com; 430 Canada Street). Price: Moderate. Quiet family-run six-room motel with fifteen nonglitzy housekeeping cottages. Heated pool; beach access. Open: May 16 through October 14.

   The Georgian (518-668-5401; www.georgianresort.com; 384 Canada Street). Price: Moderate to Expensive. Huge, modern 161-unit motor inn. Heated pool; private beach; restaurants. Open: Year-round.

   Rock Castle Resort (518-668-3011; 3229 Lakeshore Drive). Price: Inexpensive to Moderate. Rooms (ten with private bath) in a stucco-and-stone mansion; housekeeping units and cabins. Pool; trolley stop to downtown Lake George. Open: Mid-spring through mid-fall.

   Tea Island Resort (518-668-2776; www.teaislandresort.com; 3020 Lakeshore Drive). Price: Moderate. Motel, chalets, and a cottage. Private beach. Open: April 2 through November 14.

   Wingate by Wyndham (518-668-4884; www.wingateinnlakegeorge.com; 4054 NY 9L). Price: Expensive. New hotel with ninety-six units; no pets; indoor and outdoor heated pools; whirlpool; fitness center. Open: Year-round.

Paradox

Sunder Land (518-585-3520; www.sunderlandcottages.com; 248 Fraternaland Road; on Paradox Lake). Price: Inexpensive to Moderate. Seven housekeeping cabins, some with fireplaces, decks, or screened porches. No pets, no motorboats; canoes, kayaks, and rowboats available for extra charge. Bring your own bed linens. Open: June through October.

Schroon Lake

Elm Tree Cottages (518-532-7500; www.elmtreecabins.com; US 9). Price: Moderate to Expensive. Housekeeping cabins on Schroon Lake; dock space for boats; pets allowed in a couple of the units. Open: May through December.

   Maple Leaf Motel (518-532-7474; www.mapleleafmotel.com; 1370 US 9). Price: Moderate. Four new and six recently renovated motel rooms; four housekeeping cabins, one with fireplace; outdoor pool. Open: Year-round.

CHAMPLAIN VALLEY

For a complete list of accommodations in the Champlain Valley, High Peaks, and Northern Adirondacks, contact the **Lake Placid/Essex County Visitors Bureau** (518-523-2445; www.lakeplacid.com; 2610 Main Street, Lake Placid).

Keeseville

Ausable Chasm Campground (518-834-9990; www.ausablechasm.com; intersection of Route 373 and US 9). Price: Inexpensive. 135 tent and RV sites; some full hookups. Short walk to Ausable Chasm. Open: Mid-May through mid-October.

Port Kent

Port Kent Campsite (518-834-9011; www.port-kent-campsite.com; 93 NY 373). Price: Inexpensive. Numerous RV hookups and tent sites, overlooking Lake Champlain at the Port Kent Ferry. Pool; nature trails; camping cabins; playground; Laundromat. Open: Mid-May through mid-October.

Ticonderoga

Best Western Ticonderoga Inn & Suites (518-585-2378; www.bestticonderogahotel.com; 260 Burgoyne Road). Price: Expensive. Brand new lodging offering a variety of accommodations and amenities. Banquet room for weddings or conferences that seats up to 250. Indoor heated pool; day spa; fitness center; game room. Open: Year-round.

HIGH PEAKS AND NORTHERN ADIRONDACKS

Lake Placid

Adirondack Inn by the Lake (518-523-2424; www.adirondack-inn.com; 2625 Main Street). Price: Expensive. One of the newer hotels in the center of downtown Lake Placid. Heated indoor pool; whirlpool; sauna; exercise room. Open: Year-round.

    Golden Arrow Lakeside Resort (518-523-3353; www.golden-arrow.com; 2559 Main Street). Price: Expensive. Modern motor inn on the lakefront in the heart of downtown. Health club; new heated pool; private beach; inquire about special getaway packages; all rooms are nonsmoking. Open: Year-round.

    Comfort Inn (518-523-9555; 2125 Saranac Avenue). Price: Expensive. Newish pet-friendly hotel across the street from the delicious Caribbean Cowboy restaurant; a half-mile or so walk to downtown Lake Placid; close to Peninsula hiking/skiing trails. Open: Year-round.

    Crowne Plaza Resort & Golf Club (518-523-2556; www.lakeplacidcp.com; 101 Olympic Drive). Price: Expensive to Very Expensive. Recently renovated hotel overlooking the Olympic Arena. 245 units; heated pool, sauna, whirlpool; access to Jackrabbit cross-country ski trails; two championship golf courses; health club; lake view; restaurant and lounge. Open: Year-round.

    High Peaks Hostel (518-523-4951; www.highpeakshostel.com; 5956 Sentinel Road). Price: Inexpensive. The cheapest lodging to be found in town. Call about group rates. Open: Year-round.

    Hilton Lake Placid Resort (518-523-4411; www.lphilton.com; 1 Mirror Lake Drive). Price: Expensive. Large, downtown complex with three separate buildings, one on Mirror Lake. Indoor and outdoor pools; restaurant and lounge; shops; 177 units. Ask about packages for family vacations. Open: Year-round.

Northwoods Inn (518-523-1818; www.northwoodsinn.com; 2520 Main Street). Price: Moderate to Expensive. ninety-two units. New hoteliers from Cornell University's School of Hotel Administration started renovating this historic hotel in 2005. Restaurant downstairs; cozy bar upstairs. Open: Year-round.

Prague Motor Inn (518-523-3410; www.praguemotorinn.net; 6048 Sentinel Road). Price: Inexpensive to Moderate. Quiet, folksy mom-and-pop place with an amusing Queen Anne house in front of the motel units. Open: Year-round.

North Hudson

Blue Ridge Falls Campground (518-532-7863; www.blueridgefallscampsite.com; 3493 Blue Ridge Road). Price: Inexpensive. Off the main highway; pool; walk to waterfalls. Open: Spring through fall.

Ray Brook

Sherwood Forest Motor Inn (518-891-4400; www.sherwoodforestmotorinn.com; 15 Knotingham Road). Price: Inexpensive to Moderate. Not a motel at all but nice one- and two-bedroom housekeeping cabins, just off the busy highway and by the Tail O' the Pup restaurant. Most cabins have wood-burning fireplaces and views of a pretty little pond. Open: Year-round.

Saranac Lake

The Lake Flower Inn (518-891-2310; www.lakeflowerinn.com; 234 Lake Flower Avenue). Price: Inexpensive to Moderate. Clean, tidy motel with pleasant grounds; boat dockage; swimming pool; picnic area; pets welcome with fee. Open: Year-round.

Wilmington

The Hungry Trout Resort (518-946-2217; www.hungrytrout.com; 5239 NY 86). Price: Moderate to Expensive. twenty rooms. Great view; nice restaurant and R. F. McDougal's Tavern; excellent fishing on private stretch of river; fly-fishing guide service, lessons, and tackle shop. Open: Late June through October; January through mid-April.

NORTHWEST LAKES

For a complete list of lodgings in the immediate area, contact the **Tupper Lake Chamber of Commerce** (518-359-3328; www.tupperlakeinfo.com; 112 Park Street).

Tupper Lake

Pine Terrace Resort (518-359-9258; www.motelpineterrace.com; 1616 NY 30). Price: Inexpensive to Moderate. Housekeeping units and motel rooms. Pool; clay tennis courts; private beach across the road; picnic area. Open: Year-round.

Red Top Inn (518-359-9209; www.redtopinn.com; 1562 NY 30). Price: Inexpensive to Moderate. eighteen rooms. Lake view; private beach across the road; boat rentals and dockage; fishing dock. Open: Year-round.

CENTRAL AND SOUTHWESTERN ADIRONDACKS

See Chapter 9 for individual town chambers of commerce; the Central Adirondacks is cottage country, with lots of housekeeping cabins on lakes available. A sampling of motels, campgrounds, condos, and other options is listed below.

Inlet

Nelson's Cottages (315-357-4111; www.nelsonscottages.com; 128 NY 28). Price:
Inexpensive to Moderate. Twelve old-fashioned cabins named after US states set along a
sandy circular drive. The accommodations are clean and quiet; most cabins have refrigerators, grills, and picnic tables but no TVs and phones. There is a tiny beach, fine for launching a canoe or kayak. No pets allowed. Open: May through October.

Long Lake

Shamrock Motel and Cottages (518-624-3861; www.shamrockmotellonglake.com; NY
28/30). Price: Inexpensive to Moderate. Motel and neat-as-a-pin housekeeping cottages.
Private beach; picnic area. Open: June through mid-October.

North Creek

Alpine Motel (518-251-2451; www.thealpinemotel.com; 264 Main Street). Price:
Inexpensive to Moderate. Newly renovated no-frills motel close to Gore Mountain. Open:
Year-round.

    Broderick Real Estate (518-251-0103 or 1-800-309-0577; www.broderickrealestate.com;
235 Main Street). Rental agent for nicely equipped one- to four-bedroom town homes
(fireplaces, Jacuzzis, dishwashers, TV/VCR) at Pine Ridge and the Summit, both only minutes away from Gore Mountain. Open: Year-round.

Old Forge

Best Western Sunset Inn (315-369-6836; 2752 NY 28). Price: Moderate. fifty renovated
rooms. Indoor pool; tennis; putting green. Open: Year-round.

    The Forge Motel (315-369-3313; www.adirondacktravel.com/forge; 104 Lamberton
Street). Price: Moderate. sixty-one units. Lake view, the best from Room 13; pool; next to
public beach; walk to restaurants. Open: Year-round.

    Old Forge Camping Resort (315-369-6011; www.oldforgecamping.com; 3347 NY 28).
Price: Inexpensive. 200 sites on 101 acres plus cabins and cottages. Private lake; laundro-
mat; showers; convenience store; dumping station; canoes; movies; shuttle to town. Open:
Year-round.

    Water's Edge Inn and Conference Center (315-369-2484; www.watersedgeinn.com;
3188 NY 28, Old Forge). Price: Moderate. seventy-six rooms. Lakefront; indoor pool;
sauna; dock; family restaurant; across from Enchanted Forest/Water Safari park. Open:
Year-round.

5

Restaurants and Food Purveyors

Always in Good Taste

Adirondack cuisine surely lacks the instant name recognition of American Southwest or Southern cooking, and the intriguing blend of different cultures, each contributing to the table, is missing here. The food that appeared in local kitchens since the very first settlers lit their home fires was Yankee or French Canadian and dependent on what the terrain could provide. Game in abundance—moose, whitetail deer, snowshoe hare, partridge— were there for the shooting, with no laws to limit the take until the 1890s. The same was true of fish: trout, landlocked salmon, whitefish, bass, and so on. The growing season is short, often wet, and good for root crops, beans, squash, and apples. Not a lot of intrinsic excitement in these, especially if the primary seasoning is salt.

Still, nineteenth-century hotels managed to conjure up lavish menus. By the 1870s, the beginning of the modern tourist era, huge and truly remote resorts offered a dazzling array

Your table and a delicious meal await at these fine Adirondack eateries. Courtesy of the Whiteface Lodge

of meats, seafood, fruit, and vegetables. Seven-course menus listed sweetbreads, quail, fresh lobsters, and white asparagus, along with imported cheeses. It was far easier to find Stilton in Blue Mountain Lake in the nineteenth century than it is today. How did the guests do it? Nowadays we can't imagine gorging for hours on end, especially clad in a corset with whalebone stays. We can picture buttons flying across the dining room at places like the Prospect House or Paul Smith's hotel, following the seventh course. And imagine the kitchens of these resorts, with massive coal- or wood-burning stoves and barely a clear countertop in sight.

Adirondack hostelries had to keep up with their competitors in Newport or Saratoga Springs, which was entirely possible thanks to rail service and plentiful ice. Competition is a funny thing. The hotels that clamored for the affluent traveling public couldn't keep up with what roadside cabins and motels could provide. Once they had automobiles, families wanted to stay on the move, and formal dining in a chandelier-lit hall was too slow, too heavy, too much a thing of the past.

The mid-twentieth century caused many regional cuisines to step aside or go underground. Restaurants across the nation served much the same stuff: steak, pork chops, burgers. Perhaps northern New York stayed in this rut a little longer than other places. Fashion takes a while to get here and tends to linger. Hence platform shoes in revival were not greeted with as much enthusiasm as elsewhere, since many women still had a pair kicking around.

A funny thing happened to cuisine about 1998. Although a handful of creative chefs were working out their own brand of Adirondack style, the notion of putting native produce and products front and center really took hold. Flavors like maple, always in the bakers' repertoire, showed up in marinades, dressings, and soups, not cloyingly sweet but a glimpse of the smoky woods. Local artisanal cheeses from chévre to Asiago and fresh herbs gave the better places a whole new list of ingredients to assimilate. Potato farms, an agricultural mainstay of the windswept plains north of Saranac Lake and fertile Champlain Valley bottom land were planted with whole new organic crops, from garlic to baby greens to Asian vegetables.

The William West Durant *offers a gourmet meal with great views as it cruises Raquette Lake.* James Swedberg

Adirondack eating in the twenty-first century showcases a nascent regional flair, but hometown joints, fire-department barbecues, and dozens of little bakeries offer the tried and true. If you want the comfort of thick homemade lasagna with lots of red sauce, you can find those places here. If a Friday night means fish fry to your tribe, you won't go hungry. And if you like your vittles seasoned with a stunning view, you've come to the right place.

In this chapter you'll find reviews of scores of restaurants, from high cuisine to funky grab-and-go. What you won't find here is the average but not so great place that zips open a frozen portion of chicken Kiev and tries to pretend the dish is a signature creation. Our team of critics is fond of spotlighting town treasures, even if the menu is breakfast only.

Another caution: Always call ahead before venturing long distances in search of the perfect pie or best clam chowder. November and April are slow months, and many places take a breather then. Even eateries open in April—although a welcome sight—may use that month to clean out the freezer and run down the pantry stock. Monday can be a tough night for dinner out even in July or August, because there tend to be few deliveries at the start of the week. The best plan may be to hit that special someplace on a Sunday and picnic with the leftovers on Monday.

Below you will find a table listing the price code for regional restaurants. Then, on to the real tables, described in alphabetical order and by towns within the park region.

Dining Price Codes
Inexpensive: Up to $15
Moderate: $15–$25
Expensive: $25–$40
Very Expensive: Over $40

Credit Cards
AE: American Express
CB: Carte Blanche
D: Discover
DC: Diners' Club
MC: Master Card
V: Visa

Meals
B: Breakfast
L: Lunch
D: Dinner

ADIRONDACK RESTAURANTS

Lake George and Southeastern Adirondacks

BOLTON LANDING

The Algonquin
518-644-9442
www.thealgonquin.com

4770 Lakeshore Drive (about 1/2 mile south of town in Huddle Bay)
Open: Daily at 11:30, mid-April through Columbus Day; upstairs dining room closes in the fall
Cuisine: Continental, American
Serving: L, D
Price: Moderate to Expensive
Credit Cards: AE, D, DC, MC, V
Reservations: Suggested (only for upstairs

dining room Friday, Saturday, and Sunday nights)

Handicap Access: Yes

Remarks: Live music on the deck weekends in summer; boat docks

On Lake George's Huddle Bay, this bustling lakeside institution continues to attract waterfront diners all summer long. Most guests prefer to arrive by boat.

There are some drawbacks to the Algonquin: In high summer, an hour wait is possible for seating on the deck, and the background rock music can take away from the beautiful, serene vistas seen through large picture windows in the dining rooms. Be aware that service upstairs begins at 5 PM, for full entrées only (no burgers or sandwiches).

The menu's "beginnings" range from chicken wings and stuffed mushrooms to duchess pâté and baked brie. Salads include chicken Caesar, the fresh-catch salad, and Tuscan—fresh mozzarella, tomato, roasted red pepper, and roasted garlic on a bed of greens. Dinner entrées (served with a house salad) include chicken Monterey or cordon bleu, horseradish-encrusted salmon, flat-iron bourbon steak, and veal Oscar. The Greek shrimp with feta cheese, tomatoes, and herbs in a sherry sauce over linguini is quite tasty. Burgers and club sandwiches are available on the deck and in the downstairs dining room.

Cate's Italian Garden Restaurant and Bar

518-644-2041

4952 Lakeshore Drive

Open: Year-round, weekends only in winter

Cuisine: Italian American

Serving: L (from June 15 through Columbus Day), D (year-round)

Price: Moderate to Expensive

Credit Cards: AE, D, MC, V

Reservations: Yes

Handicap Access: Yes

The spacious covered terrace between the building and the street hums with the activity of a popular tourist town. Inside, the small dining room is crowded with art posters and Italian bric-a-brac and is strewn with strings of clear lightbulbs.

Kathy and Buddy Foy, on-the-spot owners, serve pizza (the best in the area) or full-course dinners. Specials are consistently delicious—be sure to ask about the lasagna.

The service is friendly and efficient, and the local, well-trained waiters are also fonts of area information. Incidentally, the cozy, charming bar is a spot of calm if that's your desire.

Mister Brown's Pub

866-385-6221

www.thesagamore.com

110 Sagamore Road

Open: Year-round; call for hours

Cuisine: American

Serving: L, D (11 AM–11 PM)

Price: Moderate to Expensive

Credit Cards: AE, D, DC, MC, V

Reservations: No

Handicap Access: Yes; elevator in building

Mister Brown's Pub is a great opportunity to enjoy a moderately priced meal at the grand Sagamore hotel. The pub—with Adirondack cedar posts, antler chandeliers, twig trim, and cozy fireplace set off by oversize armchairs—is considerably less formal than the hotel's other dining rooms. The place is named for one of the Sagamore's founding fathers, Myron Brown, born in the town of Bolton in 1837. An early developer on Lake George, he was the first manager of the Sagamore when it opened in 1893. Severely damaged by fire a decade later, the hotel was rebuilt and Brown continued as manager, helping to popularize Bolton as a summer resort.

At the ground-floor tavern, choices range from crab cakes, cheddar and ale fondue, and India Pale Ale–scented soup to a host of wraps and sandwiches and pub fare like fish and chips, buffalo wings, and cheeseburgers, as well as unusual choices like wild mushroom tortellini and diver sea scallops, and a marinated Portobello mushroom Philly cheese wrap. Daily specials include a pasta creation, "mom's favorite" (comfort food), and a catch of the day. Dinner entrées are slow-roasted maple brined turkey, pecan-crusted trout, and a barbecue rib platter. Be sure to save room for dessert: The list includes raspberry tiramisu and chocolate cake, the house favorite. Lunch offers an abridged dinner menu with starters, fresh salads, and stacked sandwiches.

We offer two words of advice about the pub and dining at the Sagamore. At Mister Brown's Pub in the early evening, your fellow diners may be children accompanied by their baby-sitters (although no one under 21 is allowed in the place after 10 PM). Parents send youngsters here while they enjoy the fancier, quieter dining rooms upstairs. Also, the Sagamore adds an 18 percent gratuity to all services, including dining checks, regardless of party size. Often the wait staff does not mention the added gratuity and an additional tip is left (unnecessarily) by unknowing customers.

If your taste is for quiet, elegant food and setting, get a reservation at the **Trillium Bis** for contemporary American cuisine. (Take note: Men are required to wear a collared shirt and jacket.) The menu includes foie gras, lobster parfait, rock shrimp Tom yum, grilled Colorado lamb rack, and the Sunday brunch is sensational.

After a round of golf, or for a fine steak and hearty home-style side dishes in an excellent dining room away from the hotel, try the **Club Grill** overlooking the golf course. Meals are also served on the Sagamore's luxury cruise boat, *The Morgan,* to accompany gorgeous Lake George views.

Pumpernickel's Restaurant
518-644-2106

www.pumpernickels.com
4571 Lakeshore Drive
Open: Daily, mid-June through Labor Day;
    call for off-season hours
Cuisine: German
Serving: L, D summer; D winter
Price: Moderate to Expensive
Credit Cards: MC, V
Reservations: Yes
Handicap Access: Yes

It's almost too bad that Pumpernickel's boasts America's largest cuckoo clock, a 10-foot-tall timepiece that was carved in Germany's Black Forest, then hung for many years in Times Square. It makes the place appear like a German theme park, and it might distract you from the food, which is very good.

German cooking has a bad reputation—heavy, greasy, inert. But in the capable hands of Chef Hans-Jurgen Winter, the wursts and the schnitzels and virtually everything on Pumpernickel's menu tastes vivid, intense, almost light. Don't miss the potato pancakes with applesauce; they're deftly fried, a crisp treat. Dinner comes with hearty soup and a decent salad bar as well as plenty of side dishes, plus a fresh loaf of pumpernickel on every table.

It's a great place to take children, of course. And it's a great place to come without children, because families with kids are usually corralled into a loft where they can watch the cuckoo clock without bothering other diners. The service is swift and pleasant. And it's the only place in the southern Adirondacks with a wide selection of the finest German beers on draft.

The new **Wooden Barrel Bar & Grill**, adjacent to Pumpernickel's (and run by the same owners), is great for late-night darts, pool, bar food—wings, wraps, burgers, and panini sandwiches—and features a bunch of draft and bottled beer. Sometimes on summer weekends there's live entertainment.

Villa Napoli

518-644-9047

www.melodymanor.com

4610 Lakeshore Drive

Open: Daily July and August; weekends only
  May through June and September
  through October

Cuisine: Italian

Serving: B, D

Price: Moderate to Expensive

Credit Cards: AE, MC, V

Reservations: Suggested

Handicap Access: Yes

Naples meets the Adirondacks in this lakeside restaurant: Frescos and paintings of quaint towns and Lake Como adorn the dining room. With heavy drapes, Venetian plaster walls, and hand-carved marble fireplace, the atmosphere is unmistakably Old Country but the view is pure North Country.

Like a foreign film, the menu is written in Italian with English subtitles. Warm rolls are served with rosemary-infused olive oil. Appetizers include sautéed artichoke hearts, steamed mussels and clams, and a large antipasto with Italian meats, vegeta-

The Sagamore's elegant Trillium Bis offers a dramatic contrast from the casual Adirondack-style Mister Brown's Pub. Courtesy of the Sagamore

bles, cheeses, and olives. Traditional pasta, veal, chicken, steak, and fish entrées offer many delicious, bountiful choices. Try the *pesce livornese*—the catch of the day sautéed with garlic, tomatoes, capers, white wine, Sicilian and Kalamata olives over spinach risotto, or the ravioli *di aragosta,* fresh lobster ravioli in a brandied pink sauce with langostino. If you're stumped about how to complement your choices with the proper beverage, the wait staff can offer suggestions for each entrée from the restaurant's generous wine list. Be sure to leave room for tiramisu, a cannoli, or cappuccino to conclude your Villa Napoli experience.

CHESTERTOWN

Friends Lake Inn
518-494-4751
www.friendslake.com
963 Friends Lake Road
Open: Year-round
Cuisine: Contemporary American
Serving: B, D
Price: Very Expensive in dining room;
    Moderate in Wine Bar
Credit Cards: AE, DC, MC, V
Reservations: Recommended
Handicap Access: Yes

This handsomely restored inn began serving the public before the Civil War and was a hotspot during Prohibition. Today Friends Lake Inn is a rewarding destination for a romantic getaway or a fine meal. The wine list is longer than the local phone book, and there's an impressive selection of American craft and imported beers. If the choices have you confused, innkeepers John and Trudy Phillips sponsor occasional wine-tasting events that pair imaginative cuisine with interesting beverages.

In the main dining room, there's a distinct difference between the summer and winter menus, with seasonal fruits and vegetables and lighter presentations favored during warm weather, though the chef incorporates fresh, organic local ingredients in his dishes year-round.

For appetizers try the scallop- and lobster-stuffed corn crêpe with vanilla bean beurre blanc, pine nuts, and chopped scallions. Entrées range from trilogy of duck (pan-seared duck breast, crisp duck confit, apple brandy duck sausage with cherry pinot noir chutney, slow-roasted fingerling potatoes, and sautéed asparagus) to braised Chilean sea bass with tomato fennel broth served over jasmine rice and caramelized fennel bulbs.

The **Wine Bar** is fine for sampling interesting food on a budget. Recommended is grilled Oscar's Adirondack Smoke House pork loin on a bed of micro greens with apples and carrot slaw. Desserts are all made on the premises and match the seasons, from fresh fruit tarts in summer to grand chocolate concoctions for the holidays. The Wine Bar also lists twenty-six wines by the glass, all also offered in the inn's wine shop, where individual bottles can be purchased. Oenophiles who can't make it to Chestertown can buy online, at www.friendslakewine.com.

A private wine cellar dining room with a large table beneath an antler chandelier is also available for parties of up to fourteen at no extra cost.

Main Street Ice Cream Parlor and Restaurant
518-494-7940
www.thechesterinn.com
6339 Main Street
Open: Daily
Cuisine: High-end deli; ice-cream parlor
Serving: L, D
Price: Inexpensive to Moderate
Credit Cards: D, MC, V
Reservations: No
Handicap Access: Yes

The ice-cream parlor's new yellow schoolhouse digs, down the street from its old headquarters on Main Street, are the perfect funky, high-ceilinged space for this upscale deli. Sandwiches and homemade soups and chili are excellent; go for the thick, complicated Reuben sandwiches layered on rye and stuffed with bacon, tomatoes, Russian dressing, cheese, and meat. Recent dinner specials have included Portobello-stuffed meatloaf and potato-crusted salmon—not your typical diner fare. Sodas come from an old-style fountain—a classic touch that draws the nostalgic.

The ice-cream treats are worth saving room for, whether it's a sundae topped with local maple syrup or a chocolate malted made with lots of real malt powder.

A gift shop offers high-end women's clothes, home furnishings, regional books, jewelry, and interesting browsing post-meal.

CLEVERDALE

Sans Souci Restaurant and Bar
518-656-9285
92 Nathan Road
Open: Year-round
Cuisine: American
Serving: D
Price: Moderate to Expensive
Credit Cards: AE, D, MC, V
Reservations: No
Handicap Access: Yes

New owners Larry Clute and Scott Parker are the daily forces behind this busy neighborhood cornerstone. This very local eatery is extremely family-friendly, noisy, and fun. The bar is partially separated and may or may not be a little quieter as exuberant neighborly greetings and conversation flow.

For starters, the chicken quesadilla is made in-house, not warehouse. Burgers, pizzas, and a full set of entrées fill the evening menu. Don't miss the daily specials board; the "mom-style" offerings are delicious.

HADLEY

Saratoga Rose Inn and Restaurant
518-696-2861
www.saratogarose.com
4136 Rockwell Street
Open: Year-round; days and hours are seasonal
Cuisine: Contemporary American
Serving: D
Price: Expensive to Very Expensive
Credit Cards: AE, D, MC, V
Reservations: Recommended
Handicap Access: Ramp in rear

Since 2004 owners Claude Belanger and Richard Ferrugio have pulled out all the stops in their effort to upgrade this Victorian inn and its amenities and invoke the high-living yet homey Gilded Age. Dining rooms occupy what used to be the parlor, library, and living room of the old mansion, and the picture lacks only a player piano in the corner cranking out a ghostly tune. In summer meals can be served on the veranda, which, with the gardens, is a popular spot for events, such as weddings. (Ferrugio also offers off-site catering for special events.)

Ferrugio's background as a successful New York City caterer—feeding the mayor's office as well as President Ronald Reagan and the New York City Ballet—means quality, creative, and "unique" (as he describes it) fine dining. His selection of delicious fare—meals with Mediterranean and Asian accents—changes according to season, but in late summer includes twin pork osso buco, black angus New York strip steak with chianti shallot sauce, and a number of heart-healthy selections, from salmon with Grande Marnier citrus sauce to Singapore curried noodles. The Rose also has an extensive wine and beer list. Ask about special dinner events that center on wine or beer tastings.

Ferrugio's other creative outlet—oil paintings—hang throughout the inn.

LAKE GEORGE

Adirondack Pub & Brewery

518-668-0002

www.adkpub.com

33 Canada Street

Open: April through December; daily in summer; Thursday through Sunday, fall and spring

Cuisine: Pub fare

Serving: L, D

Price: Inexpensive to Moderate

Credit Cards: AE, D, MC, V

Handicap Access: Yes

Remarks: Live music on most Friday and Saturday nights during the summer season; brewery tours with samples are by appointment

This casual stop has a charming North Woods atmosphere, complete with log pillars, twig screens, and fairy lights creating just enough privacy and sense of separation from the bar. Families with children are very much in evidence—not always the case at brewpubs.

You may wish to remain at the bar, however, given the tasty assortment of beers brewed on the premises. We recommend the Bear Naked Ale. The kitchen does well with a variety of thick sandwiches, stuffed wraps, and handmade burgers; the Jack Daniels steak is a local favorite. Takeout—even the beer, in growlers—is available.

Barnsider Smokehouse Restaurant

518-668-5268

www.barnsider.com

2112 US 9 (just before Waterslide World)

Open: April through November

Cuisine: American, barbecue

Serving: B (on weekends), L, D

Price: Inexpensive to Moderate

Credit Cards: AE, D, MC, V

Handicap Access: Yes

Remarks: Live music on Thursday, Friday, and Sunday in summer

The Adirondack Park is not what anyone would call ribs country, but as folks keep on discovering the family-run Barnsider, this could change. Owner-chef Ed Pagnotta's rack of pork is as scrumptious as it gets. Pagnotta's parents ran a produce market on this roadside spot, so he comes by his food savvy naturally. The method, says the chef, is "Memphis style," and involves "a process using dry rub which kind of marinates the ribs, then I throw 'em in a water smoker, and use hickory and oak for wood, which filters up through the oven and heats up the water, which I think keeps a moister flavor."

The on-site competition with those ribs includes generous halves of barbecue chicken (every bit as tender and savory with smoke), and there's smoked baked beans and brisket, too. Try the chicken 'n' ribs combo, with good corn on the cob and onion rings. Prompt, cheerful service and outdoor decks make a summer dinner at this congenial spot a real Adirondack find.

The Boathouse

518-668-3332

www.cresthavenlodges.com

3210 Lake Shore Drive at The Lodges at Cresthaven

Open: April through October

Cuisine: American

Serving: L, D (call for hours in spring and fall)

Price: Expensive

Credit Cards: AE, MC, V

Handicap Access: No

During high season the boats line up, waiting to put in at the restaurant's dock, and the food is well worth the wait, whether you arrive by Chris Craft or car. The ambiance only enhances the food; the newly refurbished main dining room is a massive post-and-beam boathouse built in the late 1800s, once owned by *New York Times* publisher Adolph Ochs, which is attractively outfitted with Adirondack details and plants.

Umbrella-shaded seating is available dock-side. The bar lines one side of the dining room and seems to do a regular business, and the overall atmosphere is casual.

The menu is loaded with delicious seafood and steak items, and Chef Paul Kuntz comes up with several excellent appetizers like crab Asiago and dinner picks that include spicy Tyler gulf shrimp simmered in Kuntz's Fra Diavalo marinara sauce over pasta and juicy steak au poivre. When the chef offers not one but four specials and comes through with quality presentations consistently, you can rest assured the kitchen is skilled and industrious. Original sauces and side dishes add enticing twists to traditional plates.

The Farmhouse at the Top of the World
518-668-3000
www.topoftheworldgolfresort.com
441 Lockhard Mountain Road
Open: Early May through October,
  Wednesday through Sunday; seven-
  course community family-style Harvest
  dinner on Thursday
Cuisine: Contemporary American
Serving: L, D
Price: Moderate to Expensive
Credit Cards: MC, V
Reservations: Yes
Handicap Access: Yes

In 2007 reviews were nothing but twinkly for the new Farmhouse, on French Mountain—part of Top of the World Golf Resort. For starters, a sustainable farm adjacent to the restaurant grows the majority of the produce that appears, in all sorts of creative combinations, on the menu. Even the cut flowers decorating the restaurant come from the farm.

The idea here is to offer fresh, "exciting"—according to Chef Kevin London—dishes made from organically grown ingredients from regional farms in an elegant atmosphere off Lake George's main

drag. Mission accomplished. The views from the Farmhouse's nineteenth-century dining room are lovely. The menu changes daily, but examples of London's entrées include Hudson Valley duck with fava, butter, and cannelloni beans; and Flying Pigs Farm pork with apple gratin and wild arugula. The lunch and bar menus have lighter fare, such as a smoked turkey sandwich with Saratoga apples and Adirondack cheese; Bouchot mussels with chilies, garlic, and thyme; and chorizo bruschetta with sherry and roasted red pepper.

This is also a fine place for a wedding or other private gathering.

George's Restaurant
518-668-5482
NY 9L, east side of Lake George
Open: Year-round; check seasonal hours
Cuisine: Steak and seafood
Serving: D
Price: Expensive
Credit Cards: MC, V
Reservations: Recommended
Handicap Access: Yes

George's is the real deal, the place steak house chains aspire to become. It is set on the east side of Lake George, a short drive from busy Canada Street. Dozens of assorted Tiffany lamps hang from the rafters to illuminate the cozy log cabin interior. The large wooden bar is separated from the dining room by colorful stained-glass windows and huge, heavy-framed mirrors cover the walls.

Clams casino, escargot in wine sauce, and stuffed mushrooms are good starters for a long list of main courses. All entrées include access to a generous salad bar stocked with typical offerings and more interesting salad combinations such as Mexican black beans, cold spaghetti, and chickpea-and-roasted-garlic. A tip: Don't let the salad bar slow you down or fill you up.

You can't go wrong with the beef here—

first-rate porterhouse, sirloin, or filet mignon. Rack of lamb and stuffed boneless pork chops are also good. Seafood entrées include broiled swordfish, salmon, and lobster tails, and seafood marinara or alfredo; the poultry menu offers chicken alfredo, parmigiana, or chicken Oscar. There's a children's menu, too.

Inn at Erlowest
518-668-5928
www.theinnaterlowest.com
3178 Lakeshore Drive
Open: Year-round; closed Mondays; hours seasonal
Cuisine: French fusion
Serving: D
Price: Very Expensive
Credit Cards: AE, D, MC, V
Reservations: Yes
Handicap Access: Yes

By far the fanciest place around, this 110-year-old mansion is the ultimate for an upscale meal in Lake George. A private residence until 1999, Erlowest is now a four-star bed & breakfast, with several elegant private dining rooms—stunning backdrops for romantic dinners, small receptions, and other affairs.

The lake itself isn't visible from the restaurant, but guests can sip pre-meal cocktails on the mansion's Grand Patio, where there's a gorgeous Lake George view. And a massive fireplace heats up the space, allowing for lingering alfresco on chilly nights.

The inn's wine list is extensive; meals are truly an experience. The menu changes each season, but starters may include duck leg confit and drumette, served warm, with microgreen tangle and pomegranate, and blood orange gastric, or the Baha cracked crab in the shell martini with ponzu-scented cocktail dressing. For a main course, try applewood smoked bacon barded prawns with roasted plum tomato confit and Yukon gold mash, or double

venison loin chop, seared and roasted, with Italian white truffle-enhanced jus and potato puree.

There is, of course, a dress code.

Mario's
518-668-2665
www.marioslakegeorge.com
429 Canada Street
Open: Daily, 4 PM–10 PM
Cuisine: American/Italian
Serving: B (in summer), D
Price: Moderate to Expensive
Credit Cards: AE, D, MC, V
Reservations: Yes
Handicap Access: No

This is the place to go if you have a hankering for familiar Italian American fare. The dining room, the service, and the food—even the clientele—are comfortably reminiscent of decades past. The fact that the restaurant has been open since 1954 under the ownership of one family contributes heavily to this nostalgia. The current chef and owner, Paul Nichols, learned many of the dishes from his grandmother Mary Mazzeo, who founded the restaurant.

On early summer evenings the place is often jammed with contented diners, many under the age of 12. The buzz of happy children is the result of an attentive wait staff working the crowd with crayons, games, and a child-friendly menu. Appetizers are delicious: The hot antipasto is a meal in itself and the homemade minestrone and pasta fagiole are good. For dinner, choose your pasta (angel hair to penne, many choices), then select from more than half a dozen sauces. Want something light like oil and garlic over linguine? No problem. Hungry? You can order a side of meatballs or sausage to add to fresh mushroom sauce. No meat? You can have a plate of pasta with red or white clam sauce.

Pizza Jerks

518-668-4411
www.pizzajerks.com
59 Iroquois Street
Open: Daily, 11 AM–10 PM
Cuisine: Pizzeria
Serving: L, D
Price: Inexpensive
Credit Cards: AE, D, MC, V
Handicap Access: Yes

Two years ago Jerks moved from Main Street to its present location on Iroquois, and business is good—very good. Locals rave about this place. In summer 2007 the pizzeria sold a whopping 35,000 slices. Pizzas are fresh, absolutely delicious, and the management swears its pies are better than anyone else's, or your money back. You can get grub to go, have it delivered, or eat in (there's Wi-Fi here).

Try the specialty pizzas, such as the Tree Hugger (fresh spinach, pesto, garlic, and onions), the Carcass (every meat in the shop), or hot subs, chicken wings, or for dessert, silly sweet stix (baked dough strips with cinnamon sugar and icing). Hats, T-shirts, vests, and other merchandise are also available.

Ridge Terrace

518-656-9274
2172 Ridge Terrace
Open: April through October
Cuisine: Continental
Serving: D
Price: Expensive to Very Expensive
Credit Cards: MC, V
Reservations: Yes
Handicap Access: Yes

This busy restaurant sits firmly in the history of the east side of Lake George. Chef/owner Ray Rios and his wife, Norma, have overseen the kitchen and dining room since 1972.

Regulars as well as summer friends celebrating a day at the Saratoga races choose this venerable eatery for dinner. Even with reservations, you are likely to spend time in the lounge. Request seating on the enclosed porch and you'll enjoy the gleam of the highly varnished log structure and serenity of the gardens.

Although the service may be uneven, the food is well prepared and generous. Ridge Terrace's menu is like time traveling—beef with béarnaise or bordelaise sauce, veal with cream sauces, entrées that were in the front line of fine restaurant cuisine thirty years ago. These dishes still work well here, but for something more contemporary try chicken al pesto or fresh broiled fish. And all selections on the separate dessert menu are made here.

A Taste of Poland

518-668-4386
375 Canada Street
Open: Daily
Cuisine: Polish
Serving: B, L, D June through October; D
    November through April
Price: Moderate
Credit Cards: MC, V
Reservations: Requested on Saturday
Handicap Access: Yes

Downtown Lake George has dozens of restaurants. None are as unique as this one and few are as tasty. Owners Jan and Joanna Kosz learned their craft in Woslaw, Poland, and brought their talent to the Adirondacks.

The extensive menu offers interesting items. If you're new to Polish cuisine, the "taste of Poland plate"—a compilation of traditional recipes laid out as a meal for two—is a fabulous tutorial. The borscht soups are tremendous: Zuerek, a sour white borscht with egg and sausage, is a standout. Many entrées feature meat paired with stewed or sauced fruit. Other dishes feature Polish pastry dough, fresh noodles, or cabbage variations. The owners emphasize that the Polish-born chef makes everything from scratch.

The wait staff is gracious and helpful; in the summer season the place employs many eastern European students, adding a decidedly non-New York atmosphere.

LAKE LUZERNE

Papa's Ice Cream Parlor & Restaurant
518-696-3667
www.papasicecream.com
35 Main Street
Open: Memorial Day through Columbus
    Day, 8 AM–9 PM
Cuisine: Ice-cream parlor; deli
Serving: B, L, D
Price: Inexpensive
Credit Cards: None
Handicap Access: Yes

Papa's is resilient. A devastating fire in 2002 almost made this cherished landmark merely a memory, but Edie "Nana" and Fred "Papa" Gardner rebuilt and the ice-cream parlor is better than ever—now a bright, airy space. The hundreds of antique bottles and old-time photos burned, but friends and customers regularly donate artifacts to be hung and displayed on Papa's walls.

Deli sandwiches and delicious salads can be ordered in the dining room or on a cozy deck out back so diners can enjoy the view of the Hudson River. A few years back celebrity chef Rachael Ray spotlighted Papa's and its old-fashioned fare on her Food Network *$40 A Day* program. (Ray is a proud Lake Luzerne native.)

Sadly, Nana passed away in 2005 and Papa has cut back on his hours, but the Gardner kids—Nana and Papa had eight children, and now numerous grand- and great-grandchildren—continue their parents' legacy of offering delicious ice-cream treats and good meals to loyal visitors.

SCHROON LAKE

Drake's Restaurant
518-532-9040
www.drakesmotel.com
1299 US 9
Open: Memorial Day through Columbus
    Day
Cuisine: Seafood/Italian/American
Serving: B (Sunday), D (late June through
    Labor Day); call for hours
Price: Moderate to Expensive
Credit Cards: AE, MC, V
Handicap Access: Yes

No-nonsense Drake's, on the north side of Schroon Lake village, has been a popular spot for almost four decades. There's a medium-size dining room with a small bar and two-table solarium off to the side. The cuisine is Italian/American, with an extensive array of seafood dishes.

Appetizers of note are steamed mussels, jumbo shrimp cocktail, and Italian-style roasted red peppers in fresh garlic and olive oil with garlic bread. For entrées, try classic Italian chicken dishes like cacciatore, parmigiana, and marsala, plus a handful of vegetarian selections like eggplant parmigiana and baked ziti. On the seafood side—all entrées are served with garden salad, potato or rice, vegetable, and roll—try the Alaskan king crab legs, seafood Newburgh, sautéed scallops, or have a big ol' New England lobster (check out your dinner victim in the tank on the way in). There is a different special each night, from surf and turf to prime rib. Good desserts—Ticonderoga bread pudding, "Chocolate Confusion," and New York cheesecake, among others—are made on premises.

The Morningstar Bistro
518-532-0707
www.morningstarbistro.com
1079 Main Street
Open: Daily, year-round

Cuisine: French bistro
Serving: B, L
Price: Inexpensive to Moderate
Credit Cards: MC, V
Reservations: No
Handicap Access: Yes

Myriam Friedman's quaint little eatery is just a block from Schroon Lake's park and public beach, though it could very well be in some bucolic corner of French countryside. Friedman is from Algeria, by way of Paris and a kibbutz in Israel, and now Adirondack crêpe lovers are rejoicing that she picked Schroon Lake to share her culinary expertise.

Sandwiches, named after old Schroon Lake hotels, are fantastic (the Scaroon is made with roasted red pepper and avocado; the Ondawa is a turkey melt; the Edgewater is topped with grilled salmon and cucumber and wasabi dressing); salads are fresh and fun; and the crepes . . . enough of a reason to head to Schroon. Order a savory crêpe—Swiss or cheddar or brie and avocado—or a sweet one (or two) filled with marmalade, Nutella and banana, lemon butter, fruit and Grand Marnier, and the list goes on.

Pitkin's
518-532-7918
1085 US 9
Open: Year-round
Cuisine: American
Serving: B, L, D
Price: Inexpensive
Credit Cards: AE, D, MC, V
Handicap Access: Yes

If only every town had a spot as good as Pitkin's—where the homemade soups are thick with real stuff (not cornstarch), pies are heavenly, service is brisk—why, we'd never leave. The cole slaw and potato salad are the best around, and then there's the barbecue. Sure, Pitkin's looks like your average North Country diner with giant lake trout

and panoramic photos on the walls, but there's authentic Texas-style barbecue, beef brisket, pork ribs, and chicken. On Thursday nights in the summer, the lines of ribs fans snake down Main Street, in anticipation of the Thursday rib special, and the wait for a table can be long. Happily, the restaurant is open all year, and you can get barbecue at lunch, even in mud season (the period after winter and before spring, when everything in the Adirondacks turns muddy).

STONY CREEK

Stony Creek Inn & Restaurant
518-696-2394
6 Roaring Branch Road
Open: Mid-April through December;
   Wednesday through Sunday
Cuisine: American
Serving: L, D
Price: Inexpensive to Moderate
Credit Cards: MC, V
Reservations: Accepted, but not necessary
Handicap Access: Yes, but not restrooms
Remarks: Live music on Friday and Sunday

This twenty-seven-year-old inn is a southern Adirondack institution, one of the neatest spots between Saratoga and Montreal. On Sunday night the joint really jumps, when there's great Mexican food and local bands.

Long a mecca for square dancers and the home stage for the regionally renowned Stony Creek Band, the inn presents everything from straight country to rhythm and blues, old-time fiddle to salsa. All this music—a rarity in the area—attracts crowds from far and wide; owner Dot Bartell says her mailing list of 800 names includes regulars from New Jersey and Vermont. Along with hot tunes, the Stony Creek Inn offers some unbeatable specials: on Wednesday, full roast beef dinner for $10 and combo dinners for $12. On Friday, two-for-$25 dinner specials, including ribs and surf and turf.

WARRENSBURG

The Grist Mill

518-623-8005
100 River Street (NY 418 just beyond the
iron bridge)
Open: Seasonal; call for hours
Cuisine: Contemporary American
Serving: D
Price: Expensive
Credit Cards: AE, MC, V
Reservations: Recommended
Handicap Access: Yes, but not restrooms
Remarks: Mill museum, screen porch din-
ing area

Almost a decade ago Chef Christopher
Lambeth took the reigns of this venerable
Warrensburg dining institution. He brings
several years of gourmet cooking experience
in Vail, Colorado, which serve him well in
maintaining a tradition of fine cuisine at the
mill. Creative sauce work (cherry demi-
glace with venison, ginger cilantro sauce
with tuna, orange tarragon sauce with
chicken) and unique accompaniments
(potato-parsnip purée, Thai shrimp fried
rice, garlic and spinach stuffing) delight and
awe even the most accomplished home cook
or well-traveled palate. Recommended
starters include asparagus wrapped in pro-
sciutto with a subtle maple glaze, eggplant
ravioli, and prawns stuffed with pine nuts in
basil cream sauce. And the entrées and
desserts are even more extraordinary.

The dining room, which shows off both
the massive 1824 mill architecture within
and the beauty of the Schroon River outside, is delightful. The mechanical chutes,
pulleys, and works of the mill, along with
an array of tools, photographs, and assorted
paraphernalia make for a museum-like, yet
unpretentious, atmosphere. The downstairs bar is charming, and the screened
riverside dining area behind the bar is
especially appealing on summer nights.

Merrill Magee House

518-623-2449
www.merrillmageehouse.com
3 Hudson Street
Open: Year-round
Cuisine: Continental
Serving: L, D
Price: Expensive
Credit Cards: AE, MC, V
Reservations: Suggested
Handicap Access: Yes

Behind a prim white picket fence and
across the street from Warrensburg's
pocket-size band shell is the Merrill Magee
House, a historic inn listed on the National
Register of Historic Places, with two
charming dining rooms and, in 2006, new
owners expanded the tavern and lounge
into a comfy space with two fireplaces.

Chef Matt Caul's meals begin with a basket of excellent homemade breads and proceed to good salads; appetizers include
baked gouda, creamy corn chowder, or
mushroom and goat cheese strudel—ask
about the nightly appetizer feature. Entrées
range from traditional rack of lamb to mussels marinara to filet mignon to fresh fish.
If you call ahead, large groups can be
accommodated—the lovely lily garden
makes an ideal setting for a wedding.

Authentic English ales and stouts are
available in the tavern, and the wine list is
quite complete.

Sapienza Pizzeria and Restaurant

518-623-5555
www.sapienzaofwarrensburg.com
4112 US 9
Open: Year-round, 10 AM–10 PM ; closed
Monday; call for seasonal hours
Cuisine: Italian
Serving: L, D
Price: Inexpensive to Moderate
Credit Cards: AE, D, MC, V
Handicap Access: Yes

Anthony Sapienza, who a few years back ran

the popular Anthony's Ristorante at his family's North Country Lodge motel, has opened a new eatery, Sapienza Pizzeria and Restaurant, in the same spot. There's lots of buzz about this place: the food is delicious, and the charismatic young proprietor plans to book big names in the entertainment world to entertain at his restaurant. In 2007 Slam Allen, Roy Book Binder, and Sam Andrew from Big Brother and the Holding Company (Janis Joplin's band) performed; ticket prices ranged from $25–$35, which included the cost of the show as well as multicourse Italian tapas.

Champlain Valley

ELIZABETHTOWN

Deer's Head Inn
518-873-6514
www.thedeershead.com
7552 Court Street
Open: Year-round; call for hours
Cuisine: Contemporary American
Serving: L (every day except Sunday), D
Price: Moderate to expensive
Credit Cards: AE, D, MC, V
Reservations: Yes
Handicap Access: Yes

This rambling inn, built in 1808 (the guest registry shows that Grover Cleveland and Benjamin Harrison stayed here), has changed hands through the centuries, but new owner Matthew Baldwin, former executive chef at Lake Placid's Mirror Lake Inn, has transformed it into a special place with creative cuisine.

Baldwin's rosemary roasted rack of lamb with brandied Dijon lamb *jus-lie* and maple syrup, and his prosciutto-wrapped cod with parmesan polenta cake, warm tomato relish, and balsamic reduction are some customer favorites. Fresh, locally grown ingredients are used whenever possible, and dishes are surprisingly affordable.

Three dining areas received a facelift

when Baldwin took the helm: The ambiance is old-school elegance—fireplace, walls hung with paintings by regional artists, tables with candles. There's a cozy pub, too, perfect for a cocktail and conversation.

ESSEX

Old Dock House
518-963-4232
Lake Shore Road
Open: Mid-May through Columbus Day
Cuisine: American
Serving: L, D
Price: Moderate to Expensive
Credit Cards: MC, V
Reservations: Yes
Handicap Access: Inside dining room only
Remarks: Boat dockage for diners

Like many of the commercial establishments in Champlain Valley villages, the Old

Deer's Head Inn chef Matthew Baldwin's rosemary roasted rack of lamb is a hit among Elizabethtown diners. Courtesy of Kelly Kilgallon

Dock is in a handsome stone building dating back to the early nineteenth century. It was converted to a restaurant in the 1930s and overlooks the landing of the popular ferry to Vermont.

The setting is lovely—in good weather, everyone sits outdoors to watch the clouds racing above Vermont's Green Mountains.

Lunch and dinner offerings are varied, although seafood dishes are favorites among diners, particularly the escargot and crab cake appetizers, the fish and chips, and dinner entrées such as the seafood pasta and shore dinner platter.

PORT HENRY

The King's Inn
518-546-7633
42 Hummingbird Way
Open: Year-round
Cuisine: American
Serving: D
Price: Moderate
Credit Cards: AE, D, MC, V
Reservations: Yes
Handicap Access: No

Restoring this stone mansion from foundation to chimney cap and creating a good restaurant in a town that has lacked such things since the heyday of iron mining ended in the 1960s has been a labor of love. The efforts have paid off: The King's Inn now has such a regional following that reservations are essential in summer.

One big, airy dining room with a stone fireplace occupies the long side of the building; across the front, with windows facing the lake, is a smaller dining room. (We prefer this space, but the other dining room is fine.)

Meals begin when your server presents you with a salad checklist; it looks like a multiple-choice quiz, which it is. Choose what things you'd like on your salad—sunflower seeds, green peppers, and black

olives, say, or tomatoes, cucumbers, and red onions—and write your name on top. This approach works like a salad bar, but with less waste. That done, order appetizers and entrées. Beef is generally good, as is broiled salmon; seafood fra diavolo, with lots of big, juicy shrimp, scallops, and clams over pasta, is generously proportioned and excellent.

Between the two dining rooms is a nice little bar, fine for lingering before dinner in cool weather. There's an old-fashioned porch with comfortable wicker furniture and a deck with a view down the hill to the lake; that's where you want to enjoy a glass of wine, dessert, or after-dinner drink on a summer night.

TICONDEROGA

The Carillon
518-585-7657
www.carillonrestaurant.com
872 NY 9N
Open: Year-round, 4 PM ; closed Wednesday
Cuisine: French/American
Serving: D
Price: Expensive
Credit Cards: AE, D, MC, V
Reservations: Yes
Handicap Access: Side entrance ramp, but
    restrooms inaccessible

Carillon is the original French name of Fort Ticonderoga, the historic site three miles from this restaurant, located in a modest roadside brown-painted wooden building. Established in 1988 by chef/owner Russ Slater, the Carillon provides hearty fare for post-fort excursions. Duffers also dine here after a day at the public golf course, just down the road. This is where to go for more upscale seafood than anywhere else in Port Henry or Ticonderoga.

Although pasta and meat are on the menu, the seafood dominates: It's always very fresh, and the catch of the day lives up to its name. The soups, especially the creamy seafood bisque, are excellent. Lean fish fillets, shrimp, and bay scallops are competently prepared without fuss and their succulent flavor shines through; the seafood pot pie is delicious. Another popular entrée is the roast duckling. The bread, appetizers, and desserts are made on the premises.

Emerald's

518-585-7435

609 Hague Road, NY 9N, at the Ticonderoga Country Club

Open: May through October

Cuisine: American

Serving: L, D

Price: Moderate to Expensive

Credit Cards: AE, D, MC, V

Reservations: Yes

Handicap Access: Yes

Inside the clubhouse at Ticonderoga Country Club, Emerald's (the former O'Leary's) serves meals in a sunporch or in a more formal dining room. The golf course is one of the most beautiful in the Adirondacks; the views of the green fairways and nearby mountains from the porch windows are breathtaking.

At lunch very good salads (grilled chicken Caesar, among others), seafood (broiled scallops are delicious), and great big sandwiches on crusty French bread are appealing. Dinner includes aged steaks, sauced chicken dishes, quality seafood, accompanied by nice salads, rolls, and seasonal vegetables.

Hot Biscuit Diner

518-585-3483

www.hotbiscuitdiner.com

14 Montcalm Street

Open: Year-round

Cuisine: American

Serving: B, L, D

Price: Inexpensive to Moderate

Credit Cards: None

Reservations: No

Handicap Access: Yes

A fire almost destroyed this cheery, checked-tablecloth place close to a decade ago, but thank heavens owners Bonnie and Orley Dixon decided to build up from the ashes. Now their son, Craig, and his wife, Valerie, are at the helm, and the Hot Biscuit's still as great as ever, and worth a stop for any meal or if you've got a sudden hankering for hot, made-from-scratch gingerbread dolloped with whipped cream or genuine tapioca pudding. Everything's homemade, from blueberry muffins to the trademark biscuits; chili and soup are tasty and a real bargain. For breakfast, go for the plump, puffy Belgian waffles topped with whipped cream and strawberries.

The country dinner plates—less than $8 and one special per day—feature ham steak, pot roast, meatloaf, or chicken and biscuits. Along with the chow, the place is a mini museum, decorated with old photos, sheet music, tools, advertising art, and local mementos.

Ye Olde Forte View Inn

518-585-7767

325 NY 22

Open: Wednesday through Sunday

Cuisine: American

Serving: L, D

Price: Moderate to Expensive

Credit Cards: None

Reservations: Yes

Handicap Access: Partial; restrooms inaccessible

Ye Olde Fort View Inn features dining on an enclosed porch overlooking Lake Champlain and Fort Ticonderoga. The view is outstanding, with rock cliffs in the foreground, the lake in middle distance, and the stone walls of the fort beyond. The inn's interior wood motif is charming and bright, and service is fast and efficient. There's an extensive sandwich menu for lunch, with creations named after historical figures who visited Fort Ticonderoga. For instance, the General Burgoyne is a lot of turkey piled on a Kaiser roll (what, you thought colonial hero Ethan Allen would be represented by turkey?), topped with a tasty sauce and veggies. Sweet-potato fries or fresh, thick homemade French fries are recommended side orders. Wings are good, too.

Seafood, steaks, and pasta are the featured dinner fare. Desserts include cheesecake and very good carrot cake and homemade pies; this is orchard country, with luscious apple pie a fall favorite.

WESTPORT

Le Bistro at the Westport Yacht Club
518-962-8777
www.bistrodulac.com
On Lake Champlain, off NY 22
Open: Mid-June through mid-September
Cuisine: French
Serving: L, D
Price: Expensive
Credit Cards: AE, MC, V
Reservations: Recommended
Handicap Access: Yes

This just might be the finest waterfront setting on either side of Lake Champlain. Guests arrive by car—or they sail right up to the concrete dock that forms the front of the outdoor dining area. Le Bistro is without a doubt one of the top 10 restaurants in the Adirondacks: simple, fresh ingredients combine in inventive, but not gimmicky, ways.

Start with ciabatta bread. Proceed to wonderful appetizers like escargot on puff pastry, *moules marinière* (mussels and shallots in white wine cream sauce), a fine country pâté, or smoked bluefish bruschetta, offered as a special. Then endive salad, or mesclun lettuce topped with Roquefort or goat cheese. Entrées are presented elegantly, in perfect (not gluttonous) portions.

The rack of lamb with rosemary and garlic sauce, filet of beef with béarnaise sauce, and duck with green peppercorns are all winners. Le Bistro may be the only spot between Montreal and Manhattan with true filet tartar on the menu. The bouillabaisse Provencal is highly recommended, and the lovely broth overflows with succulent lobster, mussels, scallops, shrimp, and clams; chicken is prepared in a different way each day. The wine list is excellent, and Continental desserts feature seasonal fruits and top-quality chocolate.

Lunch offers an excellent, reasonably priced way to sample the menu and enjoy an alfresco meal in the sun. Choices include half a lobster with tarragon mayonnaise, spinach quiche, an excellent burger, and many specials.

Normandie Beach Club
518-962-4750
www.normandiebeachclub.com
96 Furnace Point Lane
Open: Memorial Day through Columbus Day
Cuisine: Continental
Serving: B (brunch on Sunday), L, D
Price: Moderate to Expensive
Credit Cards: AE, D, MC, V
Reservations: Yes
Handicap Access: Yes

Since 2006, this resort in Westport (previous incarnations, beginning in the 1960s, were kids' language and water sports camps) has been a welcome addition to town, adding two super choices for dining in the Champlain Valley. In addition to lakeside cabins that proprietors Molly and Waldemer Kasriels rent by the week are the **Furnace Point Grill** (named after the blast furnace that stood here in the 1840s)—a fine, but casual establishment—and the more laid-back lunch spot, the **Coco Café.**

The Furnace Point Grill has a big, welcoming bar for cocktails and a dining room that seats about sixty. Steaks, seafood, chicken dishes, and salads fill the menu, and homemade bread means delicious sandwiches. The Coco Café includes a stone terrace beside awninged deck overlooking Lake Champlain, great for a light meal. Overall, the menu at both spaces is varied and uniformly good, and in summer there's regular live entertainment (check the club's Web site for dates). Locals don't miss the Sunday brunch. You can also get a basket lunch to go—perfect to take on the boat (many diners arrive via water) or the trail. Also, the beach club offers guests waterskiing, sailing, canoeing, tennis, windsurfing, and other activities.

The Kasriels have planted funky eight-foot Paulownia Empress trees around the property, and their Bernese Mountain dogs can be seen lounging about. This really is a fantastic resort, and a fun backdrop for a special event.

WILLSBORO

Upper Deck at Willsboro Bay Marina
518-963-8271
www.upperdeckrestaurant.com
20 Klein Way, Willsboro Bay Marina
Open: Daily; mid-June through Labor Day
Cuisine: American, Continental
Serving: D
Price: Moderate to Expensive

On warm summer days, these garage doors roll up to provide open-air dining at the Upper Deck, in Willsboro. James Swedberg

Credit Cards: MC, V
Reservations: No
Handicap Access: Yes

The Upper Deck's two airy dining rooms—elegantly decorated with walls of windows that are kept open in warm weather—overlook Willsboro Bay and the wooded cliffs beyond. To complement the ambiance, the chef has created menus that meld American dishes with world flavors. For example, selections include sun-dried-tomato tortillas rolled around grilled onion, zucchini, and shrimp or a grilled ham, cheese, and artichoke sandwich on a crusty roll. Soups are very good, especially the gazpacho with homegrown herbs.

For dinner, appetizers include escargot á la Bourguignon, gravlox, and a wild mushroom tart, which make nice transitions to veal scaloppini, Chesapeake Bay crab cakes, tandoori salmon, or a grilled porterhouse steak, served with an au poivre sauce of green peppercorns, shallots, demi-glace, and cognac. Three to five specials are offered each night, and vegetarians should be quite happy here. (If you can't eat milk products or wheat, call ahead; the chef will make something delicious just for you.) There's a scaled-down menu for children, an extensive wine list, and good desserts, like strawberry torte and chocolate pecan pie.

Whether relaxing before or after dinner, the cozy, well-stocked bar is an excellent place to unwind. The service is friendly and accommodating.

Turtle Island Café
518-963-7417
www.turtleislandcafe.com
3 North Main Street
Open: Year-round
Price: Moderate to Expensive
Serving: L, D
Cuisine: Freestyle cuisine
Credit Cards: AE, MC, V
Reservations: No

Handicap Access: Yes

David Martin, former chef at the Hungry Trout, in Wilmington, now operates his own popular café with delicious, imaginative cuisine, in Willsboro. At Turtle Island, Martin says he uses "both traditional ingredients as well as a global array of fresh products to create an eclectic blend of many cultures in one dish." He incorporates "a lot of fruit purees, lighter oils, fresh herbs, and various chilies to achieve flavor." The result is super. Try his artichoke hearts stuffed with goat cheese with spiced ham and seared spinach leaves for an appetizer, his osso buco for an entrée, topped off with apple crisp with pumpkin spice gelato. Martin's duck gets rave reviews, too.

The wine list here is constantly growing; microbrews are also available.

High Peaks and Northern Adirondacks

KEENE

Baxter Mountain Tavern

518-576-9990
www.baxtermountaintavern.com
10050 NY 9N
Open: Daily, year-round
Cuisine: American
Serving: L, D
Price: Moderate
Credit Cards: MC, V
Reservations: Yes
Handicap Access: Yes

Baxter Mountain Tavern is casual and comfortable, with an overstuffed couch facing a stone fireplace, a big bar, and a dining room with a view of Hurricane Mountain. Settle in with a good draft beer, like Sierra Nevada, Bass, Guinness, or Sam Adams pale ale. If you're traveling through the High Peaks with family, this place is very kid-friendly, too.

Every day there's a ravioli special; the portabella ravioli (ask for marinara sauce; the cream sauce seems overpowering) is good. Save room for dessert, which is always made on the premises and always delicious.

In winter, the couch in front of the fireplace is a cozy spot for lounging; in summer you can see the surrounding mountains from the deck.

Cedar Run Bakery

518-576-9929
2837 NY 73
Open: Daily, (6 AM–5 PM); bakery open
   until 6 PM
Cuisine: American
Serving: B, L
Price: Inexpensive to Moderate
Credit Cards: MC, V
Reservations: No
Handicap Access: Yes

What started out as a cramped bakery in a Keene strip mall has expanded into its own restaurant just a short stretch down NY 73—a bustling little café that attracts locals and visitors alike. The paninis, wraps, quiches, and soups are delicious: Expect lots of fresh, snappy, interesting combinations and a welcome twist on sides and garnishes—three-bean salads or hummus or even melon concoctions.

The baked goods are also tasty, especially the muffins, scones, and cookies; our canine reviewers seem to like the homemade dog biscuits. You can buy prebaked meals to go; request a made-to-order cake (the carrot cake melts in your mouth); or pick up gourmet teas, sodas, soup mixes, condiments, or a cup of Green Mountain coffee for the road.

Service can be pokey and this eatery's layout is a bit awkward—you may stand by the cash register in the baked goods section without being noticed by the busy wait staff hustling back and forth from the dining room or deck to the kitchen. But the food is definitely worth the wait.

KEENE VALLEY

Great Range
518-576-9069
1799 NY 73
Open: Year-round; call ahead for hours
Cuisine: International
Serving: L, D
Price: Expensive
Credit Cards: AE, D, MC, V
Reservations: Recommended
Handicap Access: Yes

Great Range is a sunny oasis in a forest of restaurants bedecked in birch bark and twigs. Owners Jason Piasecki and Elly Preston have transformed what was a cluttered climbers' hangout—the beloved Cliffhanger Café, which burned in 2006—into a bright, open cheerful space with six or so tables and a lovely bar.

Entrées—Thai vegetable curry, free-range chicken with garlic and citrus, pan-seared duck breast—are a welcome change from the typical heavy High Peaks food. Try the smoked-salmon quesadilla appetizer followed by seared scallops and risotto, paired with a glass of white from an unexpectedly varied wine list. There are lots of beer choices, too, even Japanese labels.

Ambiance is chill—calming jazz piano music over the sound system—and the service is excellent. Casual outdoor seating is available in summer—perfect for hiker-watching and taking in the mountain air. Several wine-tasting events have been a hit, one even turning into an impromptu dance party. Call to see about upcoming tastings—a fine way to pass a summer evening, but even better for dark, chilly winter nights.

Cedar Run's tasty lunches and baked goods make this Keene eatery a hot spot. Annie Stoltie

Noon Mark Diner

518-576-4499
www.noonmarkdiner.com
NY 73/Main Street
Open: Year-round, 6 AM–9 PM
Cuisine: Diner
Serving: B, L, D
Price: Inexpensive to Moderate
Credit Cards: MC, V
Handicap Access: Yes

Everybody from High Peaks backpackers to investment bankers to kids on bikes converges at the Noon Mark during a typical week, to stoke up on homemade doughnuts, cinnamon buns, pies, muffins, banana bread, soups, French fries, and whatever else is on the menu. You can order breakfast any time, if you're not up for chili made with chunks of beef round, or the trail blazer, a steak sandwich with sautéed mushrooms, onions, and peppers on a hard roll.

Dinners lean toward frozen things popped into the deep fryer, like clams or shrimp, but soup, salad, and potatoes or rice come with any choice. After a long day in the outdoors, try turkey or lasagna, and then order some homemade bread pudding or heavenly pie (worth a visit for coconut cream alone) to have for breakfast the next day. An ice-cream stand is off to one side of the huge front porch (open seasonally), if you want some walk-around dessert. Note that the Noon Mark can be jammed on summer weekends, with a half-hour wait for a table and another half hour before your meal is served.

LAKE PLACID

Aki Sushi & Japanese Restaurant

518-523-5826
2724 Main Street (across from High Peaks Cyclery)
Open: Tuesday through Sunday
Cuisine: Japanese
Serving: L, D
Price: Inexpensive to Moderate
Credit Cards: AE, D, MC, V
Reservations: Recommended for large parties

After a long day in the outdoors, stop by the Noon Mark for heavenly homemade pie. Annie Stoltie

Handicap Access: Yes

Aki is popular with locals and visitors alike. Shoehorned into a storefront near Norm's barbershop, the sushi bar and handful of tables are usually busy every night.

Recommended are rice bowls with stir-fried vegetables and shrimp or tofu, sashimi and all sorts of rolls—the specialty ones, such as the volcano roll are a big hit—some tempura, iceberg lettuce with gingery dressing, rice noodles, and wasabi. Take-out is available, and the lunch menu presents smaller versions of dinner selections.

Brown Dog Deli & Wine Bar

518-523-3036
3 Main Street
Open: Year-round, 11:30 AM—9:30 PM ; subject to seasonal closings
Price: Inexpensive to Moderate
Cuisine: Bistro
Serving: L, D
Credit Cards: MC, V
Reservations: No
Handicap Access: Yes

Part wine bar and part fancy sandwich shop, the Brown Dog offers sophisticated lunch and dinner options. At lunchtime, you fill out a form with boxes to check off for sandwiches and toppings. In the evening, wait staff take the burden of ordering from diners.

The wine selection is a plus, plenty of choices at $8 to $10 per glass, served in perilously tall stemware. Starters include excellent crab cakes with a side of baby greens, good salads with grilled chicken or shrimp, big soups, green-lipped mussels (in season), and nice crusty breads. Entrées typically include duck quesadillas, grilled chicken or salmon, beef or pork.

The ambiance is bare-table bistro, the place a Main Street storefront, and you'll feel like a Placid insider for finding this hideaway.

Caffé Rustica

518-523-7511
1936 Saranac Avenue (in the Price Chopper Plaza)
Open: Year-round, subject to seasonal closings
Price: Expensive
Cuisine: Rustic Italian/Mediterranean
Serving: L (Tuesday through Saturday), D (Monday through Saturday).
Credit Cards: AE, M, V
Reservations: No
Handicap Access: Yes

Don't let the Price Chopper–plaza digs fool you. There are delicious meals to be had in this little café, prepared by the capable hands of Kevin Gregg. Try the enormous Nicoise or duck salads, the *fungi misti* pizza (mushroom, taleggio, mixed greens, rosemary, truffle oil, and garlic), pasta scallop Provencal (seared scallops tossed with tomato, basil, capers, and artichokes in a white wine butter sauce over penne), the *pesce del gornio* (fresh catch of the evening), or the *gnocchi alla rustica* (lemon basil pesto, sun-dried tomatoes, wilted greens, and feta cheese). You just can't go wrong here.

This isn't the place to go if you're hoping for a private dinner—tables are close together like crammed-in city restaurants, so eavesdropping is all but inevitable here. But this is where you go for a fine lunch or dinner, and the wait staff is well-versed in Gregg's cuisine and the wine list, so if you have questions, ask away, especially if you're looking for the right glass of wine to pair with a meal.

The café has a handsome bar where you can get a cocktail, perhaps before venturing next door to the supermarket. In warm weather outdoor seating is available. Gregg and his team are also popular local caterers, particularly at weddings. Or you can arrange to have a private shindig at the café itself.

Caribbean Cowboy

518-523-3836
89 Saranac Avenue, behind Saranac
    Sourdough, across from HoJo's
Open: Year-round; call ahead for hours
Price: Moderate to Expensive
Serving: D
Cuisine: Caribbean/Contemporary/Fusion
Credit Cards: MC, V
Reservations: No
Handicap Access: Yes

At this bright, fun, funky place tucked
behind Saranac Sourdough, you can get a
spicy, delicious, abundant dinner for a fine
price. Start off at the bar, where Tim will
make you a mango margarita, a Painkiller (a
strong and delicious rum drink), or a Dark
and Stormy (ginger beer and dark rum),
and you get the vibe of island meets Pacific
Rim cuisine, from the able hands of Vicky
and Rob Breyette.

Appetizers include shrimp and black
bean fritters, little sweet crab cakes,
chicken satay, and sushi. Entrée selections
are plentiful and range from thick all-natu-
ral broiled burgers—the Cowboy burger is
stuffed with blue cheese—or seafood quesadillas, jerk chicken, with the salmon
burger (a nice fillet, not a processed patty),
and a different tuna, salmon, or pork special each night. Salads are enormous, and
rice or soba noodle salads are a favorite. Try
the freshly made key lime pie for dessert.

The place can be packed on nice summer evenings. Go early if you want to beat
the rush. Or what the heck—linger outside
on the patio until your table is ready.

Interlaken Inn

1-800-428-4369
www.theinterlakeinn.com
39 Interlaken Avenue
Open: Year-round
Cuisine: Contemporary American
Serving: D
Price: Expensive to Very Expensive

Credit Cards: AE, D, MC, V
Reservations: Recommended
Handicap Access: No
Remarks: Lovely old inn

A grand old small hotel tucked into a peaceful downtown neighborhood, this place has
Richard Brousseau, one of the finest chefs
in the Adirondacks, and, consequently,
fantastic food for the elegant dining room
and the informal pub. In the latter, try fresh
lump crab cakes served with orange basic
beurre blanc; buffalo shrimp with blue
cheese dipping sauce; champagne or garlic
blue cheese or black truffle fondue; or a
grilled Kilcoyne Farm grass-fed burger on a
baguette roll, topped with Great Hill Dairy
blue cheese and roasted pancetta. There's
an excellent wine and beer list, too.

In the dining room, start with the oyster
martini, pickled with lemon vodka and
topped with Meyer lemon foam, or mini
sourdough pancakes set on smoked
proscuitto, quail eggs, and maple bourbon
butter. Entrées, depending on the season—
as is the case with all of Chef Richard's
offerings—include crispy red snapper set
on an artichoke puree drizzled with a pinot
noir reduction; grilled Colorado loin lamb
chops paired with rosemary mint melon
salad and topped with crispy zucchini;
grilled strip steak that's rubbed with
coriander, set on cheddar horseradish
grits, and topped with chimichurri butter.
There's more, too, but desserts certainly
deserve a mention: rosemary crème brulee,
chocolate truffles rolled in almonds, warm
ápple Charlotte with maple syrup and
vanilla ice cream. If you overindulge, you
can always ask for a room.

Lake Placid Lodge

518-523-2700
www.lakeplacidlodge.com
Whiteface Inn Road

In 2005 a devastating fire razed the Lake
Placid Lodge, one of the finest, most elegant

restaurants in the Adirondacks. The good news is that construction on a new main lodge on the Lake Placid Lodge property is in the works—ground was broken in March 2007 and the gorgeous new building is expected to open in 2008.

Lisa G's

518-523-2093
444 Main Street
Open: Year-round
Cuisine: Contemporary American/Greek
Serving: L, D
Price: Moderate to Expensive
Credit Cards: AE, MC, V
Reservations: Recommended for large parties
Handicap Access: Yes

Locals love this restaurant in an old opera house away from Lake Placid's touristy main drag. The setting is casual—if you don't feel like eating in the dining room, enjoy your meal in the bar or, in summer, dine on the deck overlooking the Chubb River.

Proprietor Lisa G., this place's namesake, is a welcoming bolt of energy—and one of the nicest people in the North Country—who checks on customers, serves cocktails and food, and visits with everyone who walks through the door. Oh, and the food is fantastic. There are four kinds of chicken wings on the apps menu, even Greek wings that are marinated in lemon juice, olive oil, and oregano, with creamy feta dressing (wing night). Other appetizers, with polenta supporting homemade sauces, pulled chicken or short ribs, often make nice meal portions. The French fries and sweet potato fries are yummy; salads such as the new Asian (arugula, roasted peppers, grilled chicken, and chow mein noodles with miso dressing) and My Big Fat Greek Salad (huge portions of olives, feta, and chicken) are delicious; and the beans and greens entrée is rigatoni with traditional upstate NY treatment: sausage, spinach, garlic, olive oil, and white beans.

We also like the homemade ice cream, especially the raspberry graham cracker and peanut butter flavors.

There's often live music on weekends; call ahead to ask about upcoming entertainment or swing by for a drink and a game of pool and ask in person.

Veranda

518-523-3339
1 Olympic Drive (across from the Crowne Plaza hotel)
Open: Tuesday through Sunday
Cuisine: French
Serving: D
Price: Expensive to Very Expensive
Credit Cards: AE, CB, DC, MC, V
Reservations: Recommended
Handicap Access: No

A grand restaurant in a gracious old home, the Veranda may not be hip, but Chef Claude Gaucher's food is great and classically prepared. This place is worth a special trip, and eating on the deck is heavenly. A stunning panorama of the Sentinel Range marches across your field of view, with a bit of Mirror Lake in the foreground.

Downstairs are two dining rooms, each with cobblestone fireplaces; upstairs are three private dining rooms accommodating from six to forty or so guests. All are finished with handsome woodwork, wallpapers, and drapes.

Menu choices are tried and true examples of French country cuisine. Appetizers are all delectable, with the escargot, jumbo shrimp amandine, and vegetable terrine at the top of our list. The house salad (everything is à la carte) covers a dinner plate with artfully arranged shredded vegetables and greens.

The many entrées include duck breast with a duet of sauces (green peppercorn and raspberry), salmon quenelles, grilled rosemary lamb (terrific), aged steaks, and superb bouillabaisse (summer only). Desserts, all made in the Veranda's kitchen, show real finesse, such as apple tart, peach Melba, and Paris-Brest (puff paste with hazelnut cream). The wine list is extensive, although house wines by the glass are limited.

The View at Mirror Lake Inn Resort & Spa

518-302-3000
www.mirrorlakeinn.com
77 Mirror Lake Drive
Open: Year-round
Cuisine: Contemporary American
Serving: B, L, D
Price: Expensive to Very Expensive
Credit Cards: AE, D, DC, MC, V
Reservations: Suggested
Handicap Access: Yes

For years it seemed that the lovely Mirror Lake Inn was stuck in a time warp, with a stuffy, formal dining room serving unmemorable food. The good news is that former Paul Smith's College dean of the culinary arts and hospitality management program and award-winning chef Paul Sorgule has taken the reigns at the inn and revamped the entire dining experience.

The main dining room is now The View restaurant, a truly elegant backdrop for grilled veal tenderloin, breast of chicken and figs, pull braised pork, diver scallops and rhubarb, and numerous lower calorie and lower fat "spa" meals, such as pan-seared organic tofu and tri-flavored vegetarian gateau. There's also a nightly chef's feature of the day. Also new: The inn's cozy bar is now **Taste Bistro & Bar**, where you can order a fine glass of wine or microbrew with *pommes frite*, a green papaya salad, teriyaki prawns, a thin-crust pizza, or a half-pound Black Angus burger.

And for foodies, the Adirondack Festival of Food & Wine, at the Mirror Lake Inn, is very popular. Contact the inn for information about the event, which usually takes place in April.

Across Mirror Lake Drive, and owned by the inn, is the **Cottage**, a breezy little bar

The View, a new restaurant at the Mirror Lake Inn Resort & Spa, offers fine dining in the Olympic Village.
Courtesy of the Mirror Lake Inn Resort & Spa

right on the lake. It's a fine spot for enjoying a cocktail and some nachos; though there is a variety of sandwiches and salads, the kitchen is limited.

RAY BROOK

Tail O' the Pup
518-891-5092
NY 86, next to the Evergreens cabins
Open: Mid-May through mid-October
Cuisine: Barbecue
Serving: L, D
Price: Inexpensive to Moderate
Credit Cards: AE, MC, V
Reservations: No
Handicap Access: Yes
Remarks: Folk music in summer

For more than half a century, Tail O' the Pup has served happy travelers with its winning combination of good, cheap food,

Try lobsters, clams, barbecue, or burgers under the big top at Tail O' the Pup, a classic roadside eatery.
Annie Stoltie

and come-as-you-are atmosphere. You can eat at a picnic table beneath a huge tent, inside at a booth, or, depending on how busy the place is, even beep for a carhop. Bring the kids: They'll love it here, especially on the nights when there's a singer/guitarist strolling around.

The ribs and chicken are yummy, smoked and smothered with tangy, not-too-sweet sauce, and come with waffle fries, baked beans, corn on the cob (sometimes soggy), and a miniscule dab of pretty good cole slaw. On Wednesday, Thursday, and Friday nights, you can also get steamed clams or whole lobster for bargain prices. Onion rings are just the way they should be, crunchy and sweet; better order a couple of portions for the table. About half a dozen good imported and domestic beers are on tap. Oddly, the hot dogs—for which this landmark is named—are just so-so.

SARANAC LAKE

The Belvedere Restaurant
518-891-9873
102 Bloomingdale Avenue
Open: Year-round
Cuisine: American/Italian
Serving: D
Price: Moderate
Credit Cards: None
Reservations: No
Handicap Access: No

Since 1933, there's been a member of the Cavallo family in the Belvedere's kitchen, and the restaurant is known for consistently good Italian home cooking. If you've been to a Midwestern supper club, you'll recognize the ambiance: the rambling dining room, a dim bar, a crew of regulars who have their own special tables. If you don't want to feel like a tourist, this is the place. The drinks are reasonably priced, including a good selection of Italian and California wines.

Hot sausage is made right here, and provides zip to thick tomato sauces; recommended entrées are veal and peppers, chicken cacciatore, and lasagna with homemade noodles. Appetizers are few and downright quaint—celery and olives, for instance. For dessert, try spumoni or save room for cheesecake. For an excellent burger, head for the bar, and while you're there, read the newspaper clippings about a memorable day at Saratoga, when a horse named Belvedere won big—and the Cavallos were there to cash in.

Eat-N-Meet Grill & Larder

518-891-3149
www.eatnmeet.com
Open: Year-round; closed Tuesday
Cuisine: Eclectic
Serving: L, D
Price: Moderate
Credit Cards: D, MC, V
Reservations: No
Handicap Access: No

This joint on Upper Broadway is an unexpected surprise, though if you're driving past you can't miss the place, with its life-size plastic Elvis posing on the front sidewalk. Inside, the décor is decidedly funky: a busy meal counter where you place your order and pick it up; three or so modest tables—usually graced with a *New York Times* on Sunday—where you can eat your grub; and a larder with walls of exotic condiments that aren't so easy to find in the North Country, like mega-jars of saffron.

Proprietors John (who is also the chef) and Colleen Vargo subscribe to the slow-food movement, which means a constantly changing menu of fresh local seasonal fare cooked long, carefully, and to perfection. Dishes range from gyros to Jamaican curried goat stew to Chesapeake oyster stew to tacos to huge salads to pork schnitzel sandwiches to fresh fish cooked as you choose. Slow food also translates to. . . well, slow food, so if you're ravenous, call in your

order ahead or, once you're there, play a complementary round or two of mini golf at Eat-N-Meet's adjacent nine-hole course while you wait.

There's no industrial-size dishwasher in the tiny kitchen, so all meals are served in takeout containers with plastic eating utensils.

Little Italy Pizzeria

518-891-9000
23 Main Street
Open: Year-round, 10:30 AM—10 PM
Cuisine: Italian
Serving: L, D
Price: Inexpensive to Moderate
Credit Cards: None
Reservations: No
Handicap Access: Yes

What appears to be a simple pizza joint is much, much more. Venture beyond the front counter and booths in this Saranac institution—this is, after all, the town's number one takeout/delivery pizza place—and you'll find yourself in a spacious dining room with Old Country décor and tables (with paper placemats imprinted with a map of Italy) that accommodate parties from two to twenty.

What you'll get here is straight-up Italian fare—no pretension, no nonsense. Just ziti, manicotti, lasagna, chicken parmesan, spaghetti with meatballs, gnocchi, ravioli, fettuccine alfredo—all the standards. You can't go wrong with any of these dishes.

Some grumble about how long it takes the cooks to prepare takeout meals, even pizza pies, but the easiest way to avoid this is to call in your order before heading to the restaurant's Main Street headquarters. Another solution: Stay to eat. That way you can unwind in the back dining room over a glass of chianti and melt-in-your mouth hunks of garlic bread.

Morgan's II

518-897-1111

33 Broadway
Open: Year-round
Cuisine: Italian/American
Serving: L, D
Price: Moderate to Expensive
Credit Cards: D, MC, V
Reservations: No
Handicap Access: Yes

This boisterous hot spot operated in down-town Saranac Lake by a few Morgan broth-ers (siblings to legendary Dew Drop Morgan who ran the Dew Drop Inn next door for years and years, then bartended at the Lake Placid Lodge until it burned in 2005) is a super place for a drink and a brick-oven pizza. In addition to the twelve or so different pies on the menu you can get various Italian and American fare, all served by a friendly, accommodating staff.

Crews of cheerful locals gather at the bar and, consequently, the chatter in this cozy restaurant hits high volume, particularly after happy hour. But the pizza makes din-ing here worth it, and in warm weather you can escape the noise by sitting outside on the deck overlooking the Saranac River.

WILMINGTON

The Hungry Trout
518-946-2217
www.hungrytrout.com
5239 NY 86
Open: Most of the year; sometimes closed
    in March and April; call ahead
Cuisine: Continental
Serving: D
Price: Expensive
Credit Cards: AE, MC, V
Reservations: Yes
Handicap Access: Yes

A mile-long section of the legendary West Branch of the Ausable River wraps around this motel/restaurant/fly shop complex, and fine views of Whiteface Mountain and a foaming waterfall can be seen from the din-ing room. Arrive before dark, as the setting sun puts a golden glow on the hillside; the scenery is awesome and upstages the food.

The menu is extensive, with numerous trout (farm-raised) dishes, plus quality lamb, steaks, pasta, chicken, and excellent mesquite-grilled Norwegian salmon. The house salad, dressed with balsamic vinai-grette and usually served with craisins, is quite good, and desserts range from pre-mium ice creams to fruit pies.

If you'd like to sample this spot but pre-fer not to spend a bundle, try the tavern on the ground floor, **R. F. McDougall's** (as in Rat Face McDougall, a trout fly). It's casual, with antique woodsy/sporty decor, a long bar, comfortable booths, a lighter menu (excellent charbroiled burgers), and lots of good beers on hand.

Northwest Lakes

LAKE CLEAR

Hohmeyer's Lake Clear Lodge
518-891-1489
www.lodgeonlakeclear.com
6319 NY 30
Open: Wednesday through Sunday
Cuisine: German
Serving: D
Price: Expensive to Very Expensive
Credit Cards: AE, D, MC, V
Reservations: Recommended
Handicap Access: No

This charming Adirondack inn, built in 1886, was the town's first post office and an early stagecoach stop; the décor today is a pleasant European/Adirondack fusion. Bring a small group of friends for dinner so you can sample many of the interesting appetizers (marinated herring, smoked oys-ters, and pâté, for example) and homemade desserts. Soups, especially oxtail, are won-derful. All meals come with a combination of German potato pancakes, wild rice, potato dumplings, fresh vegetables, and a bowl of sweet red cabbage and green apples.

Entrée choices—usually six to eight options each night—are heirloom German recipes that showcase farm-raised venison, rabbit, duckling, pork, and veal in traditional sauces, plus sauerbraten, rouladen, and schnitzels. Also look for regional dishes like Adirondack rainbow trout or salmon. Desserts can include delicious blueberry strudel (right from the oven if your timing's good).

After dinner, take your party down to the Bierkeller to sit by the fire and digest, or play pool, Ping-Pong, or backgammon. There is an extensive variety of beers (some 125 kinds from around the world) and a good list of German, French, and California wines.

WANAKENA

The Pine Cone
315-848-2121
68 Ranger School Road
Open: Tuesday through Sunday
Cuisine: American
Serving: L, D
Price: Moderate
Credit Cards: None
Reservations: No
Handicap Access: Street-level entry

A classic North Woods tavern with respectable fare, the Pine Cone is worth a visit—if you're nearby—to check out the ceiling, plastered with baseball caps of all descriptions, about a thousand of them. Come by boat from Cranberry Lake for one of the pig roasts or barbecues; there's plenty of dock space.

The Friday fish fry (beer-battered haddock) is fine, and try the prime rib, which is quite popular. You'll find the service to be quick and friendly.

Central and Southwestern Adirondacks

BIG MOOSE

Big Moose Inn
315-357-2042
www.bigmooseinn.com
1510 Big Moose Road
Open: January through March; May through October; part of December; call for hours
Cuisine: American/Continental
Serving: B, L, D
Price: Moderate to Expensive
Credit Cards: AE, MC, V
Reservations: Recommended
Handicap Access: Yes

Overlooking Big Moose Lake is this old-time lodge, a favorite destination for year-round residents who want to go someplace special on birthdays, anniversaries, and other occasions; some people even come by seaplane for dinner. In the summer, eating on the lakeside deck is a treat; ask for a table by the windows in the winter. Proprietor Robert Hankey goes out of his way to make guests feel welcome.

The menu is hearty and interesting—one of the most extensive in the area—and the chef promises the finest, freshest ingredients in every dish (ask about the herb garden on the premises). There's fine aged beef—delicious Black Angus tenderloins, fresh seafood, rack of lamb, and a personal favorite, crisp duck. The dessert tray is full of excellent choices, so save room for peanut butter pie.

Big Moose Station
315-357-3525
Big Moose Road
Open: Spring through fall; call for hours
Cuisine: American
Serving: B, L, D
Price: Moderate

Credit Cards: AE, MC, V
Reservations: Yes
Handicap Access: Yes

This attractively restored depot for the Adirondack Railroad hasn't seen regular passenger service for years (that will change, when the line from Thendara is extended), but it's still a fine destination for hungry travelers. The down-home fare is delicious, presented in ample portions, and the setting is charming. For breakfast, try waffles or thick French toast; at lunch, hearty soups and a grilled burger or club sandwich. The daily dinner specials are always "special," including the popular Friday night fish fry.

EDINBURG

I-Go-Inn Restaurant & Bar
518-883-8900
241 South Shore Road
Open: May through September
Cuisine: Eclectic American
Serving: L, D
Price: Inexpensive to Moderate
Credit Cards: MC, V
Reservations: No
Handicap Access: Yes

Lots of folks get their I-Go meal to go, but in summer this is a perfectly nice spot to stay and dine. Stands of tall white pines surround the patio, where you can monitor the cars going by on South Shore Road. Some diners arrive here via the Sacandaga Reservoir: Park your boat at I-Go's docks and stay for some grub and the live music on summer evenings.

Staff wear Hawaiian shirts, but the food is a little bit southwestern, mostly American, with a touch Italian and Asian. "Cowboy" fare, as the southwestern recipes are categorized, includes Mom's meatloaf over smashed potatoes and topped with onion rings, and classic- or Cajun-cowboy sirloin. Other meals are the usual burgers

and wraps—try a rolled-up Rueben or BLT—or a Caesar, spinach, or Cobb salad. There are quesadillas, too; chicken, clam, and fish baskets; and fancier entrées, such as a sirloin steak encrusted with gorgonzola wasabi sauce, twin lobster tails, and chicken Florentine. The selections are endless, and the best part is that the I-Go is open until midnight to accommodate those with the late-night munchies.

INDIAN LAKE

Chili Nights
518-648-5832
NY 3
Open: Thursday through Sunday; days vary
    by season
Cuisine: Mexican
Serving: D
Price: Moderate
Credit Cards: AE, D, MC, V
Reservations: Suggested
Handicap Access: Yes

Ten years ago an unlikely place took over the front room of a local watering hole and surprised everyone by serving authentic Mexican food. There's Mexican beer on draft, Mexican sodas, fried ice cream for dessert, and an upbeat, earnest ambiance.

Appetizers include the usual suspects—nachos, guacamole, and such—but the entrée list is every bit as complete and tasty as any of the other Mexican eateries in the Adirondacks. The stuffed chilies (Anaheim chilies stuffed with corn, tomatoes, and black beans) are very popular, and a healthier baked alternative to some other heavy fried fare. If a chimichanga isn't for you, then try the steaming chili served in a bowl made of bread, or perhaps a vegetarian fajita with portabellas and sweet red peppers.

INLET

Seventh Lake House
315-357-6028

479 NY 28
Open: Year-round, except for November
Cuisine: Contemporary American
Serving: D
Price: Expensive
Credit Cards: AE, D, MC, V
Reservations: Suggested
Handicap Access: Yes

Chef/owner Jim Holt has presided here since 1989, and his varied seasonal menus continue to offer innovative dishes made from the best ingredients.

The place is elegantly simple, with white tablecloths, an imposing fireplace, and lots of picture windows facing the lake. There's a comfortable bar off to one side and a big canopied deck stretching across the back, trimmed with tiny Christmas lights. Seventh Lake House is child-friendly, especially in the summer, when the deck is open.

Appetizers are delicious, including shrimp foccacia, Thai marinated chicken strips, and crab cakes. Soups are heavenly, especially the crab bisque. You can't beat the Caesar salad. Entrées run the gamut of fresh seafood on angel-hair pasta to triple meatloaf made with beef, veal, and pork—a combination that trumps all other recipes. The Long Island duck is scrumptious; filet mignon with adobo sauce is very good. Desserts made on the premises include a flourless chocolate gateau and the Adirondack, a warm pastry made with fresh Granny Smith apples, walnuts, and maple syrup.

The Woods Inn

315-357-5300
www.thewoodsinn.com
148 NY 28
Open: December through March; May
     through October
Cuisine: American
Serving: B (for lodging guests only), L
     (depending on season; call ahead), D
Price: Moderate to Expensive
Credit Cards: D, MC, V

Handicap Access: Yes

Since it was built in 1894, the Woods Inn has undergone expansions, renovations, and passed through many hands. In 2003 the latest proprietors, Joedda McClain and Jay Latterman, completely restored the inn, returning it to its noble state—it really is something to see as you're paddling past on Fourth Lake. Original structures were winterized, new plumbing and wiring were installed, and the building's massive porches were replaced. McClain says you can see some of the best sunsets in the Adirondacks from the Woods Inn's front porch.

In 2004 a dining room and the **Laughing Loons Tavern** were open to the public, creating two fine venues for meals and a super backdrop for private parties, be they family reunions, weddings, or corporate retreats. McClain describes the meals available in the dining room as real comfort food; particularly popular are the home-style meatloaf, lamb shank, and chicken pot pie. For something lighter order a beet salad, quesadilla, or tuna tataki, served with seaweed salad.

The Laughing Loons Tavern has pub fare, such as burgers, Saranac Black & Tan beef stew, and salads. It's a cozy space—check out the tin ceiling and lounge beside the fireplace—for a drink and a round or two of pool; smokers appreciate the veranda outside the bar.

LONG LAKE

Long Lake Diner

518-624-3941
NY 30
Open: Year-round, except for holidays
Cuisine: American
Serving: B, L (6 AM–2 PM), D (Wednesday
     only, 5 PM –8 PM)
Price: Inexpensive to Moderate
Credit Cards: MC, V
Reservations: No

Handicap Access: Yes

This spotless, bright lakeside restaurant is hard to beat. The staff is friendly and fast, and it's tough to find a clunker on the menu. In the morning, go for the eggs Benedict or Belgian waffles with real maple syrup; at lunch, homemade soups, char-grilled burgers, club sandwiches, and huge Caesar salads are all good. The clam basket is tasty. Wednesday is prime rib and chicken night; on Friday you can get good fish fry in the diner's bar, referred to as the **Owl's Head Pub**.

Long View Lodge
518-624-2862
www.longviewlodge.com
NY 28N and 30
Open: Year-round; from Columbus Day
   through Memorial Day, open only on
   weekends; open every day but
   Wednesday the rest of the season
Cuisine: Contemporary American
Serving: B (depending on season; call
   ahead), D
Price: Moderate to Expensive
Credit Cards: D, MC, V
Reservations: Yes
Handicap Access: No

With a history that dates back to the mid-1800s, the Long View Lodge, on the eastern shore of Long Lake, is currently operated by Angela and Fred Fink. (Angela's great-great-grandparents actually built the original farmhouse that fed and boarded tourists here, then called the Emerson Homestead.) Sadly, as this book goes to press, the lodge is for sale, though it continues accommodating diners.

   Meals in the dining room are very nice, particularly when the fireplace is stoked; entrées include walnut-crusted chicken, Mediterranean duck, mutton Espagnole, scallops brandy, and prawns Florentine. There are also several vegetarian offerings on the menu, plus plenty of salads. Have a drink and take in the view of nearby Owls Head from the knotty pine lounge.

MAYFIELD

Lanzi's on the Lake
518-661-7711
1751 NY 30
Open: Daily year-round
Cuisine: American
Serving: L (depends on season), D
Price: Moderate to Expensive
Credit Cards: AE, D, MC, V
Reservations: Yes
Handicap Access: Yes

On the western shore of Great Sacandaga Lake, this spacious, attractive restaurant is deservedly popular. Ample docks and a long outdoor deck invite boaters. No need to dress up—the mood here is vacation casual.

   Dinner portions are large and often provide leftovers for meals the next day. Fresh fish and quality steaks are carefully prepared; vegetables, salads, and desserts are tasty, too. Lanzi's can become crowded on weekends, so reservations are recommended.

   Under the same ownership is Northville's **Sport Island Pub** (518-863-2003), with ample pasta portions, good salads, and a low-key atmosphere. It's busy in winter with snowmobilers, and popular in summer with folks who arrive by boat.

NORTH RIVER

Garnet Hill Lodge
518-251-2444
www.garnet-hill.com
Thirteenth Lake Road
Open: Year-round
Cuisine: Country American
Serving: B, L, D
Price: Moderate to Expensive
Credit Cards: MC, V
Handicap Access: Yes

Come here for the view, a sweeping vista of

pristine Thirteenth Lake and Peaked Mountain to the west. Another reason to come here is the **Miners Pub**, a fun little Irish bar that proprietors Mary Donnellan and her husband Joseph Fahey recently built that has Guinness on tap, music by a Celtic harper, fireplace, standard bar food, and the Garney Stone, a massive hunk of garnet from the nearby mines. (Yes, you can kiss it.)

There's also the **Log House Restaurant**, which offers a range of apps and entrées, though favorites are the Ruby Mountain chicken (sautéed chicken breast with spinach, cheddar cheese, and a roasted red pepper sauce), Peaked Pond trout (two rainbow trout fillets breaded with grilled pecans and walnuts and drizzled in light lemon butter sauce), and wilderness steak (a 12-oz. New York strip grilled and topped with sautéed onions and mushrooms). On weekends a piano player provides chill-out ambiance.

OLD FORGE

The Knotty Pine
315-369-6859
NY 28, across from the Thendara Golf
   Course
Open: Year-round
Serving: D
Cuisine: American
Price: Moderate
Reservations: Yes
Credit Cards: AE, MC, V
Reservations: Yes
Handicap Access: No

A treasured local place, especially for the Friday fish fry, the Knotty Pine is known for its friendly atmosphere. Cindy and Gary Isensee make everyone feel welcome. The popcorn is always hot in the machine on the corner of the bar; a real log fire glows in the dining room fireplace.

The menu includes prime rib, sirloin, beef fillets, blackened Chicken Oscar (rec-

ommended), chicken, and beef en brochette; Cajun shrimp on angel hair pasta is listed as an appetizer but makes a nice light meal. Children are welcome, and there's a special menu for them. A private dining room accommodates large parties (call to reserve).

OLMSTEDVILLE

The Owl at Twilight
518-251-4696
1322 County Route 29, next to the Alpine
   Homestead Bed & Breakfast
Open: Friday, Saturday, and Sunday; call for
   seasonal hours
Cuisine: New American/Latin
Serving: D
Price: Moderate to Expensive
Credit Cards: AE, D, MC, V
Reservations: Recommended
Handicap Access: Yes

Olmstedville, about 8 miles from North Creek, is in the town of Minerva, and Minerva's companion in Greek mythology was an owl . . . hence the name of this restaurant. With that background out of the way, on to the food: in a word, superb, and the service, likewise.

The Owl opened in winter 1999, and people wondered how the place could survive because it's off the beaten track—

Olmstedville's the Owl at Twilight has become a popular place for New American/Latin fare.

James Swedberg

unless, that is, you live in Olmstedville. But word of mouth about the restaurant's great menu and lovely co-owner/maître d'/waitress/bartender (Joanne Dwyer does it all and makes it look easy) brought in a dedicated clientele. Her husband, Rich, is in the kitchen, creating dishes with flair.

Start with the risotto of the day (billed as an appetizer but big enough for an entrée), the mussels steamed in tequila with habañero chilies, sautéed shrimp and lobster with roasted corn puree, or chive habañero rouile. Proceed to Latin-influenced entrées like seafood stew with coconut milk and plantain broth; grilled skirt steak with parsley and oregano chimichuri and sweet potato fries; or grilled rack of lamb with serano and rosemary aioli. Linger over flourless chocolate cake with homemade espresso ice cream, various flavors of sorbet, or an apple and raisin empanada with chili ice-cream *cageta*. Or head to the bar for an after-dinner glass of fine sherry, Madeira, or port. The wine list here is excellent, with delicious but obscure Italian, Spanish, and South American wines you probably won't find elsewhere in the Adirondacks.

POTTERSVILLE

The Wells House
518-494-5995
www.thewellshouseny.com
6 Olmstedville Road
Open: Year-round
Cuisine: Contemporary American
Serving: B, L, D
Price: Inexpensive to Expensive
Credit Cards: AE, MC, V
Reservations: Recommended for the
    Country
Handicap Access: Yes

In fall 2007 new proprietors Vince and Marion McCann reopened the historic Wells House, offering two separate dining facilities—the upscale **Country**, open for dinner only, and the **Once Upon A Moose Café**, a bar and lounge offering breakfast, lunch, dinner, and Wi-Fi.

Chef Dan Palmer's menus for the dining room and café are creative and fantastically ambitious. Choices will change with the seasons, and mostly fresh, local ingredients will be incorporated into all dishes. At the Country, start with oxtail soup or chilled scallops on a tarragon-seasoned grilled squash cake with saffron vinaigrette, followed by grilled medallions of venison with rosemary French toast and maple demi-glace, or roasted Loch Duart salmon with black bean sauce and tomato corn salsa. Desserts include apple fritters in caramel sauce, a pear tart, and other delicious choices.

At the café, try a thin-crust pizza or cheese fondue or a duck quesadilla or a panini. Get your comfort food to go, or enjoy it on the newly refurbished wraparound bar. While the McCanns offer a lengthy wine and beer list, at press time a liquor license is still pending because of the Wells House's proximity to a church next door.

SPECULATOR

Melody Lodge
518-548-6562
www.melodylodge.com
NY 30
Open: Year-round; Wednesday through
    Sunday in winter
Cuisine: American
Serving: L, D
Price: Moderate to Expensive
Credit Cards: AE, D, MC, V
Reservations: Suggested
Handicap Access: No

Melody Lodge feels almost like an Adirondack Great Camp, with its antiques, massive stone fireplaces, and lovely view down Page Hill toward Lake Pleasant. The rambling inn (there are ten guest rooms with shared baths upstairs) was built in 1912 as a singing school for young girls, and became a restaurant and hotel in 1937.

The lodge's menu is interesting, with unexpected choices, like salmon with artichoke and tomato salsa and roast duckling with Grand Marnier sauce. Seafood fans will be happy with the numerous fresh offerings; the only purely vegetarian entrées are eggplant parmesan and feta pasta, although a call ahead would yield something special. Steaks are good, with a delicious portabella mushroom and sirloin combination occasionally presented. There's a small, very reasonably priced wine list and a well-chosen selection of desserts, with homemade rice pudding at the top of the list.

Lighter fare in the taproom is available, too, including clams in ale, a quiche of the day, hickory-smoked spare ribs, wings, and sesame salmon salad.

THENDARA

Frankie's Taste of Italy
315-369-2400
2824 NY 28
Open: Year-round, Wednesday through Sunday
Cuisine: Italian
Serving: D
Price: Moderate to Expensive
Credit Cards: D, MC, V

Reservations: Recommended, but not accepted in summer
Handicap Access: Yes

Frankie and Tina Zammiello—who had a very successful Italian restaurant in Utica, a city known for great ethnic food—brought their authentic flavors first to Old Forge, but in spring 2007 moved their operation to a bigger space (a former fireplace shop) in Thendara. They've earned a faithful year-round following. Some patrons claim Frankie's food is "better than sex."

The pasta couldn't be fresher or the hospitality warmer. Be prepared to wait for a table in high summer. Frankie checks every plate thoroughly, and he refuses to rush diners through a meal. If you have to wait, rest assured you'll get the same personal attention as those ahead of you.

Frankie's Italian approach to a New York strip steak is inspired. Veal and chicken dishes are exceptional. But be sure someone at the table tries Riggies Anna, rigatoni with a light sauce and morsels of homemade sausage. Greens—spinach sautéed in olive oil—spiked with garlic and topped with cheese are the signature appetizer. Salad comes to the table in a huge bowl for family-style serving, accompanied by the house balsamic vinaigrette (a secret Zammiello recipe, so don't even ask). Bread—hot, crusty—comes right from the oven to your table. For dessert, there's spumoni, cannelloni, and other traditional Italian sweets.

ROAD FOOD AND QUICK BITES

Lake George and Southeastern Adirondacks
Bolton Landing's **Frederick's** is open year-round, and a casual lakeside spot for cocktails, a summertime Sunday raw bar, and live music (518-644-3484; www.fredericks restaurant.com; 4870 Lakeshore Drive). In Chestertown, **Anywhere's a Better Place to Be** (518-494-5888; www.anywheresabetterplacetobe.com; 6332 US 9) has all sorts of choices,

including the "Heart Attack Yak-Yak-Yak": four buffalo wings, two chicken tenders, three mozz sticks, and French fries. **The Garrison** (518-668-5281; 220 Beach Road, near Million Dollar Beach), in Lake George, offers a friendly bar festooned with college pennants. Here you'll find delicious lunches. For great margaritas and Mexican appetizers—and excellent homemade guacamole—try **S. J. Garcia's** (518-668-5111; 192 Canada Street). And **Cafe Vero**, serving breakfast and lunch, is one of the coolest places around (518-668-5800; 185 Canada Street). **Porreca's Restaurant & Lounge** (518-668-5259; www.nordicks.com; 2897 Lake Shore Drive) serves breakfast, lunch, dinner, and desserts it claims are "to die for." In Warrensburg, **Bill's Restaurant** (518-623-2669; 3915 Main Street) makes a fine roast-turkey sandwich and serves breakfast all day. **George Henry's** (518-623-5186; www.georgehenrys.com; 3735 Main Street) has a lengthy selection of grilled sandwiches, wraps, and, on Tuesday nights, all-you-can-eat chicken wings. **Dragon Lee** (518-623-3796; 35 Main Street, next to Stewart's) has a huge Chinese menu with decent carry-out options; sauces tend to be syrupy, so ask for spicy, not sweet. **Mountain Sun Market & Café** (518-623-4303; 3749 Main Street) is a nice place that sells homemade soups, wraps, deli sandwiches, and good coffee.

Champlain Valley

In Elizabethtown, **Arsenal Inn** (518-873-6863; 7581 Court Street) makes a good breakfast, especially if you like griddle-toasted biscuits and crisp bacon. Port Henry has the popular **Golden Palace** for Chinese takeout (518-546-7950; 3266 Broad Street). Deborah Mackey, the **Gourmet Gal** (518-585-6309; www.thegourmetgal.com; 59 Montcalm Street), serves breakfast, lunch, and dinner at her café, in Ticonderoga, and makes fresh soup, bread, and desserts. Westport's the **Galley Restaurant** (518-962-4899; www.westportmarina.com; 20 Washington Street) isn't recommended for dinner, but in summer it's a fun spot for cocktails and late-night bar food; on weekends there's usually live music. The **Inn on the Library Lawn** (518-962-8666; www.theinnonthelibrarylawn.com; 1234 Stevenson Road) serves lovely breakfasts and lunches. At the **Sportsman's Dinette** (518-963-8399; 3745 Main Street), in Willsboro, you can get reliable diner fare.

High Peaks and Northern Adirondacks

In Keene, at **Tip a Canoe** (518-576-97756; www.tip-a-canoe.net; NY 73) you can order light fare or full dinner entrées. Service is inconsistent, but that's OK on the deck, where you can sip a beer and watch the traffic flow into the High Peaks, particularly on weekends. In Lake Placid, in winter, check out Wednesday "brat nights" at the **Alpine Cellar** (518-523-2180; 2830 Wilmington Road). We love the endless German beer list and the guy in lederhosen playing the accordion. **Chair 6** (518-523-3630; www.chair6.com; 5993 Sentinel Road) has breakfast burritos, good sandwiches, salads, and soups. **Charlie's Restaurant** (518-523-9886; 157 Main Street) is a convenient place for a cocktail and a bite to eat. Expect good margaritas, tasty enchiladas, tacos, fajitas, etc., at **Desperados** (518-523-1507; 2090 Saranac Avenue, next to Top's Express). **Mr. Mike's Pizza** (518-523-9770; 2742 Main Street), owned and run by Mike and Nia Nicola, has great pizza with all kinds of exotic toppings, good eggplant parmesan, and big, delicious salads for eat-in (though there are usually huge tables of kids) or carry-out; they deliver, too. Another Nicola's enterprise, **Nicola's On Main Mediterranean Cuisine & Grill 211** (518-523-5853; www.nicolasand grill211.com; 211 Main Street), is the massive restaurant across from the Olympic Center. The food is really good here, but customers often gripe about a long wait for a table and the service. Many locals eat at the bar where customer service is super. The **Lake Placid Pub & Brewery** (518-523-3813; www.ubuale.com; 813 Mirror Lake Drive), also known as P.J.'s, is home to excellent, relatively inexpensive fare, from ribs to quesadillas to specialty burgers. Wash it down with ale or beer made on-site. **Simply Gourmet** (518-523-3111; 1983 Saranac Avenue) is simply delicious for an upscale deli lunch. In Saranac Lake, check out the **Blue Moon Café** (518-891-1210; 46 Main Street) for breakfast, lunch, or early dinner in a popular downtown hangout. Cold River Coffee is roasted downstairs, panini sandwiches or real turkey on a homemade roll are good bets. From Memorial Day to Labor Day, **Donnelly's** is, without a doubt, the place for soft-service ice cream (518-891-1404; intersection of NY 86 and 186). The **Lakeview Deli** (518-891-2101; 137 River Street) is the place to go for a quick lunch in the Adirondacks' All-America City. In summer boaters crisscross Lake Flower for the soft ice cream at **Mountain Mist Ice Cream** (260 Lake Flower Avenue). Insiders say **Sweet P's** has a fantastic chicken sandwich and crisp French fries (518-891-6733; 67 Broadway). Paul Johnson's **Bakery at Standard Falls Garden** (518-946-8328; NY 9N) is the spot for delicious lunches and pastries in warm moths, in Upper Jay. In Wilmington, the **Country Bear** (518-946-2691; 5830 NY 86) bakes good homemade bread for its French toast and sandwiches. The **Evening Hatch** (518-946-1219; 5545 NY 86) is an angler's haven—one of the waitresses has been known to decorate her long nails with paintings of trout flies—with reasonable breakfasts. **Steinhoff's Sportsman's Inn and Restaurant** (518-946-2220; www.steinhoffssportsmansinn.com; NY 86) has backwoods tavern ambiance, with a bar frequented by locals and the après-ski crowd. The bartender at the **Wilderness Inn** (the place along NY 86 bedecked year-round in lights) knows how to make a fine mixed drink; light fare ordered in the bar, such as the chicken and fish

Boaters hungry for a cone can dock behind Mountain Mist Ice Cream, in Saranac Lake. Annie Stoltie

sandwiches, is recommended, but if you want traditional meat and potatoes, hunker down in the dining room in front of the fireplace (518-946-2391; 5481 NY 86).

Northwest Lakes

In Cranberry Lake, the **Stone Diner** (315-848-2678; 7179 NY 3) is a cheerful place with good chow and ice cream. The **Cranberry Lake Lodge** (315-848-3301; www.cranberrylakelodge.com; 7202 NY 3) is popular for drinks and fried food among snowmobilers and boaters. Order some grub from the **Windfall House Bar & Grill**'s (315-848-3559; www.windfallbarandgrill.com; 550 Tooley Pond Road) pub menu. Paul Smiths's **Sampsons Bar & Grill** (518-327-5252; www.samsonsbarandgrill.com; 9667 NY 30) is a new hangout with live music, occasional jam sessions, and a decent menu. In Star Lake, the **Blue Spruce Bar & Restaurant** (315-848-2116; 4180 NY 3) is a local hangout that is revered for its burgers. **Mountain Gate Café** (315-848-9992; NY 3) has a complete and reasonably priced menu for breakfast, lunch, and dinner, plus ice cream. The **Adirondack Café** (518-856-9298; 5 N. Main Street), a.k.a. the Igloo, is a novel spot for a bite in St. Regis Falls. In Tupper Lake, **Main Street Restaurant** (518-359-7449; 79 Main Street, in "the Junction") is clean and good, with terrific

In summer anglers make up much of the Cranberry Lake Lodge's clientele; in winter it's popular with snowmobilers. Annie Stoltie

homemade soups and pies. The **Swiss Kitchen** (518-359-3513; 92 Park Street), same block as the theater, serves hearty breakfasts and diner-style lunches and dinners.

Central and Southwestern Adirondacks

The **Glenmore Hotel Bar & Grill**, in Big Moose, is a year-round hangout (popular with snowmobilers and paddlers) for drinks and burgers (315-357-4891; www.glenmorebarandgrill.com; Big Moose Road). In Eagle Bay, the **North Woods Inn** (315-369-6777; www.northwoodsinnresort.com; 4920 NY 28) has a lovely dining room that overlooks Fourth Lake. Chef Dave Thompson's menu is expansive. In Inlet, **Kirsty's Red Dog Tavern** (315-357-5502; South Shore Road) has good bar food, including chicken wings, quesadillas, and bruschetta. There's the venerable nineteenth-century **Adirondack Hotel** (518-624-4700; www.adirondackhotel.com; NY 28), in Long Lake, where hungry patrons can choose between casual meals in the Lake Street Café or a more formal setting in the Victorian dining room. **Trapper's Tavern** (518-251-2500; www.copperfieldinn.com; Copperfield Inn, 307 Main Street) is a sports bar with occasional live music; it has good burgers, sandwiches, and fries. In Northville **Klippel's Kozy Korner Café & Deli** (518-

863-8550; 221 Bridge Street) serves breakfast in the summer, and lunch and dinner year-round. Stop by for burgers and specialty sandwiches in a café setting. For basic diner fare, open for breakfast and lunch, try **Main Street Kitchenette** (518-863-4362; 132 North Main Street). In Old Forge, the **Muffin Patch** (315-369-6376; 2946 NY 28) serves breakfast, lunch, and dinner in July and August and breakfast and lunch the rest of the year. Some top picks there are Belgian waffles with pecans and strawberries, roast-pork club sandwich, spinach salad, chicken gumbo (with real okra, something most Adirondackers have yet to appreciate), and ice-cream specialties like the pecan turtle sundae or the McCauley Mountain Volcano, which is multiple scoops of ice cream with multiple toppings, perfect for a serious appetite. The best burger in Old Forge can be found at **Slickers** (315-369-3002; NY 28, near the covered bridge); we also like the nachos with guacamole and salsa.

If you're entering the Adirondacks from Amsterdam or Gloversville, here are a couple of options for inexpensive food: In Rockwood, at the very southern tip of the Adirondack Park, try the **Rockwood Tavern** (518-762-9602; 4700 NY 29) for inexpensive lunches and dinners. Pizza, served all day, is the best around. In Speculator, **King of the Frosties** (518-548-3881; NY 30) has soft-serve ice cream, as well as good burgers, salads, and excellent Filipino noodle soup. Open breakfast, lunch, and dinner. New in 2006, the **Lake House Grille**, in Wells, has an eclectic menu; live music on Saturday evenings in summer is a big draw (518-924-2424; www.lakehousegrille.com; NY 30).

The former Big Moose Supply Company, which catered to Big Moose vacationers in the early- to mid-1900s, is now the Glenmore Hotel Bar & Grill. Courtesy of Jim Autenrith

ADIRONDACK FOOD PURVEYORS

Bakeries

The Adirondack Park used to be balloon-bread heaven, but as the twenty-first century dawned, several great new bakeries have opened. Some are in remote locales so call ahead for hours. Bear in mind that some places are operating in former gas stations and might not look as cute as bake shops in the suburbs; the proof is in the pie crust—or the muffins, or the sticky buns. Also, bakeries that are open seven days a week in July and August usually cut back their hours when Labor Day rolls around.

Blue Moon Café (518-891-1310; 55 Main Street near the town hall, Saranac Lake). Nice storefront café serving full breakfasts and lunches, light evening meals, with full-service coffee bar. Homemade muffins and desserts. Open year-round.

Blues Berry Bakery (518-523-4539; 26 Main Street, next to the Palace Theatre, Lake Placid). Real European-style strudels, croissants, Napoleons, and tortes made by Rainer Schnarrs. Open year-round.

Café Sarah Bakery & Coffee Shop (518-251-5959; 260 Main Street, North Creek). Unbeatable éclairs, scones, pies, biscotti, pumpkin bread, smoothies, and coffee bar. Grab a fresh mozzarella and pesto sandwich or ham and brie with apples.

Crown Point Bread (518-597-4466; www.crownpointbread.net; 2744 Main Street, Crown Point). Yannig Tanguy makes true French country bread in a wood-fired oven; scones, sweet rolls, baguettes, and sandwiches. Open year-round.

You can't miss the dome-shape Adirondack Café, a. k. a. the Igloo, in St. Regis Falls.

Courtesy of Kelly Kilgallon

Lake Flour Bakery (518-891-7194; 23 River Street, Saranac Lake). The best baguettes around; chewy semolina bread; strawberry-cheese, chocolate, and plain croissants; bagels; homemade ice-cream sandwiches. Open Monday through Saturday winter; daily in summer.

Merrick's Bakery (518-962-2280; corner of Lewis Road and NY 22, Wadhams). Old-world-style bakery in what was once the Agway building in the middle of town. Specialties include brick-oven baked wheat, rye, and whole grain breads, and French baguettes. Open year-round.

Nathan's Adirondack Bakery (315-369-3933; Crosby Boulevard, Old Forge, around the corner from Old Forge Hardware). Nathan's is the place for wonderful, chewy bagels and bialys; the dense, crusty eight-grain bread is good, too. Cinnamon buns, sour-cream doughnuts (heaven!), bran muffins, pizza slices, and special-occasion cakes are highly recommended. Open weekends during the school year; daily in July and August.

Nicole's Gourmet Coffee Shop & Bakery (518-863-9119; 102 North Main Street, Northville). Fresh-baked goods, and specialty coffee and tea. Open year-round.

Seneca's Trading Post (518-597-4422; NY 9N near the road to the bridge, Crown Point). Don't let the funky-looking exterior deter you: There's good baking going on here. Excellent coffee cakes with sweet fillings; nice round loaves of sunflower seed bread. Try whatever's fresh out of the oven.

Sherwood Forest Bakery (518-924-7825; www.sherwoodforestbakery.com; Sunset Circle, Wells). Focaccia, Jewish rye, bagels, Kaiser rolls, semolina, and other fresh-baked goods. Open year-round.

Soulshine Bagel (518-523-9772; 2526 Main Street, Lake Placid). Fresh chewy bagels, breakfast and lunch sandwiches on homemade bread, super veggie burgers. Open year-round.

Spruce Mountain Bakery and Pizza (518-623-2911; US 9, between Chestertown and Warrensburg). Seen from the highway, Spruce Mountain Bakery looks too sad, but do check it out. The Danishes and other gooey, sweet rolls are very good, and the light, buttery onion rolls are excellent. Real, crusty, Italian bread is made every morning; the cannolis are first-rate. Open year-round.

BREWPUBS

Adirondack Pub & Brewery (518-668-0002; www.adkpub.com; 33 Canada Street, Lake George). On-site brewing; seven flavors to pick from on tap. Lunch and dinner are served; call ahead because hours shift with the seasons.

The Great Adirondack Steak & Seafood Company (518-523-1629; www.greatadirondacksteakandseafood.com; 34 Main Street, Lake Placid). Fresh microbrews made on premise brewery (seven-barrel microbrews; tours offered). Lunch and dinner available; tourists pack the place and the restaurant doesn't take reservations, so arrive early.

Lake Placid Pub & Brewery (518-523-3813; www.ubuale.com; 14 Mirror Lake Drive, across from the Mirror Lake beach). A half dozen ales and beers on tap at all times, some brewed in the back of the restaurant, including very strong and popular Ubu Ale and Lake Placid IPA. Pub-style lunch and suppers are available; there's a deck overlooking Mirror Lake for summer sipping.

CANDY

Candy Cottage (315-369-2310; 3031 Main Street, Old Forge). All sorts of candy, but the fudge gets the highest marks.

The Candy Man (800-232-4626; www.candymanonline.com; NY 86, Wilmington; and 61 Main Street, Lake Placid). There are no shortcuts here, no high-tech approaches; the Candy Man even makes all the fillings in its Wilmington shop and covers them with a generous layer of chocolate. Dark chocolate, especially with coffee cream filling, is quite good. The sugar-free candies get high marks for tasting remarkably like the real thing. Open year-round; mail orders available.

Croghan Candy Kitchen (315-376-3014; www.lcida.org/cndykchn; NY 812, Croghan). Just outside the Blue Line, but famous for old-fashioned candy. The Beaver Tails, cordial cherries, and hand-dipped chocolates are superb. Open year-round.

R. Chocolate (518-523-9919; 153 Main Street, Lake Placid). Exotic chocolates, truffles, pastries, bagels, and more, made on the premises. Open year-round.

DELICATESSENS, CAFÉS, AND GOURMET SHOPS

Adirondack General Store (518-494-4408; www.adkgeneralstore.com; 899 East Shore Drive, Adirondack). Good soups and sandwiches; interesting salads. Open year-round.

Brick Oven Café (518-359-2112; www.brickovencafe.net; 10 Cliff Avenue, Tupper Lake). Paninis, soups and salads, wraps, frappes, espresso, and homemade baked goods. Open year-round.

Greens & Beans (518-354-8160; 3 Bloomingdale Avenue, Saranac Lake). Coffee, tea, sandwiches, wraps, smoothies. Open year-round.

Kalil's Grocery (315-357-3603; NY 28, Inlet). This independent grocery makes splendid tabouli, hummus, cole slaw, and potato salad in its deli, and has authentic pita bread sent up from a Lebanese bakery in Utica. You can buy other great local products here, too: garlic burst salsa made by Seventh Lake House and some truly incendiary hot sauce from the Red Dog Tavern. Open year-round.

Lakeview Deli (518-891-2101; 137 River Street, Saranac Lake). Exceptional sandwiches, heat-up dinners, fresh salads, gourmet treats like spinach-artichoke dip, fine coffees, Rockhill bread, and exotic sodas are on tap at the Lakeview, just across the street from Lake Flower. The friendliest service in the area. Open year-round.

North Creek Deli & Marketplace (518-251-2977; 282 Main Street). Good sandwiches, homemade bread, gifts, clothing, and books. Open year-round.

Saranac Sourdough (518-523-4897; 2126 Saranac Avenue, across from Howard Johnson's, Lake Placid). Good sandwiches (Cuban pork, real roast turkey, etc.) on craft bread or hard rolls baked on the premises; interesting salads, including roast eggplant and antipasto; great big cookies, muffins, and sweets. Take home a loaf of the raisin brioche for great toast; leftovers make wonderful bread pudding. Sit at one of the half-dozen tables for breakfast, lunch, or dinner, or place your order to go. One drawback to an otherwise fine place: The service can be really slow (and sometimes temperamental) no matter the time of day, or whether you wish to take out or eat in. Call in your order ahead for best results. Open year-round.

Simply Gourmet (518-523-3111; 1983 Saranac Avenue, Lake Placid). Simply delicious sandwiches, wraps, and baked goods; deli; gourmet goods; eat-in or takeout. Open year-round.

Standard Falls Garden (518-946-8328; NY 9N; Upper Jay). In summer try Paul Johnson's fantastic lunches—the menu changes daily. Also available: Johnson's fresh-baked bread, pastries, and muffins. Open Memorial Day through Labor Day.

Town & Country Gourmet (518-576-9731; 1888 Main Street, Keene Valley). Imported condiments, fine coffee, candy, bread, and frozen entrées perfect for feeding unexpected guests in style. A remarkably extensive selection of Silver Palate sauces, designer chips, exotic cheeses, fancy soft drinks, and summer dinner fare to take home. You can spend some serious cash here. Good sandwiches, salads, and soups to eat on the deck or take away. Open year-round.

Villa Vespa (518-523-9789; 2250 Saranac Avenue, Lake Placid). Great homemade Italian sauces, frozen and dry pastas, and ready-to-heat entrées are available in a bright, clean shop (the first floor of a Victorian home). Salads are good, ample enough for two; risotto, lasagna, and eggplant parmigiana portions likewise. Entrées generally include chicken cacciatore, sole, and a meat-based special. The mushroom raviolis—about 3 inches in diameter—are wonderful. Open year-round.

Village Meat Market (518-963-8612; 3609 Essex Road, Willsboro). Great sandwiches; homemade breads, rolls, and doughnuts. Open year-round.

FARM MARKETS AND ORCHARDS

For information about Adirondack producers, visit www.adirondackharvest.com or call Cornell Cooperative Extension at 518-561-7450 in Clinton County; 518-962-4810 in Essex County; and 518-483-7403 in Franklin County. Adirondack farmers' markets can be found at www.adirondackfarmersmarkets.com; the New York State Department of Agriculture and Markets has a list of statewide markets at www.agmkt.state.ny.us.

Roadside stands are everywhere in the temperate Champlain Valley; look along NY 22 from July through October for good local produce, including Silver Queen corn and heirloom tomatoes.

Adirondack Buffalo Company (518-532-9466; www.adirondackbuffalocompany.com; 3187 Blue Ridge Road, North Hudson). Dorreen and Steve Ossenkop raise a herd of forty or so American bison. Bison products, produce, and other goods are available. Open: Summer, 10 AM–6 PM .

Ben Wever Farm (518-963-8372; 445 Mountain View Drive, Willsboro). Grass-fed beef, poultry, eggs, vegetables, and honey. Open: Summer.

Bessboro Orchards (518-962-8609; NY 9N and 22, Westport). Lou Gibbs has worked hard to establish his small, high-quality orchard and offers many varieties of eating apples that he sells as they're picked. Open: Fall.

Champlain Apiaries (518-963-7593; Essex). Bill Raus and Loretta Suprenant make honey and ice cream; carriage rides by appointment. Call for hours.

Clover Mead Farm (518-834-7306; 938 Mace Chasm Road, Keeseville). Sam Hendron makes artisan cheeses from his Jersey milk cows. On-farm shop. Open: June through October.

Eagle Mills (518-883-8700; NY 29, Broadalbin, 5 miles east of intersection of NY 29 and 30). Water-powered cider mill with bakery. Special events fall weekends, including an antique tractor show in October. Open: Wednesday through Sunday in the fall.

Forrence Orchards (518-643-9527; NY 22, Peru). One of the best-known orchards for McIntosh apples, but also growing Honeycrisp, Gala, Cortland, Empire, Macoun, and Delicious. Open: Daily in the fall.

Gunnison's Lakeshore Orchards (518-597-3363; NY 9N and 22, Crown Point). Honey, jams, cider doughnuts, salad dressings, and all kinds of apples, including Honeycrisp, Gala, Empire, Ida Red, Jonagold, and McIntosh, are available at this impressive roadside orchard. Of course, October is the best time for a visit, but even if you're traveling the highway in the winter, stop in. Gunnison's will ship gift packs to anywhere in the country, in late fall. Open: Monday through Saturday year-round.

Harris Hives (518-656-3420; Kattskill Bay, Lake George). Local honey, available from the source or from numerous outlets around the southeastern Adirondacks, including Common Corners and Oscar's Smoke House. Call for hours.

Harvest Hill Farm (518-963-1127; 691 Sunset Drive, Willsboro). Michael and Laurie Davis. Vegetables and herbs; free-range poultry. Call ahead.

King's Apple Orchard (518-834-7943; Mace Chasm Road, off US 9, Keeseville). This orchard opens in August, offering Tydemans and other early apples; later on in the fall and through December, you can get Paula Red, McIntosh, Cortland, Empire, and Red Delicious apples. Call ahead.

Lakeview Orchards (518-661-5017; 133 County Highway 123, Mayfield). Pick-your-own blueberries and apples, plus cider, maple syrup, honey. Early apples include McIntosh, Macoun, and Empire, followed by Red and Gold Delicious, Cortland, Jonagold, Northern Spy, and Rhode Island Greening. Open: Daily in the fall.

Laughing Duck Farm (518-962-4508; www.laughingduckfarm.com; 792 NY 22, Wadhams). Owner Don McCormick grows micro-greens and fresh-cut natural herbs. Call ahead.

Ledgetop Orchards (518-597-3420; Lake Road, off NY 22, Crown Point). Not too far from the Crown Point bridge, you pick your own sour pie cherries in July, gather drops from the apple orchard in late September, and select the perfect jack-o-lantern pumpkin at the farm stand in October. The stand offers Cortland, Empire, Red Delicious, McIntosh, and Kendall (think of a crunchier Mac) apples beginning in early September.

Maple Grove Farm (518-547-9511; www.nycedarworks.com; 162976 NY 22, Putnam Station). Farm-raised pork, chicken, turkeys, and lamb. Fresh vegetables and honey. Call ahead.

Nettle Meadow Farm (518-623-3372; www.nettlemeadow.com; 484 South Johnsburg Road, Warrensburg). Owner Laurie Raynald makes fresh goat cheese. Call ahead.

Pray's Family Farms (518-834-9130; 391 NY 9N, Keeseville). People come from miles around when the strawberries ripen at Pray's, usually in mid-June. Beside the berries (there are blackberries and raspberries, too), the roadside stand sells homegrown vegetables of all kinds, right up to pumpkin season. The baked goods are delicious. Check out the jack-o-lantern display around Halloween. Call ahead.

Rehoboth Homestead (518-643-7822; www.rhomestead.com; 66 Jabez Allen Road, Peru). Organic produce, poultry, and cut flowers. Call ahead.

Rivermede Farm (518-576-2021; 49 Beede Road, Keene Valley). Owner Rob Hastings sells brown eggs, maple syrup from the farm's sugar bush, and fresh beans, broccoli, herbs, leaf lettuce, asparagus, new potatoes, scallions, squash, tomatoes, carrots, and more from his High Peaks area farm. Wreaths, trees, and gift baskets in winter. Nice farm stand on NY 73. Call ahead.

Rulf's Orchard (518-643-8636; 531 Bear Swamp Road, Peru, off NY 22). Excellent farm stand with vegetables, baked goods (great apple pies), and a variety of apples in the shop or to pick yourself: McIntosh, Macoun, Cortland, Northern Spy, Mutsu, and Spartan. Open year-round.

Tucker Farms, Inc. (518-327-3408; www.tuckertaters.com; 56 Hobart Road, Gabriels). Pick your own strawberries plus Asian vegetables. Down the road is Tuckers Taters, for red, white, blue, and gold spuds. In fall the corn maze is great for kids. Call ahead.

Underwood Herbs (518-425-3306; 172 Chase Road, Chateaugay). Owner Jane Desotelle grows and sells fresh herbs, dried herbs and teas; wild food and medicinal plants. Open: May through October; call ahead for hours.

Valley View Farms (518-585-9974 or 518-585-6502; Hagur Road, NY 9N, Ticonderoga). Just south of the Ticonderoga Country Club you can enjoy another aspect of the country: pick-your-own strawberries mid- to late June, red raspberries in late July, and blueberries spanning both seasons. (Note that fruit ripening depends on the weather; if spring is late and cold, it's best to call ahead to be sure the berries are ready for you.) There's also a farm stand with fresh vegetables open about June 20 through late September.

HEALTH FOODS

Bean's Goods (518-523-4676; www.beansgoods.com; 183 Newman Road, Lake Placid). Bulk organic grains, fruits, nuts, seeds, coffee, tea, and herbs. Lines of animal cruelty–free and environmentally safe products and organic body care available. Fresh local produce on Tuesday and Friday.

Nori's Natural Foods (518-891-6079; 65 Main Street, Saranac Lake, near the downtown parking lot, behind Sears). Nori's has a natural-food deli with daily lunch specials and excellent salads, plus all you'd expect from a good health-food store: bins of grains and flours; jugs of oil, honey, and maple syrup; canisters of herbs; and all sorts of organic and earth-friendly products.

MAPLE SYRUP

Upstate New York is a leading producer of high-quality maple syrup, and Adirondack syrup tastes no different from the Vermont stuff, which seems to get all the glory. Across the park, you can buy local syrup in craft shops, general stores, and farm stands; listed below you'll find a sampling of a few syrup processors who sell directly from their homes and sugar bushes. There are many more folks who make syrup, and they often advertise that fact with a large lithographed tin sign showing a maple leaf.

If you'd like to learn about sap, taps, and boiling off, the **Uihlein-Cornell Maple Sugar Project** (518-523-9337; 60 Bear Cub Road, Lake Placid), a joint project of the New York State College of Agriculture at Cornell University and Henry Uihlein, is open most weekday afternoons from spring through fall. Admission is free; in March and April, you can observe the entire process from the tree to the finished product. The **Up Yonda Farm Environmental Education Center** (518-644-9767; www.upyondafarm.com; Bolton Landing) also has special maple-sugar season demonstrations, as do **Paul Smith's College** (518-327-6227; www.paulsmiths.edu), in Paul Smiths, and the **Adirondack Museum** (518-352-7311; www.adkmuseum.org), in Blue Mountain Lake. The New York State Maple Producers Association includes maple events and lists of products and producers by county on its Web site, www.nysmaple.com.

Adirondack Gold Maple Farm (518-623-9718; 90 Bear Pond Road, Athol). Maple sugar and other candies.

Black Creek Farms (315-346-6566; 7029 Black Creek Road, Croghan). Retail and wholesale maple syrup, cream, maple butters, candies, and gift baskets.

Brandy Brook Maple Farm (518-594-8849; 439 Brandy Brook Road, Ellenburg Center). Maple syrup.

Leadley's Adirondack Sugar Bush (518-548-7093; NY 30, Speculator). Retail maple syrup.

Maple Hill Farm (518-863-4188; Tennantville Road, Edinburg). Retail maple syrup, maple cream, and candy.

Toad Hill Maple Farm, in Athol, offers maple syrup, maple candy, and maple cream, plus tours of its sugaring operation. Courtesy of Kelly Kilgallon

McComb's Oak Hill Maple Farm (518-548-6105; Elm Lake Road, Speculator). Syrup and other maple products.

Mud Road Sugar House (518-863-6313; 261 Mud Road, Ephratah). Syrup, maple cream, and maple candy.

Parker Family Maple Farm (518-493-6761; www.parkerfamilymaple.com; 1043 Slosson Road, West Chazy). Maple candy, cream, cotton candy, and jelly.

Peaceful Valley Maple Farms (518-762-0491; 116 Lagrange Road, Johnstown). Full line of maple products.

South Meadow Farm Maple Sugarworks (518-523-9369; www.maplesugarworks.com; 67 Sugarworks Way, Lake Placid). Full line of maple products.

Toad Hill Maple Farm (518-623-4744; www.toadhillmaple.com; 151 Charles Olds Road, Athol). Maple syrup, maple candy, and maple cream.

Valley Road Maple Farm (518-623-9783; www.valleyroadmaplefarm.com; 190 Valley Road, Thurman). Syrup, cream, candy, and sugar.

Meat Markets

Jacobs & Toney (518-623-3850; 3872 Main Street, Warrensburg). The front of the building proclaims "Meat Store of the North," and the folks here pride themselves on prime beef cut to order, fresh pork, chicken, lamb, and homemade fresh sausage. Open year-round.

Oscar's *Adirondack* Mountain Smoke House (800-627-3431; www.oscarssmoked meats.com; 22 Raymond Lane, Warrensburg). For more than half a century, the Quintal family has been smoking up a storm—wonderful hams, sausages, cheese: in all, about 200 different smokehouse products—in a shop just off Warrensburg's main street. You can get smoked trout, boneless smoked chicken breast, smoked lamb, and eight kinds of bacon. Chorizo and andouille sausage are great, from the freeze case. Oscar's blends a variety of flavored cheese spreads, and the shop has gourmet crackers, condiments, and mixes. It's also a terrific butcher shop for fresh meat and bratwurst, weisswurst, knockwurst . . . all kinds of wieners and wursts. Open year-round; online mail-order catalog available.

Shaheen's Super Market (518-359-9320; 252 Park Street, Tupper Lake). A family-run store staffed by genuinely friendly folks who still carry grocery bags out to your car, Shaheen's is known for quality meats cut to order. Occasionally, homemade Lebanese specialties appear in the cooler; the *kibbe* is very popular and sells out within hours. Open year-round.

Two Brother's Meat Market (518-585-2522; 81 Montcalm Street, Ticonderoga). Fresh cut meats and deli; "the meatiest subs around." Open year-round.

SPECIAL EVENTS: BARBECUES AND COMMUNITY SUPPERS

Throughout the Adirondacks, civic organizations, fire departments, historical societies, and church groups put on a variety of public suppers. Don't be shy! Visitors are welcome at these affairs, and furthermore, the food is generally inexpensive and delicious.

A North Country favorite is the chicken barbecue, with half chickens marinated in a tangy lemon-based sauce cooked outdoors over the coals. The trimmings are usually an ear of roasted sweet corn, potato salad, cole slaw or tossed salad, roll, watermelon wedge, and coffee. There are also steak roasts, clambakes, pig roasts, and buffets. Listed below (in chronological order) are some of the annual feasts found in the Adirondacks; check local newspapers for more.

Secret Recipe Chicken

Chances are if you asked a local grillmeister for the chicken barbecue sauce recipe, you'd be told it was a family heirloom not to be shared with casual visitors. Actually most of the Adirondack barbecues rely on variations of the Cornell University recipe; since 1949, the Poultry Science Department of the school has distributed close to a million copies of it. Below you'll find that secret marinade so that you can replicate smoky, lemony chicken at home.

I cup good cooking oil
I pint cider vinegar (some folks use lemon juice and vinegar)
3 Tbsp. salt (or less, to taste)
I Tbsp. Bell's (or other) poultry seasoning
½ tsp. black pepper (or more, to taste)
I egg

Beat the egg vigorously. Then add the oil and beat again to emulsify the sauce. Add other ingredients. Dunk chicken halves in the sauce and let marinate in the refrigerator for a few hours. While grilling over hot coals, baste each side.

The sauce will keep in the refrigerator for about a week. Enough for eight to ten half chickens. Leftover barbecued chicken makes superb chicken salad.

Newcomb Lions Club Chicken Barbecue (518-582-3211; Newcomb). At the Newcomb Town Beach, on Lake Harris, off NY 28N, first Saturday in July.

North Creek Fire Department Chicken Barbecue (518-251-2612; North Creek). At the North Creek Ski Bowl, off NY 28, first Saturday in July.

Chilson Volunteer Fire Department Chicken Barbecue (518-585-6619; Ticonderoga). At Elks Field, NY 22, fourth Sunday in July.

Keene Valley Fire Department Open House and Chicken Barbecue (518-576-4444; Keene Valley). At the firehall, on Market Street, last Sunday in July.

Newcomb Fire Department Steak Roast and Parade (518-582-3211; Newcomb). Rib-eye steaks, burgers, corn, hot dogs, and salads, at the Newcomb Town Beach, last Sunday in July.

Penfield Museum Heritage Day Chicken Barbecue (518-597-3804; Ironville). On the museum grounds, third Saturday in August.

Plump Chicken Inn (518-251-2229; Minerva Historical Society, Olmstedville). Chicken and biscuits, homemade pickles and salads, real mashed potatoes, plus live music and costumed serving wenches, at Minerva Central School, third Saturday in August.

Lewis Volunteer Fire Company Ox Roast (518-873-6777; Lewis). At the firehall, US 9, last Saturday in August.

Keene Fire Department Open House and Chicken Barbecue (518-576-4444; Keene). At the firehall, on East Hill Road, last Saturday in August.

Indian Lake Pig Roast (518-648-5112; Indian Lake Volunteer Fire Department, Indian Lake). Succulent roast pork and stuffing, steamed clams, homemade clam chowder, corn, and burgers, held at the firehall, on NY 28, Saturday before Labor Day.

Westport Marina Labor Day Lobsterfest (518-962-4356; Westport). Lakeside feasting at Westport Marina. Advance tickets necessary; first Saturday in September.

Blue Mountain Lake Volunteer Fire Department Chicken Barbecue (518-352-7710; Blue Mountain Lake). Organized by a vegetarian, but plenty of mouth-watering food for hungry carnivores, at the firehall, NY 28, first Sunday in September.

Hopkinton Turkey Pie Supper (315-328-4684; Hopkinton Town Hall, NY 11B). This fundraiser, which has been organized annually for four decades, benefits the Hopkinton Congregational Church and takes place the second Saturday in September.

Speculator Lions Club Roast Beef Fall Dinner (518-548-4521; the Inn at Speculator). Benefits Lions Charities, the third weekend of October.

WINE AND LIQUOR STORES

You can purchase wine and liquor in numerous shops throughout the park. Some of the smaller places are adjacent to taverns, or even the owners' homes; you may have to ring a buzzer to have them open up for you. Note that New York State liquor stores and grocery stores that sell beer and wine coolers can't sell alcohol until after noon on Sundays.

A handful of shops stand out for their good selection of domestic and imported wines and knowledgeable staff. In Lake George, **Duffy's Wines & Liquor Store** (518-668-2103; 46 Amherst Street, opposite Price Chopper) is a convenient spot to stock up on spirits. Plus, they deliver. In Lake Placid, **Outpost Wine & Spirits** (518-523-5898; in the Price Chopper plaza) has an excellent selection and a friendly, helpful staff. Although it has less to choose from, **Terry Robards's Wines and Spirits** (518-523-9072; 243 Main Street) is also worth a visit; Robards was a columnist for the *Wine Spectator*. North Creek has **Adirondack Spirits** (518-251-3898; Main Street). In Saranac Lake, **Saranac Lake**

Discount Liquors (518-891-4104; 40 Main Street), has friendly service. There's also **High Peaks Wine & Spirits** (518-891-0400; www.highpeakswine.com; 251 Broadway), where the clerks really know their stuff. There's lots to choose from at **Adirondack Wine & Liquor** (518-891-4556; 153 Lake Flower Avenue) and case discounts are available. Farther south in the Adirondacks, in Speculator, Elizabeth Gillespie at **Speculator Spirits** (518-548-7361; NY 30) knows her grapes, and her tiny shop offers an astonishing variety of wines. In Inlet, talk to Maryann and Dan Ryan at the **Wine Shop** (315-357-2477; 155 NY 28, next door to the movie theater) for advice about great German, French, Australian, and domestic wines. Tupper Lake's **Ray's Liquor Store** (518-359-3450; 4 Demars Boulevard) is modest looking but has a surprising selection of excellent wine at competitive prices.

6

Culture

From Folkways to Fine Arts

Culture—seen as noble endeavors like fine arts, literature, classical music, theater, ballet—may have been beyond the reach of the old-time Adirondack woodsman and his family, but the wild landscape inspired many a visiting painter, writer, and composer. It could be argued, too, that because of popular fiction, weekly national magazines such as *Harper's* and *Every Saturday,* and Currier and Ives prints, the Adirondacks was much better known as a particular place 130 years ago than it is today.

Consider *The Last of the Mohicans.* The harrowing trip from what's now called Cooper's Cave, in Glens Falls, to the fort at Ticonderoga went along the Hudson River, crossed over the Tongue Mountain range, skirted the west side of Lake George, and reached Lake Champlain at its narrowest spot. The adventure is now firmly etched in American letters, but few of us connect the journey with actual sites in the Adirondacks. James Fenimore Cooper visited Warrensburg and Lake George in 1824 to research his story and observe the landscape. Many of his landmarks are inaccessible today, but you may catch a few glimpses if you follow in his tracks, on modern-day US 9.

Visual artists recorded the region in a state of bucolic grace, before the iron industry's charcoal kilns darkened the skies and lumbermen cut the forests; beginning in 1830, and on up through the turn of the twentieth century, the countryside practically swarmed with painters. Thomas Cole, Frederic Church, and other Hudson River School artists depicted perfect scenes of glowing mountains, shimmering lakes, and tiny villages. Frederic Remington, who was born just north of the Adirondacks, in Canton, New York, sketched trappers' cabins and lumber camps near Cranberry Lake. The English painter A. F. Tait also showed the manly side of the wilderness, in oil paintings of groups of hunters and fishermen and portraits of their prey. Many of Tait's images were used for Currier and Ives

From 1918 to 1934 Georgia O'Keeffe spent summers at her husband Alfred Stieglitz's family estate in Bolton Landing, where she painted wildflowers, barns, clouds, and the wild moods of Lake George.
Private collection

lithographs, but the popularity of those Adirondack prints also created demand for Tait imitators; more than one-hundred different Currier and Ives images illustrate scenes of the region, from maple-sugaring parties to ice fishing to humble log farmsteads.

Winslow Homer painted woodsmen in Keene Valley and at the North Woods Club, near Minerva, in a terse, impressionistic style that helped cinch his career as America's premier watercolorist. His illustrations of guides and lumberjacks that appeared in weeklies brought the backwoods to urban homes. Harold Weston, who lived most of his life in Keene Valley, made bold, burly oils of the High Peaks that were exhibited widely from the 1920s to the 1970s, and now reside in major collections throughout the world. Rockwell Kent spent his last decades at his farm near Au Sable Forks, painting the Ausable River Valley and designing houses for friends. David Smith, one of the best-known sculptors of the modern age, lived in Bolton Landing; today, in a field overlooking Lake George, many of his abstract sculptures remain. Unfortunately, the property is rarely open to the public.

Composers found their muse in the woods and waters, too. A few parlor ditties made the rounds in the late-nineteenth century, like "Floating for Deer" and "The Adirondacks: A Gallop." And the immense popularity of canoeing in the 1890s created a whole new genre of songs celebrating the sport, such as "Paddlin' Madeline Home." But more important, two of the finest modern composers, Charles Ives and Béla Bartók, both spent extended periods working in the Adirondacks. Ives created the Concord piano sonata while visiting Elk Lake, and began the *Universe Symphony,* one of his last major works, while at the summer home of his wife's family, in Keene Valley. Bartók wrote the *Concerto for Orchestra* at a modest cottage in Saranac Lake, where he was taking the "cure" for tuberculosis.

With only a few exceptions, women are notably absent from this list of resident and visiting artists. Poet Jeanne Robert Foster grew up in grinding poverty in Johnsburg and went on to be an editor of the *Transatlantic Review.* Her circle of friends included Ezra Pound, T. S. Eliot, and John Butler Yeats, father of the Irish poet. Her poetry-and-prose memories of her youth were published in *Adirondack Portraits: A Piece of Time.* Painter Georgia O'Keeffe experienced Lake George with her photographer husband, Alfred Stieglitz, creating elemental scenes of water, rock, sky, and undulating hills. Although her Adirondack tenure was a short period in a long and productive life, this region launched O'Keeffe's signature style.

Traditional women's work—needlecrafts like fine samplers, coverlets, and quilts, so revered in other parts of the country—is rare here. Farm wives made clothing and bedding, but relatively few examples of these have survived the hard pioneer life. Instead, folk arts from the nineteenth-century Adirondacks reflect the lumbering days, in songs and tall tales, and the Gilded Age, in rustic furniture and decorative items local carpenters and blacksmiths made for the Great Camps. Traditional music can be heard at many of the arts centers listed elsewhere in this chapter; the best place to see rustic furniture in quantity and quality is at the Adirondack Museum, in Blue Mountain Lake. Throughout the park the icons of North Country material culture are ubiquitous: the guideboat, pack basket, lean-to, and Adirondack chair. The art of storytelling is also alive and well in informal gathering places and on stage.

The cultural scene in the Adirondacks is remarkably diverse, showcasing native skills and crafts and honoring the fine artists who visited the region. There's real community pride in libraries, arts centers, theater companies, historic-preservation groups, museums, and musical ensembles. But beyond the good feelings and active schedules, there's also a level of excellence that rises above sometimes-humble settings. The following descriptions will tell you where to go in search of history and the arts throughout the park, but you'll have to call or check Web sites to get a current schedule of events. Local radio stations and weekly papers offer calendars of events; *Adirondack Life* magazine and www.adirondacklife.com have a bimonthly calendar, "Inside & Out," which covers the entire Adirondack Park, but always call ahead to confirm ticket availability and location of an event. Web sites for tourism offices listed in Chapter 9 usually contain schedules of cultural events.

ARCHITECTURE

Compared to touring Vermont, with its many postcard-pretty villages, old-house hunting in the Adirondack Park may be disappointing to the historic-preservation buff. Bear in mind that settlements, especially in the central Adirondacks, are considerably newer than New England towns, and that the communities dating back to the 1700s along Lakes George and Champlain were destroyed during the French and Indian and Revolutionary Wars. Devastating fires before 1900 in towns such as Tupper Lake and Indian Lake obliterated hundreds of prosperous businesses and attractive homes. However, along the eastern edge of the park, there are several lovely towns with fine buildings dating back two centuries.

The celebrated Adirondack rustic style of architecture, which borrowed designs from Swiss chalets, English half-timber buildings, pioneer cabins, and even Japanese tea-houses, isn't easy to view from the comfort of an automobile. You'll find rustic lodges and boathouses in all their twiggy glory mainly on remote lakeshores. **Sagamore Great Camp** (315-354-5311; wwwsagamore.org), the former Vanderbilt summer estate near Raquette Lake, and **White Pine Camp** (518-327-3030; www.whitepinecamp.com), the summer White House of Calvin Coolidge, in Paul Smiths, on Osgood Pond, are two Great Camps you can easily see. Visiting **Santanoni Preserve** (518-897-1302; www.dec.ny.gov), near Newcomb, requires a 10-mile round trip without a car, but it's well worth the effort. You can reach the impressive rustic complex by walking, cross-country skiing, snowshoeing, biking, or riding a horse-drawn wagon.

Adirondack Architectural Heritage (518-834-9328; www.aarch.org; 1790 Main Street, Keeseville) is a parkwide nonprofit organization devoted to historic preservation. Tours of public and private sites in summer and fall, lectures, workshops, and technical assistance to building owners are just a few of the programs and services it offers.

Lake George and Southeastern Adirondacks

For many travelers, Warrensburg is the gateway to the Adirondacks. Along Main Street (US 9), there are stately nineteenth-century homes, from Greek Revival and Gothic cottages to Italianate villas and Queen Anne mansions. The oldest building in Warrensburg, diagonally across from the car dealership on US 9, is a former blacksmith shop, dating back to 1814. Along the Schroon River (NY 418 West), you can see remnants of the village's industrial center in several old mill buildings; the **Grist Mill** (518-623-8005; 100 River Street), now an excellent restaurant, still has grindstones, conveyors, chutes, and grain-grinding apparatus, plus a great river setting. Also on US 9, Chestertown has a historic district with colorful Greek Revival houses and restored storefronts.

Champlain Valley

Essex County is rich in architectural sights. Beginning in the south, the town of Ticonderoga is a major destination for history lovers. Fort Ticonderoga is about 2.5 miles north of the village on NY 22, but you can find the crumbling walls and rusting cannons of

Fort Mount Hope by exploring near the old cemetery on Burgoyne Street, not far from the village waterworks. At the head of the main drag, Montcalm Street, is a replica of John Hancock's Boston home, built by Horace Moses in 1926. Moses made his fortune with the Strathmore Paper Company and funded many town beautification projects, including the Liberty Monument, a bronze statue by Charles Keck that's in the center of the traffic circle across from Hancock House. **Pride of Ticonderoga** (518-585-6366; www.prideofticonderoga.org; 111 Montcalm Street), a nonprofit revitalization organization, offers a walking tour brochure that highlights Ticonderoga's bustling nineteenth-century industrial history.

At Crown Point, there were several fortifications along the lake harkening back to the French occupation of the Champlain Valley in the 1730s; near today's bridge to Vermont, off NY 22, is Fort Crown Point. West of Crown Point is Ironville, a well-preserved gem of an early-nineteenth-century community, with several white clapboard homes, a lovely church, numerous farm buildings, and peaceful, tree-shaded roads. On the way to Ironville, in Factoryville, you'll see the only octagonal house in the Adirondacks.

Historic markers erected by New York State abound along NY 22 as you approach Port Henry. The original settlement here supplied lumber for the forts at Crown Point and for Benedict Arnold's naval fleet. Later, the discovery of abundant iron ore shaped the town. Evidence of this prosperity appears in an ornate downtown block, elaborate churches, and the exuberant high Victorian Moriah Town Office building, formerly the headquarters of the Witherbee, Sherman & Co. Iron Company. In the carriage house next to the town offices the **Iron Center** (518-546-3587) is a museum dedicated to local mining and railroads.

The Essex County seat is Elizabethtown, founded in the 1790s. The county courthouse complex is impressive, and about half a mile away are brick buildings built by the illustrious Hand family, which produced a dynasty of civic leaders and attorneys, including Supreme Court Justice Learned Hand. The well-preserved Greek Revival Hand House and the Hands' freestanding law office are on US 9, near the flashing light. About 8 miles east of E'town, along Champlain's shore, is Westport, which was first settled in 1770. Buildings from that era have all disappeared, but a few homes near the lake on Washington Street, off NY 9N and 22, were built in the 1820s. Westport was a vital port, shipping iron, lumber, wool, and other farm products before the Civil War, and a thriving summer community afterward. Following NY 22, you pass Gothic cottages and impressive stone houses overlooking the lake. Between Westport and Essex, on NY 22, is the tiny farm community of Boquet, with its odd little octagonal schoolhouse, occasionally open to the public.

The Adirondack community richest in architectural treasures is undoubtedly Essex; it's as if the clock stopped here in 1856. There are wonderful Dutch Colonial, Georgian, Federal, and Greek Revival buildings in excellent repair throughout the town: check under "Historic Buildings and Districts" for more information. Continuing on NY 22, Willsboro and Keeseville contain many historic buildings. Keeseville has several homes made of buff-pink native sandstone that date back to the 1830s, and buildings in the full range of nineteenth-century styles from Dutch Colonial to Federal and Greek Revival to Gothic Revival and Romanesque. The Stone Arch Bridge over the Ausable River, built in 1842, is the largest single-span arch bridge in the country. From the bridge you can see the huge factory buildings that made horseshoe nails, an indispensable product of the nineteenth century.

The monograph *Crossing the River,* published by the **Friends of the North Country** (518-834-9606), highlights historic bridges in Essex County, and makes an excellent driving tour. Another interesting driving tour for the historic Boquet River is published by the **Boquet River Association** (518-873-3688; www.boquetriver.org); the loop begins just off the Northway and follows the river through Elizabethtown, Wadhams, Whallonsburg, Boquet, and Essex to its northernmost point, at Willsboro, and then goes south to Reber and Lewis. A map with interpretive signs along the route has been published by the **Champlain Valley Heritage Network** (1-866-843-5253) and highlights historic sites, farmsteads, local industries, and vistas from Keeseville to Ticonderoga.

High Peaks and Northern Adirondacks

The Ausable River Valley holds many historic buildings that are visible along roadways. South of Keene Valley, it's worth a quick detour off NY 73 at St. Hubert's to see the massive Victorian inn, the Ausable Club. It is "members only" inside the building, but you can get a rare glimpse of the kind of hostelry that visitors once enjoyed throughout the Adirondacks. North on US 9, between Upper Jay, Jay, and Au Sable Forks, there are fine Federal-style stone and brick houses and churches; in Jay, the sole remaining covered bridge in the Adirondacks, built in 1857, was dismantled in 1997 and rebuilt with an adjacent park in 2007. It's a fine place for a stroll, a picnic, and a popular spot for a dip in the Ausable River (John Fountain Road, 1/4 mile off US 9).

   The Olympic Village—Lake Placid, that is—has only a few buildings left from its earliest days, when the settlement of North Elba, near the ski jumps, was an iron-mining center: One that's easy to spot on Old Military Road is the Stagecoach Inn. Another, off Old Military, is John Brown's Farm.

   In Saranac Lake, which was incorporated in 1892, the tuberculosis industry inspired its own architecture, manifested in "cure porches" and "cure cottages." The group **Historic Saranac Lake** (518-891-4606, www.historicsaranaclake.org) sponsors lectures, concerts, and tours from time to time highlighting buildings of note; ongoing restoration projects include the cure cottage used by composer Béla Bartók and the 1894 laboratory of tuberculosis pioneer Dr. E. L. Trudeau.

   Tucked back in the woods at Loon Lake, partly visible from County Road 99, is a surprising collection of cottages and other elaborate buildings designed by celebrated architect Stanford White.

   North of Newcomb on County Road 25, en route to the Upper Works trailhead for the High Peaks, is the Adirondac blast furnace, an immense stone monolith built in 1854 that produced high-quality iron. Continuing on the road, you'll pass a faded white farmhouse—now being restored—that was the office of an early iron-mining concern. (The other deserted buildings nearby belonged to the 1890s Tahawus Club.)

   On Upper Saranac Lake, which straddles the High Peaks and Northwest Lakes regions of this book, there are fine examples of rustic architecture, but you'll need a canoe to paddle by **Wenonah Lodge**, **Prospect Point** (now a Christian summer camp), **Camp Wonundra** (now "The Point," a sumptuous inn; 1-800-255-3530; www.thepointresort.com), **Pinebrook**, **Eagle Island** (now a Girl Scout camp), and **Sekon Lodge**. Don't expect more than a tantalizing peek at these places hidden by the trees, and for heaven's sake, don't go ashore on private lands.

The Adsit log cabin, on Willsboro Point, was built by Yankee settlers in the 1790s. James Swedberg

Northwest Lakes

For boathouse fans, Upper St. Regis Lake, near Paul Smiths, has many lovely waterfront buildings, in high rustic, cobblestone, and shingle style. You'll need a boat to make this tour, and you'll have to paddle several miles from the public put-in on Keese Mill Road, west of Paul Smith's College. Also, a reminder—respect landowners' privacy by staying away from docks and shore.

Central and Southwestern Adirondacks

The heart of the Adirondacks has few pre–Civil War buildings, but it's home to a vernacular architectural style that honors French Canadian and Yankee traditions in steep-roofed, simple homes. Olmstedville, off NY 28N, has a cluster of Greek Revival storefronts and houses from the 1840s. Farther south, on NY 30, Wells has nicely restored Victorian-era homes along the Sacandaga River. For rustic architecture, a boat tour of Raquette Lake on the *W. W. Durant* (315-354-5532), a replica of an old steamboat, allows glimpses of Great Camps such as **Pine Knot** (the first rustic camp designed by William West Durant), **Camp Echo**, and **Bluff Point** (the former Collier estate). **Great Camp Sagamore** (315-354-5301, www.sagamore.org) occasionally offers tours of nearby rustic estates, as does **Adirondack Architectural Heritage** (518-834-9328; www.aarch.org).

ARTS CENTERS & ARTS COUNCILS

The arts scene is surprisingly lively in this, New York's most rural area, thanks in part to the long-time leadership of the New York State Council on the Arts. Through grants from the state council to arts presenters, producers, and nonprofit galleries, and a re-grant program to fledgling and volunteer organizations, all kinds of arts programs can be found in all kinds of towns.

Adirondack Art Association

518-963-8309
Schoolhouse Gallery, Essex
Open: Spring through Fall
Open: Daily

This community gallery showcases regional professional artists in solo and group exhibitions, from quilts to photography and watercolor paintings to designer crafts.

Adirondack Lakes Center for the Arts

518-352-7715
www.adk-arts.org
NY 28, next to the post office, Blue Mountain Lake
Open: Year-round

Since 1967 this multi-arts center has brought a full palette of programs to Blue Mountain Lake, population 150 (give or take). The Adirondack Lakes Center for the Arts, a former garage, has presented hundreds of concerts, including performances by the Tokyo String Quartet, Doc Watson, Tony Trischka, Paul Taylor, the Seldom Scene, Odetta, Livingston Taylor, and more. There have been sand mandala workshops as well as classes on the art of the Japanese tea ceremony.

Exhibitions include contemporary paintings, sculpture, photography, and crafts; Adirondack furniture; children's art; and traveling shows. Complementing the shows are intensive workshops for adults, on weekends in fall and winter and weekdays in summer. Programs for kids range from crafts, dance, and music workshops to family presentations of storytelling, New Vaudeville, and magic.

Arts Center/Old Forge
315-369-6411
www.artscenteroldforge.org
NY 28, Old Forge
Open: Year-round
Remarks: Gift Shop open daily in July and August; during exhibitions the rest of the year

The Arts Center/Old Forge is the oldest community-arts organization in the region, and the organization continues to grow, change, and pursue new directions. At press time a 27,000-square-foot eco-friendly facility—already a model for renewable energy—is under construction. It will house expanded programs in visual and performing arts, ecology, and early childhood education.

Annual events include the Adirondacks National Exhibition of Watercolors (August–September) and the October quilt show. The arts center hosts visiting theater troupe productions; classical concerts as well as bluegrass, folk, and jazz programs are staples in a packed performance schedule.

In summer, there are local history outings and lectures and presentations by artists, naturalists, and writers. Throughout the year, the arts center shows contemporary American and foreign films and offers workshops for adults and children, from boat building to basketry, jewelry making to the healing arts.

Arts Council for the Northern Adirondacks
518-962-8778
www.artsnorth.org
NY 22, Westport
Open: Year-round

Launched as an advocacy group for local artists and craftspeople, for twenty years the Arts Council for the Northern Adirondacks has published its comprehensive *Annual Arts Directory,* also available online, listing exhibitions, lectures, fairs, music, theater, dance performances, and children's programs. In addition, the organization offers grants to working artists, presents traditional and contemporary musicians from the region in different towns, and sponsors traveling juried art shows.

Bluseed Studios
518-891-3799
www.bluseedstudios.org
24 Cedar Street, Saranac Lake
Open: Year-round

Ever since 2002, a 7,000-square-foot 1930s train warehouse has been home to a bustling arts scene—it's an oasis for artists and the community. Between its must-see exhibitions, studio space, weekend and one-day workshops—everything from printmaking and letter-press to ceramics and photography—and eclectic music series that features regional and national performers such as Eliza Gilkyson and Martin Sexton and every musical genre you can think of, the place is hopping all year. Bluseed's popular "open-minded" mic nights draw all sorts of entertainers.

Fulton Chain of Lakes Performing Arts Council, Inc.
315-357-3799
P.O. Box 680, Inlet
Open: Summer

For a decade the Fulton Chain group has brought professional musicians to small central Adirondack communities that may never have seen the likes of a piccolo or timpani. Each summer—always the last Friday in July—the council sponsors a concert featuring the entire Syracuse Symphony Orchestra in a tent overlooking Fourth Lake.

Lake George Arts Project
518-668-2616
www.lakegeorgearts.org
Old County Courthouse, 1 Amherst Street, Lake George
Open: Year-round

The Lake George Arts Project (LGAP) is decidedly hip. Over the years, it has organized contemporary sculpture shows on the frozen lake, in tree-shaded Shepard Park, and alongside the scenic highway up Prospect Mountain. The offices and gallery are on the ground floor of the old courthouse in the center of town; special exhibitions featuring artists with national renown are scheduled monthly. LGAP offers free outdoor concerts; sponsors a popular day of rock and roll and chili cook-offs called Bands and Beans (March), the sizzling Lake George Jazz Festival (September), and the Black Velvet Art Party (November), a celebration of terminal tackiness.

Lake Placid Center for the Arts
518-523-2512
www.lpartscenter.org
17 Algonquin Drive, Lake Placid
Open: Year-round

The Lake Placid Center for the Arts (LPCA) has metamorphosed through different identi-ties, beginning as the Center for Music, Drama, and Art; then as an accredited two-year arts school; and next as the summer campus for the Parsons School of Design. Now a multiarts center with a community focus, the facility is topnotch. The center boasts a theater that seats about 300, well-equipped studios, and a bright, airy gallery. Exhibitions are slated throughout the year, with two juried shows for regional artists and craftspeople.

Presentations include visiting theater groups; contemporary American and foreign films; folk, blues, and zydeco music; dance-company residencies; gala programs by soloists of the New York City Ballet; and excellent classical and chamber performances. The Lake Placid Sinfonietta plays here on Sunday evenings in July and August.

The LPCA also is home to the Community Theater Players, who offer three or four shows annually. For kids, in July and August, there's the free "Young and Fun" performance series on weekday mornings.

Lower Adirondack Regional Arts Council

518-798-1144
www.larac.org
7 Lapham Place, Glens Falls
Open: Year-round

The Lower Adirondack Regional Arts Council (LARAC), formed in 1972, is based just out-side the Blue Line in Glens Falls, and it supports the arts in Warren and Washington Counties. LARAC showcases the art of regional and visiting artists in its gallery and juried arts-and-craft shows and sells their work in its retail shop. It provides grants to local tal-ents and arts programs; presents concerts at City Park in Glens Falls; and hosts workshops, theater, and meeting space for such groups as the Adirondack Audubon Society and the Hudson Valley Watercolor Society.

The Lake George Arts Project's Lake George Jazz Festival is one of the hottest events in the park. Delfeayo Marsalis performs in Shepard Park. Courtesy of the Lake George Arts Project; photograph by Andrzej Pilarczyk

Sacandaga Valley Arts Network

518-321-3468
www.svanarts.org
Box 660, Northville
Open: Year-round

The Sacandaga Valley Arts Network (SVAN), serving those in the Sacandaga River watershed in the south-central Adirondacks since 1997, spreads its knowledge and philosophy through programs ranging from group shows of internationally acclaimed artists to drum circles to quilt and film clubs to watercolor and photography classes. A coffeehouse series brings music to the region in winter; in summer, alfresco performances at Northville Park provide audiences with a variety of music—gospel, bluegrass, country, folk, and rock. SVAN also sponsors a classical music series at the Batchellerville Presbyterian Church, in Edinburg.

Tannery Pond Community Center

518-251-2505
www.tpcca.org
228 Main Street, North Creek
Open: Year-round

Opened in 2002, the state-of-the-art Tannery Pond Community Center is home to North Creek's cultural scene. It hosts chamber music players and theater groups, and houses a gallery that features work by regional artists. The facility has four multipurpose meeting rooms, a caterer's kitchen, and a two-story, 150-seat auditorium.

In summer kids, ages 5 to 18, can enroll in the center's Art and Nature Camp, where they take fieldtrips to collect natural pigments for painting, learn to make Raku pottery, create shadow puppets, build floating boat sculpture, and participate in other wilderness-inspired projects.

Upper Jay Art Center

518-946-8315
www.upperjayartcenter.com
Recovery Lounge, Upper Jay Upholstery, NY 9N, Upper Jay
Open: Year-round

At first this place was an underground scene—locals gathering at brothers Scott and Byron Renderer's Upper Jay Upholstery to hear the Renderers and their friends play music. But nowadays the shop's 1920s former Model-T factory headquarters, just across the Ausable River from what was the Land of Makebelieve theme park, is a thriving arts spot drawing more and more culture seekers.

At press time the Renderers have applied for nonprofit status, turning their funky, cavernous space, called the Recovery Lounge in the hours they aren't upholstering furniture, into an arts center. Impromptu performances by regional acts as well as visiting groups will continue, as will Arts Nights, drawing hundreds of people to see paintings, sculpture, and films by local artists, some of whom are nationally recognized, such as photographer Nathan Farb and painters Harold Weston and Paul Matthews. Recent theater productions at the Recovery Lounge include David Mamet's *American Buffalo* and an adaptation of Keene-based writer Russell Banks's *The Fisherman*. In the works: filmmaking, acting, fine arts, and dance classes.

CINEMA

During the silent-film era, the Adirondacks provided a backdrop for popular films, including *The Shooting of Dan McGrew, The Wilderness Woman, Glorious Youth,* and dozens more; the movie industry thrived for more than a decade in unlikely places such as Saranac Lake, Plattsburgh, and Port Henry. There were cowboy scenes at Ausable Chasm, "Alaskan" trapper cabins in Essex County farmyards, and adventures supposedly set in South America, Siberia, and Switzerland. As the cameras rolled, Washington crossed the frozen Delaware—somewhere on the Saranac River.

In 1941, Alfred Hitchcock's only comedy, *Mr. and Mrs. Smith,* was set at the Lake Placid Club. A few years later, *Lake Placid Serenade,* which featured dizzying reels of figure skating and Roy Rogers as king of the Placid winter carnival, was a commercial success. In 1958, scenes of *Marjorie Morningstar* were shot in Schroon Lake; local extras were paid the princely sum of $125 per day.

The stars came back to the Adirondacks for *The Good Shepherd* (2006), starring Matt Damon, Angelina Jolie, William Hurt, and Robert De Niro. Sagamore Great Camp was the setting for several scenes, including a spectacular opening shot of the main lodge.

Today there are many places where you can catch foreign, classic, and first-run films. Several vintage theaters have been lovingly restored in recent years. **The Lake Placid Film Forum** (518-523-3456; www.lakeplacidfilmforum.com) runs a silent film series using the Palace Theater and its magnificent Robert Morton theater organ. The Film Forum, held in early June each year, has screenings, panel discussions, and workshops in various Lake Placid venues led by critics, screenwriters, actors, and directors. Participants have included Steve Buscemi, Kyra Sedgewick, Martin Scorsese, Russell Banks, among others. The Hollywood buzz is louder than the blackflies in springtime.

Lake George and Southeastern Adirondacks

Carol Theater (518-494-0005; Riverside Drive, Chestertown). First-run films; children's matinees. Open Memorial Day–fall.

Strand Theater (518-532-9300; Main Street, Schroon Lake). Restored Art Deco building, with state-of-the-art sound system. Open May–October, plus some off-season weekends.

Champlain Valley

Champlain Valley Film Society (518-963-8662; www.cvfilms.org). Nonprofit organization that features movies year-round, at venues in Essex, Elizabethtown, Westport, and Willsboro. In August, Ballard Park, in Westport, is backdrop for the society's films.

High Peaks and Northern Adirondacks

Hollywood Theatre (518-647-5953; Main Street, Au Sable Forks). Newly restored two-screen Art Deco theater. Recent releases and independent films. Open year-round; call for schedule.

Lake Placid Center for the Arts (518-523-2512; Saranac Avenue, Lake Placid). Foreign and contemporary American film series in fall, winter, and spring.

Palace Theater (518-523-9271; Main Street, Lake Placid). Art Deco stenciling in the lobby and displays of Lake Placid movie memorabilia. Current American releases, four screens. Open daily, year-round.

Northwest Lakes

State Theater (518-359-3593; www.tupperlakemovies.com; Park Street, Tupper Lake).
Recent releases.

Central and Southwestern Adirondacks

Strand Theatre (315-369-2792; www.strandoldforge.com; NY 28, Old Forge). Beautiful
vintage cinema with three screens. Two or three shows nightly in each theater; children's
matinees; occasional foreign films in cooperation with the Arts Center/Old Forge.

Tamarack Movie House (315-357-2001; NY 28, Inlet). Recent films five nights a week.
Closed for a month in fall and a month in spring; call for schedule.

CRAFTS AND FINE ARTS INSTRUCTION

Weave a traditional Adirondack pack basket, spin a skein of wool, tie a trout fly, build a
guideboat or master digital photography, paint en plein air, or sculpt vases in numerous
centers across the park. Classes for adults range from one- or two-day intensive programs
to week-long sessions; prices vary. Always call ahead to register for these workshops.

Lake George and Southeastern Adirondacks

Lake George Arts Project (518-668-2616, www.lakegeorgearts.org; Old County
Courthouse, Lake George). Bookbinding and letterpress workshops, among many others
offered to adults. Open year-round.

Up Yonda Farm Environmental Education Center (518-644-9767,
www.upyondafarm.com; NY 9N, Bolton Landing). Kids build bluebird and butterfly houses
and other crafts. Open year-round.

High Peaks and Northern Adirondacks

Adirondack Mountain Club Heart Lake Program Center (518-523-3441; www.adk.org;
Adirondack Loj Road, Lake Placid). Painting, photography, and traditional craft classes that
make use of a spectacular natural setting for both materials and inspiration. Open year-round.

Bluseed Studios (518-891-3799, www.bluseedstudios.org; 24 Cedar Street, Saranac
Lake). Letterpress, photography, ceramics, drawing, and other classes for adults. Open
year-round.

Lake Placid Center for the Arts (518-523-2512; www.lpartscenter.org; Saranac Avenue,
Lake Placid). Watercolor painting, photography, basketry, jewelry making, figure drawing,
and other classes for adults. Open year-round.

Newcomb Adirondack Park Agency Visitor Interpretive Center (518-582-2000,
www.adkvic.org; NY 28N, Newcomb). Weekend classes in Adirondack basketry, fly tying,
watercolor painting, and nature photography. Also children's programs on most Saturdays.
Open year-round.

Northwest Lakes

Paul Smiths Adirondack Park Agency Visitor Interpretive Center (518-327-3000;
www.adkvic.org; NY 30, Paul Smiths). Workshops similar to the Newcomb Center, above.

Central and Southwestern Adirondacks

Adirondack Lakes Center for the Arts (518-352-7715; NY 28, Blue Mountain Lake).
Painting, photography, guideboat building, woodcarving, rug hooking, rustic furniture
making, basketry, and other crafts. Open year-round.

Adirondack Photography Institute (216-531-2155, www.adkpi.org; Inlet).
Photography—digital and traditional—workshops taught by expert instructors at various
venues. Open year-round.

Arts Center/Old Forge (315-369-6411; NY 28, Old Forge). Watercolor painting,
wooden boat building, quilting, pottery, rug making, lampshade making, basketry, and
more. Open year-round.

DANCE

Since 1987 the **Lake Placid Center for the Arts** (518-523-2512) has sponsored the
Rebecca Kelly Ballet (www.rebeccakellyballet.com) in residence each summer. Here the
company develops new ballets and works with kids in its OnStage performance summer
day camp. In the fall the sensual and athletic **Elisa Monte Dance** company spends three
weeks in residence at the LPCA. The arts center also presents modern dance concerts,
including stars of the New York City Ballet, throughout the year.

ELDERHOSTEL

The Adirondack Park is a favorite learning laboratory for Elderhostel, the international educational organization for people over age 60. These inexpensive, informal, noncredit courses
last five or six days and cover history, nature, folklore, and even culinary arts, in sessions led
by local experts. Some Elderhostel programs have included digital photography, birding,
canoe building, trail maintenance, landmark preservation, and regional architecture.

Adirondack sites for Elderhostel programs include **Sagamore Great Camp** (315-354-
5311; www.sagamore.org), in Raquette Lake; **Adirondack Mountain Club** (518-523-3441;
www.adk.org), at the **Heart Lake Program Center**, outside Lake Placid; **Fort Ticonderoga**
(518-585-2821; www.fort-ticonderoga.org); and the **Sagamore** (518-644-9400;
www.thesagamore.com), in Bolton Landing. For more information contact Elderhostel (1-
800-454-5768; www.elderhostel.org).

HISTORIC BUILDINGS AND DISTRICTS

More than two dozen sites in the Adirondack Park are on the National Register of Historic
Places; oddly enough, all of the state land—the Adirondack Forest Preserve—is a historic
district, although there are very few important buildings left on these lands for reasons too
complicated to explain fully here. Suffice it to say that once private land becomes public
property, the terrain is to be returned to a natural condition, and structures must be
destroyed. At least, that's the usual scenario. Santanoni Preserve, a 115-year-old rustic
enclave described earlier in this chapter, has been stabilized thanks to the efforts of
Adirondack Architectural Heritage and the Town of Newcomb.

Listed below is a selection of architecturally significant places, forts, interesting homes,
and local preservation organizations.

Lake George and Southeastern Adirondacks

Marcella Sembrich Opera Museum
518-644-2431 or 518-644-9839
www.operamuseum.org
Lake Shore Drive/NY 9N, Bolton Landing
Open: Mid-June through Labor Day; daily 10–12:30, 2–5:30
Admission: $2

During the early decades of the twentieth century, Bolton Landing was a mecca for opera stars and composers, such as Louise Homer, Samuel Barber, and Gian Carlo Menotti. From 1921–1935, Marcella Sembrich, a Polish soprano, made her home here. Born Marcella Kochanska, she was a European sensation, and in 1898, she joined New York's Metropolitan Opera. Sembrich founded the vocal departments of the Juilliard School in Manhattan and the Curtis Institute in Philadelphia; during the summers, a select group of students came to her cottage studio. The studio, now a charming little museum, houses a collection of music, furniture, costumes, and opera ephemera related to Sembrich's brilliant career, including tributes from the leading composers of the day. Don't miss a stroll around the lakeside trail for a peaceful moment. Music lectures and concerts by young composers are held on summer afternoons and evenings; curator Richard Wargo is a highly regarded opera composer.

Champlain Valley

Crown Point State Historic Site
518-597-4666
739 Bridge Road, Crown Point
Open: May through October; Wednesday through Monday, 9–5
Handicap Access: Yes
Admission: Adults, $3; seniors, $2; children 12 and under, free

Poking into Lake Champlain, there's a thumb-shape point that parts the waters, with Bulwagga Bay to the west and the long reach of the lake on the east. The sweeping view to the north once provided an ideal spot for guarding the territory. The French built a gargantuan stone octagon here in 1734, Fort St. Frederic, which was attacked repeatedly by the British in 1755–1758 and finally captured by them in 1759. Colonial forces launched their assault on the British ships in Lake Champlain from Crown Point in 1775.

In 1910, the ruins of the French, British, and colonial forts were given to New York State. There's an excellent visitor center that explains the archaeology and political history of this haunting promontory through exhibits and audiovisual programs, and several miles of interpretive trails winding around stone walls and redoubts.

Essex Community Heritage Organization
518-963-7088
Station Road, Essex
Open: Year-round, 9–5

During the brief peaceful period between the French and Indian War and the American Revolution, William Gilliland, an Irish immigrant, bought up huge tracts of land along

Lake Champlain. He envisioned a string of prosperous communities, and by 1770, had established Essex. Unfortunately, the town lay smack in the path of General Burgoyne as British troops marched from Canada to Saratoga and, just a decade after the settlers arrived, their town was destroyed.

By 1800, Essex was again thriving thanks to iron mining, stone quarrying, a tannery, shipbuilding, and other commerce. By 1850, the population of the town was 2,351, but when railroads came to eastern New York, in the 1870s, fortunes changed for Essex and other lakeside towns. The 1850s marked the peak of the town's prosperity.

Thereafter the population dwindled steadily to its current level of about a thousand residents. Because of this decline, and the lack of economic opportunities, there was little need for new housing; old buildings were preserved out of necessity. Today Essex contains one of the most intact collections of pre–Civil War buildings in the Northeast. The Essex Community Heritage Organization has published an excellent booklet describing the dozens of fine homes, inns, and commercial buildings in town, and a self-guided walk through town in summer or fall is a delightful way to spend a day.

Penfield Homestead Museum

518-597-3804
www.penfieldmuseum.org
Old Furnace Road, off NY 74, Ironville
Open: June through Columbus Day, Thursday through Sunday, 11–4
Admission: Adults, $4; children, $2
Handicap Access: Partial

A sign in the front yard of the homestead makes an astonishing claim: The site purports to be the birthplace of the Electrical Age. In 1831 Allen Penfield used a crude electromagnet to separate iron ore from its base rock, thus testing electricity in an industrial application for the first time.

Ironville today is a lovely, quiet spot so different from its heyday as the center of a major iron industry in 1830–1880, when smoke from the smelters filled the skies and the clatter of rock crushers ceased only after dark. The complex is an open-air museum dedicated to the local mines, forges, and old railroads, with an eclectic historical collection in the homestead itself, a white-clapboard Federal building, circa 1826. The other buildings along the lane in town are mainly Greek Revival, in excellent condition; there's a self-guided walking tour of the 550-acre grounds that takes you for a nice hike in the woods to find remnants of the days of iron. In mid-August, the museum sponsors Heritage Day, a festival of traditional crafts and skills, with wagon rides and a chicken barbecue. In October, there's the Penfield's Apple Folkfest, a celebration that includes crafts, music, and every kind of apple dessert imaginable.

High Peaks and Northern Adirondacks

Historic Saranac Lake

518-891-4606
www.historicsaranaclake.org
89 Church Street, Suite 2, Saranac Lake
Open: Year-round

The health care history of Saranac Lake is unique, and in 1980, Historic Saranac Lake was launched to commemorate the special architecture that evolved to help tuberculosis patients get fresh air and sunlight. Numerous cure cottages and sanatorium-related buildings have been recognized on the National Register of Historic Places. The group has published a walking tour, presents lectures and conferences, and is a key player in restoring the village's railroad station, a stop on the Adirondack Scenic Railroad, as well as tuberculosis-treatment pioneer Dr. Edward Trudeau's laboratory.

John Brown Farm
518-523-3900
115 John Brown Road, Lake Placid
Open: Year-round

In 1849, abolitionist John Brown came to North Elba, near Lake Placid, to help Gerrit Smith foster a self-sufficient enclave for free black citizens. Smith owned more than 100,000 acres across northern New York, and his plan was to give forty acres to each would-be African American homesteader. The idea may have been doomed from the start since the families—many of them from northern cities—were not prepared to farm in the harsh climate or work the rugged, unprepared ground. Most of the residents of "Timbuctoo," as it became known, left within a few years of their arrival. Brown himself lived only a few years at the farm, leaving his family for months at a time to pursue a failing wool business and work on antislavery concerns. After his final adventure in Harper's Ferry, Virginia (modern-day West Virginia), Brown was executed on December 2, 1859.

John Brown's humble farmstead, near Lake Placid, tells about the abolitionist's life in the Adirondacks.
James Swedberg

In 1870 the property was acquired by a group of the abolitionist's admirers. Today the farmhouse and outbuildings, managed by New York as a state historic site, contain exhibits related to John Brown's life, and his "body lies a-mouldering in the grave" nearby. John Brown's birthday, May 1, brings a major gathering of people to the site sponsored by the Westport-based group, John Brown Lives! (518-963-4618).

Robert Louis Stevenson Memorial Cottage and Museum
518-891-1462
www.pennypiper.org
11 Stevenson Lane, Saranac Lake
Open: July 1 through Columbus Day, Tuesday through Sunday, 9:30–noon, 1–4, or year-round by appointment
Admission: $5

In 1887–1888, Robert Louis Stevenson took the "cure" for tuberculosis in Saranac Lake. He slept in an unheated porch all winter and took in plenty of fresh air while hiking and skating. During his Adirondack stint, Stevenson wrote a dozen essays for *Scribners,* started *The Master of Ballantrae,* and worked on *The Wrong Box,* a collaborative effort with Lloyd Osbourne. In a letter to Henry James, the Scotsman described his tiny cottage: "Our house . . . is on a hill, and has sight of a stream turning a corner in the valley—bless the face of running water!—and sees some hills too, and the paganly prosaic roofs of Saranac itself; the Lake it does not see, nor do I regret that; I like water (fresh water, I mean) either running swiftly among stones, or else largely qualified with whiskey."

The Stevenson Society was founded in 1916 to commemorate the writer's life and works; one of the group's original projects was to interest Gutzon Borglum, the sculptor best known for creating Mount Rushmore, in designing a bronze bas-relief depicting Stevenson—now displayed next to the cottage's front door. The society still manages the property and museum, which has displays of Stevenson letters, photographs, memorabilia, and first editions, and sponsors readings and lectures.

Northwest Lakes

Beth Joseph Synagogue
518-359-3580
Lake Street, Tupper Lake
Open: July through August, Tuesday through Friday, 11–3

Built in 1905, Tupper Lake's temple is an elegant structure made of simple pine boards and tall arched windows. Beth Joseph once served an active congregation, but after the 1930s, attendance declined. Scout troops met in the basement, and for a time, a group of Baptists even worshipped there because they didn't have a church of their own. In 1959, the synagogue closed and stood vacant for twenty-five years.

Community interest in the historic building was rekindled by a summer resident who encouraged former temple members to get the structure listed on the National Register of Historic Places and begin restoration work. Local people of all religions pitched in with donated labor, materials, and funds; the ornate embroidered velvet Torah covers were painstakingly restored by a local weaver. Today the facility hosts art exhibitions, concerts, lectures, and other events.

Central and Southwestern Adirondacks

Sagamore Great Camp
315-354-5311
www.sagamore.org
Sagamore Road, off NY 28, Raquette Lake
Open: Memorial Day through October
Tours: Call or visit the Web site for a schedule
Admission: Adults $12; Children $6

Adirondack entrepreneur William West Durant built Sagamore, a massive rustic lodge, along the lines of a Swiss chalet, in 1897, and sold it to Alfred G. Vanderbilt Sr in 1901. Even though the Vanderbilts spent much of their time elsewhere, Sagamore was a self-sufficient village in the heart of the wilderness, with its own farm and a crew of craftsmen to supply furniture, hardware, and boats. Today, the millionaires' complex—main lodge, dining hall, rustic guest cottages, casino/playhouse, open-air bowling alley, and boathouse—and the artisans' barns, carriage house, workshops, and blacksmith shop are open to the public. Two-hour tours are presented by college interns and other volunteers; a highlight is sending a vintage bowling ball down the lane toward the pins to demonstrate the loop-de-loop ball return.

Sagamore is in a gorgeous setting on Sagamore Lake, 4 miles off the main state highway on a rough dirt road. Besides tours, the Great Camp sponsors workshops and conferences; is available for overnight accommodations; has a small gift shop and café; and can be hired for special events like wedding receptions and family reunions. The Sagamore was the backdrop for scenes from director Robert DeNiro's 2006 film *The Good Shepherd,* starring Angelina Jolie and Matt Damon.

Lecture Series

An Adirondack education is possible through numerous public lectures at libraries, museums, town halls, and other sites. The **Lake George Association** (518-668-3558; www.lakegeorgeassociation.org) and **Lake George Land Conservancy** (518-644-9673; www.lglc.org) sponsor year-round talks about local ecology and wildlife in Lake George and Bolton Landing, respectively. The **Wadhams United Church of Christ** (518-564-2293), in Wadhams, has a popular lecture series in a traditional lyceum format. The **Atmospheric Science Research Center** (518-946-2142) on Whiteface Mountain, in Wilmington, presents natural history and science lectures on Tuesdays in July and August. The **Wildlife Conservation Society** (518-891-8872) in Saranac Lake hosts talks throughout the year by wildlife experts on bears, loons and other animals. Tupper Lake–based **Adirondack Public Observatory** (www.apobservatory.org) volunteers give summer evening lectures at the Natural History Museum of the Adirondacks, a.k.a. the Wild Center, also in Tupper Lake. At the **Visitor Interpretive Centers** in Paul Smiths (518-327-3000; www.adkvic.org) and Newcomb (518-582-2000) there are nature, history, and arts presentations year-round. The **Huntington Lecture Series**, in July and August, sponsored by the Adirondack Ecological Center (a major research facility associated with the State University of New York's College of Environmental Science and Forestry), at the Adirondack Park Agency Visitors Information Center in Newcomb, offers an excellent assortment of programs on current environmental topics, as well as fishing, landscape photography, and natural history. **St. William's on Long Point**, in Raquette Lake (315-354-4265; www.stwilliamsonlongpoint.org), a small, shingled church built by William West Durant in 1890, offers summer lectures and concerts in a nineteenth-century church. There is boat access only, so if you don't have one, call ahead to get a ride.

Libraries

There are dozens of public libraries inside the Adirondack Park, and visitors are always welcome, rain or shine. In this wired age, what used to be hallowed halls for books have evolved into key places for visitors and residents to check their e-mail, post photos and videos, and blog about their adventures. And some have Wi-Fi, so you'll often find cars gathering in the library parking lot at all hours to take advantage (Old Forge, for one). Most libraries have books as downloads for MP3 players through cooperating library systems.

Several libraries are known for their special collections of regional books, classic and children's videos, and even mini museums. Many libraries offer children's programs, readings by regional writers, films, travel lectures, how-to sessions, concerts, and even good used books for sale. A sampling of libraries with noteworthy collections, exemplary programs, and fine buildings follows.

Lake George and Southeastern Adirondacks

Caldwell Lake George Library (518-668-2528; 340 Canada Street, Lake George). Films, lectures, workshops.

Horicon Free Public Library (518-494-4189; 6604 NY 8, Brant Lake). Tiny, picturesque cobblestone building perched on the edge of the lake.

Champlain Valley

Black Watch Memorial Library (518-585-7380; Montcalm Street, Ticonderoga). Designed as a medieval-looking "shrine to literacy" in 1905 and named after the 42nd Highland Regiment, which fought at Ticonderoga in 1758.

Paine Memorial Free Library (518-963-4478; 1 School Street, Willsboro). Lovely brick building overlooking the Boquet River. Numerous summer programs, from art exhibitions to traditional craft demonstrations. Ask a librarian about the library's popular "bridge cam."

Westport Library Association (518-962-8219; 6 Harris Lane, Westport). Look for the clock tower. Great old building with fireplaces, antique woodwork, natural lighting, high ceilings, comfy couches, and several computers with Internet access. Lecture series and occasional concerts on the library lawn.

High Peaks and Northern Adirondacks

Keene Valley Library (518-576-4335; www.kvvi.net; 1796 NY 73, Keene Valley). Excellent local history and mountaineering collection with monographs, maps, photographs, and rare books.

Lake Placid Library (518-523-3200; www.lakeplacidlibrary.org; 67 Main Street, Lake Placid). Story hours for children; good general collection.

Saranac Lake Free Library (518-891-4190; www.nc3r.org/slfl; 100 Main Street, Saranac Lake). Extensive Adirondack collection in the William Chapman White Room, open by appointment. Brown-bag luncheon lecture series, evening lectures; gallery featuring local artists; Charles Dickert Memorial Wildlife Museum open in July and August.

Northwest Lakes

Goff Nelson Memorial Library (518-359-9421; 41 Lake Street, Tupper Lake). Good Adirondack collection available to readers; crafts and local history exhibits; lectures.

Joan Weill Adirondack Library (518-327-6211; Paul Smith's College, NY 86 and NY 30, Paul Smiths). Impressive college library, also open to the public. Books, magazines, historical collections, regional archives, and electronic wizardry. Coffee shop downstairs; concert space upstairs.

Central and Southwestern Adirondacks

Johnsburg Library (518-251-4343; 219 Main Street, North Creek). General collection and computer stations.

Northville Public Library (518-863-6922; 341 South Third Street, Northville). A relatively new library supported by the nonprofit Friends of the Northville Public Library.

General collections, lecture series, and story time programs for preschoolers.

Old Forge Library (315-369-6008; 220 Crosby Boulevard, Old Forge). Adirondack collection, lecture series, writers' workshops, storytelling festival, exhibitions, children's programs, performances by Adirondack storytellers.

Raquette Lake Free Library (315-354-4005; 1 Dillon Road, Raquette Lake). Charming turn-of-the-century building with window seats and fireplace; lectures and special programs.

Town of Indian Lake Library (518-648-5444, indianlake.sals.edu/; Pelon Road, Indian Lake). General collection, with lectures and special programs year-round.

MUSEUMS

1812 Homestead Farm & Museum
518-963-4071
112 Reber Road North, Willsboro
Open: May through September, Daily 10–5, or by appointment
Admission: Donation suggested

The past is present at this early farm complex, with an original homestead, barn, and schoolhouse. Families can try making candles, cooking in an open hearth, or gathering eggs. You can meet the farm's resident oxen, sheep, and pigs. Demonstrations include blacksmithing, spinning, gardening, shingle-making, quilting, and other old-time skills. In season, the farm makes apple cider and maple sugar; call ahead to learn about special events like Pioneer Harvest Celebration. Recommended for kids ages 6 to 12.

Adirondack History Center Museum
518-873-6466
www.adkhistorycenter.org
7590 Court Street/US 9, Elizabethtown
Open: Memorial Day through Columbus Day; Monday through Saturday, 9–5, Sunday, 1–5
Admission: Adults $5; $4 seniors, $2 children 6–18
Handicap Access: Yes
Remarks: Gift shop

If all the military skirmishes along Lake Champlain have blurred into one confusing cloud of cannon smoke, the Essex County Historical Society's museum has a nifty sound and light show that puts the battles into a geographical and chronological context. That's not the only reason to visit: The Adirondack History Center interprets local pioneer life—mining, farming, trapping, logging—through its permanent exhibits and showcases contemporary local artists during the summer.

There's a stagecoach that once carried passengers from Elizabethtown to Keene, a fire tower that you don't have to climb a mountain to enjoy, a roomful of dolls, and the wonderful Colonial Garden of perennials and herbs. For Adirondack and genealogical scholars, there's an excellent library open by appointment year-round.

The Adirondack Museum

518-352-7311

www.adkmuseum.org

NY 28 & 30, Blue Mountain Lake

Open: Memorial Day through mid-October 15, open daily; open weekends the rest of the
    year

Admission: $15 adults; $8 children ages 6–12; discounts available for seniors and groups

Handicap Access: Yes

Remarks: Book and gift shop; snack bar

If your last trip to the Adirondack Museum was on a rainy day ten years ago, it's high time
you went back. Simply put, no visit to the Adirondacks is complete without seeing this cultural icon. Perched on the side of Blue Mountain and overlooking the island-studded lake,
this is a major outdoor museum that is user-friendly, scholarly, beautiful, amusing, and
superlative in every way. Not surprisingly, the place has been described by *The New York
Times* as "the best museum of its kind in the world."

The museum's theme is interpreting man's relationship to the Adirondacks, and it does
so in twenty-plus exhibit buildings. Adjacent to the entrance is a theater showing *The
Adirondacks: The Lives and Times of an American Wilderness,* an award-winning film. In the
galleries of the main building, there are changing exhibits of paintings; in 2007–2008
Adirondack rustic architecture and decorative arts were the special exhibitions.

The Adirondack Museum, in Blue Mountain Lake, is a regional institution.

Courtesy of the Adirondack Museum

There are scores of wooden boats, including fine Adirondack guideboats and a Gold Cup racer; there are dozens of carriages, sleighs, and wagons. You can glide through August Belmont's private railroad car and imagine yourself en route to your very own Great Camp, or you can picture the other extreme of Adirondack life, in displays covering agriculture and logging. In "Woods and Waters: Outdoor Recreation in the Adirondacks," you'll find hunting and fishing gear. On Merwin Hill, Bull Cottage—a nice example of everyday rustic architecture—showcases rooms of rustic furniture.

The museum is a great place for children who can read and understand historical ideas; there are audio- and videotape stations that add depth to the displays. One suggestion, though: Parents should keep a close eye on young ones who may be tempted to touch fragile artifacts. The Marion River Carry locomotive, in the center of the campus, is a good place to let active kids be themselves.

"The Great Outdoors" is a new exhibit building devoted entirely to interactive sections for kids: snowshoes to try on fake snow, a tent to scramble into, a climbing wall to scale, fishing poles with magnets to catch (and release) your own faux brook trout or bass.

The museum comes alive with craft demonstrations, music, and storytelling on selected days. Opened in August 2007, the "Dog Days of Summer" features agility contests, sheep-herding demonstrations, dogs at work—and guests can even bring their own dogs for this special event. The Rustic Furniture Fair in September showcases fifty-plus builders so that visitors can decide how to begin their own Adirondack collections.

It's probably a natural response to plan a visit to the Adirondack Museum on a rainy day, but thousands of other folks think along the same lines, and the place can get crowded. Far better to pick a gorgeous day when you can savor the view and the many outdoor displays, and see the exhibits without having to jockey for position.

In the works at press time is an 8,000-square-foot Tri-Lakes branch of the Adirondack Museum to be built in Lake Placid.

Vintage Watercraft

In 1843 John Todd visited the lonely settlers in Long Lake and wrote, "Their little boats were their horses, and the lake their only path." Traditional wooden boats, especially the guide-boat, performed a major role in nineteenth-century work and play. At several affairs across the park, you can get a taste of this era, and enjoy beautifully restored guideboats, canoes, sail-boats, and even classic powerboats.

The **No-Octane Regatta** (518-352-7311, www.adkmuseum.org), a June affair, cospon-sored by the Adirondack Museum and Traditional Arts of Upstate New York at Little Wolf Lake, in Tupper Lake, attracts a glorious array of muscle- and wind-powered watercraft. There are builders' exhibits and lectures. The main attrac-tion is on the waterfront, where boats are dis-played. There are old-fashioned contests, including canoe jousting, where standing

Canoe-camping, 1890s: sailing canoe with canvas tent hung from its spars, at the Adirondack Museum.
Courtesy of the Adirondack Museum

contestants try to knock one another out of canoes with long, padded poles, and the hurry-scurry race, where participants' boats are anchored out in the lake: The competitors run from the beach, swim to the boats, clamber in, then paddle or row to the finish line. You won't believe your eyes when you see a war canoe—propelled by eight or ten paddlers—pull a water skier off the fire department's dock. New events include a pack canoe race and dog-paddle event in which each boat must have a dog passenger.

Saranac Lake hosts the early-summer **Willard Hanmer Adirondack Guideboat Races** (518-891-1990, www.saranaclake.com), on Lake Flower. Check out quintessential Adirondack vessels during this competition, for show and sale.

In July the **Fulton Chain Rendezvous of the Antique and Classic Boat Society** (315-369-3552, www.oldforgeny.com) welcomes exhibitors and members, with a dockside show at the Old Forge waterfront, and a grand parade—everything from old Fay & Bowens and Chris-Crafts, to HackerCrafts and Gar Woods—through the channel that marks the beginning of the eight lakes.

The **Lake George Rendezvous** (518-885-0146) happens in August in the village of Lake George. Expect plenty of the classics, rumbling and gleaming on a lake that's no stranger to snazzy vessels. In September 2007 the **International Antique Classic Boat Society** held its annual meeting in Lake George, which included a show featuring about 125 boats.

Fort Ticonderoga
518-585-2821
www.fort-ticonderoga.org
30 Fort Ti Road, off NY 22, Ticonderoga
Open: Mid-May through mid-October, daily 9–5
Admission: $12; children 7–12 $6; under 7 free; senior and group discounts
Handicap Access: Yes
Remarks: Museum shop, snack bar, picnic grove

High above Lake Champlain is a must-see for Adirondack visitors: Fort Ticonderoga. In 1755, the French built a fort, Carillon, on the site, and for the next quarter century, the stone fortification was a key location in the struggle to claim North America. The Marquis de Montcalm defended the site against numerous British invaders until 1758, when Lord Jeffery Amherst captured the fort. Ticonderoga was British territory until Ethan Allen and the Green Mountain Boys took the fort "in the name of Jehovah and the great Continental Congress," during the American Revolution.

In the early 1800s, the Pell family acquired the ruins and fields where the soldiers once camped. Work was begun in 1908 to rebuild the barracks and parade grounds, making Fort Ticonderoga the nation's first restored historic site (in contrast, Colonial Williamsburg's restoration dates back to the 1930s).

Inside the barracks are exhibits on the French and Indian War and the American Revolution, from intricately inscribed powderhorns to blunderbusses, cannons, and swords. The grim side of winter warfare is clear (some youngsters love the gory stuff), and there's little glorification of the ordeal of battle. Below the barracks is the subterranean kitchen, which supplied thousands of loaves of bread every day to the standing army. Beneath the walls, on a broad plain facing the lake, is the King's Garden, a beautiful spot that's been cultivated for hundreds of years and is open for tours (call for hours). The walled

English-style garden dates back to the 1920s and is one of a handful of American places recognized by the Garden Conservancy. At press time the Pavilion, which was a hotel in the 1830s, is being restored.

There's plenty of action at the fort in the summer, from tours from costumed interpreters, demonstrations of black-powder shooting, and cannon firing to fife-and-drum drills; many of the demonstrators are local teenagers who are happy to explain what they're up to. On some weekends, there are encampments of regiments reenacting battles, or bagpipe-band concerts.

The fort is set in a spectacular spot with a magnificent view of the lake, but don't end your visit there. It's worth a side trip up Mount Defiance, near town, to get an even higher perspective. From the top of that hill, a show of British cannons so intimidated the officers at Ticonderoga and Fort Independence, a fort across the lake in Vermont, that colonial troops fled both strongholds. (Shots were never fired.) Bring a pair of binoculars and a picnic lunch.

A view of Fort Ticonderoga from Mount Defiance. Courtesy of Fort Ticonderoga; photograph by John Tichy

Natural History Museum of the Adirondacks (aka The Wild Center)

518-359-7800

www.wildcenter.org

45 Museum Drive, Tupper Lake

Open: Year-round

Admission: $14 adults; $9 children ages 4–14; discounts available for seniors and groups

Handicap Access: Yes

Remarks: Wild Supply Company gift shop; café

There was plenty of eye-rolling among locals when folks first suggested a natural history museum in Tupper Lake. But after years of planning and then building, nobody can argue with the magnificence of the brand new Natural History Museum of the Adirondacks, a slick, state-of-the-art facility that's also referred to as the Wild Center.

If you're interested in the Adirondacks and its natural world, set aside time during your visit to see this place, its live exhibits—more than 900 live animals, some that scurry, slither, and swim in and out of the museum via a gorgeous reflective pond—walking trails, guided-treks by knowledgeable staff, nature films, lectures, workshops, you name it. Stars of the museum are a pair of adorable otters.

This place hosts climate conferences, high-end private parties and weddings, and a Fourth of July extravaganza WildFest—an annual gathering to promote eco-friendly living that includes exhibits, all sorts of activities, and national recording stars who are dedicated to the cause.

Tupper Lake's new Natural History Museum of the Adirondacks is a slick, cutting-edge science-based facility with walking trails, live exhibits—including otters—and staff-led lectures and workshops.

Courtesy of the Natural History Museum of the Adirondacks

Six Nations Indian Museum

518-891-2299

1462 County Road 69/ Buck Pond Campsite Road, Onchiota

Open: July 1 through Labor Day, Tuesday through Sunday, 10–6, or by appointment

Admission: $2; $1 children

Native people did travel to the Adirondacks for spring fishing, summer gathering, and fall hunting: The mountains, forests, and lakes offered abundant resources. At many local institutions this information is overshadowed by all the other stories those museums have to tell, but at Six Nations, the kaleidoscopic collection of baskets, beadwork, quill work, tools, weapons, paintings, drums, cradle boards, hats, pottery, and clothing all celebrate the lives and times of the Haudenosaunee (Iroquois). Artifacts fill cases, line the walls, hang from the ceilings; take the time to look closely and you'll be rewarded.

Lake George and Southeast Adirondacks

In Warren County you'll find numerous small museums to visit. The **Bolton Historical Museum**, in Bolton Landing (518-644-9960, boltonhistorical.org; NY 9N), is housed in a former Catholic church. Nineteenth-century photos of Lake George hotels by Seneca Ray Stoddard give a taste of the Gilded Age; more contemporary photos show sculptor David Smith at work in his Bolton Landing studio. There's an assortment of furniture, clothing, agricultural implements, and items relating to the town's days as a summer retreat for musical superstars.

In Brant Lake, the **Horicon Museum** (518-494-7286; NY 8) is a well-kept nine-room farmhouse full of antiques, agricultural implements, prints, photos, toys, and dolls; open from Memorial Day through Labor Day. The **Frances Kinnear Museum** (518-696-4520; 2144 Main Street), open year-round in an 1880s Victorian Lake Luzerne home, is similarly chockfull of local memorabilia; the town is also home to two summer museums: the **Pagenstacher Pulp Mill Museum** (518-696-2645; Mill Street), set in a park near the lake, and the **School House Museum** (518-696-3051; Main Street). In Chestertown, local history comes alive from July to August at the **Town of Chester Museum of Local History** (518-494-2711; Town Hall, Main Street/US 9), with neat displays on village life. Ask about photographer "Its" Sumy, a Japanese bachelor who took endearing pictures of people and events in the area from the late 1930s to the 1960s.

In Lake George, in the old courthouse, the **Lake George Historical Association Museum** (518-668-5044; 290 Canada Street) contains three floors of exhibits, including 1845-vintage jail cells in the basement. Also in Lake George is **Fort William Henry Museum** (518-668-5471; www.fwhmuseum.com; Canada Street), a restored log fortress dedicated to French and Indian War history, with life-size dioramas, assorted armaments, and lots of action: military drills, musket and cannon firing, fife-and-drum bands. The fort is open daily, 9–6, spring through fall.

In Schroon Lake, the **Schroon–North Hudson Historical Society** (518-532-7615; 1144 US 9) is open Wednesday through Sunday from June through Labor Day. Stony Creek's **Stony Creek Historical Museum** (518-696-5211; Lanfear Road & Creek Center) celebrates this place's past in a historic home.

In Warrensburg, the **Warrensburg Museum of Local History** (518-623-2928; 3797 Main Street) highlights the town's early industries, from garment factories to saw mills.

Champlain Valley

Ticonderoga is home to Stan Burdick's **Ticonderoga Cartoon Museum** (518-585-7015; www.ticonderogacartoonmuseum.com; Ticonderoga Community Building, Lower Montcalm Street), which is packed with old political cartoons, comic book characters, and animation art. It's open Monday, Wednesday, and Friday, 2–4. Also in town are two local-history museums: the **Heritage Museum** (518-585-2696; www.ticonderogaheritagemuseum.org; Bicentennial Park) and the **Historical Society** (518-585-7868; www.thehancockhouse.org; Hancock House, 6 Moses Circle), located in a replica of John Hancock's Boston home. The Heritage Museum depicts nineteenth-century industries, including paper- and pencil-making, in a Victorian office building, once head-quarters of the old Ticonderoga pulp and paper company. (Contact the museum for hours.) Hancock House was the first home of the New York State Historical Association (now in Cooperstown), and the house has several period rooms illustrating social history from the 1700s to the turn of the twentieth-century. There's an extensive research library open by appointment year-round; regular hours are Wednesday through Saturdays, 10–4. Pick up the brochure "Marker and Monument Tour Guide" when you're in Ticonderoga for con-nect-the-dots historical trivia, and you'll learn about such figures as the Jesuit martyr Isaac Jogues (died by torture), Lord George Howe (died by musket ball), and Horace Moses (died a millionaire).

In Essex, just a minute's walk from the ferry landing, **Greystone Mansion** (518-963-8058; NY 22) is open year-round by appointment only. The 1853 house is packed with the Empire-style antiques and decorative arts that a wealthy Essex family of the time would cherish, providing a real contrast to the rustic or Victorian embellishment usually associ-ated with the Adirondacks.

High Peaks and Northern Adirondacks

In Lake Placid, the depot for the Adirondack Scenic Railroad is home to the **Lake Placid–North Elba Historical Society Museum** (518-523-1608; 242 Station Street). There's a nostalgic country store display, sporting gear and memorabilia from the 1932 Olympics, and a music room honoring residents Victor Herbert and Kate Smith. Open June through September, Wednesday through Sunday, 10–4.

In the Olympic Center is the **Lake Placid Winter Olympic Museum** (518-523-1655; www.orda.org), open daily year-round. Photographs, vintage films, equipment, trophies, clothing, and memorabilia illustrate the two sets of Olympic competitions that have come to town.

Tucked away in the basement of the Saranac Lake Free Library, the **Charles Dickert Memorial Wildlife Museum** (518-891-4190; 100 Main Street) is open some weekday mornings in July and August, with displays of hundreds of stuffed mammals, birds, and fish native to the Adirondacks.

Central and Southwestern Adirondacks

Riley's House—next door to Riley's Tavern—in Piseco, is home to the **Piseco Lake Historical Society** (518-548-4812; Old Piseco Road), a collection of antiques and ephemera open Saturday and Sunday in summer. In Edinburg, the **Nellie Tyrell Museum** (518-863-2034; www.edinburg-hist-soc.org; County Road 4) is an old schoolhouse with displays showing life before the creation of the Great Sacandaga Reservoir in the 1930s. Northville has two museums right on South Main Street: the **Gifford Valley Schoolhouse**,

The Lake Placid Winter Olympic Museum has sports memorabilia from the 1932 and 1980 Winter Games. The 1980 U.S. Olympic hockey team beat the USSR in the "Miracle on Ice."
Courtesy of the Olympic Regional Development Authority

behind the municipal offices, and the **Paul Bradt Museum** (518-863-4040 ext. 22), which is filled with North American taxidermied wildlife and housed inside the village office complex. The outdoor museum complex near Caroga Lake, the **Caroga Historical Museum** (www.carogamuseum.org; London Bridge Road), recreates pioneer life in the southern Adirondacks in a farmstead, schoolhouse, and country store.

In Olmstedville, the **Minerva Historical Society** (518-251-2229; Main Street) is open July through Columbus Day; displays honor artists who visited the area, such as Winslow Homer. In Old Forge, the **Town of Webb Historical Association** (315-369-3838; Main Street) has exhibits on railroads, resorts, rustic furniture, and early industries in its **Goodsell Museum**, which is open year-round. On the edge of town is the **Forest Industries Exhibit Hall** (315-369-3078; 3311 NY 28), with displays on forest management, logging history, and dioramas, open Memorial Day through Columbus Day.

BEYOND THE BLUE LINE

North of the park, in Chazy, is a quirky private museum, the **Alice T. Miner Colonial Collection** (518-846-7336; www.minermuseum.org; 9618 US 9). Located in a three-story mansion, it houses a fine textile collection, china and glass, rare books, colonial furniture, and strange curiosities from around the world. The Alice is open Tuesday through Saturdays, 10–4. In Plattsburgh, the **Kent-DeLord House Museum** (518-561-1035; www.kentdelordhouse.org; 17 Cumberland Avenue) is a nicely restored late-eighteenth-century home. Also in Platt, on the old air-force base, is the new **Champlain Valley Transportation Museum** (518-566-7575, cvtmuseum.com; 12 Museum Way). It was originally planned as a Lozier museum, but has expanded to include the history of handmade watercraft, steam ferries, rail cars, and all forms of military transportation. Near Malone is the **Wilder Homestead** (518-483-1207; www.almanzowilderfarm.com; Stacy Road, Burke), the setting for the novel *Farmer Boy*, by Laura Ingalls Wilder. The farmstead was the home of the author's husband, Almanzo Wilder, in the mid-1800s.

South of the park, in Johnstown, but pertinent to Adirondack studies is the **Johnson Hall State Historic Site** (518-762-8712; Hall Avenue). The restored 1763 Georgian mansion was the home of Sir William Johnson, who served as superintendent of Indian affairs for the northern colonies; the Adirondack fur trade was a mainstay of his wealth. Also nearby is the Georgian-style **Old Fort Johnson** (518-843-0300, www.oldfortjohnson.org; on NY 5 and 67), finished in 1749. This is where Johnson lived during the French and Indian War. The Colonial Market Fair is a popular event at Johnson Hall in June, and the site hosts reenacted encampments of frontiersmen, Canadian fur traders, and Native people.

The guidebook *Adirondack Odysseys* (Adirondack Museum and Berkshire House Publishers, 1997) details a hundred historic sites from the Mohawk Valley to the St. Lawrence River, with capsule histories of the region and information useful to traveling families.

MUSIC

Traditional North Country music is represented by dance and fiddle tunes that have roots in French Canadian and Irish music, and by ballads of the lumber woods, like "Blue Mountain Lake," "The Jam on Gerry's Rocks," "The Wild Mustard River," and "Once More A-Lumbering Go."

Come all you good fellers
Wherever you be
Come sit down a while and listen to me
The truth I will tell you without a mistake
About the rackets we had around Blue Mountain Lake . . .

To hear authentic old-time instrumental music, look for the occasional fiddle jamborees or square dances, sponsored by arts groups and towns: The **Forest, Field, and Stream Festival** in September at the Adirondack History Center (518-873-6466, www.adkhistorycenter.org), sponsored by the Arts Council for the Northern Adirondacks, features traditional music. **The New York State Old Tyme Fiddlers' Association and Fiddlers' Hall of Fame** (315-232-4681), based in Redfield, outside the Blue Line, in Lewis County, promotes concerts within the Adirondack region. **Otis Mountain Music Festival** (518-962-8687, www.otismountain.com), held in August, brings a weekend of bluegrass, country, and old-time music, plus mandolin, guitar, and fiddle workshops, to Elizabethtown.

Nearly every town with a summer tourist

African American musicians entertain a group of canoeists, Lake George.
Seneca Ray Stoddard photograph, private collection

draw presents outdoor or indoor musical programs. A few examples include the following: In the Champlain Valley, Westport's Thursday night **Ballard Park Concert Series** (518-962-8778, www.artsnorth.org), featuring all types of music overlooking Lake Champlain. If you're traveling to the High Peaks, in Jay, the **Jay Entertainment and Music Society** (518-946-7362, www.jemsgroup.com) presents music and other programs, on Saturday evenings at the village green. In the northern Adirondacks, Saranac Lake has music on Friday nights at **Riverside Park**, on Lake Flower (518-891-1990; www.saranaclake.com). In the southern Adirondacks, at Northville's park, the **Sacandaga Valley Arts Network** (518-321-3468; www.svanarts.org) sponsors concerts and open mic nights. To hear folk songs and ballads, jazz riffs, and recitatives, check with music presenters listed below:

Lake George and Southeastern Adirondacks

Lake George Arts Project
518-668-2616
www.lakegeorgearts.org
Old County Courthouse, 1 Amherst Street, Lake George
Open: Year-round

On the second weekend in September, the Lake George Jazz Festival, in Shepard Park, is the place to be. The bands—often Latin or Afro-Caribbean stars—are topnotch, the vibe is cool, and the price is free. The arts project also sponsors music in the village park on summer nights, from reggae to blues to Celtic rock.

Luzerne Music Center
518-696-2771
www.luzernemusic.org
Luzerne Music Center, Lake Tour Road, 1.3 miles off NY 9N, Lake Luzerne
Open: July and August

Members of the Philadelphia Orchestra (who also perform at the Saratoga Performing Arts Center in July and August) present a superb chamber music concert series on Monday nights. Artistic directors of the center are Toby Blumenthal, piano, and Bert Phillips, cello, and they pride themselves on bringing internationally acclaimed soloists to join the resident ensembles. The music center is also a summer camp for gifted young musicians, and the free student/faculty recitals held Fridays, Saturdays, and Sundays are definitely worth a listen.

Schroon Lake Arts Council
518-532-9259
www.schroonlakearts.com
Dock Street, Boathouse Theatre, Schroon Lake
Open: July and August

On the lakeshore, yet within walking distance of downtown Schroon Lake, the Boathouse Theater and the adjacent bandstand are fitting spots to hear traditional music. The arts council presents evening concerts, open jams, and dance performances in the historic boathouse, and a festival of folk music, storytelling, and rustic crafts each August.

Seagle Music Colony

518-532-7875
www.seaglecolony.com
999 Charley Hill Road, Schroon Lake
Open: June through August

Oscar Seagle, famed tenor and voice teacher, established this country retreat in 1915. Vocal music is still the primary program, with coaching and master classes in opera and musical theater for conservatory students and aspiring performers. Every Sunday evening in the summer, the nondenominational Vespers concerts showcase exceptional choral singing; public concerts featuring scenes from opera and musical theater are held June through August.

Champlain Valley

Meadowmount School of Music

518-873-2063
www.meadowmount.com
Lewis-Wadhams Road, Lewis
Open: June through August

A short list of founder Ivan Galamian's Meadowmount School of Music's alumni gives a hint of the talent nurtured in the hills of the Boquet Valley: Yo-Yo Ma, Itzhak Perlman, Pinchas Zukerman, Michael Rabin, Lynn Harrell, Jaime Laredo, and Joshua Bell. Distinguished faculty, visiting artists, and promising students—ages 8 through 30—give free concerts at the camp's 500-seat Ed Lee and Jean Campe Memorial Concert Hall on Wednesday, Friday, and Sunday, at 7:30 PM, while the annual scholarship-benefit concert features world-famous string and piano players. Meadowmount is a rare treasure, and if you're visiting the eastern Adirondacks, the programs are certainly worth the drive.

Ticonderoga Festival Guild

518-585-6716
www.ticonderogafestivalguild.org
Montcalm Street, Ticonderoga
Open: July and August

An enormous striped tent in the center of town is the festival guild's summer home; under the big top there are weekly performances of music, dance, and theater, with concerts on Tuesday nights, and "Arts Trek" kids' shows on Wednesday mornings.

High Peaks and Northern Adirondacks

Hill and Hollow Music

518-293-7613
www.hillandhollowmusic.com
550 Number 37 Road, Saranac
Open: Year-round

Angela Brown and Kellum Smith bring fine, mostly classical, music to an off-the-beaten-path corner of the northeastern Adirondacks, offering a dozen or more concerts a year in the Church in the Hollow, an old Methodist church on NY 3 in Saranac that has excellent acoustics, and at other area venues. Past performers have included the Tokyo String Quartet, the Baltimore Consort, Soovin Kim, and musicians-in-residence the Biava Quartet. Hill and Hollow also sponsors community dance programs and coordinates special events that weave dance with food and historical reenactment—a combination that draws many local followers.

Jay Entertainment and Music Society
518-946-7362
www.jemsgroup.com
Village green, Jay
Open: Year-round

Ever since 1987 Jay Entertainment and Music Society (JEMS) has worked to organize free summertime music and entertainment at the town's hub, at the village green—Saturday evening acts that include rock and roll, blues, folk, and storytelling. At press time JEMS is expanding its program by renovating a former firehouse on the green to serve as the Amos & Julia Ward Theater, a 130-plus-seat structure to support concerts, art exhibitions, workshops, and other community events year-round. A winter coffeehouse music series at the theater is in the works.

Lake Placid Institute for Arts and Humanities
518-523-1312
www.lakeplacidinstitute.org
Various locations, Lake Placid
Open: Year-round

Take a walk on a summer evening in downtown Lake Placid and you'll likely hear the sound of classical musicians practicing new works. The Lake Placid Institute offers an adult Chamber Music Seminar, giving string players and pianists a chance to perform and study with world-class faculty in various local venues.

   The Institute is far more than just music, however. There are residencies for cutting-edge playwrights (New Dramatists program), poetry and nonfiction events for kids, an artists' roundtable, ongoing workshops in ethics, and an annual children's literature conference.

Lake Placid Sinfonietta
518-523-2051
www.lakeplacidsinfonietta.org
Various locations, Lake Placid
Open: July and August

In 1917, the Sinfonietta was established as the house orchestra at the Lake Placid Club, playing for the guests at the exclusive resort. Now the chamber orchestra is a valued community resource, presenting free Wednesday night Pops in the Park concerts in the Paul White Memorial Shell in Mids Park, overlooking Mirror Lake in the center of town (7 PM; bring a lawn chair), children's programs at the Lake Placid Center for the Arts, and concerts on stages across the Adirondack Park. On Sunday nights, the Sinfonietta performs its Symphony Series at the Lake Placid Center for the Arts.

Loon Lake Live
518-891-0757
www.loonlakelive.org
Venues in Loon Lake and Saranac Lake
Open: July and August

Launched in 1994, Loon Lake Live presents small classical ensembles in cozy spaces like
Loon Lake's Jewish Center, the Saranac Lake Free Library, and Harrietstown Hall, in Saranac
Lake. Each concert, played by fine, professional musicians, is preceded by a workshop
(suitable for children and adults) with the performers; programs are delightfully informal.

Central and Southwestern Adirondacks

Upper Hudson Musical Arts
518-251-3751
www.adirondackensemble.org
Tannery Pond Community Center, North Creek
Open: Year-round

Throughout the year, Upper Hudson Musical Arts provides professional chamber music
concerts at Tannery Pond Community Center, in North Creek. Performers have included
the Adirondack Ensemble, groups from Schroon Lake's Seagle Music Colony, the Saratoga
Chamber Players, and the Manchester Chamber Orchestra.

Beyond the Blue Line
Saratoga Springs isn't too far beyond the Adirondack Park, and the **Saratoga Performing
Arts Center** (518-587-3300; www.spac.org; Saratoga Springs) is a wonderful outdoor set-
ting for the Philadelphia Orchestra, the Newport Jazz Festival–Saratoga, the new Saratoga
Chamber Music Festival, and endless rock and pop offerings—Bruce Springsteen, Lucinda
Williams, and James Taylor, to name a few past performers. From mid-June through Labor
Day, SPAC is busy practically every night. (See Chapter 3 for more information.)

NATURE CENTERS

The Adirondack Park has two excellent state-funded facilities that explain the region's natural history through permanent exhibits, public programs, workshops for children and
adults, and offer extensive trails for hiking, snowshoeing, and cross-country skiing. Works
by regional artists are featured in rotating exhibitions. **The Adirondack Park Agency
Visitor Interpretive Center** (VIC) in Paul Smiths (518-327-3000) has a wonderful butterfly house with flowers, plants, and indigenous insects, and also sponsors the Great
Adirondack Birding Celebration in June and the Adirondack Wildlife Festival in August.
The VIC in Newcomb (518-582-2000) is home to the Huntington Lecture Series, with talks
by ecological experts; check out its guided backcountry trips. You can also snowshoe its
trails on your own through old-growth forest. Both centers are active year-round and can
be previewed at www.adkvic.org.
   Up Yonda Farm (518-644-9767; www.upyondafarm.com; NY 9N, Bolton Landing) is a
lovely lake-view property that functions as an environmental education center. The site,

The Adirondack Park Agency Visitor Interpretive Centers include exhibitions, workshops, hiking, snowshoe and cross-country-ski trails and, in Paul Smiths, the Native Species Butterfly House.
Courtesy of the Adirondack Park Agency Visitor Interpretive Center

operated by Warren County, is busiest during warm weather, with guided trail walks, after-dark tours, and programs on birds, bats, butterflies, and other beasts.

SEASONAL EVENTS

Throughout the Adirondack Park, special occasions celebrate local traditions and old-time North Country culture. The events listed below (in chronological order and listed by region) emphasize history, music, storytelling, crafts and skills, or a combination of the arts. You'll also find annual athletic contests, such as the White Water Derby and the Whiteface Mountain Uphill Footrace listed in Chapter 7; craft fairs and antique shows are noted in Chapter 7, and affairs with a gustatory focus, like the Newcomb Steak Roast, are outlined in Chapter 5.

Lake George and Southeastern Adirondacks

Lake George Winter Carnival (518-240-0809; www.lakegeorgewintercarnival.com) spans from January through February, with kid-oriented activities, fireworks, music, races, and polar bear plunge.

Bands 'n Beans (518-668-2616; www.lakegeorgearts.org) is a Lake George Arts Project benefit that includes numerous local bands and a massive chili cook-off at Roaring Brook Ranch, in Lake George, in March.

Americade (518-798-7888; www.tourexpo.com) is reportedly the world's largest multi-brand motorcycle-touring rally. Held in and around Lake George in early June, there are guided rides on Adirondack back roads, seminars, swap meets, contests, music, parades, and banquets. Bikes range from tasteful special-edition Harleys worth tens of thousands of dollars to rusty "rat bikes" that look like found-object sculptures.

Summerfest (518-668-5755; www.lakegeorgechamber.com) features music, arts and crafts, and games for kids in Shepard Park, in Lake George, on the last weekend in June.

Stony Creek Mountain Days (518-696-3575; www.stonycreekny.org) highlight Adirondack skills and pastimes with lumberjack contests, craft demonstrations, square dancing, and storytelling, followed by fireworks, held in Stony Creek the first weekend in August.

Adirondack Folk Music Festival (518-532-9259; www.schroonlakearts.com) is an all-day affair in Schroon Lake that also includes rustic furniture and crafts, in mid-August.

Warren County Country Fair (518-623-3291; www.warrensburgchamber.com) is a family-oriented fair, with the usual 4-H and agricultural exhibits, a horse show, historical displays, traditional music, a pony pull, carnival rides, and fish-and-wildlife exhibits, held in August at the fairground on Horicon Avenue outside Warrensburg.

Fiddlers' Jamboree (518-623-9961; www.thurman-ny.com) is a high-spirited September weekend of bluegrass and fiddle bands, dancing, workshops, and kids' activities.

Champlain Valley

Trashy Art Day (518-873-3688; www.boquetriver.org), in Elizabethtown, in May, brings concerned citizens together to collect trash along the Boquet River and build sculptures from their gleanings.

Grand Encampment of the French and Indian War at Fort Ticonderoga (518-585-2821; www.fort-ticonderoga.org) features hundreds of make-believe French, Scottish, and colonial troops, Native American scouts, and camp followers in authentic costumes, in late June.

For a quarter century Lake George has been host to Americade, the world's largest multibrand motorcycle-touring rally. Courtesy of Americade

Old-Time Folkcraft Fair (518-963-4478), on the lawn of the Paine Memorial Library, in Willsboro, is a showcase for local artisans and a chance to learn traditional North Country skills, in late July.

Essex County Fair (518-962-8650; www.essexcountyfair.org), in Westport, has harness racing, livestock and agricultural displays, a midway, educational programs by Cooperative Extension, music, and lots of cotton candy. The fair runs in late July.

Otis Mountain Music Festival (518-962-8687; www.otismountain.com), in Elizabethtown, features bluegrass and folk performers, workshops, and camping in a beautiful setting, in September.

Forest, Field, and Stream Festival (518-873-6466; www.adirondackhistorycenter.org), at the Adirondack History Center Museum, in Elizabethtown, happens during the height of fall color, in September, with a full slate of storytelling, old-time music, craft demonstrations, black-powder shooting, and participatory programs for children.

Apple Folkfest at the Penfield Museum (518-597-3804; www.penfieldmuseum.org), in Ironville, features traditional crafts, music, animals, and activities for children, in early October.

High Peaks and Northern Adirondacks

Saranac Lake Winter Carnival (518-891-1990; www.saranaclake.com), in February, is reputedly the oldest winter carnival in the country. On the shore of Lake Flower, there's an awesome ice palace, dramatically lit by colored spotlights each evening; events include ski races, a parade, concerts, theater, and kids' activities.

Round the Mountain Festival (518-891-1990; www.macscanoe.com), in Saranac Lake is a spring celebration centered around a canoe race that circles Dewey Mountain, with bluegrass bands and a barbecue, all on the second Saturday in May.

Lake Placid Film Forum (518-523-3456; www.lakeplacidfilmforum.com), early in June, brings directors, screenwriters, and indie film producers together to meet and greet the public each year. Venues throughout Lake Placid, including the Palace Theatre, show films from morning to midnight.

I Love Barbeque Festival (www.ilbbqf.com) means a tasty barbecue competition sanctioned by the Kansas City Barbecue Society, with vendors and two full days of music by local bands at Lake Placid's speed skating oval at the beginning of July.

Jay Studio Tour (518-946-2824; www.jaystudiotour.com), in July, involves a dozen artisans in Jay who open their studios to the public for demonstrations.

Oktoberfest (518-946-2223; www.whiteface.com), at the end of September, draws Bavarian culture-lovers to Whiteface Mountain, in Wilmington, for oom-pah-pah and *gemütlichkeit*. There's live music and German-style dancing, a crafts fair, ethnic food and beer booths, children's activities, and rides on the ski area's chairlift to view the fall foliage.

Northwest Lakes

WildFest (518-359-7800; www.wildcenter.org) is a Fourth of July event at the Natural History Museum of the Adirondacks, in Tupper Lake, that features national recording stars, such as Martin Sexton and Ralph Stanley, and outdoor exhibits exploring climate change and sustainable living.

Woodsmen's Days (518-359-9444; www.woodsmensdays.com), in Tupper Lake, highlight old-time lumber skills and underline the importance of logging in the Adirondack economy today. There's a parade with sparkling log trucks hauling the year's biggest, best logs; contests for men and women (ax throwing, log rolling, and speed chopping), beast (skidding logs with draft horses), and heavy equipment (precision drills for skidders and loaders); clowns and games for kids. It's all on the second weekend in July, in the municipal park on the lakefront in Tupper Lake.

Adirondack Wildlife Festival (518-327-3000; www.adkvic.org), at the Adirondack Park Agency Visitor Interpretive Center in Paul Smiths, offers guided wildflower walks, wildflower craft workshops, wildflower cooking demonstrations, and art programs for kids, in late July.

Central and Southwestern Adirondacks

Indian Lake Winter Festival (518-648-5112; www.indian-lake.com), on Presidents' Weekend in February, mixes local history programs with outdoor events such as cross-country-ski treks, downhill races at the town ski area, snowmobile poker runs, and snow-shoe events throughout Indian Lake and Blue Mountain Lake. There's music and sometimes square dancing in the evenings, plus community suppers.

Olde Home Days and Carnival (518-548-4521), in Wells, held in August, with a parade featuring horse-drawn wagons, antique cars, floats, and marching bands. Expect all kinds of music, plus a carnival and a craft fair.

Fox Family Bluegrass Festival (315-369-6869; www.foxfamilybluegrass.com), at Old Forge's McCauley Mountain, presents the town's own bluegrass stars plus other national bands, in early August.

Kribstock (518-696-4445; www.kribsmusic.com) is a grassroots gathering to benefit the Southern Adirondack Musicians' Fund, which sends money to musicians who don't have health insurance after an accident or illness. Blues, rock, and roots bands gather to play at this day-long festival in Corinth in early August.

Adirondack Authors' Fair at Hoss's Country Corner (518-624-2451; www.hossscountrycorner.com), in Long Lake, is a great opportunity to meet and greet dozens of regional writers, held under a huge tent in mid-August.

Upper Hudson Bluegrass Festival (518-251-2240; www.upperhudsonbluegrass.com), in August, brings fine bluegrass acts to North Creek.

Teddy Roosevelt Weekend (518-582-3211; www.newcombny.com), in Newcomb, Minerva, and North Creek, celebrates Teddy Roosevelt's wild ride to the presidency with historical programs, train rides, and sports contests, in early September.

Adirondack Gathering for Family Talk and Tales (315-369-6008), at McCauley Mountain, in Old Forge, sponsored by the Old Forge Library, hosts a gathering of regional storytelling masters in early September.

Rustic Furniture Fair (518-352-7311; www.adkmuseum.org), in September, at the Adirondack Museum, in Blue Mountain Lake, features the work of talented craftsmen from across the Adirondacks and beyond. Also, demonstrations, rustic designs sale, music, and food.

Adirondack Balloon Festival (www.adirondackballoonfest.org), in late September, brings hundreds of international hot-air balloons, music, and kids' activities to Lake George, Queensbury, and Glens Falls.

Gore Mountain Harvest Festival (518-251-2411; www.goremountain.com), in early October, in North Creek, has scenic gondola rides, crafters, straw maze, music, and kids' activities.

Harvest Festival (518-624-3077), in Long Lake's Sabattis Park, serves up family fun with games for kids, apple-cider making, a craft show, and apple pies galore, usually on the Saturday before Columbus Day.

THEATER

Lake George and Southeastern Adirondacks

Adirondack Theatre Festival
518-798-7479
www.atfestival.org
Charles R. Wood Theater, 207 Glen Street, Glens Falls
Open: Summer; occasional winter shows in other venues
Handicap Access: Yes

The Adirondack Theatre Festival was launched in 1995. Founders of the company were involved with the original production of the Broadway hit *Rent,* and bring real sophistication to their shows, performed in a 274-seat theater that was converted from an old Woolworth department store. The season begins in June, with five or six shows, children's workshops, and new play readings. Summer 2007's big hit was *Tick...Tick...Boom!,* an autobiographical musical by Pulitzer Prize–winning composer Jonathan Larson.

The Bridge Theater
518-499-2435
www.bridgetheater-whitehall.com
Lock 12 of the Champlain Canal, Whitehall
Open: Summer, Friday and Saturday

An old bridge transformed into a cozy sixty-seat performing space is probably one of the more unusual backdrops for a summertime theater series. Artistic director Martin Kelly's latest Saturday night productions include revues *The Styne Way* and *Whither Whitehall*; on Friday evenings seats are replaced by tables and chairs for a cabaret.

Lake George Dinner Theater
518-668-5762 ext 411
www.lakegeorgedinnertheatre.com
Holiday Inn, 2223 Canada Street, Lake George
Open: Mid-June through mid-October

For more than forty seasons this Actors Equity company has presented one show a season in a semiproscenium setting; a sample from past playbills includes *Oil City Symphony, Shear Madness, Over the River and Through the Woods,* and *On Golden Pond.* Productions are thoroughly competent, as is the food at the Holiday Inn's banquet room.

Champlain Valley

Depot Theatre
518-962-4449
www.depottheatre.org
Delaware & Hudson Depot, NY 9N, Westport
Open: June through September

Westport's Delaware & Hudson depot has found new vitality as home to a fine professional acting company. The former freight room—with newly installed air conditioning—comes alive with four or five plays each summer: 2007's smash hits were *Hank Williams: Lost Highway* by Randal Myler and Mark Harelik, and *The Memory of Water* by Shelagh Stephanson. Each year, a new musical debuts, and performance-art pieces by visiting actors are scheduled midweek. Local artists display their work in the lobby. Depot Theatre offers matinees for each of its shows—a nice option on a rainy day—but be sure to call ahead for tickets.

Shakespeare Festival
518-962-8383
Ballard Park, Westport
Open: First weekend in September

Every Labor Day weekend American Studio Theater presents a Shakespeare production at Ballard Park, in Westport. The acting and the scenery are equally fantastic. Past productions include *Much Ado About Nothing, Twelfth Night,* and *The Merry Wives of Windsor.*

Other Organizations
The region is also home to two community theater organizations: **The Essex Theatre Company** (518-524-7708; www.essextheatre.org), which was formed in 1993 to showcase local talent. Productions in recent summers were held at the Masonic Lodge and included *The Glass Menagerie, Wizard of Oz,* and musical cabarets. **The Boquet River Theatre Festival** (518-572-4193; www.brtf.com) presents original children's theater at the Whallonsburg Grange Hall.

High Peaks and Northern Adirondacks

Community Theatre Players, Inc.
518-523-2512
Lake Placid Center for the Arts, 17 Algonquin Drive, Lake Placid
Open: Year-round

An amateur group founded in 1972, CTP mounts three or four shows a year at the Lake Placid Center for the Arts and other venues. Productions—consistently good—have included *Babes in Toyland* (written by Lake Placid summer resident, Victor Herbert), and most recently, *Brighton Beach Memoirs*, by Neil Simon.

Pendragon Theatre
518-891-1854
www.pendragontheatre.com
15 Brandybrook Avenue, Saranac Lake
Open: Year-round
Handicap Access: Yes

This highly successful local troupe was awarded the prestigious Governor's Art Award, and has received acclaim for performances at the Edinburgh International Arts Festival, the Dublin Theatre Festival, and in Stockholm at the English-Speaking Theater. During the summer and fall, Pendragon puts on three or four shows in repertory format; in 2007 shows included *The Fantasticks, Lend Me a Tenor,* and *The Clean House*. During the school year and in winter, actors tour local classrooms and perform in regional venues.

Pendragon, anchored by husband-and-wife team Bob Pettee and Susan Neal, was founded in 1981. Performances are worth a special trip.

Central and Southwestern Adirondacks

Our Town Theatre Group
518-251-2938 or 518-494-5280
www.ottg.org
Tannery Pond Community Center, 228 Main Street, North Creek
Opens: Year-round
Handicap Access: Yes

This amateur troupe founded by Lyle Dye performs at its permanent headquarters at Tannery Pond Community Center, in North Creek, and occasionally takes its shows on the road. A recent production includes Neil Simon's *Fools*. All who are involved in this community-based organization—actors, costumers, stagehands, and ushers—are volunteers.

WRITERS' PROGRAMS

The **Adirondack Center for Writing** (518-327-6278; www.adirondackcenterforwriting.org; Paul Smith's College, Paul Smiths) schedules workshops, readings, book signings, literary contests; hosts children's literature seminars, in-school programs, publishing conferences, lectures by authors including Andrea Barrett and Terry Tempest Williams; sponsors a prison-writing program; and has a comprehensive listing of opportunities for writers for the Adirondacks and beyond. **Fiction Among Friends** (518-623-9305; www.persisgranger.com) hosts an Adirondack Mountain Writers' Retreat, in

The power of books. "Absorbed" by Seneca Ray Stoddard. Private collection

Thurman, that offers workshops and an in-residence component. **Wiawaka Holiday House Women's Retreat** (518-668-9690; www.wiawaka.org), in Lake George, offers poetry and other writing workshops, and hosts readings by regional authors. The **Writer's Voice** (518-543-8833; www.silverbay.org), a nationwide program of the YMCA, has a center at Silver Bay Association, on the northern end of Lake George. Workshops and readings (funded by the Lila Wallace-Reader's Digest Fund and the National Endowment for the Arts) by highly regarded poets, travel writers, novelists, and essayists are slated for spring and summer. The **Old Forge Library** (315-369-6008) offers summer writing workshops, readings, and an authors' fair with dozens of Adirondack writers.

7

RECREATION

A Land for All Seasons

Adirondack woods and waters beckoned to nineteenth-century visitors with promises of a primeval wilderness overflowing with fish and game. City "sports" relied on Adirondack guides to row them down lakes, lead them through forests in pursuit of deer or moose, cook them hearty meals, and finally tuck them into balsam-bough beds at night. The popular press swelled with accounts of these manly Adirondack adventures, and by the 1870s, the North Country was a great destination for thousands.

In those rough-and-tumble days, hunting and fishing were the prime recreational pursuits. Hiking through the woods was something done as a last resort: "[I]f there is one kind of work which I detest more than another, it is tramping; . . . How the thorns lacerate you! How the brambles tear your clothes and pierce your flesh!" wrote William H. H.

Guideboat at Forked Lake. Private collection

Murray in his 1869 best seller, *Adventures in the Wilderness.* Boating was simply a method of transportation, to go from one campsite to the next or a necessary component of a hunting or fishing trip. Later, near the turn of the twentieth century, recreational canoeing swept the nation (the idea of using Native American watercraft for fun came across the Atlantic from England).

Despite Murray's opinion, hiking or mountain climbing for pleasure was a nineteenth-century notion that coincided with the growth of grand hotels across the Adirondacks. Walking in the woods—dressed in long skirts, shirtwaists, high boots, wool stockings, gloves, hats, and veils—was fine for ladies; they could hire their own guides, too, to take them up High Peaks or into pristine scenes. Hiking was healthful: Breathing in pine-scented, ozone-laden air was regarded as a tonic for frail, dyspeptic, or consumptive patients.

Winter, however, was no time for fun. Getting around in the snow and cold was hard work; the idea of going outside to play when temperatures were below freezing was thought sheer folly—until Melvil Dewey, of Dewey Decimal System fame, created the Lake Placid Club in the early 1900s and thereby launched America's first full-service winter resort, complete with skiing, skating, sleigh riding, snowshoeing, and backcountry bonfires to ward off the chill.

With the advent of the automobile, recreation in the Adirondack Park changed. No longer were the lake country and High Peaks inaccessible to the masses; no longer did the exodus north take long days and large sums. Vacations were within reach of almost every working person, and with the help of a reliable Ford or Chevy, so was the Adirondacks. In the wake of this new, more democratic summer vacation approach, the huge hotels closed one by one, to be replaced by motels and housekeeping cabins. The New York State Conservation Department responded to new tourist demand by creating car-camping havens under the pines.

Today in the Adirondack Park, whether you come for health, adventure, solitude, or just plain fun, you'll find that outdoor recreation opportunities are limited only by your imagination. Nowhere else east of the Mississippi is there such a variety of sport: wilderness canoeing, backcountry hiking, rock climbing, downhill and cross-country skiing, fishing, big-game hunting . . . the list goes on. If you want to get away from civilization, this is indeed the place; there are nearly three million acres of public lands to explore. In that regard, the Adirondack Park compares favorably to the national parks, and there's an added bonus: There's no entry fee when you cross the Blue Line. You may hike or mountain bike, bird watch, canoe or kayak, rock-climb, ski tour or snowshoe in the Forest Preserve without having to buy a permit.

If your taste runs to a round of golf or watching a chukker of polo, you'll find those here, too. There are tour boats to ferry you around scenic lakes, and pilots to hire for flying above the mountaintops. The Adirondacks might also be regarded as the birthplace of two of the cornerstones of American popular culture: theme parks and miniature golf.

In this chapter you'll find descriptions of myriad diversions, along with suggestions on how to find the right gear, and who to call for additional details. What you won't find in this chapter are specific instructions on where to begin or end a particular hike, climb, or canoe trip; it's important that you take the responsibility to read guidebooks and study maps. Each season a few unprepared outdoors folk become unfortunate statistics due to errors in judgment. The Blue Line encircles a wonderful park, but if you get lost, we can't "just turn the lights on" (as one urban dweller suggested to forest rangers involved in a search) to find you.

ADIRONDACK GUIDES

An Adirondack woodsman "falls so to speak out of his log cradle into a pair of top boots, discards the bottle for a pipe, possesses himself of a boat and a jackknife and becomes forthwith a full-fledged experienced guide," wrote an observer in 1879. William H. H. Murray described guides as, "A more honest, cheerful, and patient class of men cannot be found the world over. Born and bred, as many were, in this wilderness, skilled in all the lore of woodcraft, handy with the rod, superb at the paddle, modest in demeanor and speech, honest to a proverb, they deserve the admiration of all who make their acquaintance." Of course, not everyone agreed with him—one nineteenth-century writer declared "a more impudent, lazy, extortionate, and generally offensive class . . . would be hard to find"—but Murray's view became the popular ideal.

The Adirondack Guides' Association was established in 1891 as a backwoods trade union to adopt uniform pay (then about a dollar a day) and follow the state's new game-protection laws. Nowadays, the Department of Environmental Conservation (DEC) licenses hundreds of men and women as guides for rock climbing, hunting, fishing, and whitewater rafting. Guides pass a written exam that tests woods wisdom, weather awareness, and safety situations; they must also know first-aid and CPR.

There are several hundred guides who are members of a select group within the DEC-licensees: the **New York State Outdoor Guides Association** (www.nysoga.com). These folks make a point of preserving wild resources as well as helping clients find the right places for hunting, fishing, camping, and climbing; many guides practice low-impact camping and offer outdoor education.

Under the separate sports headings in this chapter, you'll find a sampling of licensed guides for different outdoor activities.

BICYCLING

As the twenty-first century unfolds, promising all kinds of technological marvels, plain old bicycling is undergoing a renaissance in the region. New publications and maps plus new trail systems provide excellent information. Highways, byways, and skidways offer challenges, variety, and great scenery for road and mountain bikers; May through October are the best months. In April, road bikers might find that the snowbanks are gone, but a slippery residue of sand remains on the road shoulders. Likewise, springtime backcountry cyclists might discover patches of snow in shady stretches of woods or muddy soup on sunnier trails. At the other end of the year, note that big-game season begins in October, and some of the best mountain-biking destinations are also popular hunting spots.

The most complete guidebook for all-terrain cyclists is *25 Mountain Bike Tours in the Adirondacks* by Peter Kick (Backcountry Publications). Amusing and informative, the book outlines really tough single-track routes requiring map-and-compass and advanced riding skills as well as adventures suitable for families. Some of the trips include rides on the Adirondack Scenic Railroad, in Thendara, to get to starting points. (See the "Scenic Railroads" section elsewhere in this chapter.) You can also do a bike/train combo with the Upper Hudson Scenic Railroad from North Creek to Riparius. Also available is Gary Thomann's *Mountain Biking in the Adirondacks: 25 Trail Riding Adventures* (North Country Books), with trips for beginner, intermediate, and advanced cyclists.

The most comprehensive book for road cyclists is *25 Bicycle Tours in the Adirondacks:*

Road Adventures in the East's Largest Wilderness by Bill McKibben, Sue Halpern, Barbara Lemmel, and Mitchell Hay (Backcountry Publications). It describes loop trips in wonderful detail, with an eye toward scenic and historic destinations like Willsboro Point, a thumb of land sticking into Lake Champlain, with great views coming and going. Free guides offer more riding options: Boquet River Association's **Historic Boquet River Bike Trails** (518-873-3688; www.boquetriver.org; Essex County Government Center, Elizabethtown) outlines excellent road trips with historical stops; **Essex County Visitors Bureau** (518-523-2445; www.lakeplacid.com; Olympic Center, Lake Placid) has a selection of backcountry bike trips of varying difficulty on its Web site. (From the home page click on "What to do," then "Outdoor Adventure," and finally, "Two-Wheel Traveling.") **Franklin County Tourism** (518-483-9470; www.adirondacklakes.com; 10 Elm Street, Malone) publishes a brochure describing off-the-beaten-path treks that's available at the office and online; and the **Whiteface Regional Visitors Bureau** (518-946-2255; www.whitefaceregion.com), in Wilmington, has a new brochure with area mountain bike trails. Also, **Lake Champlain Bikeways** (802-652-2453, www.champlainbikeways.org; Local Motion, 1 Steele Street #103, Burlington, Vermont) has identified a network of routes around the lake, with interpretive maps available online or at the LCB clearinghouse, in Burlington. Check out the **"Speculator Loop"** on Speculator's Web site; www.adrkmts.com, where you can download a map and trail information (or call 518-548-4521). The *Annual Guides to the Great Outdoors,* published by *Adirondack Life* magazine, list dozens of bike trips; back issues are available (518-946-2191; www.adirondacklife.com). For still more trip ideas, ask at regional bike shops; many sponsor guided rides or have their own maps of local favorites. Check www.bikeadirondacks.org for an online atlas.

As mountain biking continues to grow in popularity, the Inlet–Old Forge area has emerged as a center for the sport. Old Forge welcomes pedalers to explore its extensive

Mountain biking continues to grow in popularity. There are extensive ski and snowmobile trails throughout the park that provide gnarly, bumpy rides. Courtesy of the Olympic Regional Development Authority

snowmobile trails; call the **Central Adirondack Association** (315-369-6983; www.caany
.com; Main Street, Old Forge) for a map. Inlet is perched on the edge of the Moose River
Recreation Area, which is laced with old logging roads and fantastic trails. Check out
www.inletny.com for a list of loops of varying difficulty. In spring and fall the town hosts
mountain-bike weekends that attract hundreds of cyclists. Lift-serviced biking is available at
both of the New York State–owned ski areas, **Gore Mountain** (518-251-2441;
www.goremountain.com; Peaceful Valley Road, North Creek) and **Whiteface Mountain** (518-
946-2233; www.whiteface.com; NY 86, Wilmington). Some ski trails—as you'd suspect—are
gnarly, scary, bumpy rides, but both areas have traverse routes and woods roads, too.

All-terrain bicycles are barred from wilderness and primitive areas in the Adirondack
Park, but many wilderness hiking trails are inappropriate for bikes, anyhow: too steep, too
narrow, too wet, too rocky. In the state-land areas designated as wild forest, you'll find old
logging roads that make excellent bike routes, and in most of these places, you'll find far
fewer people.

Road cyclists will discover that many state highways have wide, smooth shoulders. You
won't have to contend with much traffic in May and June or September and October, except
on weekends, but be aware that main roads become quite busy with all kinds of vehicles
from log trucks to sightseeing buses to RVs throughout the summer. Also, be prepared for
any long trips: Check topographical as well as highway maps for significant hills on your
proposed route. Always carry plenty of water and a good tool kit. *Wear a helmet!*

Rules of the Trail

• Ride on open trails only. Respect trail and road closures and avoid trespassing on private lands.
  Wilderness areas are closed to cycling.

• Leave no trace. Even on open trails, you should not ride under conditions where you will leave evidence of your passing. Practice low-impact cycling by staying on the trail and not creating any new
  ones. Pack out at least as much as you pack in.

• Control your bicycle. There is no excuse for excessive speed.

• Always yield the trail to hikers and others. Make your approach known well in advance; a friendly
  greeting or a bell works well.

• Never spook animals. Give them extra room and time to adjust to your presence; use special care
  when passing horseback riders.

• Plan ahead. Know your equipment, your ability, and the area in which you are riding, and prepare
  accordingly. Be self-sufficient; carry the necessary supplies and tools you may need.

—From the International Mountain Bicycling Association

BICYCLE DEALERS AND OUTFITTERS

Lake George and Southeastern Adirondacks

Beach Road Outdoor Supply (518-668-4040; 2239 Canada Street, Lake George). Seasonal
bike rentals.

High Peaks and Northern Adirondacks

High Peaks Cyclery (518-523-3764; www.highpeakscyclery.com; 2733 Main Street, Lake Placid). Road and mountain bike sales, repairs, and rentals. Ask about group rates and minitriathlon series.

LeepOff Cycles (518-576-9581; 23 Market Street, Keene Valley). Road, mountain, and cross-bike sales, service, and guided trips.

Maui North (518-523-7245; www.mauinorth.net; 134 Main Street, Lake Placid). Road and mountain bike sales, bike gear, and rentals.

Placid Planet (518-523-4128; www.placidplanetbicycles.com; 2242 Saranac Avenue, Lake Placid). Good inventory of new and used bikes and repairs; occasional group rides; excellent service.

Central and Southwestern Adirondacks

Beaver Brook Outfitters (518-251-3394 or 1-888-454-8433; www.beaverbrook.net; 2349 NY 28, Wevertown). Mountain bike rentals.

Garnet Hill Lodge (518-251-2444; www.garnet-hill.com; Thirteenth Lake Road, North River). Cross-country-ski trail network converts to bike loops in the off-season; citizen races; shop; bike rentals for use on Garnet Hill trails only.

Pedals & Pedals (315-357-3281; www.pedalsandpetals.com; NY 28, Inlet). Bikes for sale and rent; repairs. Sponsors a major mountain-bike race in spring. Ask here for trip suggestions in the Moose River Plains.

Village Rental and Sales (518-548-7368; www.villagerentalsny.com; NY 8, Speculator). Bike rentals and simple repairs.

Beyond the Blue Line

In Plattsburgh, **Wooden Ski and Wheel** (518-561-2790; www.woodenskiandwheel.com; 4614 US 9, Plattsburgh) is a professional shop for new bikes, tune-ups, equipment; repair classes offered. Also in Plattsburgh, **Maui North** (518-563-7245; www.mauinorth.net; 31 Durkee Street) sells road and mountain bikes, and equipment. In Saratoga Springs, **Blue Sky Bicycles** (518-583-0600; www.blueskybicycles.com; 71 Church Street) sells and repairs bikes, and offers clinics. **Elevate Cycles** (518-587-0455; www.elevatecycles.com; 35 Van Dam Street) focuses on mountain bike sales and repair, but is competent with road bike sales and maintenance, too.

BOATING

Scores of lovely Adirondack lakes have public launches for motor- and sailboats. Many are free, operated by the New York State Department of Environmental Conservation or villages; individual businesses may charge a nominal fee. You'll find these launch sites marked on regional road maps. Many state campgrounds (listed under "Camping" later in this chapter) have boat ramps. If you have a reserved campsite, there's no extra charge to launch a boat, and if you'd like to make a short visit to Lake Eaton, Buck Pond, or Eighth Lake, for example, you pay the day-use fee. Note also that motorboats (over 10 hp) and sailboats (longer than 18 feet) used on Lake George must have a permit, available from local marinas or the Lake George Park Commission (518-668-9347; Box 749, Lake George).

Marinas and boat liveries offer another chance for folks with trailers to get their boats in the water. Many more options are open to canoeists and kayakers who can portage their boats a short distance, so look under "Canoeing" for further information.

The *New York State Boater's Guide* contains the rules and regulations for inland waters, and is available from offices of the New York Department of Transportation. Some statewide laws for pleasure craft follow:

- You must carry one personal flotation device for every passenger in your boat. Children under 12 are required to wear life jackets while on board.

- Any boat powered by a motor (even canoes with small motors) and operated mainly in New York State must be registered with the Department of Motor Vehicles.

- When traveling within 100 feet of shore, dock, pier, raft, float, or an anchored boat, the speed limit is 5 mph. (Maximum daytime speed limits are 45 mph, and nighttime, 25 mph, although on many lakes with rocky shoals, or on water bodies that are also popular with nonmotorized craft, lower speeds are prudent.)

- Powerboats give way to canoes, sailboats, rowboats, kayaks, and anchored boats.

- The boat on your right has the right-of-way when being passed.

- Running lights must be used after dark.

- Boaters under 16 must be accompanied by an adult, or, if between 10–16 and unaccompanied, they must have a safety certificate from a New York State course.

- Boating under the influence of alcohol carries heavy fines and/or jail sentences.

- Littering and discharging marine-toilet wastes into waterways is prohibited.

Eurasian Milfoil

A new invasive species is spreading throughout Adirondack waters: Eurasian water milfoil. This leafy underwater plant grows luxuriantly in hundreds of lakes, creating a nearly impenetrable tangle that can stop a small outboard in its tracks. Paddling through a milfoil jungle is no fun, either. Eurasian milfoil chokes out native plants that offer better food and cover to fish, and once established, this invader is very tough to eradicate.

It's clear that this milfoil, like zebra mussels, was brought into its new habitat inadvertently by recreational boaters. If you've taken your boat through milfoil-infested waters, clear the weeds off the prop and trailer carefully when your boat is on land, pulling off leaves and stems. Even tiny fragments can grow quickly into 10-foot-long underwater vines.

Zebra Mussels

A tiny, striped mollusk from the Caspian Sea was accidentally introduced into Michigan's Lake St. Clair in the 1980s when a European freighter discharged its ocean-water ballast. From there, zebra mussels (*Dreissena polymorpha*) have been spread by recreational boaters to Lakes Erie, Ontario, Champlain, and a portion of Lake George. Some beaches have become treacherous because the shells are razor-sharp.

Zebra mussels can clog water-intake pipes, colonize historic shipwrecks, attach themselves to navigational markers in such quantity that the buoys sink, and damage boat hulls. Besides affecting human-made objects, the nonnative mussels have the potential to irrevocably change a lake's ecology. The mussels' free-swimming larvae are so small that thousands can be found in a boat's live well or cooling system and even bait buckets, and if these contaminated waters are released into lakes and rivers, the mussels may spread into new territory.

Canoes and car-top boats usually don't harbor the mussels because they're not left at anchor long enough for mussels to attach and because these boats don't carry water when transported from one lake to the next. Trailerable boats, especially inboards, pose a greater risk, but boat owners can minimize that by flushing the cooling system on land thoroughly before launching in a new lake, and rinsing the boat hull and trailer. To be doubly safe, you can use a mild bleach solution for the rinse, or let the boat and trailer dry out completely on a hot, sunny day.

Marinas and boat liveries offer a variety of services; complete listings are available from tourist-information booklets published by Warren, Essex, Clinton, Franklin, Fulton, Herkimer, and Hamilton Counties (see Chapter 9).

BOAT TOURS

There are nearly 3,000 Adirondack lakes, ponds, and reservoirs to explore, but if you'd prefer not to be your own helmsman, practically every water body of significant size has a cruise vessel. Prices vary widely depending on the length of the tour, and what kind of frills come with it—music, dancing, and champagne, for example. Most boats can be chartered for special events like receptions and parties; some captains are licensed to perform weddings, too.

The season generally runs from early May through October. Note that many of the boats are enclosed, so this is an activity you can try on a drizzly day. Whether you choose sunshine, clouds, or moonlight for your cruise, call ahead for a reservation.

Lake George and Southeastern Adirondacks
Lake George Shoreline Cruises (518-668-4644; www.lakegeorgeshoreline.com; 2 Kurosaka Lane, Lake George). Several boats to choose from, including the adorable *Horicon* and the new *Adirondac;* narrated daytime and dinner cruises. Wedding cruises available; the *Horicon* departs at dusk on Thursdays in the summer for fireworks cruises.

Lake George Steamboat Company (518-668-5777; www.lakegeorgesteamboat.com; Steel Pier, Lake George). Three enclosed boats, including the huge *Lac du Saint Sacrement* and the paddle wheeler *Minne-ha-ha*. The *Mohican* makes a four and one-half hour-long tour of the lake daily in the summer and navigates through the Narrows, among the islands each afternoon. In addition to shorter narrated trips, boats have cocktail lounges and offer dinner, pizza, and moonlight cruises with live music. Wedding packages are available.

Champlain Valley
Carillon Cruises (802-897-5331; www.carilloncruises.com; Fort Ticonderoga, Ticonderoga). Historic tour on the *Carillon,* which presents narrated tours near Fort Ticonderoga and longer cruises to Whitehall, New York, and Vergennes, Vermont.

Lake Champlain Ferries (802-864-9804; www.ferries.com). Car ferries between Essex, New York, and Charlotte, Vermont; Port Kent, New York, and Burlington, Vermont; and

Plattsburgh, New York, and Grand Isle, Vermont. Passengers without cars are welcome.

Ticonderoga Ferry (802-897-7999; NY 74, Ticonderoga). Inexpensive scenic trip across Lake Champlain on a small cable-operated car ferry.

High Peaks and Northern Adirondacks

Lake Placid Marina Boat Tours (518-523-9704; 24 George and Bliss Road, Lake Placid). Scenic narrated (don't believe everything they tell you) trips on Lake Placid aboard the enclosed, classic wooden boats *Doris II* (1950) and *Lady of the Lake* (ca. 1929).

Central and Southwestern Adirondacks

Blue Mountain Lake Boat Livery (518-352-7351; www.boatlivery.com; NY 28, Blue Mountain Lake). Narrated rides through the Eckford Chain of Lakes aboard three restored wooden launches, the *Neenykin*, the *Toowaloondah*, and the *Osprey*.

Dunn's Boat Service (315-357-3532; www.dunnsboats.com; 1500 Big Moose Road, Big Moose Lake). Tours of the setting of *An American Tragedy* aboard *Grace*, a beautiful inboard.

Norridgewock III (315-376-6200; www.beaverriver.com; 150 Norridgewock Lake Road, Eagle Bay). Tours and water taxi service on Stillwater Reservoir; access to Beaver River, the most isolated community in the park.

Old Forge Lake Cruises (315-369-6473; www.oldforgecruises.com; NY 28, Main Street, Old Forge). Narrated 28-mile cruise on the Fulton Chain of Lakes aboard the *Uncas* or the *Clearwater*. Also weekend shuttles to Inlet from Old Forge for lunch or exploring town. Passengers can ride on the *President Harrison*, a 20-foot vessel used to deliver letters and packages on the longest running freshwater mail boat route in the country.

Raquette Lake Navigation Co. (315-354-5532; www.raquettelakenavigation.com; Pier I, Raquette Lake). Lunch, brunch, and dinner cruises—by reservation only—aboard the posh *W. W. Durant*.

CAMPING

Sleeping under the stars on a remote island, in the bugless confines of a recreational vehicle, or nestled within a cozy backpacking tent deep in the forest—camping possibilities in the Adirondacks cater to all tastes. The **Department of Environmental Conservation**, or DEC (518-402-9428; www.dec.ny.gov), operates forty-some public campgrounds, most of which are on beautiful lakes or peaceful ponds, and all of which are open from Memorial Day through Labor Day. Many campgrounds open earlier, and some operate late into the fall.

The smaller places (those with one-hundred sites or fewer) tend to be quieter; some campgrounds accommodate upwards of 400 families and can resemble little cities in the woods. However, camping in the North Country is still very much a wholesome experience. The only hassles you may encounter might be from persistent chipmunks and red squirrels that regard your picnic table as their personal lunch counter.

Facilities at state campgrounds include a picnic table and grill at each site, water spigots for every ten sites or so, and lavatories. Not every campground has showers. Many facilities have sites for mobility-impaired campers, with hard-surface areas, water spigots at wheelchair height, and ramps to rest rooms. Most campgrounds have fishing docks for wheelchairs.

Camping is allowed year-round on state land, but you need a permit to stay more than three days in one backcountry spot or if you are camping with a group of more than six people. Special regulations apply in the High Peaks Wilderness Area. These permits are available from forest rangers. Some locations such as Stillwater Reservoir, Lows Lake, Little Tupper Lake, or Lake Lila have designated primitive camping spots with fire rings and/or privies. You may camp in the backcountry provided you pitch your tent at least 150 feet from any trail, stream, lake, or other water body. (See "low-impact camping," below.)

Along the Northville–Lake Placid Trail and on popular canoe routes you'll find lean-tos for camping. These three-sided log structures are an Adirondack icon. A handy guide with useful tips for family trips as well as destinations is Barbara McMartin's book *Adventures in Camping: An Introduction to Adirondack Backpacking* (North Country Books).

Reservations can be made for a site in the state campgrounds by contacting **Reserve America** (800-456-CAMP; www.reserveamerica). Its Web site includes details about every state campground, as does the DEC's campsite listings on its site, so you can see for yourself if site #4 at Lake Durant is on the water. (It is.) If you can't find what you're looking for on Reserve America's site, contact the campground itself.

You may book a place for a single night or as long as three weeks and charge it to your credit card. DEC campgrounds will cheerfully take you on a first-come, first-served basis if space is available; before July 4 and after September 1, it's usually easy to find a nice site without a reservation. In 2007, campsites cost about $12–$22 per night; the reservation fee is $9. Day-use fees are about $6 per carload, and at most places bicyclists or hikers can enter at no charge. Senior or access-disability discounts are available for specific campgrounds.

DEC public campgrounds do not supply water, electric, or sewer hook-ups for recreational vehicles. If you require these amenities, there are privately owned campgrounds in

Setting up camp near Follensby Clear Pond. Courtesy of Mark Bowie

many communities. Check Chapter 5 for these facilities. Also, some towns offer public camping; check with local tourist-information offices, listed in Chapter 9.

PUBLIC CAMPGROUNDS

Camping fees listed are for 2007.

Lake George and Southeastern Adirondacks

Eagle Point (518-494-2220; US 9, Pottersville). On Schroon Lake. Boat launch; showers; swimming. Camping fee: $18.

Hearthstone Point (518-668-5193; 3298 Lakeshore Drive, Lake George). On Lake George. Showers; swimming. Camping fee: $18.

Lake George Battleground (518-668-3348; 2224 US 9, Lake George). Historic site. Showers; easy walk to downtown and tour boat docks. Camping fee: $18.

Lake George Islands (Numerous sites on Narrow Island, 518-499-1288; Glen Island, 518-644-9696; and Long Island, 518-656-9426; 18 Boathouse Lane, Bolton Landing). Access by boat; tents only; swimming. No dogs allowed. Camping fee: $18.

Luzerne (518-696-2031; 892 Lake Avenue, Lake Luzerne). On Fourth Lake. A Hudson River impoundment. Showers; swimming; canoe and rowboat launch; no powerboats allowed. Camping fee: $18.

Rogers Rock (518-585-6746; 9894 Lake Shore Drive, Hague). Historic site on Lake George. Boat launch; access to rock climbing cliff. Camping fee: $18.

Trouble Bruin

As humans have become comfortable sleeping out in the wilds, some wild animals have learned to recognize coolers, packs, tents, even car trunks as potential food sources. Hungry black bears or pesky raccoons may not be in evidence when you set up camp, but it's best to take all precautions. If your site has a metal locker for food storage, use it. Otherwise, stash your supplies and cooking gear well away from your tent: put it in a pack or strong plastic bags and suspend it between two trees with a sturdy rope at least 20 feet off the ground. Tie it off by wrapping several times around one tree and tie a complicated knot; bears have been known to swat down food stashes within their reach, climb saplings, and even bite through ropes. Don't try to outsmart bruin by putting your food in an anchored boat away from shore; bears swim well. In some places, the campsite caretaker can give you an update on the bear situation. Also, special poles for bear bags can be found in some High Peaks Wilderness campsites. Bear-proof canisters for food can be rented at places like EMS, in Lake Placid. However, there are reports that some bears have learned how to rip tops off these sturdy tubes. As soon as humans think they have outsmarted the bears the wild ones come up with creative solutions.

If a bear does visit your camp, loud noises (yelling, banging on pots, loud whistles) usually discourage it. Attacks are extremely rare in the Adirondacks; do keep your dog under control in the event of a close encounter of the ursine kind.

Champlain Valley

Ausable Point (518-561-7080; 3346 Lake Shoe Road, Peru). On Lake Champlain. Showers; swimming; boat launch. Near wildlife refuge; good place to explore by canoe; great beach for kids. Camping fee: $18.

Crown Point (518-597-3603; 784 Bridge Road, Crown Point). On Lake Champlain. Showers; boat launch. Across from fort. Next to good visitor information center. Camping fee: $14.

Lincoln Pond (518-942-5292; 4363 Lincoln Pond Road, Elizabethtown). Swimming; showers; canoe or rowboat rentals; no powerboats allowed. Camping fee: $14.

Paradox Lake (518-532-7451; 897 NY 74, Paradox). Swimming; showers; canoe or rowboat rentals; boat launch. Camping fee: $14.

Poke-O-Moonshine (518-834-9045; 135 US 9, Chesterfield). Showers; access to hiking and rock climbing on Poke-O-Moonshine Mountain. Camping fee: $12.

Putnam Pond (518-585-7280; 763 Putts Pond Road, Ticonderoga). Swimming; showers; canoe or rowboat rentals; boat launch. Access to Pharaoh Wilderness Area. Camping fee: $14.

Scaroon Manor (518-623-3671; US 9, Schroon Lake). New, beautiful property—formerly the site of a classy 1950s resort. Several accessible sites; lovely beaches. Call for camping fee.

Sharp Bridge (518-532-7538; 4390 US 9, North Hudson). On Schroon River. Showers; access to Hammond Pond Wild Forest. Camping fee: $14.

High Peaks and Northern Adirondacks

Buck Pond (518-891-3449; 1339 County Route 60, Onchiota). Swimming; showers; canoe or rowboat rental; boat launch. Camping fee: $16.

Lake Harris (518-582-2503; 291 Campsite Road, Newcomb). Swimming; showers; boat launch. Near Visitor Interpretive Center nature trails. Camping fee: $14.

Meacham Lake (518-483-5116; 119 State Campsite Road, Duane). Swimming; showers; horse trails and barn; some primitive sites accessible by foot only; boat launch. Good place to see bald eagles in summer. Camping fee: $16.

Meadowbrook (518-891-4351; 1174 NY 86, Ray Brook). Showers; no swimming. Closest campground to downtown Lake Placid. Camping fee: $14.

Saranac Lake Islands (518-891-3170; 58 Bayside Drive, Saranac Lake). Access by boat; tents only. Beautiful sites. Camping fee: $18.

Taylor Pond (518-647-5250; 1865 Silver Lake Road, Au Sable Forks). Boat launch. Camping fee: $12.

Wilmington Notch (518-946-7172; 4953 NY 86, Wilmington). On the West Branch of the Ausable River. Great area for fly-fishing; fairly close to Lake Placid. Camping fee: $14.

Northwest Lakes

Cranberry Lake (315-848-2315; 243 Lone Pine Road, Cranberry Lake). Swimming; showers; rowboat or canoe rentals. The easy hike up Bear Mountain begins from this campground. Camping fee: $16.

Fish Creek Pond (518-891-4560; 4523 NY 30, Saranac Lake). Swimming; showers; canoe or rowboat rentals; boat launch; nature and beginner camper programs. Camping fee: $18.

Rollins Pond (518-891-3239; NY 30, near Fish Creek Pond campsite). Showers; canoe or rowboat rentals; boat launch. Camping fee: $16.

Central and Southwestern Adirondacks

Alger Island (315-369-3224; 303 Petrie Road, Old Forge). On Fourth Lake. Access by boat; tents only. Camping fee: $14.

Brown Tract Pond (315-354-4412; Uncas Road, Raquette Lake). Canoe to Raquette Lake or Fulton Chain. Swimming; canoe or rowboat rentals; no powerboats allowed. Camping fee: $14.

Caroga Lake (518-835-4241; 3043 NY 29A, Gloversville). Swimming; showers; boat launch. Camping fee: $16.

Eighth Lake (315-354-4120; NY 28, between Raquette Lake and Inlet). Swimming; showers; canoe or rowboat rentals; boat launch. Camping fee: $18.

Forked Lake (518-624-6646; 381 Forked Lake Campsite Lane, Long Lake). Primitive walk-in or canoe-in sites; launch for cartop boats. Camping fee: $14.

Golden Beach (315-354-4230; NY 28, Raquette Lake). On Raquette Lake. Swimming; showers; boat or canoe rentals; boat launch. Camping fee: $16.

Indian Lake Islands (518-648-5300; off NY 30, Sabael). Access by boat; tents only; boat launch. Camping fee: $16.

Lake Durant (518-352-7797; NY 28 & 30, Blue Mountain Lake). Swimming; showers; canoe rentals; boat launch; handicap accessible campsite. Access to Blue Ridge Wilderness and Northville–Lake Placid Trail. Camping fee: $16.

Lake Eaton (518-624-2641; NY 30, Long Lake). Swimming; showers; canoe or rowboat rentals; boat launch. Camping fee: $16.

Lewey Lake (518-648-5266; NY 30, Sabael). Swimming; showers; canoe or rowboat rentals; boat launch. Camping fee: $16.

Limekiln Lake (315-357-4401; Limekiln Lake Road, Inlet). Swimming; showers; canoe or rowboat rentals; boat launch. Access to Moose River Recreation Area. Camping fee: $16.

Little Sand Point (518-548-7585; Old Piseco Road, Piseco). On Piseco Lake. Swimming; canoe or rowboat rentals; boat launch. Camping fee: $16.

Moffit Beach (518-548-7102; Page Street, Speculator). On Sacandaga Lake. Swimming; showers; canoe or rowboat rentals; boat launch. Camping fee: $18.

Nicks Lake (315-369-3314; 278 Bisby Road, Old Forge). Remote lakeside location. Swimming; no motorboats; trout fishing; nearby hiking trails. Camping fee: $18.

Northampton Beach (518-863-6000; 328 Houseman Street, Mayfield). On Great Sacandaga Lake. Swimming; showers; canoe or rowboat rentals; boat launch. Camping fee: $18.

Point Comfort (518-548-7586; Old Piseco Road, Piseco). On Piseco Lake. Swimming; showers; canoe or rowboat rentals; boat launch. Camping fee: $16.

Poplar Point (518-548-8031; Old Piseco Road, Piseco). On Piseco Lake. Swimming; canoe or rowboat rentals; boat launch. Camping fee: $16.

Sacandaga (518-924-4121; NY 30, Northville). On Sacandaga River. Swimming; showers; no powerboats. Camping fee: $16.

Tioga Point (315-354-4230; NY 28, Raquette Lake). On Raquette Lake. Access by boat; some lean-tos, although it's best to bring a tent. Beautiful spot. Camping fee: $14.

CAMPS

Famous folks spent their summers at Adirondack camps: Vincent Price was a counselor at Camp Riverdale, on Long Lake; Bonnie Raitt is an alum of Camp Regis, on Upper St. Regis Lake; G. Gordon Liddy went to Brant Lake Camp; Arlo Guthrie and his mother, a dance instructor, enjoyed many seasons at a Raquette Lake camp; Demi Moore and Bruce Willis enrolled their kids at Long Lake Camp for the Arts.

Throughout the Adirondacks summer camps offer a wide range of programs. There are high-adventure canoeing, backpacking, and rock-climbing camps, with emphasis on self-reliance in the wilderness. There are also very comfortable camps that offer nice cabins, good food, and fine arts or technology programs. Some camps are truly Great Camps—in the architectural sense—housed in impressive vintage estates. And several camps offer family sessions so that everyone can share in the fun.

If you're in the Adirondacks during July or August, and would like to visit a particular camp with your prospective happy camper, you should call ahead; also, many camps will send DVDs or have live Web cams to give you a taste of the action. If you want to let your fingers do the walking, check out these Web sites: www.acacamps.org for camps accredited by the American Camping Association; www.nycamps.org, which has descriptions of camps and links to their individual Web sites; or www.camppage.com/newyork, with similar links to camp home pages.

CANOEING AND KAYAKING

Paddlers agree: The Adirondack Park offers some of the best canoeing and kayaking in the Northeast. Some might argue that the region rivals the Boundary Waters Canoe Area in

The Adirondacks has unlimited opportunities for paddlers—and their friends. Courtesy of Mark Bowie

Minnesota for excellent backcountry tripping. For thrill seekers, there's serious whitewater (with rapids up to Class V) on the Upper Hudson, the Moose, portions of the Schroon, and other rivers; for flatwater fans, there are long trips linking lakes, such as the 44-mile route from Long Lake to Tupper Lake, the 35-mile trip from Old Forge to Blue Mountain Lake; the 25-mile trip from Osgood Pond to Lake Kushaqua; or the Old Forge to Lake Champlain stretch of the 740-mile Northern Forest Canoe Trail, which begins in Old Forge and ends in northern Maine. In the St. Regis Canoe Area it's possible to paddle for weeks on end and visit a different pond or lake each day. There's even a three-day race, the Adirondack Canoe Classic, which covers 90 miles of water in a long diagonal from the Fulton Chain of Lakes to Saranac Lake village (see the listing under "Annual Events" in this chapter).

Options have improved considerably in recent years, with New York State's acquisition of beautiful, motorless Little Tupper Lake and Rock Pond (1998), and the myriad whitewater rivers that formerly belonged to Champion International Company (1999). In 2006, more lakes opened to paddlers, such as Round Lake, adjacent to Little Tupper Lake. Four-mile-long Little Tupper Lake offers gorgeous paddling, swimming, and loon-watching, with several primitive campsites you can reserve from the registration box at the parking lot. The Champion purchase is primarily in the northern Adirondacks, and includes some very challenging Class IV–V runs on the Deer, St. Regis, and other rivers. The Department of Environmental Conservation's Northville office (518-863-4545) has an excellent guide to the William C. Whitney Area, which encompasses Little Tupper Lake.

Given that the possibilities seem unlimited, you may wonder how a newcomer chooses where to go. Three guidebooks cover Adirondack destinations for human-powered watercraft: *Adirondack Canoe Waters: North Flow* by Paul Jamieson and Donald Morris (Adirondack Mountain Club); Adirondack Mountain Club's *Canoe and Kayak Guide: East–Central New York State;* and *Fun on Flatwater: Family Adventures in Canoeing* by Barbara McMartin (North Country Books). Both *Adirondac* and *Adirondack Life* magazines frequently publish articles describing canoe trips; check a local library for back issues or contact the publications (listed in Chapter 9). Some articles are archived on www.adirondacklife.com. The bimonthly newspaper *Adirondack Explorer* (www.adirondackexplorer.org) features paddling trips. There's also a fine topo sheet, Adirondack Canoe Map, published by Adirondack Maps, in Keene Valley, that shows several routes (518-576-9861; www.adirondackmaps.com). Adirondack Paddler's Map, a waterproof and tear-proof guide for multiday trips with enough details for navigating, includes trailheads, portages, and white-water ratings across the region. It's available at St. Regis Canoe Outfitters, in Saranac Lake (888-775-2925), or online, at www.canoeoutfitters.com.

The Department of Environmental Conservation (518-891-1200; www.dec.ny.gov; NY 86, Ray Brook NY

Little Tupper, a motorless lake, is a mecca for canoeists and kayakers. James Swedberg

12970) has pamphlets that describe canoe routes, including the Bog River area near Tupper Lake, Stillwater Reservoir, and many others; ask for *Adirondack Canoe Routes* or the "official map and guide" of the area you wish to paddle. The excellent twenty-four-page booklet *Guide to Paddling Adirondack Waterways* is available by calling 1-800-487-6867. Some tourist information offices, such as the Saranac Lake Chamber of Commerce (518-891-1990; www.saranaclake.com), offer useful brochures and maps; ask for Canoe Franklin County. Searching online for the "William C. Whitney Area" and other public lands leads to basic access information, but these simplified charts are not suitable for navigating. Always consult U.S. Geological Survey topographic maps for the area you're traveling through.

When you're planning any trip, allow an extra day in case the weather doesn't cooperate. Remember that you're required to carry a life jacket for each person in the boat; lash an extra paddle in your canoe, too. Bring plenty of food and fuel, a backpacker stove, and rain gear. A poncho makes a good coverall for hiking, but you're far better off with rain jacket and pants in a canoe, since a poncho can become tangled if you should dump the canoe. Do sign in at the trailhead registers when you begin your trip.

If you're still overwhelmed by making a decision about where to go, consult one of the outfitters or guides listed below. (These are folks specializing in canoeing or kayaking and offer lightweight, good-quality equipment; many boat liveries and marinas also rent canoes.)

And if you're eager to try canoeing but just aren't sure of your abilities, there are plenty of places where you can get lessons in flatwater or whitewater techniques. **Old Forge's Paddlefest** (315-357-6672; www.mountainmanoutdoors.com), in mid-May, has demonstrations and more than a hundred different boats to try. **Blue Mountain Outfitters** (518-352-7306) and **Lake George Kayak Company** (518-644-9366) schedule demo days. For lessons, hire a guide for one-on-one sessions or check with your local Red Cross office for water safety courses and basic canoe instruction.

Each summer the State University of New York at Plattsburgh hosts a **Lake Champlain Sea Kayak Institute** (518-564-5292) that includes workshops, demos, and a race around Valcour Island.

You Give Me Fever

The cool, clear water may seem like the ideal thirst quencher, but please resist the temptation to drink freely from Adirondack lakes, rivers, ponds, and streams. Sadly, due to careless campers and occasional animal pollution, these wild waters may harbor a microscopic parasite known as *Giardia lamblia*, which can cause bloating, diarrhea, cramping, and vomiting. *Giardiasis*—also known as Beaver Fever—is easily diagnosed (with a stool sample) and treated (with quinicrine or Flagyl), but it's better to avoid the ailment in the first place. Practice good campsite sanitation. Treat all drinking water by boiling ten minutes, by using a specially designed *Giardia*-proof filter, or with chlorine or iodine tablets.

CANOE OUTFITTERS AND TRIP GUIDES

Lake George and Southeastern Adirondacks

Adirondack Mountain Club Member Services Center (518-668-4447; www.adk.org; 814 Goggins Road, Lake George). Spring, summer, and fall canoe workshops in different locations for all ages; guided canoe tours for women, youth, and Elderhostel groups.

Lake George Kayak Company (518-644-9366; www.lakegeorgekayak.com; Main Street, Bolton Landing). Canoes, kayaks, paddling accessories, and gear to buy or rent; lessons; demonstrations; tours.

Wild Waters Outdoor Center (518-494-4984; www.wildwaters.net; 1123 NY 28, The Glen). Canoe and kayak instruction for youth and adults; whitewater clinics for men and women; kayak camp for youth; lodging available.

High Peaks and Northern Adirondacks

Adirondack Lakes and Trails Outfitters (518-891-7450; www.adirondackoutfitters.com; 541 Lake Flower Avenue, Saranac Lake). Canoes, kayaks, tents, and gear to buy or rent; paddling instruction.

Adirondack Rock and River Guide Service (518-576-2041; www.rockandriver.com; Alstead Hill Lane, Keene). Whitewater kayaking instruction; guided trips; lodging.

Cloud-splitter Outfitters (518-582-2583; NY 28, Newcomb). Canoe and kayak rentals.

High Peaks Mountain Adventures (518-523-3764; www.highpeaksma.com; High Peaks Cyclery, 331 Main Street, Lake Placid). Canoe and kayak rentals, lessons, and guided trips.

Jones Outfitters Ltd. (518-523-3468; www.jonesoutfitters.com; 331 Main Street, Lake Placid). Canoe and kayak sales and rentals.

Middle Earth Expeditions (518-523-9572; www.adirondackrafting.com; NY 73, Lake Placid). Guided wilderness trips.

St. Regis Canoe Outfitters (518-891-1838; www.canoeoutfitters.com; 73 Dorsey Street, Saranac Lake). Trip outfitter; guided trips; canoe instruction; car shuttles. In the heart of the St. Regis Canoe Area.

Tahawus Guide Service (518-891-4334; Box 424, Lake Placid). Guided canoe—ask about the 35-foot war canoe—and traditional guideboat trips.

Northwest Lakes

Adirondack Canoes and Kayaks (518-359-2174; www.capital.net/com/adkcanoe; 96 Old Piercefield Road, Tupper Lake). Its Web site asks, "Why are you on the Internet when you should be paddling?" Rentals, tours, car shuttles, paddling instruction.

Mac's Canoe Livery (518-891-1176; www.macscanoe.com; 5859 NY 30, Lake Clear). Complete year-round outfitter and guide service; wilderness education; scheduled trips and races; sales and rentals.

Raquette River Outfitters (518-359-3228, www.raquetteriveroutfitters.com; 1754 NY 30, Tupper Lake). Complete trip outfitter; canoe repairs; guided trips; car shuttles. Satellite shop in Long Lake.

St. Regis Canoe Outfitters (518-891-1838; www.canoeoutfitters.com; Floodwood Road, Lake Clear). Trip outfitter; guided trips; canoe instruction; car shuttles. In the heart of the St. Regis Canoe Area.

Central and Southwestern Adirondacks

Beaver Brook Outfitters (888-454-8433; www.beaverbrook.net; 2349 NY 28, Wevertown). Canoe and kayak center offers sales, rentals, and guided trips.

Blue Mountain Outfitters (518-352-7306; www.adirondacks.com/bluemtoutfitters; 144 Main Street, Blue Mountain Lake). Complete trip outfitter; guided trips; car shuttles; sporting goods shop; canoe rental and sales. Boats can be delivered to Lake Durant campground.

Haderondah Company (315-369-3868, www.haderondah.com; 3011 Main Street, Old Forge). Canoe sales; guide service.

Mountainman Outdoor Supply Company (Inlet: 315-357-6672, NY 28; Old Forge: 315-369-6672, NY 28; www.mountainmanoutdoors.com). Kayak and canoe rentals and sales, camping gear, books, maps. Primary sponsor of the annual Paddlefest at Inlet's Arrowhead Park.

Stillwater Shop (315-376-2110; www.stillwaterreservoir.com; 2590 Stillwater Road, Stillwater Reservoir, Lowville). Canoe rentals; camping supplies for sale.

Tickner's Moose River Canoe Outfitters (315-369-6286; www.ticknerscanoe.com; Riverside Drive, Old Forge). Complete trip outfitter; canoe instruction; canoe rentals and sales; special River and Rail excursion with Moose River paddle and return via the Adirondack Scenic Railroad.

Whitewater Challengers (800-443-7238; www.whitewaterchallengers.com; NY 28, Old Forge). Canoes and kayaks for sale and rent; kayaking clinics. Also summer rafting trips with picnics.

DIVING

No amount of wishful thinking could turn the chilly Adirondack depths into crystal-clear Caribbean seas, but there is plenty to discover beneath the waves in Lake George. In fact, it's the site of New York's first underwater heritage preserve and home to numerous eighteenth- and nineteenth-century shipwrecks.

In the works since 2007 is the **Underwater Blueway Trail**, which aims to promote and preserve New York's maritime heritage. Shipwrecks and rock formations will be marked with buoys, guiding lines, and signage. Volunteers for this project include members of Batteaux Below, historians and divers who created dive sites in Lake George beginning in the 1990s. Three sites on the bottom of Lake George already have preserve status: the 52-foot British artillery ship the *Land Tortoise,* which sank in 1758; the Sunken Fleet of 1758, smaller bateaux used to transport troops; and the 45-foot tour boat *Forward* that sank in the 1930s, today used as an underwater classroom for beginner divers.

The following dive operators can help with equipment, instruction, and maps to the Underwater Blueway Trail: **Adirondack Scuba Champlain** (518-884-4056, www.adirondackscuba.com; 98 Rowland Street, Ballston Spa); **Diamond Divers** (518-505-3483, www.divelakegeorge.com; Bolton Landing); **Dive Center** (518-562-3483, www.divechamplain.com; 4013 US 9, Plattsburgh); and **Jones' Aqua Sports** (518-963-1150, 482 Willsboro Point Road, Willsboro). The **New York State Divers Association** (www.scubany.org) also provides scuba diving resources.

FAMILY FUN

Alongside countless pristine natural attractions, the Adirondack Park offers plenty of human-made amusements and privately owned curiosities. Ausable Chasm, a spectacular gorge of carved sandstone cliffs near the park's northeastern corner, is one of the country's oldest tourist destinations, dating back to 1870. Since the 1930s, visitors have filled their pockets with glittering garnets at the Barton Mines tour. Santa's Workshop, near Whiteface Mountain, is touted as the oldest theme park in the world, dating back to 1946, and it is the place to mail your Christmas cards, since the postmark reads "North Pole, NY." On the other end of the spectrum, there are new-wave fun parks with towering water slides and pools that generate their own whitecaps. The **Olympic Regional Development Authority** (518-523-1655; www.orda.org) offers an Olympic Sites Passport ($29 in 2007), which provides VIP entry to all Lake Placid region Olympic venues.

If sliding down a frozen chute is something the kids want to try and the bobsled price tag is a bit much, Lake Placid's toboggan run, near the Mirror Lake beach, is a cheap thrill. It's open winter weekends, weather permitting; check with the **North Elba Parks Department** (518-523-2591).

You'll find miniature golf courses listed under a separate heading, Olympic spectator events outlined under "Olympic Sports," and annual races and competitions later in this chapter. Described below is a potpourri of places to go and things to do.

Price Code

Adult Admission:	Inexpensive	Moderate	Expensive
(Children's tickets are less)	under $9	$10–$15	over $16

Lake George and Southeastern Adirondacks

Adirondack Extreme Adventure Course (518-494-7200; www.adirondackextreme.com; 35 Westwood Forest Lane, Bolton Landing). Brand new high-wire treetop adventure park with ropes courses and zip lines for adults and kids. Open in weather above 20 degrees. Expensive.

Dr. Morbid's Haunted House (518-668-3077; www.drmorbid.com; 115 Canada Street, Lake George). Spooky fun; screaming encouraged. Open Memorial Day through Halloween. Inexpensive.

House of Frankenstein Wax Museum (518-668-3377; www.frankensteinwaxmuseum.com; 213 Canada Street, Lake George). From the *Phantom of the Opera* to modern horrors. Open daily Memorial Day through Columbus Day. Inexpensive.

Magic Forest (518-668-2448; www.magicforestpark.com; US 9, Lake George). Rides and games; Santa's Hideaway; and home to the Adirondack Park's only diving horse, Lightning. Open Memorial Day through Labor Day. Moderate.

Natural Stone Bridge & Caves (518-494-2283; www.stonebridgeandcaves.com; 535 Stone Bridge Road, Pottersville). Caves; stone archway; mineral shop; playground and picnic area; mining activities. Open daily Memorial Day through Columbus Day. Inexpensive.

Water Slide World (518-668-4407; US 9 and 9L, Lake George). Wave pool; water slides; bumper boats. Daily mid-June through Labor Day. Expensive.

Champlain Valley

Ausable Chasm (518-834-7454; www.ausablechasm.com; US 9, Ausable Chasm). Deep sandstone gorge, open as a tourist attraction since the 1870s. Hike through the formations,

Ausable Chasm has been open as a tourist attraction since the 1870s. Private collection

then ride a raft or inner tube down 2 miles of rapids. Check out the new rim walk. Open daily mid-May through mid-October. Moderate.

High Peaks and Northern Adirondacks

Adirondack Park Agency Visitor Interpretive Centers (518-327-3000; www.adkvic.org; NY 30, Paul Smiths; and 518-582-2000; NY 28N, Newcomb). Great places for hiking well-marked trails, with lots of workshops and programs for preschoolers to senior citizens. Open daily except Thanksgiving, Christmas, and New Year's Day; no admission charge for trails or exhibits.

Adirondack Scenic Railroad (518-891-3238; www.adirondackrr.com; 19 Depot Street, Saranac Lake). Ten-mile trip from Saranac Lake to Lake Placid. Open Memorial Day through Columbus Day. Moderate.

Avalanche Adventures (518-523-1195; www.avalancheadventures.com; 194 Saranac Avenue, Lake Placid). Small family center that includes climbing wall, mini golf, caving maze, and bungee jump. Open year-round. All-inclusive pass, expensive.

High Falls Gorge (518-946-2278; www.highfallsgorge.com; NY 86, Wilmington). Waterfalls and trails on the Ausable River. Open July and August, and in winter for spectacular snowshoeing. Moderate.

Santa's Workshop (518-946-2212; www.northpoleny.com; NY 431, Wilmington). Reindeer; craft demonstrations; corny singing and dancing; Santa; rides. Pageant and craft shops open some winter weekends. Don't expect slick Disney World offerings; this place suits the nostalgic set with small children. Open daily Memorial Day through Columbus Day. Expensive.

Tucker Farm's Autumn Corn Maze (518-327-5054, www.tuckertater.com; 112 Hobart Road, Gabriels). Corn maze with varying themes; in 2007 it was designed with medieval features, including a castle, dragon, and knight. Open August through early November. Inexpensive.

Whiteface Mountain Gondola Ride (518-946-2223; www.whiteface.com; NY 86, Wilmington). Cloudsplitter gondola recommended for fall foliage. Open late June through Columbus Day. Moderate.

Central and Southwestern Adirondacks

Adirondack Scenic Railroad (315-369-6290; www.adirondackrr.com; NY 28, Thendara). Excursions from Thendara to Minnehaha or Carter Station, about 4 and 6 miles, respectively. Bike and rail or canoe and rail combinations. Train robberies, Halloween ride, other special events. Open May through November. Inexpensive.

Barton Garnet Mine Tours (518-251-2706; www.garnetminetours.com; Barton Mines Road, North River). Tours of open-pit mines; rock collecting; mineral shop. Open June through Columbus Day. Moderate.

Calypso's Cove (315-369-6145; 3183 NY 28, Old Forge). Arcade, bumper boats, batting cages, driving range, mini golf, go-karts. Open Memorial Day through Columbus Day. Moderate.

Enchanted Forest/Water Safari (315-369-6145; 3183 NY 28, Old Forge). New York's largest water theme park; a real blast for teenagers and younger kids. Try the Black River if you like your rides dark, wet, and fast. Open daily Memorial Day through Labor Day. Expensive.

Gore Mountain Northwoods Gondola Skyrides (518-251-2411; www.goremountain.com; Peaceful Valley Road, North Creek). Open fall weekends. Moderate.

McCauley Mountain Chairlift Ride (315-369-3225; www.mccauleyny.com; McCauley Mountain Road, Old Forge). Open daily June 25 through Labor Day; weekends Memorial Day through June 24. Inexpensive.

Upper Hudson Scenic Railroad (518-251-5334; www.uhrr.com; 3 Railroad Place, North Creek). Ride the round-trip or bike to Riparius and ride back. Kayak and canoe shuttles back upstream. There are plans for this excursion to eventually connect to Saratoga Springs, offering wonderful views between Lake Luzerne and The Glen. Open May through October, two runs daily. Inexpensive.

Beyond the Blue Line

New York's largest theme park—**Six Flags The Great Escape Fun Park** (518-792-6568; www.sixflags.com; US 9, Lake George)—is visible from the Northway, just south of Lake George village. It's an awesome complex with one-hundred rides, shows, and attractions; the Comet roller coaster is regarded as one of the world's classic thrills. Open daily June through Labor Day, plus some spring and fall weekends. Expensive. New adjacent **Great Escape Lodge & Indoor Waterpark** (888-708-2684) means thrills year-round. Expensive.

FISHING

Brook trout, lake trout, landlocked salmon, muskellunge, great northern pike, pickerel, walleye, smallmouth bass, largemouth bass, bullhead, whitefish, and assorted panfish are all native to Adirondack waters; toss in the exotics like brown trout, rainbow trout, splake, tiger musky, and kokanee, and an angler's alternatives approach Neptune's harvest. Of course, we can't guarantee that you'll actually catch anything. But with preparation—like reading a guidebook or calling one of the hotlines or spending a day with a guide on remote waters—you may be able to tell the story about the big one that *didn't* get away.

Quite the catch!
Courtesy of the Adirondack Collection, Saranac Lake Free Library

Begin your fishing education with the *New York State Freshwater Fishing Regulations Guide,* published by the Department of Environmental Conservation and available at DEC offices, sporting goods stores, tourist information centers, online (www.dec.ny.gov), or by mail (DEC, 625 Broadway, Albany, New York 12233). The free booklet details all the seasons and limits for various species. Everyone 16 and older who fishes in the Adirondacks must have a New York fishing license, which can be purchased at sporting goods stores and town offices. Nonresidents can get special five-day licenses; state residents 70 and older may get free licenses.

The DEC site also has helpful hotlines for anglers, describing the top fishing spots and what's hitting where on which kind of bait. Plus, there's information about the toxic build-up of mercury in fish. The site lists certain fish species in the Adirondacks that should not be consumed by children or pregnant women.

If you'd like to read about fishing, county and town tourism offices listed in Chapter 9 have the lowdown on local angling. You can find Dennis Aprill's *Good Fishing in the Adirondacks* (Countryman Press) in bookstores, and you can order I Love New York's comprehensive *Adirondack Fishing* guide at www.fishadk.com.

To get in the proper frame of mind for fishing, nothing beats a trip to a local fish hatchery. In the southeastern Adirondacks, the **Warren County Fish Hatchery** (518-623-2877; 145 Fish Hatchery Road, Warrensburg) is open daily with a nice picnic grove. In the Champlain Valley, the **Essex County Fish Hatchery** (518-597-3844; Creek Road, Crown Point) is also open every day. The only fish ladder in the park is on the Boquet River (School Street, Willsboro); if you time it just right in the fall, you can watch big salmon ascend the watery staircase. In the Northwest Lakes the **Adirondack Fish Hatchery** (518-891-3358; NY 30, Saranac Inn) specializes in raising landlocked salmon for stocking lakes.

Acid rain has had an effect on fishing in the southwestern quadrant of the Adirondack Park, where there's more precipitation and thinner soils. About two-hundred lakes and ponds that once supported fish are now devoid of them; research has shown it's not the direct effects of low pH levels, but acidic waters leaching toxic minerals from the soil that cause problems. Efforts to combat acidification by applying lime have shown some effect on small ponds. Biologists are also breeding trout that can survive in more acidic waters, but as yet these creatures have not been widely stocked. The good news is that more than two thousand lakes and ponds and countless miles of rivers and streams have stabilized at pH levels that support fish and all kinds of wildlife. For more information about acid rain, its effects, and what you can do to offset its spread, contact the DEC's **Division of Air Resources** (518-402-8452; 625 Broadway, Albany, NY 12233).

FISHING GUIDES, SCHOOLS, AND OUTFITTERS

Lake George and Southeastern Adirondacks

Adirondack Fishing Adventures (518-494-5770; www.adirondackcharters.com; Schroon River, Chestertown). Charter boat on Lake George and Schroon Lake, fly-fishing guides for interior ponds.

Adirondack Trout & Salmon (518-859-5035; www.adktroutguide.com; Lake Shore Drive, Lake George). Fly-fishing expeditions.

Ann's Bait & Tackle Shop (518-644-9989; Norowal Road, Bolton Landing). Charters and guides available.

Cherokee Trout Charters (518-644-2920; Main Street, Bolton Landing). Guided fishing trips on Lake George.

E & R Sport Fishing Charters (518-747-6987; www.lakegeorge-fishing.com; NY 9N, Diamond Point). Guided lake trout, salmon, and bass fishing.

Lake George Fly Fishing School (518-798-3494; 1571 US 9, Lake George). Instruction and trips.

Lockhart Charter Fishing & Guide Services (888-848-5253; www.fishlakegeorge.com; 2 Lake Road, Diamond Point). Ice-fishing and regular season trips on Lake George for salmon, lake trout, and northern pike; backcountry trips.

Mike's Lake George Fishing Charters (518-623-3288; 710 NY 28, Warrensburg). Charter boat on Lake George; sport-fishing guide.

Risky Business Fishing Charters (518-623-9582; 14 Meadowlark Lane, Warrensburg). Sport-fishing guide.

Rod Bender's Charters (518-668-5657; www.captjj.com; P.O. Box 76, Diamond Point). Guided light-tackle and ice fishing.

Ted's Charter Fishing Service (518-668-5334; NY 9N, Diamond Point). Charter boat for salmon, lake trout, bass on southern Lake George.

No-Kill Fishing

Angling for fun rather than for the frying pan is catching on across the country, especially in trout waters. If you'd like to match wits with a wild piscine, and then send it back to live for another day, here are some tips for catch-and-release fishing.

Use a barbless hook or take a barbed hook and bend down the barb with a pair of pliers. Be gentle landing your fish; some anglers line their nets with a soft cotton bag. When removing the hook, it's best not to handle the fish at all, since you can disturb the protective coating on the skin. If you have to touch the fish, wet your hands first, don't squeeze the body and don't touch the gills. If you can, extract the hook without touching the fish: hold the hook's shank upside down and remove it. Usually, the creature will swim happily away. If your fish is tired, you can cradle it gently, facing upstream so that water flows through the gills, or if you're in a lake, move it back and forth slowly as a kind of artificial respiration.

A 5-mile-long section of the West Branch of the Ausable River between Lake Placid and Wilmington is designated for catch-and-release fishing only. With the no-kill rules in effect for a decade, the action on the river has been transformed; the fly-fishing here can be the stuff dreams are made of. Also, Little Tupper Lake—home to a rare strain of brook trout—is designated for artificial lures and catch-and-release only. Don't even whisper the word "baitfish" if you plan to wet a line in Little Tupper or nearby Rock Pond.

Champlain Valley

Adirondack-Champlain Guide Service (518-963-7351; www.adirondackchamplain guideservice.com; 46629 NY 22. Long Pond Lodge, Willsboro). Guided trips on Lake Champlain and backcountry lakes.

Adventure Guide Service (518-963-4286; www.adventureguideservice.com; 37 Maple Street, Willsboro). Guided fly-fishing or spin-casting outings.

High Peaks and Northern Adirondacks

Adirondack Angler Guide Service (518-524-3364; www.adkangler.com; 161 Neil Street, Saranac Lake). Guided fly-fishing and light-tackle spin-casting trips; boat charters.

Adirondack Mountain Club (518-523-3441; www.adk.org; Adirondak Loj, Lake Placid). Fly-fishing workshops.

Adirondack Sport Shop/Francis Betters Guide Service (518-946-2605; www.adirondackflyfishing.com; NY 86, Wilmington). Fly fishing on the Ausable River; fly-fishing and fly-tying instruction; new tackle shop—a quarter mile from previous location—plus small café and basic motel.

Blue Line Sports, LLC (518-891-4680; 81 Main Street, Saranac Lake). Tackle and camping gear.

Bunkhouse Guide Service (518-946-2602; PO Box 377, Wilmington). Guided fly-fishing.

The Hungry Trout (518-946-2217; www.hungrytrout.com; NY 86, Wilmington). Fly shop; fly-fishing instruction; access to private section of the Ausable River. Ask about day-long trips to Twin Ponds. Lodging and two restaurants on the premises.

Jones Outfitters (518-523-3468; www.jonesoutfitters.com; 2733 Main Street, Lake Placid). Fly-fishing instruction; guide service; rod and reel repairs; Orvis shop.

Middle Earth Expeditions (518-523-7172; www.adirondackrafting.com; 4529 Cascade Road, Lake Placid). Guided fly- and spin-fishing trips.

The Mountaineer (518-576-2281; www.mountaineer.com; NY 73, Keene Valley). Fly-fishing school; fishing equipment.

Placid Bay Ventures Guide & Charter Service (518-523-2001; www.placidbay.com; 2187 Saranac Avenue, Lake Placid). Charter boat on Lake Placid; wilderness fishing trips; lodging.

Tahawus Guide Service (518-891-4334; NY 86, Ray Brook). Fishing trips to remote streams; corporate retreats.

Northwest Lakes

Adirondack Fishing Inc. (518-327-3133; www.adirondackfishing.net; 549 NY 86, Paul Smiths). Guided fishing trips; popular nighttime trout trips.

Packbasket Adventures (315-848-3488; www.packbasketadventures.com; 12 South Shore Road, Wanakena). Guided fishing trips. Fly-fishing and ice-fishing packages available. Bed & breakfast.

Central and Southwestern Adirondacks

Adirondack Mountain & Stream Guide Service (518-251-3762; Hardscrabble Road, Olmstedville). Wilderness fishing trips.

Beaver Brook Outfitters (888-454-8433; www.beaverbrook.net; 2349 NY 28, Wevertown). Guided trips; Orvis equipment; fly-tying and fly-fishing lessons.

Dave's Bait and Tackle (518-863-8318; 247 Bunker Hill Road, Mayfield). All-season tackle; cleaning station; fishing charter service.

North Country Sports (518-251-4299; Thirteenth Lake Road, North River). Fly-fishing and spin-fishing shop.

Outback Outfitters Guiding Service (518-251-5731; www.outbackoutfitter.com; P.O. Box 152, North River). Fly-fishing trips; lodging.

Thomas Akstens (518-251-2217; Bartman Road, Bakers Mills). Fly-fishing instruction; Adirondack patterns for bass and trout flies. Guide service on the Ausable and backcountry ponds.

Walleye Wizard Guide Service (518-725-8609; P.O. Box 287, Mayfield). Specializing in walleye fishing on Great Sacandaga Lake; boat charters.

Wharton's Adirondack Adventures (518-548-3195; Oxbow Lake Road, Lake Pleasant). Guided wilderness fishing trips.

GOLF

Savor the green rolling hills, craggy peaks, deep blue lakes, and bracing air—the Adirondacks does recall Scotland's landscape just a wee bit. Perhaps then it's no surprise

The Sagamore golf course, in Bolton Landing, was designed and built under Donald Ross's personal supervision in 1928. Courtesy of the Sagamore

that there are dozens of courses tucked in mountain valleys throughout the park. Once upon a time, there were even more golf tracks than are open today, links that were attached to grand hotels and exclusive private clubs. The book *Adirondack Golf Courses . . . Past and Present* (Adirondack Golf), compiled by Whiteface Inn golf pro Peter Martin, outlines the history of regional golf with dozens of old photographs and anecdotes. The annual publication *New York Golf* (Divot Communications) describes course upgrades, tournaments, and personnel and is available at selected pro shops. The only golf school near the Adirondacks is the **Adirondack Foothills Golf Academy** (315-831-5222; www.golfadirondacks.com; Alder Creek Golf Course, NY 12, Alder Creek), with two- and three-day packages that include lodging in Alder Creek's elegant old clubhouse, meals, and instruction.

Adirondack golf courses today range from informal, inexpensive, converted cow pastures to challenging, busy, championship links. At most places, you don't have to reserve a tee time, and at only a few are golfers required to rent carts.

Price Code for Greens Fees (for nine holes):

Inexpensive	Moderate	Expensive	Very Expensive
under $15	$15–$25	Over $25	Over $40

Lake George and Southeastern Adirondacks
1000 Acres Golf Club (518-696-2444; www.1000acres.com; 465 Warrensburg Road, Stony Creek). Nine holes; par 35; 3,900 yards. Inexpensive.

Bend of the River Golf Course (518-696-3415; 5 Park Avenue, Hadley). Nine holes; par 35; 2,700 yards. One of the first courses to open in the spring. Expensive.

Country Meadows Golf (518-792-5927; www.countrymeadowsgolf.net; NY 149, Fort Ann). Twelve holes; driving range. Inexpensive.

Cronin's Golf Resort (518-623-9336; www.croninsgolfresort.com; Golf Course Road, Warrensburg). Eighteen holes; par 70; 6,100 yards. Cottages on site. Inexpensive.

Green Mansions Golf Club (518-494-7222; www.greenmansionsgolf.com; 207 Darrowsville Road, Chestertown). 9 holes; par 36; 2,700 yards. Moderate.

Queensbury Country Club (518-793-3711; 907 NY 149, Lake George). Eighteen holes; par 70. Expensive.

The Sagamore (518-644-9400; www.thesagamore.com; Federal Hill Road, Bolton Landing). Eighteen holes; par 70; 6,900 yards. Designed by Donald Ross; challenging and lovely. Very Expensive.

Schroon Lake Municipal Golf Course (518-532-9359; Hoffman Road, Schroon Lake). Nine holes; par 36; 3,000 yards. Moderate.

Top of the World (518-668-3000; www.topoftheworldgolfresort.com; 441 Lockhart Mountain Road, Lake George). Nine holes; par 36; 2,900 yards. Moderate.

Champlain Valley
Cobble Hill Golf Course (518-873-9974; US 9, Elizabethtown). Nine holes; par 35; 3,000 yards. Completed in 1897; great views of the High Peaks. Inexpensive.

Harmony Golf Club, Port Kent Golf Course (518-834-9785; 95 North Street, Port Kent). Nine holes; par 30; 2,000 yards. Close to Vermont ferry. Inexpensive.

Moriah Country Club (518-546-9979; Broad Street, Port Henry). Nine 9 holes; par 32; 2,100 yards. Opened in 1900. Inexpensive.

Ticonderoga Country Club (518-585-2801; www.ticonderogacountryclub.com; US 9, Ticonderoga). Eighteen holes; par 71; 6,300 yards. Expensive.

Westport Country Club (518-962-4470; www.westportcountryclub.com; Liberty Street, Westport). Eighteen holes; par 72; 6,200 yards. Challenging; beautiful views. Very expensive.

Willsboro Golf Club (518-963-8989; 140 Point Road, Willsboro). Nine holes; par 35; 2,600 yards. Inexpensive.

High Peaks and Northern Adirondacks

Ausable Club (518-576-4411; www.ausableclub.org; 137 Ausable Road, St. Huberts). Nine holes; Scottish links-type course. Open to nonmembers in September only, Monday through Thursday. Inexpensive.

Ausable Valley Country Club (518-647-8666; www.avgolfcourse.com; 58 Golf Course Road, Au Sable Forks). Nine holes; par 34; 2,700 yards. Inexpensive.

Craig Wood Golf Course (518-523-9811; www.craigwoodgolfclub.com; Cascade Road, Lake Placid). Eighteen holes; par 72; 6,500 yards. Named after Lake Placid native Craig Wood, who won both the U.S. Open and Masters in 1941. Expensive.

Crowne Plaza Resort & Golf Club (518-523-2556; www.lakeplacidcp.com; Mirror Lake Drive, Lake Placid). Two eighteen-hole courses: the Mountain course, and the Links course. Lunch at the clubhouse is excellent. Very expensive.

High Peaks Golf Course (518-582-2300; Santanoni Drive, Newcomb). Nine holes; par 33; 2,600 yards. New in 2005; magnificent High Peaks views. Inexpensive.

Saranac Inn Golf & Country Club (518-891-1402; www.saranacinn.com; 125 County Route 46, Saranac Inn). Eighteen holes; par 72; 6,600 yards. Beautifully maintained course. Very expensive.

Saranac Lake Golf Club (518-891-2675; NY 86, Ray Brook). Nine holes; par 36; 3,000 yards. Inexpensive.

Whiteface Club Golf Course (518-523-2551; 373 Whiteface Inn Lane, Lake Placid). Eighteen holes; par 72; 6,500 yards. Challenging course; beautiful views. Very expensive.

Northwest Lakes

Clifton-Fine Golf Course (315-848-3570; 4173 Main Street, Star Lake). Nine holes; par 36; 2,800 yards. Inexpensive.

Tupper Lake Golf & Country Club (518-359-3701; Country Club Road, Tupper Lake). Eighteen holes; par 71; 6,200 yards. Inexpensive.

Central and Southwestern Adirondacks

Brantingham Golf Course (315-348-8861; Brantingham Road, Brantingham Lake). Eighteen holes; par 71; 5,300 yards. Moderate.

Cedar River Golf Course (518-648-5906; www.cedarrivergolf.com; 180 West Main Street, Indian Lake). Nine holes; par 36; 2,700 yards. Inexpensive.

Inlet Golf Course and Country Club (315-357-3503; NY 28, Inlet). Eighteen holes; par 72; 6,000 yards. Expensive.

Lake Pleasant Golf Course (518-548-7071; NY 8, Lake Pleasant). Nine holes; par 35; 2,900 yards. Moderate.

Nick Stoner Golf Course (518-835-4211; 1803 NY 10, Caroga Lake). Eighteen holes; par 70; 5,800 yards. Moderate.

Sacandaga Golf Club (518-863-4887; NY 30, Sacandaga Park, Northville). Nine holes; par 36; 3,000 yards. Inexpensive.

Thendara Golf Club, Inc. (315-369-3136; www.thendaragolfclub.com; off NY 28, Thendara). Eighteen holes; par 72; 6,000 yards. Expensive.

Wakely Lodge & Golf Course (518-648-5011; 110 Cedar River Road, Indian Lake). Nine holes; par 34; 2,500 yards. Inexpensive.

HIKING AND BACKPACKING

Walk on the wild side. The Adirondack Park has more than 2,000 miles of marked hiking trails leading to pristine ponds, roaring waterfalls, spectacular peaks, ice caves, and hidden gorges; perhaps the toughest choice for an Adirondack visitor is selecting where to go.

There are dozens of guidebooks to help you make that decision. The *Discover the Adirondacks* series (Lakeview Press) by the late hiker-historian Barbara McMartin and coauthors divides the park into eleven regions and describes the natural and human histories of dozens of different destinations; beside marked trails, McMartin suggests basic bushwhacks to reach great views. The guidebooks published by the Adirondack Mountain Club (ADK) slice the Adirondacks into six sectors; there's also a volume dedicated to the 132-mile Northville–Lake Placid Trail. Dennis Aprill's *Paths Less Traveled* (Pinto Press) notes dozens of small peaks to scale, with interesting wildlife or natural features. For details on these books, check the bibliography in Chapter 9, and for local sources, consult the bookstore section in Chapter 8.

For even more reading on tramps and treks, there's *Adirondac* magazine, published by ADK; *Adirondack Life* magazine, especially its *Annual Guides to the Great Outdoors,* outlines plenty of good long walks; the newspaper *Adirondack Explorer* features excursions all over the park; and the Department of Environmental Conservation has free guides to trails in wilderness and wild forest areas.

Buzz Off

Springtime in the Adirondacks can be lovely, but this earthly paradise has a squadron of tiny, persistent insects to keep humans from overwhelming the countryside. We speak here of blackflies. Bug season is usually late May through June, although its duration depends on the weather. If you are planning an extended hike, golf outing, streamside fishing trip, horseback ride, or similar activity, you'll want to apply insect repellent, wear light-color clothing (blue, especially dark blue, seems to attract blackflies), and tuck in your pant legs and shirt: The Adirondack red badge of courage is a bracelet of bites around the ankles or waist. Avoid using perfume, shampoo, or scented hairspray—these products broadcast "free lunch!" to hungry little buggers.

There's a pharmacy of lotions and sprays that use varying amounts of DEET (diethyl-meta-toluamide) as the active ingredient, but note that products containing more than 25% DEET should not be applied to children's skin. DEET should not be used at all on infants. A recent article in the *New England Journal of Medicine* cited a University of Florida study that tested the effectiveness of various repellents. Deep Woods Off, with about 20% DEET, won hands down. Off Skintastic, with far less DEET, was also very effective. Products with citronella failed miserably. If you don't want to use DEET, look for bug repellent with a soybean oil base.

Some people love Avon's Skin-So-Soft bath oil for confounding insects. Fabric softener sheets, like Bounce, can be tucked into your hatband to keep flies away from your face. Some Adirondackers prefer pine-tar based bug dopes, like Ole Woodsman, that also have the lasting aroma of authenticity; after a good dose of Ole Woodsman, your pillows and sheets will be scented, too. If these fail, there are bug jackets and pants, veils, and even crusher-type hats with lightweight netting attached.

If you're searching online, the Great Outdoor Recreation Pages (www.gorp.com) have a good selection of Adirondack hikes listed by area, like Keene Valley or Old Forge. Descriptions include length, difficulty, and directions to trailheads, but this information should be supplemented by a real topographical map. Saranac Lake's Web site, www.saranaclake.com, contains a bunch of "short and relaxing" walks plus more strenuous local hikes, like Mount Baker, an easy summit with a great view.

The Adirondack woods are free of many of the natural hazards that you need to worry about in other locales. There's some poison ivy in the Champlain Valley and parts of the High Peaks, but very little in the northwest lakes and central and southern Adirondacks. Rattlesnakes are found in the Tongue Mountain range near Lake George, and occasionally in the Champlain Valley; keep your eyes open when crossing rock outcrops on warm, sunny days. These Eastern timber rattlers are quite shy and nonaggressive, but do take care not to surprise one.

In some parts of the park, you can leave the trailhead and not see another person until you return to your car and look in the rearview mirror. The Five Ponds Wilderness Area, between Stillwater Reservoir and Cranberry Lake, is especially remote. Parts of the

Bear Mountain, overlooking Cranberry Lake, is an easy hike for kids. Annie Stoltie

Northville–Lake Placid Trail are many miles from the nearest road; passing through the West Canada Lakes or Cold River areas, you might go several days with just the cry of the loon or howl of the coyote for company. Going end-to-end on this long trail requires a minimum of ten days, and a solid amount of backcountry knowledge, but you can pick shorter sections for three-day junkets. Parts of the High Peaks—especially from southern access points—offer similar overnights. It's possible to find solitude even in the middle of the busy summer season if you select the right destination. Lest we make it sound too daunting, there are plenty of easy hikes of 2- to 5-miles that traverse beautiful terrain throughout the park. The DEC's High Peaks Unit Management Plan limits group size, prohibits campfires, and requires that dogs be leashed in this 226,000-acre wilderness; contact the DEC's Ray Brook office (518-897-1200) for the rules.

Don't assume that just because the Adirondacks doesn't reach the height of the Rockies that it's all easy strolling; paths can be steep and treacherous; weather is downright changeable. Wherever you choose to go, be prepared. Your pack should contain a flashlight, matches, extra food and water, map, compass, and extra clothes (wool or fleece for warmth; leave the cotton at home). At most trailheads, there's a register for signing in. Forest rangers rely on this data to estimate how much use a particular area receives; and, in the unlikely event that you get lost, the information about when you started, where you were planning to go, and who you were with would be helpful to the search team.

For neophyte hikers, the trails at the **Adirondack Park Agency Visitor Interpretive Centers at Newcomb** (518-582-2000; www.adkvic.org) and **Paul Smiths** (518-327-3000) are ingeniously designed to offer a wide range of nature in a relatively short distance, and you won't be too far from the building no matter how long you travel. You can join a guided trip to learn about wildflowers, mushrooms, trees, or birds. There are also wheelchair-accessible trails at both centers.

Several organizations and guide services lead trips and give map-and-compass, woodcraft, and low-impact-camping workshops.

Low-Impact Camping

Wilderness camping in the old days relied on techniques like digging deep trenches around tents, cutting balsam boughs for backwoods beds, sawing armloads of firewood, and burying garbage and cans. For camp clean-up, we used to think nothing of washing dishes in the lake, and scrubbing ourselves vigorously with soap as we cavorted in the shallows. All of these activities left a lasting mark on the woods and waters; today it's important to leave no trace of your visit.

Low-impact camping is perhaps easier than old-fashioned methods once you grasp the basics. Most of the skills are simply common sense: think of the cumulative effects of your actions when you set up camp and you're on your way to becoming a responsible wilderness trekker.

Choose a site at least 150 feet away from the nearest hiking trail or water source, and try to select a place that will recover quickly after you leave. Separate your tent from your cooking area to avoid attracting animals and to distribute the impact of your stay. When you leave, tidy up. Be sure the spot is absolutely clean of any trash—even stuff we commonly regard as biodegradable, such as banana peels—and spread dirt or dead leaves around any trampled areas.

Use a portable stove for backcountry cooking rather than a campfire. (Use only dead and down wood in the Forest Preserve; cutting trees on state land is prohibited.) Plan your meals so that you don't have extra cooked food; if no one in the party can assume the role of "master of the clean plate

St. Regis Mountain fire tower. Courtesy of Mark Bowie

club," then pack out all your leftovers. Wash your dishes and your body well away from streams and lakes using a mild vegetable-based soap.

How to sh-t in the woods is something to consider; nothing kills that "gee, isn't it terrific out here in the wilderness" feeling more than finding unmistakable evidence of other humans. Bring a shovel or trowel and bury that hazardous waste at least 6 inches down and 150 feet from the nearest water. Lean-tos and some backcountry campsites have privies; use them.

HIKING GUIDES AND ORGANIZATIONS

Adirondack Connections (518-359-2911; www.adirondackconnections.com; 78 Dugal Road, Tupper Lake). Guided hikes; backpack, paddling, skiing, or snowshoeing trips.

Adirondack Foothills Guide Service (518-359-8194; www.adkfoothills.com; Saranac Lake). Guided hikes: camping, hiking, canoeing, kayaking, fishing, hunting.

Adirondack Mountain Club (518-668-4447; www.adk.org; 814 Goggins Road, Lake George). Hikes with naturalists; fall foliage hikes; wilderness overnights; weekends for women, youth, and senior citizens. Many programs in the High Peaks at the **Heart Lake Program Center at Adirondak Loj**, in Lake Placid (518-523-3441; Adirondack Loj Road, Lake Placid).

Adirondack Park Agency Visitor Interpretive Centers (518-327-3000; www.adkvic.org; NY 30, Paul Smiths; 518-582-2000; NY 28, Newcomb). Guided hikes; nature trails; ecology programs for adults and children.

Bear Cub Adventure Tours (518-523-4339; Lake Placid). Guided hikes; paddling and fishing trips; ski tours.

Middle Earth Expeditions (518-523-7172; www.adirondackrafting.com; 4529 Cascade Road, Lake Placid). Backpack and day trips.

Packbasket Adventures (315-848-3488; www.packbasketadventures.com; 12 South Shore Road, Wanakena). Custom backcountry trips.

Piseco Guide Service (518-548-4442; Piseco). Camping, hiking, and canoeing in the southern Adirondacks.

Trailhead Lodge (518-863-2198; www.adirontreks.com; 206 Washburn Road, Benson). Workshops in GPS and map-and-compass skills, survival classes.

Trek Headwaters Guides (www.headwatersguides.com; 622 Lake Flower Avenue, Saranac Lake). Nature education, family backpacking, camping in canvas yurts.

Wilderness Education Association (518-891-2915; North Country Community College, 23 Santanoni Avenue, Saranac Lake). Excellent workshops and seminars in wilderness issues and techniques for trip leaders.

Tick, Tick, Tick

Cases of Lyme disease have been recorded in the Adirondacks, and hikers should take precautions against exposing themselves to deer ticks (*Ixodes dammini*). The ticks can be found in deep woods, although they prefer to stay on their host animals, whitetail deer and deer mice. Dogs—especially exuberant ones that go crashing through the brush—are more at risk than humans; you can have your pet inoculated against Lyme disease.

New York State has approved the sale of Permanone, a tick repellent that can be applied to clothing. Be careful! It's a very strong material that should not be placed on your skin or pets. You can minimize your exposure to ticks by wearing long pants (with cuffs tucked into your boots) and long-sleeve shirts, using a good insect repellent, and staying on the trail. If you wear light-color clothing, the ticks are easier to spot, and you can check yourself and your kids for the vermin while you're in the woods.

Deer ticks are very tiny, no bigger than a sesame seed. They don't fly. If you find an eight-legged crawling creature on your body, it could be a spider, a wood tick (not a carrier of Lyme), or an arachnid locally called a "ked," which, despite its scary-looking crablike pincers, is harmless.

Humans face the highest risk of tick contact in spring. If you find a tick attached to your skin, pull it out steadily with a pair of tweezers or your fingers, grasping as close to the tick's mouth as you can.

Save the creature in a jar—your doctor will probably want to see it. Apply a topical antiseptic to the bite. A tick must feed for several hours before the disease is transmitted.

If you see on your skin a clear area encircled by a red rash and are feeling flu-like symptoms, you may have contracted Lyme disease. Visit your doctor or a medical center for a Lyme test, but be aware that it takes several weeks after a bite for your body to show antibodies. Lyme symptoms mimic many other ailments so it's difficult to get an accurate diagnosis; most medical practitioners will begin a course of antibiotics if they believe you've been exposed.

HORSEBACK RIDING AND WAGON TRIPS

New York's North Country may not have the wide, open spaces of the Wild West, but there are hundreds of miles of wilderness horse trails to explore, and plenty of outfitters to put you on a reliable mount. The possibilities range from hour-long rides to overnight guided backcountry forays; if you have your own horse, the Department of Environmental Conservation (DEC) has trail networks across the park, and even operates campgrounds that accommodate man and beast. For a handy booklet describing these trails, contact the DEC (518-897-1200; www.dec.ny.gov). One rule applies for bringing in out-of-state horses: proof of a negative Coggins test is necessary. If you plan to camp more than three nights in the Forest Preserve, or in a group of six or more, you'll need a permit from the local forest ranger.

Hay rides, sleigh rides, and wagon trips are available in many communities. Listed below are outfitters and teamsters who offer wagon trips and places to ride. In general, local stables are open only during warm weather.

If you enjoy just watching horses, there are two excellent annual horse shows in Lake Placid, located a canter away from the Olympic ski jumps: the **Lake Placid Horse Show** in late June and the **I Love NY Horse Show** (518-523-9625; www.lakeplacidhorseshow.com; 514 Cascade Road, Lake Placid) immediately afterward. At both, the emphasis is on Olympic-level competition for hunters, jumpers, and riders. There are weekend polo games at the **Bark Eater Inn** (518-576-2221; www.barkeater.com; Alstead Hill Road, Keene), starting in late June. Admission is free; the Adirondackers play against teams from Saratoga Springs and Vermont. If you're an accomplished rider, you may even be able to join in a pick-up game. Polo lessons are available. See Chapter 3 for more equine options.

A legacy of the dude-ranch days in the southeastern Adirondacks, **Painted Pony Rodeo** (518-696-2421; www.paintedponyrodeo.com; Howe Road, Lake Luzerne) presents professional rodeo competitions Wednesday, Friday, and Saturday nights in July and August, rain or shine. This is the home of the country's oldest weekly rodeo, complete with trick riding and roping, clowns and novelty acts; there's more equine action, particularly riding through acres and acres of trails, at **1000 Acres Ranch Resort** (518-696-2444; www.1000acres.com; 465 Warrensburg Road, Stony Creek).

RIDING OUTFITTERS AND STABLES

Lake George and Southeastern Adirondacks

1000 Acres Ranch Resort (518-696-2444; www.1000acres.com; 465 Warrensburg Road, Stony Creek). Guided trail rides.

Bailey's Horses (518-696-4541; NY 9N, Lake Luzerne). Western trail rides; lessons; hay wagon or carriage rides around Lake Vanare; winter trail rides; trips to Lake George horse trails by reservation.

Bennett Stables (518-696-4444; NY 9N, Lake Luzerne). Trail rides.

Circle B Ranch (518-494-4888; www.circlebranch.com; 771 Potterbrook Road, Chestertown). Wagon, sleigh, and hayrides.

Circle L Ranch (518-623-9967; 869 High Street, Athol). Horse-pack outfitter; half- and full-day trips.

Rydin'-Hy (518-494-2742; Sherman Lake, Warrensburg). Trail and sleigh rides.

Saddle Up Stables (518-668-4801; www.ridingstables.com; 3515 Lake Shore Drive, Lake George). Trail rides.

Champlain Valley

Paradise Horseback Riding (518-834-5046; 164 Mace Chasm Road, Keeseville). Riding lessons.

Willow Hill Farm Camp (518-834-9746; www.willowhill.com; 75 Cassidy Road, Keeseville). Summertime riding instruction for kids.

High Peaks and Northern Adirondacks

Circle 7 (518-582-4191; NY 28N, Newcomb). Wagon trips to Santanoni Preserve by reservation only; hunting and fishing pack trips.

Emerald Springs Ranch (518-891-3727; www.emerald-springs.com; 651 NY 186, Saranac Lake). Horseback riding; equestrian classes; horse breeding.

High Peaks Stables (518-582-2260; 5788 NY 28N, Newcomb). Horseback riding and horse boarding; wagon trips to Santanoni Preserve; sleigh rides; hunting trips to Moose Pond.

The Ranch (518-891-5684; www.dude-ranches.com; Forest Home Road, Lake Clear). Horseback riding; sleigh rides; equestrian camp.

Sentinel View Stables (518-891-3008; Harrietstown Road, Saranac Lake). English and Western lessons; jumping instruction; bridle trails.

Wilson's Livery Stable (518-576-2221; Alstead Hill Road, Keene). Western or English trail rides by the hour or day; wagon and sleigh rides; polo games; open year-round.

Central and Southwestern Adirondacks

Adirondack Saddle Tours (877-795-7488; www.adkhorse.com; 5 Uncas Road, Eagle Bay). Trail rides into Pigeon Lake Wilderness Area; pack-horse trips into Moose River Recreation Area; cookout rides to Cascade Lake. Most half-day rides include a swim; bring a lunch. Open year-round.

PUBLIC HORSE TRAILS

Lake George and Southeastern Adirondacks

Lake George Trail System. East side of Lake George, off Pilot Knob Road; 41 miles of carriage roads on an old estate; lean-tos.

    Lake Luzerne. Off Route 9N near Lake Luzerne hamlet; on Fourth Lake; campsite (518-696-2031), with corral; 5 miles of trails on state land that connect with many miles of privately owned trails.

    Pharaoh Lake Horse Trails. Pharoah Lake Wilderness Area, East of Schroon Lake. 12 miles of sandy woods roads; lean-tos.

High Peaks and Northern Adirondacks

Cold River Horse Trails. Six miles east of Tupper Lake off NY 3; very difficult 13- and 32-mile-loop dirt trails; lean-tos and corral. Connects with easier Moose Pond and Santanoni trails.

    Meacham Lake. Three and a half miles north of Paul Smiths, off NY 30; 10 miles of trails, although they include two separate dead-end routes; lean-tos and barn.

    Moose Pond Trail. Starts at Santanoni trailhead just north of Newcomb off NY 28N; 10 miles.

    Raquette Falls Horse Trail. Branches off Cold River Trail; 1.6 miles.

    Santanoni Trail. North of Newcomb off NY 28N; 10-mile round-trip. Hitching trails and two wagon teams that transport people.

Northwestern Lakes

Saranac Inn Horse Trail System. Off NY 30 near Saranac Inn; several short trails to ponds in the St. Regis Canoe Area; 11-mile round-trip on the Fish Pond Truck Trail.

Central and Southwestern Adirondacks

Independence River Wild Forest. Off Number Four Road near Stillwater Reservoir; assembly area at Chases Lake Road, off NY 12, Greig, 28 miles of sand roads; connects with Otter Creek; barn.

    Moose River Recreation Area. Between Indian Lake and Inlet off NY 28, 28-mile dirt road plus many miles of old logging roads; campsites.

    Otter Creek Trails. Near Greig, off NY 12; nearly 50 miles of sandy roads; connects with Independence River.

    William C. Whitney Area. Between Tupper Lake and Long Lake, off NY 30. Horse campsites and more trails in development; sandy roads.

HUNTING

Native Americans, colonial scouts, and nineteenth-century travelers regarded the Adirondacks as happy hunting grounds. Early accounts describe shooting deer year-round for cooking at camp and for swank Manhattan restaurants. Old pictures show small groups of men displaying dozens of dead bucks; the moose—never truly abundant in the Adirondacks—probably disappeared in part due to over-hunting. (Other factors were loss of habitat and diseases transmitted by deer.) Market hunting has been outlawed for more than a century.

The Adirondack Guides Association was a major force in pushing the state to enact hunting laws that would ensure that deer would not face near extinction like the moose.

Hunting is a popular, regulated pursuit each fall in many Adirondack counties. Beside deer, there are seasons for black bear (the 2006 bear take for the Adirondack Park was more than 300), snowshoe hare, coyote, bobcat, and other small mammals, plus ruffed grouse, woodcock, wild turkey, and waterfowl. The booklets outlining game seasons are available from DEC offices, through the agency's Web site (www.dec.ny.gov) or by writing (625 Broadway, Albany, New York 12233); licenses can be purchased from sporting goods stores, town offices, or the DEC. Nonresidents may purchase five-day licenses. If you have never had a New York State hunting license, you must show proof that you have attended a hunter education course. Turkey hunting requires a special stamp from the DEC; waterfowl hunters must possess a Federal Migratory Bird Hunting Stamp.

In general, big-game seasons begin with early bear (mid-September through mid-October); archery for deer or bear (late September through mid-October); muzzleloading for deer or bear (one week in mid-October); and regular big-game season (third Saturday in October through the beginning of December). Bow and black-powder hunters may take antlerless deer; during regular season, it's bucks only in the Adirondack Park.

Wild turkeys, brought back to habitat in the southeastern Adirondacks, have been very successful moving into new territory such as mixed hardwood forest in the central Adirondacks. Toms are sought after in spring and fall seasons, but these birds are very wary and tough to track.

Wilderness, primitive, and wild-forest areas are all open to hunting. Hunters—even if they have a brand-new, state-of-the-art GPS unit—should be proficient with map and compass. Global-positioning units don't always work well in thick forest, and batteries do wear out.

Listed below are some licensed guides who specialize in hunting.

HUNTING GUIDES

Lake George and Southeastern Adirondacks
Northwoods Wilderness Guide Service (518-532-9745; www.newyorktroutfishing.com; 59 Deer Camp Road, Schroon Lake). Big and small game.

    Trout Brook Guide Service (518-532-7089; Main Street, Schroon Lake). Big and small game.

Champlain Valley
Adirondack-Champlain Guide Service (518-963-7351; www.adirondackchamplain guideservice.com; Long Pond, Willsboro). Big game, grouse, and snowshoe hare.

High Peaks and Northern Adirondacks
Adirondack Foothills Guide Service (518-359-8194; www.adkfoothills.com; P.O. Box 345, Saranac Lake). Big-game hunting.

    Brett Lawrence (518-576-9857; Adirondack Street, Keene Valley). Guided hunting trips.

    Bunkhouse Guide Service (518-946-2602; P.O. Box 377, Wilmington). Guided duck hunting.

    Little Black Brook Upland Birds (518-523-2161; Little Black Brook Farm, Haselton Road, Wilmington). Grouse and woodcock; meals available.

Middle Earth Expeditions (518-523-7172; www.adkhunting.com; 4529 Cascade Road, Lake Placid). Big game; lodging.

Stillwaters Guide Service (518-523-2280; Cascade Road., Lake Placid). Big game; bow hunting; snowshoe hare with beagles.

Central and Southwestern Adirondacks

Adirondack Mountain & Stream Guide Service (518-251-3762; www.adirondackmountainandstream.com; Hardscrabble Road, Olmstedville). Big game; snowshoe hare with hounds.

Adirondack Saddle Tours (877-795-7488; Uncas Road, Inlet). Pack-horse hunting trips.

Kittler Creek Outfitters (518-848-0698; 140 Ridge Road, Northville). Whitetail deer and bear hunting; snowshoe hare hunting with hounds.

Outback Outfitters Guiding Service (518-251-5731; www.outbackoutfitter.com; P.O. Box 152, North River). Big and small game; lodging.

Speculator Guide Service (518-548-7343; P.O. Box 107, Speculator). Small game.

ICE SKATING

Considering that the surface of Adirondack waters exist more months of the year in solid rather than liquid state, it's no wonder that ice skating is a popular pastime here. The modern sport of speed skating was launched in Saranac Lake and Lake Placid: In the early 1900s, more world records were set—and broken—by local bladesmen than at any other wintry place. Nowadays, there's backcountry skating on remote lakes and ponds or skating on plowed rinks in the towns and even indoor figure skating or hockey on Zamboni-maintained ice sheets.

If you'd like to try wilderness skating, wait until January. Cold, clear, still weather produces the most consistent surface. Ice that's two inches thick will support one person on skates, but it's better to wait for at least three inches to form, since currents and springs can create weak spots. Ice is thinner near shore, and be sure to steer clear of inlets, outlets, and other tributaries. In the Champlain Valley, Webb-Royce Swamp near Westport is a terrific place to skate. Ponds in the High Peaks are often good for skating by New Year's Day, especially if there's been little snow. You can scout Chapel Pond, off NY 73 south of Keene Valley, or the Cascade Lakes, on the same road, north of Keene, or Heart Lake, at the end of the Adirondack Loj Road. Ask locally for more favorite places.

Many towns offer lighted rinks with warming huts; check with tourist offices for hours. Long Lake's public rink is one of the better ones, and it's conveniently located on NY 30 between a pizzeria and a hotel. At Indian Lake, the town has built a great hockey rink at the foot of the ski hill, off NY 30. There's free skating on an indoor rink in **Fern Park**, in Inlet (1-866-464-6538); Old Forge has ice skating at its **North Street Recreation Center** (315-369-6983). Lake Champlain towns such as Ticonderoga and Westport often have good (or not so good, depending on the weather) skating. In Lake Placid, you can enjoy terrific ice outdoors most evenings at the **Olympic Speed Skating Oval**, on Main Street, or you can skate in the **Olympic Arena** (518-523-1655; www.orda.org; 2634 Main Street) at scheduled times for a small charge. If you want to try speed skating, you can get rental skates, a lesson, and ice time in Lake Placid. You can also try curling with the **Lake Placid Club** (518-327-3223). Lake Placid's Olympic ice gets lots of attention in annual Can-Am Hockey tournaments, camps, and clinics. Hockey fans can check out the Olympic Regional Development Authority's Web site, www.orda.org, for schedules. Tupper Lake (518-359-2531; McLaughlin Street) maintains rinks for hockey and skating; **Saranac Lake's Civic Center** (518-891-3800) has good ice indoors and an active youth hockey program.

Dimon Sports (518-523-1729; www.dimonsports.com; 6197 Sentinel Road, Suite 1, Lake Placid) specializes in hockey and speed and figure skates, outfits, and equipment. You can rent skates here or at the speed skating oval. Many of the sporting-goods stores throughout the region stock skates for children and adults.

Nordic skating is another sport that's gaining popularity and involves gliding long distances on frozen lakes and rivers on special blades that snap into cross-country-ski boots. Lake Champlain is a Nordic-skating mecca; always check ice conditions before setting out.

MINIATURE GOLF

If the thought of all that howling wilderness makes your kids scream for more familiar entertainment, perhaps one of the many mini golf links can fill the bill. Throughout the park, there are countless opportunities to sink little bitty putts after avoiding windmills, dead ends, and loop-de-loops; several are listed below, but you may want to call ahead for hours. Historians take note: Miniature golf was reputedly launched in downtown Lake George at the intersection of Beach Road and US 9 in the early years of the twentieth century. Lake George remains the Pebble Beach of Adirondack minis, and half a dozen courses are nearby. You can try **Around the World in 18 Holes** (518-668-2531; www.aroundtheworldgolf.com; Beach Road); **Lumberjack Pass Mini Golf** (518-793-7141; www.lumberjackminigolf.com; US 9); **Gooney Golf** (518-668-2589; www.goonygolf.com; US 9); **Pirate's Cove** (518-668-0493; www.piratescove.net; 2115 US 9); **Putts N Prizes** (518-668-9500; 8 Beach Road); and **Magic Castle Indoor Golf** (518-668-3777; 273 Canada Street). Farther up the road in Schroon Lake, is the **Narrows Pizza Miniature Golf Course** (518-532-7591; US 9), and you won't have to worry about what's for dinner after the round.

For the High Peaks and Northern Adirondacks area, there are mini golf links on both sides of Saranac Avenue, in Lake Placid: **Avalanche Adventures** (518-523-1195; www.avalancheadventures.com; 194 Saranac Avenue), with its eighteen-hole indoor course and eighteen-hole outdoor course, and **Pirate's Cove** (518-523-5478; www.piratescove.net; 1980 Saranac Avenue). Attached to Saranac Lake's funky restaurant **Eat N Meet Grill** (518-891-3149; www.eatnmeet.com; 139 Broadway) is a nine-hole mini golf course. Restaurant patrons can play a free round while they wait for their food. In the central Adirondacks go to Old Forge to choose from **Nutty Putty Miniature Golf** (315-369-6636; Main Street); **Over the Rainbow** (315-369-6565; NY 28); or **Calypso's Cove** (315-369-6145; www.watersafari.com; NY 28).

OLYMPIC SPORTS

Lake Placid is the only place in North America that has hosted two Winter Olympic Games, in 1932 and 1980. During the '32 Games, the American team won the bobsledding events, took silver and bronze medals in speed skating, hockey, figure skating, and bobsledding, and thus was regarded as the unofficial Olympic champion. In 1980, Eric Heiden garnered five gold medals in speed skating, and the U.S. hockey team won the tournament following a stunning upset over the Russians in the semifinal round. The legacy of Olympic glory lives on here, at the Olympic Training Center on Old Military Road, where hundreds of athletes eat, sleep, and work out in a high-tech setting, and in several specialized sports facilities in and around Lake Placid. Every season competitors come to town for coaching and practice.

There's just one place in the Northeast where you, too, can ride a real bobsled on an Olympic run: the **Olympic Sports Complex at Mount Van Hoevenberg**, a few miles from downtown Lake Placid. This thrill does not come cheap; in 2007 it was $55–$65, depending on the season, for the longest minute you'll ever spend. (Note that the sleds are piloted by professional drivers.) Rides are available Christmas through early March, depending on the track conditions. The "Summer Storm," a bobsled with wheels, shoots down the track when there's no ice on it. Call the **Olympic Regional Development Authority** (ORDA) for details (518-523-1655; www.orda.org; Olympic Center, Lake Placid).

Watching international luge, skeleton, and bobsled competitions is almost as exciting as trying it yourself, and perhaps easier on the cardiovascular system. Races are held nearly every winter weekend. Dress warmly for spectating; you'll want to walk up and down the mile-long track to see and hear the sleds zoom through. At some vantage points, sliders fly by nearly upside-down, and the racket of the runners is a lesson in the Doppler effect. You'll definitely want to see several push starts, where track stars have a decided advantage.

In the Olympic Arena, at the center of Lake Placid, you can watch youth and collegiate ice hockey tournaments, exhibition NHL games, figure-skating competitions, and skating exhibitions like "Stars on Ice," year-round. Since 1993, stars such as Kristy Yamaguchi and Scott Hamilton have come to Lake Placid in November and December to practice for national touring; ask at the arena about watching rehearsals. Indoor short-track speed-skating is incredibly exciting.

Ski jumping on the 90- and 120-meter jumps is thrilling; seeing people fly through the air is far more impressive in person than the sport appears on television. If watching from the bleachers, dress warmly. The 120-meter jump tower has a sky deck accessible by elevator and chairlift that provides the perfect spot to watch jumpers and surrounding mountains from above. In spring 2007 the elevator cost $5 for adults (the chairlift closes this time of year); in summer the chairlift and elevator cost $10, $14 on event days. Annual favorite competitions are the Fourth of July Ski Jump and October Flaming Leaves Festival (with blues, brews, and BBQ); these are Lake Placid spectator events where you will avoid hypothermia. Also, at the jumping complex (known as MacKenzie–Intervale), you can watch the U.S. freestyle skiers training in warm weather. The skiers go off jumps, tumble through the air, and land in a huge aerated pool of 750,000 gallons of water with their skis still attached.

At Whiteface Mountain, you can see occasional international freestyle and downhill and slalom races. In March check out men's and women's World Cup snowboard cross and parallel giant slalom races at the Olympic mountain. Or you can try riding the slopes yourself—look later in this chapter for more information on skiing and snowboarding in the Adirondacks.

RACES AND SEASONAL SPORTING EVENTS

Adirondack Sports & Fitness (518-877-8788; www.adksportsfitness.com; 15 Coventry Drive, Clifton Park) is an excellent source both for upcoming races and results of everything from snowshoe to cross-country-ski events to paddle fests to the Prospect Mountain Uphill Run.

Events are listed in chronological order within each region.

Lake George and Southeastern Adirondacks

New Year's Day Polar Plunge Swim (518-240-0809; www.lakegorgewintercarnival.com; Shepard Park, Lake George). Hundreds of brave swimmers plunge into icy Lake George.

Prospect Mountain Road Race (518-668-2195; Prospect Mountain Memorial Highway, Lake George). Five and a half miles uphill all the way, in early May.

Open Water Swim Marathon (18-543-6811; www.swimlakegeorge.com). Swim 41-km from Shepard Park to Hague in early July.

Adirondack Distance Run (518-792-7396; www.adirondackrunners.com). Ten-mile road race along Lake Shore Drive, in early July.

Lake George Triathlon (www.adktri.org). A shorter version of the real thing, in early September.

Adirondack Marathon Distance Festival (888-724-7666; www.adirondackmarathon.org). Twenty-six-mile run around Schroon Lake, in September.

Champlain Valley

Rotary International Fishing Classic (518-563-1000). Sponsored by Plattsburgh Rotary Club, covering all of Lake Champlain; weigh stations at Port Henry, Westport, and Willsboro, in late May.

Montcalm Mile Run (518-585-6619; www.lachute.us; Ticonderoga). Foot race down Ticonderoga's main street on the Fourth of July.

High Peaks and Northern Adirondacks

Adirondack International Mountainfest (518-576-2281; www.mountaineer.com; the Mountaineer, Keene Valley). Clinics, slide shows, and lectures by renowned ice and rock climbers, in mid-January.

Lake Placid Loppet (518-523-1655; www.orda.org; Olympic Regional Development Authority, Lake Placid). Twenty-five- and 50-kilometer citizens' races at Mount Van Hoevenberg, in late January.

Empire State Winter Games (518-523-1655; ORDA, Lake Placid). Figure skating, luge, bobsled, speed skating, ski jumping, cross-country skiing, and other events, in Lake Placid, in early March.

Pond Skimming (518-946-2223; www.whiteface.com; Whiteface Mountain, Wilmington). Skiers and snowboarders attempt to jump across a pool of freezing water, in April.

'Round the Mountain Canoe Race (518-891-1990; Saranac Lake Chamber of Commerce, Saranac Lake). Ten-mile canoe race on Lower Saranac Lake and the Saranac River, in early May.

Whiteface Mountain Uphill Footrace (518-946-2255; www.whiterace.com; Wilmington). An 8.3-mile race up the Whiteface Mountain Veterans Memorial Highway, on the second Sunday in June.

Watch Olympic hopefuls make death defying flips and spins at the Freestyle Aerial Training Center, in Lake Placid. Courtesy of the Olympic Regional Development Authority

Willard Hanmer Guideboat and Canoe Races (518-891-1990; Saranac Lake Chamber of Commerce, Saranac Lake). Races on Lake Flower for guideboats, canoes, rowing shells, war canoes, and kayaks, in early July.

Ironman USA (518-523-2665; www.ironmanusa.com; Lake Placid). The real deal: 2-plus-mile swim in Mirror Lake; 112-mile bike race from Lake Placid to Keene and back, twice; followed by a marathon. The best international competitors converge for this grueling event. in July.

Can-Am Rugby Tournament (518-891-1990; www.canamrugby.com; Saranac Lake Chamber of Commerce, Saranac Lake). North America's largest rugby meet, with more than 100 teams competing in fields throughout Lake Placid and Saranac Lake, in early August.

Olga Memorial Footrace (518-891-0375; www.saranaclake.com; Saranac Lake). Five- and 10-kilometer runs in Riverside Park, in August.

Summit Lacrosse Tournament (518-441-8228; www.lakeplacidlax.com). Teams of kids, old-timers, men, and women compete at the North Elba Horse Show Grounds, in mid-August.

Northwest Lakes

Chilly Ski Fest (518-327-3000; www.adkvic.org; Paul Smiths). January event at the Adirondack Park Agency Visitor Interpretive Center that combines skiing with a chili cook-off.

Great Adirondack Birding Festival (518-327-3000; www.adkvic.org; Adirondack Park Agency Visitor Interpretive Center, Paul Smiths). June birding extravaganza with trips— with an emphasis on boreal species—lectures, and workshops.

Woodsmen's Days (518-359-9444; www.woodsmendays.com; Tupper Lake Woodsmen's Association). Ax-fling, pole-climbing, sawing, carving, horse pull, chain-saw carving, and skidding competitions, plus clinics and demos, in July.

Tinman Triathlon (518-359-3328; www.tupperlakeinfo.com). Sponsored by Tupper Lake Chamber of Commerce; 1.2-mile swim, 56-mile bike, 13.1-mile run beginning at the Tupper Lake Municipal Park, in July.

Adirondack Arc Marathon to Tupper Lake (518-891-2744; www.macscanoe.com). Thirty-mile flatwater race in August from Saranac Inn to Tupper Lake.

Central and Southwestern Adirondacks

Snowflake Derby (315-369-6983; www.oldforgeny.com; Old Forge). A weekend carnival of races, parades, and fireworks, in February.

Hudson River Whitewater Derby (518-251-2612; www.whitewaterderby.com). Sponsored by North Creek Chamber of Commerce. Slalom race and Chuck Severance Memorial Downriver Race for canoes and kayaks on Saturday; Whitewater Derby Downriver race from North Creek to Riparius on the Hudson on Sunday; first weekend in May.

Adirondack Paddlefest (315-369-6672; www.adirondackpaddlefest.com). Canoe and kayak weekend with instruction, boats to try, and clinics, mid-May, in Old Forge.

Speculator Seaplane Fly-in (518-548-4521; www.speculatorchamber.com). A seaplane extravaganza held in June, on Lake Pleasant.

Black Fly Challenge (315-357-3281; www.inletny.com). Forty-mile NORBA-sanctioned mountain-bike race through the Moose River Plains, in June.

XTerra Off-Road Triathlon (518-251-2444; www.garnet-hill.com; Thirteenth Lake Road, North River). One-kilometer swim, 20-kilometer mountain bike, and 8-kilometer trail run, in June.

Adirondack Birding Festival (518-548-3076; www.adirondackbirds.com; at venues across Hamilton County). Birding hikes and paddles, lectures, and other events, in June.

Piseco Lake Triathlon (518-548-4521; www.adrkmts.com; Speculator). Half-mile swim, 11.5-mile bike, and 3-mile run, in July.

Race the Train (518-251-2602; www.uhrr.com, Riparius). Run along the Upper Hudson River Railroad, in August.

Mark 7 Road Races (www.campmark7.org; 315-369-6983; Old Forge). Five- and 10-km races, in August.

Adirondack Canoe Classic (518-891-2744; www.macscanoe.com). Sponsored by the Saranac Lake Chamber of Commerce. 90-mile three-day canoe race from Old Forge to Saranac Lake village, in early September.

Moose River Festival (315-369-6983; www.nyriverfestivals.com; Old Forge). Extreme race for kayaks and closed canoes through Class IV and V rapids, in October.

Reindeer Roundup (518-863-4974; www.laplandlake.com; Lapland Lake Cross Country Ski Center, Benson). Ten-kilometer citizens' cross-country-ski race; Empire State Games qualifier, before Christmas.

Rock Climbing

Plenty of steep, arduous rock walls can be found in the High Peaks, and scattered cliff faces are hidden in the central Adirondacks. Possibilities for rock and ice climbers abound, from nontechnical scrambles up broad, smooth slides to gnarly 700-foot pitches in the 5.11+ difficulty range. Adirondack climbers—from wannabes to folks with permanently chalky palms—all depend on a thick green guidebook, *Climbing in the Adirondacks: A Guide to Rock and Ice Routes* (Adirondack Mountain Club) by Don Mellor. This book is indispensable since the approaches to many of the best climbs involve a hike or bushwhack to the base. It also outlines hundreds of climbs and explains the local ethic on clean wilderness climbing: Leave as little trace as possible and place a minimum of bolts. New in 2008 is Jim Lawyer and Jeremy Haas's *Adirondack Rock,* a guide to new climbing routes and a remapping of old ones (for availability, call 315-677-5272 or visit www.adirondackrock.com).

Climbers can get tips in a few places. **The Mountaineer** (518-576-2281; www.mountaineer.com; NY 73, Keene Valley) sells climbing gear, topo maps, and guidebooks; advice is free. Many climbers' questions can be answered at the **Adirondack International Mountaineering Festival** each January, sponsored by the Mountaineer. Hardware and software for climbing can also be found in Lake Placid at **Eastern Mountain Sports** (518-523-2505; www.ems.com; 2453 Main Street) and **High Peaks Cyclery** (518-523-3764; www.highpeakscyclery.com; 2733 Main Street), which has an indoor climbing wall.

To learn the basics of climbing or to polish your skills if you've had some experience, a handful of guide services specialize in helping you climb higher:

Adirondack Alpine Adventures (518-576-9881; www.alpineadven.com; 10872 NY 9N, Keene). Rock- and ice-climbing guide service; instruction for women, small groups, or individuals.

Adirondack Mountain Club (518-523-3441; www.adk.org; Adirondack Loj, Lake Placid). Weekend workshops for beginners and intermediates; lodging.

Adirondack Mountain Guides (518-576-9556; www.adirondackmountainguides.com; Keene). Rock- and ice-climbing instruction for all levels of climbers.

Adirondack Rock and River (518-576-2041; www.rockandriver.com; Alstead Hill Road, Keene). Rock- and ice-climbing guide service; instruction for beginners to experts; natural indoor climbing wall; nice lodging.

The High Peaks

Dozens of mountaintops rise 4,000 feet or more above sea level in the Adirondack Park. You don't need to be a technical climber to enjoy the views, but you should be an experienced, well-prepared hiker capable of putting in at least a 12-mile round trip. For trail descriptions and access points, consult the *Guide to Adirondack Trails: High Peaks Region* (Adirondack Mountain Club) or James R. Burnside's *Exploring the 46 Adirondack High Peaks* (North Country Books). The following "Forty-Six" are in the area bounded by Newcomb on the south, Elizabethtown on the east, Wilmington on the north, and the Franklin County line on the west.

Peak	Elevation (in feet)	Peak	Elevation (in feet)
1. Mount Marcy	5,344	24. Mount Marshall	4,380
2. Algonquin Peak	5,115	25. Seward Mountain	4,347
3. Mount Haystack	4,961	26. Allen Mountain	4,347
4. Mount Skylight	4,924	27. Big Slide Mountain	4,249
5. Whiteface Mountain	4,866	28. Esther Mountain	4,239
6. Dix Mountain	4,839	29. Upper Wolf Jaw	4,185
7. Gray Peak	4,830	30. Lower Wolf Jaw	4,173
8. Iroquois Peak	4,830	31. Phelps Mountain	4,161
9. Basin Mountain	4,826	32. Street Mountain	4,150
10. Gothics Mountain	4,734	33. Sawteeth Mountain	4,150
11. Mount Colden	4,734	34. Mount Donaldson	4,140
12. Giant Mountain	4,626	35. Cascade Mountain	4,098
13. Nippletop Mountain	4,610	36. Seymour Mountain	4,091
14. Santanoni Peak	4,606	37. Porter Mountain	4,085
15. Mount Redfield	4,606	38. Mount Colvin	4,085
16. Wright Peak	4,580	39. South Dix Mountain	4,060
17. Saddleback Mountain	4,528	40. Mount Emmons	4,040
18. Panther Peak	4,442	41. Dial Mountain	4,020
19. Table Top Mountain	4,413	42. East Dix Mountain	4,006
20. Rocky Peak Ridge	4,410	43. Blake Peak	3,986
21. Hough Peak	4,409	44. Cliff Mountain	3,944
22. Macomb Mountain	4,390	45. Nye Mountain	3,944
23. Armstrong Mountain	4,390	46. Cousachraga Peak	3,820

(Elevations from *Of the Summits, Of the Forests*, Adirondack Forty-Sixers)

The Adirondack Forty-Sixers is an organization dedicated to these High Peaks. To earn the members' patch, you must have climbed all of the mountains listed above. The group performs trail work and

Visitors can drive up Whiteface Mountain Veterans Memorial Highway, park, then climb the stairs—or take an elevator—to the summit. Courtesy of the Olympic Regional Development Authority

education projects; for information, write to Adirondack Forty-Sixers, P.O. Box 180, Cadyville, NY 12918, or visit www.adk46r.org.

And More Peaks

In other parts of the park there are mountains nearly as high, with sweeping vistas of forests and lakes. A short list of pinnacles with marked trails and open summits or fire towers follows. Note that there are plenty more mountains in the park; ask locally for favorite vantage points.

Peak	Elevation (in feet)	Closest Town
Snowy Mountain	3,899	Indian Lake
McKenzie Mountain	3,832	Lake Placid
Lyon Mountain	3,830	Chazy Lake
Wakely Mountain	3,770	Indian Lake
Blue Mountain	3,759	Blue Mountain Lake
Hurricane Mountain	3,678	Keene
Pillsbury Mountain	3,597	Speculator
Ampersand Mountain	3,552	Saranac Lake
Vanderwhacker Mountain	3,386	Minerva
Crane Mountain	3,254	Johnsburg
Pharoah Mountain	2,557	Schroon Lake

ROWING

The Adirondack guideboat is the preeminent rowing machine for the region, and you'll find a selection of boat builders in Chapter 8.

Most of the small- to medium-size Adirondack lakes are suitable for rowing. Lakes with quiet bays—Indian, Paradox, Forked, Star, Long, Lake Pleasant, and others—offer several miles of open water, yet have less powerboat traffic than say, Lake George or Schroon Lake. You'll also find that early morning or early evening, when the winds are relatively calm, are the best times to row. Do carry a flashlight if you go out at dusk. Mirror Lake, on the backside of downtown Lake Placid, is not open to motorboats, so there's another fine possibility for rowers.

SAILING

The big lakes—George, Champlain, and Great Sacandaga—offer good sailing in the midst of beautiful scenery and have marinas for an evening's dockage or equipment repairs. In fact, any lake with a public launch is open to sailboats; the most suitable craft for bouldery-bottom Adirondack lakes are those with centerboards you can pull up in a jiffy. Even then, remember to keep an eye out for unmarked rocks! Sailing on island-studded waters can be tricky, since in the lee of an island you stand a good chance of being becalmed. Wind can whip shallow lakes into white-capped mini-oceans, too. A portable weather radio should be included in your basic kit; Adirondack forecasts (out of Burlington, Vermont) can be found at 162.40 megahertz.

You can purchase Coast Guard charts for Lakes George and Champlain, but not for most of the small interior lakes. Some USGS topographical maps have troughs and shoals marked, but these maps are of limited use to sailors. Your best bet is to ask at boat liveries for lake maps, or at least find out how to avoid the worst rocks.

For hardware, lines, and other equipment, check in the beginning portion of this chapter for a list of marinas. In the Lake George area, **Yankee Boating Center** (518-668-2862; www.yankeeboat.com; 3578 Lakeshore Drive, Lake George) is well stocked with everything from the essentials to brand-new boats. It also has a sailing school, and rents day sailers and cruisers. On Lake Champlain, **Westport Marina** (518-962-4356; www.westportmarina.com; 20 Washington Street, Westport) has a good selection of sailing supplies and rentals.

The Sagamore (866-385-6221; www.thesagamore.com; 110 Sagamore Road), in Bolton Landing, has a sailing school, and **Y-Knot Sailing** (518-656-9462; www.yknotsailing.org), at YMCA Camp Chingachgook, in Pilot Knob, offers sailing instruction, races, and workshops to sailors of all levels of experience and physical ability.

SCENIC FLIGHTS

If climbing a mountain isn't for you, yet you still seek a bird's-eye view, why not charter a small plane to soar above the wilds? Several pilots offer sightseeing flights at a reasonable price: a fifteen- to twenty-minute flight covering about 50 miles of territory costs less than the average evening out. You can make arrangements for longer flights, but in 2007 a typical short trip cost about $100 for a family of four. Seaplane services are also equipped to take canoeists, fishermen, and hunters into ponds and lakes. Listed below are a few fixed-wheel and seaplane services for private charters; you *must* call ahead for a reservation.

For a bird's-eye view of peaks and lakes, charter a seaplane. James Swedberg

Adirondack Flying Service (518-523-2473; www.flyanywhere.com; 73 Cascade Road, Lake Placid). Scenic flights over the High Peaks; air taxi.

Bird's Seaplane Service (315-357-3631; 275 NY 28, Inlet). Scenic flights; hunting and fishing charters.

Helms Aero Service (518-624-3931; Town Beach, Long Lake). Scenic seaplane flights; hunting and fishing charters.

Payne's Air Service (315-357-3971; Seventh Lake, Inlet). Scenic flights; hunting and fishing charters.

SCENIC HIGHWAYS

We may be biased, but we think that most Adirondack byways are pretty darn scenic: Even Interstate 87—the Northway—won an award as "America's Most Beautiful Highway" the year it was completed. Specifically, we're talking here about roads up mountains so that everyone can enjoy the view. In the Lake George area, **Prospect Mountain Veterans Memorial Highway** (518-668-5755; www.visitlakegeorge.com; off US 9 near Lake George village) snakes up a small peak to offer a terrific one-hundred-mile view stretching from the High Peaks to Vermont and the Catskills. Not too far from Lake Placid, **Whiteface Mountain Veterans Memorial Highway** (518-946-2223; www.whiteface.com; off NY 431, Wilmington) has a great view, too, looking down on other summits and silvery lakes. Both are state-operated toll roads open daily from late May through the fall.

SKIING: CROSS-COUNTRY AND SNOWSHOEING

The Adirondack Park is paradise for cross-country skiers. Most winters there's plenty of snow, upwards of 100 inches, especially in the higher elevations or west of the Champlain Valley. A wide range of destinations entices skiers, from rugged expeditions in the High Peaks to gentle groomed paths suitable for novices, plus hundreds of miles of intermediate trails. Many of the marked hiking trails on state land are not only suitable for cross-country skiing or snowshoeing, they're actually better for winter recreation since swampy areas are frozen, and ice-bound ponds and lakes can be easily crossed.

For suggestions on backcountry ski trails, consult *Classic Adirondack Ski Tours* by Tony Goodwin (Adirondack Mountain Club), or any of the books in the *Discover the Adirondacks* series (Lake View Press) by Barbara McMartin. *Adirondack Life* magazine outlines ski treks in its winter issues; if your local library has back issues, a treasure trove of potential ski trips is at your fingertips.

Many of the designated wilderness and wild-forest areas (described on pages 272-276) offer great ski touring on marked but ungroomed trails. State campgrounds—closed to vehicles from November through May—offer quiet, woodsy, snow-covered roads with gen-

New York Central ski trains made Old Forge the winter place to be in the 1930s and 1940s.
Courtesy of Ted Comstock, Saranac Lake

tle grades; places like Lake Durant, near Blue Mountain Lake, and Lake Eaton, near Long Lake, are popular with local skiers and usually have set tracks. Another option for exploring the wild wintry woods is to hire a licensed guide; check under "Hiking and Backpacking" earlier in this chapter for backcountry trip leaders.

Before setting out on any of these wilderness excursions, prepare your pack with quick-energy food; a thermos filled with hot tea or cocoa; extra hat, socks, and gloves; topo map and compass; matches; flashlight; and space blanket. Dress in layers of wool, polypropylene, or synthetic pile. Don't travel alone. Sign in at the trailhead register. Let friends know your destination and when you plan to return.

Many towns maintain cross-country-ski trails, and the **Adirondack Park Agency Visitor Interpretive Center at Paul Smiths** (518-327-3000; www.adkvic.org) has many miles of easy trails. At the **Newcomb VIC** (518-528-2000), the trails are not quite so great for skiing, but you can try snowshoeing at no charge.

The **Jackrabbit Trail** (518-523-1365; 301 Main Street, Lake Placid) is a superb resource, some 35 miles of groomed trails connecting Keene with Lake Placid, Saranac Lake, and Paul Smiths; eventually the route may extend to Tupper Lake. The trail combines old logging roads, abandoned rail lines, and trails and is named for Herman "Jack Rabbit" Johannsen, who laid out many ski routes in the 1920s. From some of the hotels in downtown Placid, you can strap on your skis and just head for the woods. There's even guided inn-to-inn skiing sponsored by some lodgings; check with your host if you're staying in the High Peaks. The Jackrabbit Trail joins with many of the commercial ski-touring areas and traverses the McKenzie Mountain Wilderness Area between Whiteface Inn and Saranac Lake. Note that dogs are not welcome on groomed portions of the Jackrabbit Trail, nor at the privately owned ski centers.

Beside wilderness trails and informal town ski trails, there are some excellent cross-country-ski areas with meticulously groomed tracks and rental equipment. You'll find a variety of ski areas listed below; we suggest calling ahead for information about snow cover. Many of the touring centers offer lessons, and the **Adirondack Mountain Club** (518-523-3441; www.adk.org; Adirondak Loj, Lake Placid) schedules backcountry- and telemark-skiing workshops.

Mount Van Hoevenberg (518-523-8824; www.adirondacksikidog.com), in Lake Placid, offers skijoring clinics, where you can learn to cross-country ski with your dog. Check out reindeer-joring demonstrations at **Lapland Lake Nordic Vacation Center** (518-863-4974; www.laplandlake.com), in Benson.

CROSS-COUNTRY-SKI CENTERS AND TRAIL NETWORKS

Lake George and Southeastern Adirondacks
Caroline Fish Memorial Trail (518-494-2722; Dynamite Hill, NY 8, Chestertown). Eleven-kilometer town trail; lighted for night skiing.

Friends Lake Cross-Country-Ski and Snowshoe Center (518-494-4751; www.friendslake.com; 963 Friends Lake Road, Chestertown). Thirty-two-kilometer groomed trails; rentals; instruction.

Rogers Rock State Campsite (518-623-1200; NY 9N, Hague). Ten-kilometer groomed trails; part of trail lit for night skiing.

Schroon Lake Ski Trails (518-532-7675). Backcountry skiing in Pharaoh Lake and Hoffman Notch wilderness areas.

Warren County Trails (518-623-5576; Hudson Avenue, Warrensburg). Sixteen-kilometer trails along the Hudson River.

High Peaks and Northern Adirondacks

Adirondak Loj (518-523-3441; www.adk.org; Adirondack Loj Road, Lake Placid). Twelve-kilometer backcountry trails; connect with numerous challenging wilderness trails; guided tours; lessons; food; lodging.

Bark Eater X-C Ski Center (518-576-2221; www.barkeater.com; Alstead Hill Road, Keene). Twenty-kilometer groomed trails; connects with Jackrabbit Trail; rentals; lessons; lodging.

Cascade Ski Touring Center (518-523-9605; www.cascadeski.com; NY 73, Lake Placid). Twenty-kilometer groomed trails; connects with Jackrabbit Trail; night skiing; rentals; lessons; ski shop.

Cunningham's Ski Barn (518-523-4460; www.cunninghamskibarn.com; 209 Main Street, Lake Placid, and 1 Main Street, North Creek). Groomed trails in North Creek and outside of North Creek at Beaver Meadows; rentals; lessons; full ski shop.

Dewey Mountain (518-891-2697; www.deweyskicenter.com; NY 30, Saranac Lake). Twenty-kilometer groomed trails; night skiing; lessons; guided tours.

Cross-country skiers explore the trails at Lapland Lake Nordic Vacation Center, in Benson.
Courtesy of Lapland Lake Nordic Vacation Center

Olympic Sports Complex at Mount Van Hoevenberg (518-523-2811; www.orda.org; NY 73, Lake Placid). Fifty-kilometer groomed Olympic trail system; connects with Jackrabbit Trail; rentals; lessons; ski shop.

Northwest Lakes

Cranberry Lake Trail (315-386-4000; NY 3, Cranberry Lake). Backcountry trails.

Deer Pond Loop (518-359-3328; NY 30, Tupper Lake). Fifteen-kilometer backcountry loop.

Cold, Cold, Cold

In the old days, folks caught unprepared in the wilds occasionally died of "exposure." Today, we call that same condition hypothermia (literally "low temperature"), and it remains a serious concern in cool, moist climates year-round. Even on a summer day, a lightly clad hiker can suffer from hypothermia after getting caught in the rain. In winter, unaccustomed strenuous exercise coupled with the wrong kind of clothing can lead to hypothermia.

Hypothermia is caused when the body loses warmth faster than it can produce heat. The normal body-core temperature of 98.6 degrees fahrenheit decreases to a dangerous level, which happens when the body is inadequately insulated by clothing. Precipitating events can be a dunking in cold water or soaking in steady drizzle. To compensate for heat loss, the body tries to produce more warmth, which burns up energy. As energy reserves dwindle and muscles become exhausted, hypothermia sets in.

Signs of hypothermia arrive in stages: First, the person feels and acts cold. He or she may shiver, have trouble with manual dexterity, or show bluish skin color. Next, shaking becomes uncontrollable, and the person starts to behave erratically, acting sluggish, apathetic, or cranky. The victim may stagger or seem off balance. Some folks refer to the "Umble Rule"—watch out when a companion begins to stumble, mumble, grumble, and fumble.

The final stage of hypothermia is a true medical emergency. The skin feels cold to the touch; shivering has stopped; limbs may be frostbitten. The victim may seem uncaring about survival. The treatment of all stages of hypothermia is basically the same—add heat. Warm the person with your hands, body-to-body contact, a fire. Provide hot liquids: tea, soup, cocoa, or any nonalcoholic beverage. For a person in severe hypothermia, prevent additional heat loss and get the victim to a medical facility quickly.

A few ounces of prevention go a long way in avoiding hypothermia. Dress in layers, especially clothing made of wool, polypropylene, or synthetic pile, all of which insulate when wet. ("Cotton kills," forest rangers say.) Bring spare hats, mittens, socks, overpants, windbreaker. Pack plenty of high-energy food and warm liquids. Put an "instant heat" packet in a pocket. Watch out for your friends and be honest about your abilities. Know when to turn back.

Frostbite and its cousin, frostnip, are not hypothermia. The terms refer to flesh actually freezing, and it's usually fingers, toes, ears, nose, or chin that are affected. Frostbite can occur quickly; look for skin appearing waxy. One test for frostbite is to pinch the affected part gently and watch for the color to change. Unaffected flesh will revert to its normal color, but frozen parts remain whitish and feel hard and cold.

At the first sign of frostbite, warm the affected part at body temperature. You can warm your hands by sticking fingers in your mouth, by placing them in an armpit or between your legs; ears and cheeks can be warmed with a dry hand; feet can be warmed up with the help of a buddy's body. Do not rub a frostbitten part; you can cause severe tissue damage since there are actual ice crystals in the cells. Don't use temperatures above 110 degrees fahrenheit for warming, as excessive heat can cause greater damage. (Be very careful using a pocket hand warmer.) Avoid refreezing frostbitten parts.

Deep frostbite should not be thawed. It sounds grim, but it's better to walk out on frozen feet than it is to thaw them and then try to shuffle along. Severe frostbite is a medical emergency that will need evacuation and lengthy hospitalization to repair circulatory damage.

Central and Southwestern Adirondacks

Adirondack Woodcraft Ski Touring Center (315-369-6031; Rondaxe Road, Old Forge). Fifteen-kilometer groomed trails; night skiing; rentals; ski shop.

Fern Park Recreation Area (315-357-5501; Loomis Road, Inlet). Twenty-two-km groomed trails; night skiing.

Garnet Hill Ski Center (518-251-2444; www.garnet-hill.com; thirteenth Lake Road, North River). Fifty-kilometer groomed trails; connects with trails in Siamese Ponds Wilderness Area; rentals; lessons; ski shop; food; lodging. Hire a guide for a great back-country trip that goes off the back side of Gore Mountain to Garnet Hill.

Gore Mountain (518-251-2411; Peaceful Valley Road, North Creek). Eleven-kilometer groomed trails; rentals; lessons; ski shop; food.

Lapland Lake Nordic Vacation Center (518-863-4974; www.laplandlake.com; 139 Lapland Lake Road, Benson). Forty-kilometer groomed trails; rentals; lessons; ski shop; food; lodging.

McCauley Mountain (315-369-3225; www.oldforgeny.com; McCauley Mountain Road, Old Forge). twenty-kilometer groomed trails at downhill area plus skiing at Thendara Golf Club; rentals; lessons; food.

Speculator Cross-Country-Ski Trails (518-548-4521; Elm Lake Road, Speculator).

CROSS-COUNTRY-SKI OUTFITTERS AND SHOPS

High Peaks and Northern Adirondacks

Blue Line Sports, LLC (518-891-4680; 81 Main Street, Saranac Lake). Ski rentals and sales; sporting goods; maps.

Cascade Ski Touring Center (518-523-9605; www.cascadeski.com; NY 73, Lake Placid). Rentals; lessons; ski shop; full-moon ski parties.

Eastern Mountain Sports (518-523-2505; www.ems.com; 2453 Main Street, Lake Placid). Cross-country, telemark, and backcountry equipment; gear; guidebooks; maps.

High Peaks Cyclery (518-523-3764; www.highpeakscyclery.com; 2733 Main Street, Lake Placid). Cross-country, telemark, and backcountry equipment for sale and rent; snowshoe rentals; outdoor gear and books.

Maui North (518-523-7245; www.mauinorth.net; 134 Main Street, Lake Placid). Ski and snowboard rentals and sales; gear.

The Mountaineer (518-576-2281; www.mountaineer.com; NY 73, Keene Valley). Cross-country, telemark, and backcountry equipment; gear; guidebooks; maps.

Central and Southwestern Adirondacks

Beaver Brook Outfitters (888-454-8433; www.beaverbrook.net; 2349 NY 28, Wevertown).
Cross-country ski and snowshoe sales and rentals; outdoor clothing; guidebooks.

    Cunningham's Ski Barn (518-251-3215; NY 28, North Creek). Groomed trails in North
Creek and outside of North Creek at Beaver Meadows; downhill and cross-country-ski
sales and rentals; clothing.

    Inlet Ski Touring Center (315-357-6961; South Shore Road, Inlet). Racing and touring
equipment; lessons; repairs; trails connect with Fern Park.

    Mountainman Outdoor Supply (315-357-6672; NY 28, Inlet; and 315-369-6672; NY
28, Old Forge; www.mountainmanoutdoors.com). Hiking, camping, snowshoe, and cross-
country-ski gear sales and rentals.

Beyond the Blue Line

Wooden Ski and Wheel (518-561-2790; www.woodenskiandwheel.com; 4614 US 9,
Plattsburgh). Cross-country-ski equipment; repairs; outdoor gear.

Skiing: Downhill and Snowboarding

Skiing has been a part of Adirondack life since the 1930s. Weekend ski trains brought
thousands of folks to Old Forge and North Creek. In North Creek they could "ride up and
slide down." The "ride up" was in school buses equipped with wooden ski racks mounted
on the outside, and the "slide down" was on twisty trails carved out of the forest near
Barton Mines, across from the present-day slopes on Gore Mountain.

At 3,430 feet, Whiteface Mountain boasts the greatest vertical drop in the East.
Courtesy of the Olympic Regional Development Authority

Today there are a couple of high-profile mountains with challenging slopes and extensive snowmaking: Whiteface and Gore, both operated by the Olympic Regional Development Authority. There are also nice little mountains where the emphasis is on family fun rather than on the trendiest gear. A few towns, like Indian Lake and Newcomb, run free downhill areas for residents and guests. Of course, you won't find human-made snow there, and you'll have to remember dormant skills for managing a poma lift or a rope tow, but you can have a blast with the kids and beat the crowds.

Naturally, downhill season in the Adirondacks depends on the weather. Often snowmaking begins in early November, and some trails may open by Thanksgiving, but it can be Christmas week before the snow is reliable throughout an entire ski area. Many people prefer spring conditions when there's corn snow and bright sunshine. Whatever the weather, it's not a bad idea to call ahead for the ski conditions before you go.

Compared to ski areas in Vermont or the Rockies, the Adirondack ones seem undeveloped. The emphasis at the hills is on skiing and snowboarding, not on hot-tub lounging, nightlife, or après-ski ambiance. At the base of a mountain, you won't find condos or designer restaurants for fancy meals and lodging, you have to go to town. Listed below are some downhill ski areas within the Adirondack Park.

Price Code

Downhill Ski Areas	Inexpensive	Moderate	Expensive
(Weekend lift ticketsfor an adult)	under $20	$20–$40	over $40

High Peaks and Northern Adirondacks

Mount Pisgah

518-891-0970
Mount Pisgah Road, off Trudeau Road, Saranac Lake
Trails: 1 main trail; 4 side trails
Lifts: 1 T-bar
Vertical drop: 300 foot.
Snowmaking: Yes
Price: Inexpensive
Open: Tuesday through Sunday; weekdays 3–9 PM; Saturday and Sunday, 10 AM–5 PM

If you've read *The Bell Jar*, you're acquainted with Mount Pisgah. Sylvia Plath skied there in the 1950s and chronicled her spectacular tumble in the book. Since then, the hill was operated on-again, off-again until the late 1980s, when volunteers restored the slopes. Their efforts encouraged public officials to revitalize the area. The mountain today is still very much a family ski area, with a friendly atmosphere and slopes geared to intermediate skiers. One section called "Suicide" falls somewhere between a modest drop-off and a mini-headwall; 10-year-olds think it's awesome.

There's snowmaking for most of the hill, thanks to local fundraising efforts, and a ski school, patrol, and base lodge. Pisgah is one of the few places left in the Adirondacks where you can enjoy night skiing; local residents often hit the slopes after work.

Whiteface Mountain

518-946-2233

www.whiteface.com

5021 NY 86, Wilmington

Trails: 76

Lifts: 8 chairlifts; high-speed gondola

Vertical drop: 3,430 feet

Snowmaking: 98 percent

Price: Expensive

Open: Daily 8:30 AM–4 PM

New York governor Averill Harriman dedicated Whiteface Mountain, a state-owned facility, in 1958; the event was marred slightly when the chairlift he was riding came to a dead halt, and Harriman had to be rescued by ladder from his lofty perch.

The Olympic mountain has the longest vertical drop in the East and lots of intense, expert skiing. Cloudspin, one of the black-diamond trails, is long and hard with big bumps; Wilderness, another toughie, is the site of international mogul competitions. Intermediate skiers have dozens of challenging trails, with the 3-mile-long Excelsior at the top of the list. Skiing the mountain's double black-diamond slides when they're open is a real adventure. Whiteface is big enough—but not a place you can get lost in—to accommodate scads of skiers without building up long lift lines.

There's an excellent Kids Kampus—play-and-ski program for tots—and a first-rate ski school. Whiteface is constantly expanding offerings for snowboarders, including a quality half-pipe and terrain parks. In 2007 World Cup snowboard athletes competed here. Other

Boarders are accommodated at North Creek's Gore Mountain. Courtesy of the Olympic Regional Development Authority

races, on boards and skis, happen during the season—check www.whiteface.com for a calendar of events.

There are three lodges for food, drink, and discussing the slopes, plus a full ski shop with rentals. Although a weekend adult ticket is more than $60, there are sizable midweek discounts, special promotions, and ladies' days.

Central and Southwestern Adirondacks

Gore Mountain

518-251-2411
www.goremountain.com
Peaceful Valley Road, off NY 28, North Creek
Trails: 75
Lifts: 7 chairs; 3 surface lifts; 1 high-speed gondola
Vertical drop: 2,100 ft.
Snowmaking: 97%
Price: Expensive
Open: Daily 9 AM–4 PM

Near North Creek, the cradle of North Country alpine skiing, is the other state-owned Adirondack ski hill: Gore Mountain, which opened in 1964. Since 1984, Gore has been managed by the Olympic Regional Development Authority, as is Whiteface Mountain. Under ORDA, snowmaking has been installed over virtually all of the mountain, and trails have been widened.

Gore is intermediate heaven, with wide-open cruising runs, such as Showcase, Sunway, and Twister, on the lower part of the mountain, accessible from the high-speed gondola or triple chair. Mogul mavens and expert skiers can find good sport on Rumor and Lies, some of the steepest trails in the East. The high-speed gondola is a godsend on frigid days. Shredders have plenty to get excited about at Wild Air, the state-of-the-art snowboard park. The Saddle Lodge offers a nice mid-mountain place to linger, with food, beverages, fireplaces, and a heck of a view.

The mountain has an excellent snow sports school for all ages, and, new in 2008, Gore's Lincoln Logs Welcome Center, which houses a daycare, a ski-and-play program for preschoolers, and rentals. The Base Lodge has a cozy lounge, with a pub and food court. Citizen racers can join in NASTAR competitions every weekend, while snurfer wannabes can take snowboarding lessons.

A recent development is revitalization of North Creek's original Ski Bowl, an easy slope to ski, plus terrain park with half-pipe, and lift-serviced tubing.

McCauley Mountain

315-369-3225
www.oldforgeny.com/mccauley
McCauley Mountain Road, off Bisby Road, Old Forge
Trails: 21
Lifts: 5 (1 double chair, 2 T-bars, 1 rope tow, 1 poma lift)
Vertical drop: 633 feet
Snowmaking: 65%

Price: Inexpensive
Open: Wednesday through Monday, 9 AM–4:15 PM

Hank Kashiwa, the international racing star and ski designer, learned his first snowplow turns here; his brilliant career is something folks in Old Forge still talk about. Actually, the Town of Webb school has produced three U.S. Olympic ski-team members, thanks to good coaches and the welcoming intermediate slopes at the local hill.

This little mountain has heaps of natural snow, due to a microclimate that can produce 200 inches or more during an average winter. Helmers and Olympic, both of which have snowmaking, are the most difficult runs. Intermediates can sample Upper God's Land, a ridge trail; Sky Ride, a wide route serviced by the double chair; or the gentle, sweeping Challenger. The lift crew feeds the deer here, so even nonskiers can enjoy a visit. You'll find all the amenities at McCauley: a ski school, rentals, food, and drink.

Beyond the Blue Line

There's good skiing just outside the Adirondack Park, too. **Titus Mountain** (518-483-3740; www.titusmountain.com; 215 Johnson Road, Malone) has 27 trails, 1,200 vertical feet, 8 chairlifts, night skiing, and snowmaking on 90% of the runs. To the west, **Snow Ridge** (315-348-8456; www.snowridge.com; off NY, Turin) has 22 trails and gets about 230 inches of natural snow a year. Snowmaking has been installed on some trails.

SNOWMOBILING

Deep blankets of snow, miles of old roads, active local clubs, and support from town trail-maintenance programs add up to excellent snowmobiling in many parts of the park. A hub of snowmobile activity is Old Forge, which offers 500-plus miles of groomed, packed trails and issues more than 14,000 snowmobile permits each winter. (Permits are available from the Tourist Information Center on NY 28 in the center of town or by going to www.old forgeny.com.) Trails in Old Forge spread out like a river with numerous tributaries. You can connect with the Inlet trails to the east, or the Independence River Wild Forest and Big Moose trails to the north, and Forestport and Boonville routes to the south. These trails meet still other trails, so that you can continue farther east from Inlet to Indian Lake or Speculator, and then from Speculator to Wells, or you can go from Inlet to Raquette Lake, and then on to Long Lake and Newcomb. Confused? There's information listed below to help you track down maps and brochures, or even find a guide. For Indian Lake snowmobiling go to www.ilsnow.com.

Beside the Old Forge–Inlet area, which receives more than 15 feet of snow during an average winter, there are more than 400 miles of snowmobile trails in the Tupper Lake–Saranac Lake–Lake Placid area, and near Cranberry Lake, there are scores of miles of trails. Many trail networks throughout the park cross private timberlands as well as the state forest preserve. Public lands designated as wild forest areas are open to snowmobiling; wilderness areas are not. (You'll find descriptions of these areas near the end of this chapter.) The DEC is a clearinghouse for snowmobile rules and regulations in the park, and offers snowmobile trail maps; its Web site, www.dec.ny.gov, also has links to sites with Adirondack snowmobile trails. For detailed maps of local trails, contact **Long Lake Parks, Recreation and Tourism Department** (518-624-3077; www.longlake-ny.com); **Indian Lake Chamber of Commerce** (518-648-5112; www.indian-lake.com); **Inlet Information**

Office (315-557-5501; www.inletny.com); and **Adirondacks Speculator Region Chamber of Commerce** (518-548-4521; www.speculatorchamber.com).

As with any winter pursuit, planning and preparation help make a successful outing. Know your machine; carry an emergency repair kit and understand how to use it. Be sure you have plenty of gas. Travel with friends in case of a breakdown or other surprise situations. Never ride at night unless you're familiar with the trail or are following an experienced leader. Avoid crossing frozen lakes and streams unless you are absolutely certain the ice is safe. Some town or county roads are designated trails; while on such a highway, keep right, observe the posted snowmobile speed limit, and travel in single file.

Your basic pack should contain a topographic map and compass as well as a local trail map; survival kit with matches, flashlight, rope, space blanket, quick-energy food, and something warm to drink; extra hat, socks, and mittens. Although a sip of brandy may give the illusion of warming you up, alcohol impairs circulation and can hasten hypothermia. And an arrest for snowmobiling under the influence carries with it severe penalties.

SNOWMOBILE RENTALS AND GUIDES

For navigating unfamiliar territory during a full day's riding, a knowledgeable leader is a real asset. In some communities, you can rent a sled, but this service is not widespread. For example, in the eastern Adirondacks you can book a guided tour or rent snowmobiles from ¼ **Mile Ranch** (518-696-3113; www.halfmileranch.com), in Lake Luzerne, and **Bolton Landing Snowmobile Tours** (518-644-9941). In Lake Placid, **Lake Placid Snowmobiling, Inc.** (518-523-3596; www.lakeplacidsnowmobiling.com) or **Snow Tours, Inc.** (518-523-3415).

Near Old Forge, several dealers, in addition to selling and repairing sleds, rent snowmobiles: **Old Forge Sports Tours** (800-854-1202); **Clark's Marina** (315-357-3231; www.clarksmarina.com; Inlet); and **Don's Polaris** (315-369-3255; www.donspolaris.com; NY 28, Old Forge). Also, check out **Village Rentals, Sales & Service** (518-548-RENT; www.villagerentalsny.com; Speculator) and **Adirondack Mountain Sports** (518-648-0215; www.adirondackmountainsports.com; Indian Lake).

SPAS

Who said this chapter was only outdoor recreation? In a few select resorts, you can sit for a day at the spa, or if time is short, there's the **Speedy Spa** (518-523-5500; www.lpspeedyspa.com), in Lake Placid. At this quick stop, you can get a massage or manicure, among other treatments. **Mountain Moon Day Spa** (518-523-8864; www.mountainmoon.us), in Lake Placid, offers massages, pedis, manis, and other treatments, too. Check local papers for massage therapists; several practice in the High Peaks and around Chestertown and Old Forge.

The most extensive spas are at **The Sagamore** (800-358-3585; www.thesagamore.com), in Bolton Landing, the **Mirror Lake Inn Resort and Spa**(518-523-2544; www.mirrorlakeinn.com), in Lake Placid, and the **Whiteface Lodge** (518-523-0560; www.thewhitefacelodge.com), in Lake Placid.

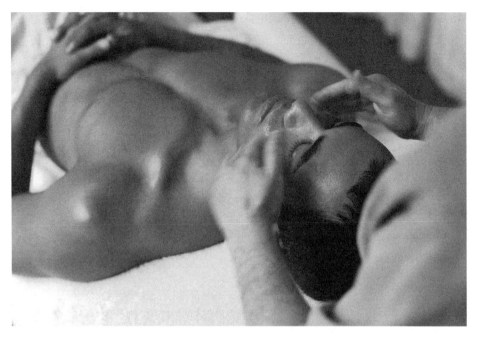

There are several full-service spas in the Adirondacks. The Mirror Lake Inn Resort and Spa's body treatments contribute to a restful Lake Placid vacation. Courtesy of the Mirror Lake Inn Resort and Spa

Whitewater Rafting

The wild, remote Upper Hudson River provides some of the East's most exhilarating whitewater: nearly 17 miles of continuous Class III to V rapids. From 1860 to 1950, river drivers sent logs downstream every spring to sawmills and pulp mills, and they followed along behind the churning, tumbling timber in rowboats to pry logjams loose. Since the mid-1970s, the Hudson's power has been rediscovered for recreational purposes, with numerous rafting companies making the trip from Indian River, just south of Indian Lake, to North River.

Reliable water levels are provided by a dam release below Lake Abanakee, courtesy of the town of Indian Lake. Releases begin about April 1 and last through Memorial Day. Since 2000, the season has increased, with summer and fall dam releases.

Although you don't need whitewater paddling experience to enjoy a trip down the Hudson, you do need to be age 14 or older, in good physical condition, and a competent swimmer. The outfitters supply you with wetsuit, paddle, life jacket, and helmet; they also shuttle you to the put-in, give on-shore instructions in safety and paddling techniques, and serve a hot meal at the end of the trip. Rafters should bring polypropylene underwear to wear under the suits; wool hats, gloves, and socks; sneakers; and dry, warm clothing for after the trip. (Springtime Adirondack air can be chilly, and the water temperature is truly frigid.)

A licensed guide steers each raft and directs the crew. This trip is not for passive passengers; you're expected to paddle—sometimes hard and fast—as the guide instructs. The Hudson Gorge is an all-day adventure, containing four to five hours of strenuous exercise, with the 2007 price, depending on the season, of $70–$110 per person.

Several rafting companies also offer short, fun trips on the Sacandaga River near Lake Luzerne. These junkets float 3.5 miles and last about an hour. Dam releases make the stream navigable all summer, and the cost is about $20–$25 per person. On the other end of the spectrum is the Moose River from McKeever to Port Leyden; this is a 14-mile beast absolutely for experienced whitewater paddlers only. The Moose is runnable after spring ice-out, and the charge is about $100 per person.

WHITEWATER OUTFITTERS

Adirondac Rafting Company (518-523-1635; www.lakeplacidrafting.com; 7 Patch Lane, Lake Placid). Hudson River trips from April through October.

Adirondack River Outfitters Adventures (1-800-525-RAFT; www.aroadventures.com; Box 649, Old Forge). Trips on the Hudson and Moose Rivers in spring; Hudson, Black, and Sacandaga Rivers in summer.

Adirondack Wildwaters Inc. (518-696-2953 or 800-933-2468; Box 801, Corinth). Hudson River trips in spring; Moose River trips in April.

Adventure Sports Rafting Company (800-441-RAFT; www.adventuresports rafting.com; Main Street, Indian Lake). Hudson River trips in spring, summer, and fall; spring trips on the Moose.

Beaver Brook Outfitters (1-888-454-8433; www.beaverbrook.net; 2349 NY 28, Wevertown). Hudson River trips April through October.

Hudson River Rafting Company (1-800-888-RAFT; www.hudsonriverrafting.com; NY 28, North Creek). Black, Hudson, and Sacandaga River trips in spring, summer, and fall; Moose River trips in April and May.

The North Creek Rafting Company takes its customers on a wild ride through the Hudson River Gorge.
James Swedberg

Middle Earth Expeditions (518-523-7172; www.adirondackrafting.com; 4529 Cascade Road, Lake Placid). Hudson River trips and overnight float-in fishing trips.

North Creek Rafting Company (1-800-989-RAFT; www.northcreekrafting.com; 9 Ordway Lane, North Creek). Whitewater rafting trips on the Hudson, Moose, Boreas, and Salmon Rivers; yoga retreats and live music overnight trips available; vegetarian lunch options.

Wild Waters Outdoor Center (518-494-4984; www.wildwaters.net; 11223 NY 28, The Glen). Hudson River trips in spring; Moose River trips in spring; Sacandaga River trips in summer. Excellent kayak workshops.

WILDERNESS AREAS

"Where man is only a visitor who does not remain," is a phrase contained within legislation that defined the sixteen wilderness areas of the Adirondack Park in the early 1970s. These portions of the Forest Preserve are 10,000 acres or larger and contain little evidence of modern times. Wilderness areas are open to hiking, cross-country skiing, hunting, fishing, and other similar pursuits, but seaplanes may not land on wilderness ponds, nor are motorized vehicles welcome. Listed below are Adirondack wilderness areas.

More than a quarter-million acres of former paper company lands may be open to the public in the next few years. Champion International, International Paper, and Finch, Pruyn & Company properties have been sold, with some state land acquisitions expected. Check with the Department of Environmental Conservation for new opportunities throughout the North Country.

Lake George and Southeastern Adirondacks
Pharaoh Lake. 46,000 acres; east of Schroon Lake hamlet. Extensive trail system; thirty-six lakes and ponds; lean-tos; views from Pharaoh and other nearby mountains.

High Peaks and Northern Adirondacks
Dix Mountain. 45,000 acres; southwest of Keene Valley. Adjacent to High Peaks wilderness; rock climbing at Chapel Pond; views from Noonmark, Dix, and many other mountains.

Giant Mountain. 23,000 acres; between Elizabethtown and Keene. Roaring Brook Falls; extensive hiking trails; views from Rocky Peak Ridge, Giant, and other mountains.

High Peaks. 226,000 acres; between Lake Placid and Newcomb. Excellent trail network; rock climbing at Wallface and other peaks; small lakes and ponds; views from Mount Marcy, Algonquin, and numerous other summits. Some interior destinations (Lake Colden and Marcy Dam) and peaks are very popular, to the point of being overused; more than 12,000 people climb Mount Marcy every year.

Jay Mountain. 7,100 acres; east of Jay. Lengthy ridge trails.

McKenzie Mountain. 38,000 acres; north of Ray Brook. Trails for hiking and cross-country skiing; Saranac River; views from McKenzie and Moose Mountains.

Sentinel Range. 23,000 acres; between Lake Placid and Wilmington. Small ponds for fishing; few hiking trails; views from Pitchoff Mountain. This area is remote and receives little use.

Northwest Lakes
St. Regis Canoe Area. 20,000 acres; west of Paul Smiths. Fifty-eight lakes and ponds for

canoeing; views from St. Regis and other mountains; trail network for hiking and cross-country skiing.

Central and Southwestern Adirondacks

Blue Ridge. 46,000 acres; south of Blue Mountain Lake. Contains several miles of the Northville–Lake Placid Trail for hiking and cross-country skiing; Cascade, Stephens, Wilson, Mitchell, and other trout ponds.

   Five Ponds. 101,000 acres; between Cranberry Lake and Stillwater Reservoir. Numerous ponds; canoeing on the Oswegatchie River; many acres of old-growth forest; some hiking trails. This area receives little use. Extensive damage from 1995 storm blowdown of thousands of trees; inquire locally before planning a trip.

Waterfalls

Throughout the Adirondacks, the combination of streams and rivers and mountainous terrain provides numerous waterfalls. Some are spectacularly high, like T-Lake, which is taller than Niagara; others, like Buttermilk Falls, near Long Lake, are just a two-minute walk from the car. Listed below are just a few of the cascades you can visit.

Falls name	Description	Nearest town
Auger Falls	Gorge on the Sacandaga River; easy hike from NY 30	Wells
Blue Ridge Falls	On The Branch; visible from Blue Ridge Road.	North Hudson
Bog River Falls	Two-tier falls at Big Tupper Lake; visible from County Road 421	Tupper Lake
Buttermilk Falls	Raquette River; easy hike	Long Lake
Cascade Lake Inlet	Rock falls above Cascade Lake; 4-mile hike from Big Moose Road	Big Moose
Falls Brook	One-mile hike	Minerva
The Flume	On West Branch Ausable River; visible from NY 86	Wilmington
Hanging Spear Falls	Opalescent River; remote wilderness	High Peaks
High Falls	Oswegatchie River; remote	Cranberry Lake
OK Slip Falls	Hudson River; highest vertical drop in the Adirondacks	Indian Lake
Raquette Falls	Raquette River; remote	Tupper Lake
Rockwell Falls	Sacandaga RiverLake	Luzerne
Shelving Rock	On Knapp estate; 4-mile hike	Pilot Knob
Split Rock Falls	Boquet River; access from NY 73	Elizabethtown
T-Lake Falls	Steep; remote, dangerous	Piseco
Wanika Falls	Chubb River; remote lean-to nearby	Lake Placid

Ha De Ron Dah. 27,000 acres; west of Old Forge. Small ponds and lakes; hiking and cross-country-ski trails around Big Otter Lake. This area receives little use.

Hoffman Notch. 36,000 acres; between Minerva and the Blue Ridge Road. Ponds and trout streams; a few hiking trails. This area is used mostly by fishermen and hunters.

Nehasane Primitive Area. 6,000 acres; lovely Lake Lila; near Long Lake.

Pepperbox. 15,000 acres; north of Stillwater Reservoir. Few trails; difficult access; mostly wetlands; excellent wildlife habitat.

Pigeon Lake. 50,000 acres; northeast of Big Moose Lake. Numerous lakes, ponds, and streams; trails for hiking and cross-country skiing.

Siamese Ponds. 112,000 acres; between North River and Speculator. Canoeing on Thirteenth Lake; Sacandaga River and numerous trout ponds; trails for hiking and cross-country skiing.

Silver Lake. 105,000 acres; between Piseco and Wells. Silver, Mud, and Rock Lakes; southern end of the Northville–Lake Placid Trail. This area receives little use.

West Canada Lakes. 157,000 acres; west of Speculator. Cedar, Spruce, West Canada Lakes, and 160 other bodies of water; portions of the Northville–Lake Placid Trail and other hiking trails. One of the largest roadless areas in the Northeast.

William C. Whitney. 15,000 acres; Little Tupper Lake and Rock Pond for excellent paddling and camping; miles of woods roads for cross-country skiing; several remote ponds. Between Long and Tupper Lakes.

WILD FOREST AREAS

More than a million acres of public land in the park are designated as wild forest, which are open to snowmobile travel, mountain biking, and other recreation. Some of the wild forest areas are listed below.

Lake George and Southeastern Adirondacks

Lake George. On both the east and west shores of the lake, north of Bolton Landing. Contains the Tongue Mountain Range on the west, and the old Knapp estate, with 40+ miles of hiking and horse trails, on the east.

Wilcox Lake. West of Stony Creek. Miles of snowmobile trails and old roads; ponds and streams for fishing.

Don't Touch That Critter!

In recent years rabies cases have been reported in the northern and southeastern corners of the Adirondacks. The disease seems to be spread by raccoons, foxes, and skunks in upstate New York.

If you come across a wild animal acting unafraid or lying passively, by all means stay away from it. Don't touch dead creatures you may find. However, humans are not at great risk for rabies exposure since contact with sick wildlings can be avoided.

Dogs must be inoculated against rabies. Keep your pet under control when traveling through the woods.

Champlain Valley

Hammond Pond. Between Paradox and Moriah, with old roads for hiking and ponds for fishing.

High Peaks and Northern Adirondacks
Debar Mountain. Between Loon Lake and Meacham Lake. Horse trails; hiking; fishing in the Osgood River.

Saranac Lakes. West of Saranac Lake village. Excellent canoeing; island camping.

Northwest Lakes
Cranberry Lake. Between Cranberry Lake and Piercefield. Snowmobile and hiking trails; trout ponds.

Central and Southwestern Adirondacks
Black River. Between Otter Lake and Wilmurt. Ponds and streams.

Blue Mountain. Northeast of Blue Mountain Lake. Contains part of the Northville–Lake Placid Trail; Tirrell Pond; views from Blue Mountain.

Ferris Lake. Between Piseco and Stratford. Dirt roads for mountain biking and driving through by car; numerous ponds and streams.

Independence River. South of Stillwater Reservoir. Dirt roads; Independence River; snowmobile trails; beaver ponds.

Jessup River. Between the south end of Indian Lake and Speculator. Miami and Jessup Rivers, and Lewey Lake; views from Pillsbury Mountain; trails for snowmobiling, hiking, and mountain biking.

Moose River Plains. Between Indian Lake and Inlet. Dirt roads; numerous ponds and streams; Cedar River and Cedar River Flow; primitive car-camping sites; snowmobile trails. If you want to see moose, this is the place.

Sargent Ponds. Between Raquette Lake and Long Lake. Trout ponds; hiking trails; canoe route between Raquette Lake and Blue Mountain Lake.

Shaker Mountain. East of Canada Lake. Dirt roads; hiking, cross-country skiing and mountain-biking routes.

Vanderwhacker Mountain. Northwest of Minerva. Fishing on the Boreas River; views from Vanderwhacker Mountain.

WILDLIFE

Viewing the bears at the town dump was a time-honored pastime for generations of tourists, but local landfills closed during the early 1990s and ended this quaint practice. To be honest, watching a sow and her cubs rip through garbage bags wasn't all that pleasant. Nowadays, the Adirondack Park offers a great variety of wildlife in their natural habitats to observe.

With marsh and mountain, field and forest to explore, experienced birders might be able to see a hundred different species in day. (Back in the 1870s, young Theodore Roosevelt and a friend compiled and published a bird guide to the northern Adirondacks listing some ninety-plus native birds they had seen.) In late spring, warblers in all colors of the rainbow arrive, and the best places to watch for them is along edges where habitats meet, such as woods on the border of a wetland, or along a brushy field. A variety of song-birds, including kingbirds, flycatchers, grosbeaks, waxwings, thrushes, wrens, and sparrows all nest here. The Adirondacks has the best Bicknell's Thrush habitat in the Northeast.

Many interior lakes and ponds are home to kingfishers, ducks, herons, and loons; listen and watch for that great northern diver in the early morning and at dusk. Peregrine falcons and bald eagles, absent from the park for much of the twentieth century, have been reintroduced. Cliffs in the High Peaks are now falcon eyries, and you should be able to spot a bald eagle or two near Tupper Lake, Meacham Lake, or Franklin Falls Pond. In the evening, listen for owls: the barred owl, known by its call, "Who cooks for you, who cooks for you," is quite common. In the fall, look up to see thousands of migrating Canada and snow geese. Wild turkeys—absent from the Adirondacks until the 1990s—are positively ubiquitous, especially along roadsides in the central Adirondacks.

Birders can participate in the **Great Adirondack Birding Festival**, at the Adirondack Park Agency Visitor Interpretive Center (518-327-3000; www.adkvic.org), in Paul Smiths, in June. Activities include birding trips, with an emphasis on boreal species, lectures, and workshops. **The Adirondack Birding Festival** (518-548-3076; www.adirondackbirds.com), also in June, but in venues across Hamilton County, involves birding hikes and paddles, lectures, and other events.

Small mammals are numerous: varying hares, weasels, mink, raccoons, fisher, pine martens, otters, bobcats, porcupines, red and gray fox. Coyotes, with rich coats in shades of black, rust, and gray, can be seen in fall, winter, and spring, and their yips and yowls on a summer night can be thrilling to the backcountry campers' ears. About fifty lynx from the Northwest Territories were released in the High Peaks in the 1980s, to restore the big cats to their former range, but it appears now that few survived.

Whitetail deer are seemingly everywhere, especially in the early spring before the fawns are born. In Old Forge, even in front yards facing busy Main Street, does are as common as squirrels.

About one-hundred moose live here now, definitely restocking themselves and raising calves in the central Adirondacks and northwest lakes. The best place to see moose is—no surprise—Moose River Recreation Area, where bulls can be seen in fall from woods roads. If you encounter one of these draft-horse size guys, do not approach! They tend to be very cranky during rutting season.

Many of the state campgrounds are good places to observe wildlife, especially aquatic birds and mammals. Ask the caretaker about where to see resident otters, ducks, loons, ospreys, and you may be rewarded with a wonderful vacation experience.

YOGA

Yoga studios have popped up across the park. The following offer year-round classes and will instruct students privately: Mary Bartel at **Inner Quest Yoga & Wellness Center** (518-891-9944; www.innerquestyoga.net; 238 Broadway, Saranac Lake); **Iyengar Yoga with Karen Stolz** at the Keene Valley Fitness Center and the Adirondack Day Spa in Lake Placid (518-576-9562; www.yogawithkarenstolz.com; P.O. Box 179, Keene); and Susanne Murtha at **Yoga in the Adirondacks** (518-251-3015; www.yogaintheadirondacks.com; 2 Coulter Road, Bakers Mills).

The Sagamore's fitness center has daily classes (1-866-385-6221; www.thesagamore.com; 110 Sagamore Road, Bolton Landing); and in July and August **Yoga on the Mountain** yoga classes are offered at the top of Little Whiteface (518-946-2223; www.whiteface.com; Whiteface Mountain, Wilmington)—call ahead and ride the gondola to the top.

8

Shopping

Woodsy Whimsy to Practical Gear

Designer-label devotees, mall rats, and outlet gypsies may find themselves at sea on an Adirondack vacation. Shopping here ranges from quirky to funky to woodsy, with nada a Prada in sight. True Adirondack style—substance over style and function over form—predates the Ralph Lauren look by a century. Today, in shops across the park, you can get hearty woolens and practical gear without worrying whether you are setting or following the trend.

Emblematic of the region's classic designs is the always-in-season Adirondack chair, available from woodworkers in shops large and small. You can get the country seat in basic pine or beautiful native hardwoods, with rockers or curved backs, as a settee or porch swing, or even hinged so the whole thing folds for storage.

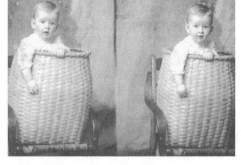

An Adirondack pack basket can carry your gear, your game, your grandkids. Courtesy of Ted Comstock, Saranac Lake

Rustic furniture, from simple tables to sculptural headboards, remains an authentic product line crafted by artisans who search the woods for the right piece of crooked yellow birch, the ideal cedar sapling. For a song (almost), you can purchase a rustic picture frame—or you can spend a small fortune on a museum-quality piece. Adirondackana (a term that describes housewares with a woodsy motif, historic collectibles, prints, books, and native crafts) is the specialty of fine stores that have been in business since the 1950s.

During the past thirty years, handcrafts have enjoyed a renaissance in the region. Typical items range from ash-splint pack baskets to chenille scarves to contemporary jewelry depicting miniature fishing lures. Some artisans rely on Adirondack wood to fire their kilns, or Adirondack wool for their yarns, or even quills from native porcupine for their jewelry. Other craftspeople are here for quiet lifestyles and natural inspiration and may not necessarily use indigenous items in their work. Items can be purchased in shops and galleries and at individual studios and fairs, noted in this chapter.

For book lovers, there are shops offering contemporary novels, trashy paperbacks for a rainy day, wholesome tales for kids, and a plethora of how-to, where-to, and why-to publications. If you can't find it on the shelves, just ask—these independent bookstores can order most anything in print. In some emporiums, you'll find new and old books combined with other things like health foods, tobacco, or hardware, making for an excellent afternoon's browsing.

Dozens of antique shops are located in the park, with concentrations around Warrensburg, the Champlain Valley, and Lake Placid. From Stickley rockers to postcards, moose antlers to Georgian silver, squeeze boxes to cheese boxes, there's bound to be a dealer who has what you're looking for at a fair price. Don't miss the first-rate antique shows, which you'll find listed here under "Fairs and Flea Markets."

General stores are still the real deal in North Country towns, supplying the goods for daily life from fresh milk to rain ponchos to crescent wrenches, and maybe even a wedding present. We like to think that the definition of an authentic general store would be a place where you could buy truly everything—from socks to dessert—you'd need for a week in the wilds.

The waters of the Adirondack Park attract many small-craft aficionados to special gatherings and to the fine traditional boat exhibit at the Adirondack Museum (described in Chapter 6). Boat builders who make guideboats—a sleek rowboat—along with guys who create everything from ultralight canoes to runabouts are listed in this chapter.

You won't find the modern suburban shopping mall inside the Adirondack Park, however. For that consumer experience you need to go south, to Aviation Mall (off I-87, Glens Falls), the big-box retailers of Wilton (I-87 Exit 15, Saratoga Springs), or north, to Champlain Centres (off I-87, Plattsburgh), or west, to Watertown, Utica, Syracuse, and beyond. Schroon Lake, Old Forge, and Lake Placid have old-fashioned main streets that you can stroll for serious window shopping; in recent years the historic village of Essex has blossomed into a delightful destination with galleries and boutiques. Canada Street, Lake George's main drag, is a Day-Glo kaleidoscope of T-shirt sellers, ice-cream stands, and souvenir joints; if you can't decide what to get the folks back home there's a psychic advisor who might be able to help.

ADIRONDACKANA

The word defines all kinds of material things that complement the countryside and evoke textures: bark, wood grain; smells: balsam, cedar; tastes: maple, apple; forest colors: deep green, gold, sienna. For a sampling of Adirondackana, you need to travel to the heart of the park.

Lake George and Southeastern Adirondacks

LAKE GEORGE
Ralph Kylloe Antiques and Rustics Gallery (518-696-4100; www.ralphkylloe.com; 1796 NY 9N). Established in 1995, enormous shop with exceptional rustic furniture and décor for the home. Open year-round; worth a special trip.

Ralph Kylloe's giant log cabin, near Lake George, is packed with antiques and furniture. James Swedberg

You can find Adirondack tchotchkes in shops throughout the park. Courtesy of Kelly Kilgallon

High Peaks and Northern Adirondacks

KEENE VALLEY

The Birch Store (518-576-4561; www.birchstore.com; 1778 Main Street, near the Noon Mark Diner). Antiques, hip clothing, cards, lotions, and interesting jewelry combined with traditional Adirondack camp furnishings: blankets, birch-bark baskets and frames, chairs, balsam pillows, and wicker ware in a classy vintage storefront. Open daily, year-round.

LAKE PLACID

Adirondack Craft Center (518-523-2062; www.adirondackcraftcenter.com; 2114 Saranac Avenue). Decorative work by more than 300 artisans.

Adirondack Decorative Arts & Crafts (518-523-4545; 2512 Main Street). Delightful four-story shop with a huge inventory—everything from birch-bark-patterned table linens to one-of-a-kind twig furniture, oiled canvas jackets, bark lampshades, jewelry, and Lightfoot's soap. The best source for woodsy cabinet hardware. Open year-round; worth a visit.

Adirondack Museum Store (518-523-9074; www.adkmuseum.org; 2477 Main Street). Books, prints, cards, clothing, jewelry, housewares. Open year-round.

Adirondack Store and Gallery (518-523-2646; www.theadirondackstore.com; 109 Saranac Avenue, W. of Cold Brook Plaza). This place launched the Adirondackana trend decades ago. If you're looking for anything—pottery, wrapping paper, doormats, sweaters, stationery, cutting boards—emblazoned with loon, trout, pinecone or moose motifs, search no further. There's an excellent selection of Adirondack prints by Winslow Homer and Frederic Remington; antique baskets and rustic furniture; camp rugs and blankets; woodsy ornaments for the Christmas tree, including minute Adirondack chairs. Be sure to visit the basement. Open daily, year-round. Gift registry.

RAY BROOK

The Ray Brook Frog (518-891-3333; www.raybrookfrog.com; NY 86). Everything you could ever need for the rustic home: furniture, lighting, pillows and throws, rugs, signs, clocks, coasters, picture frames, baskets, kitchen stuff, art, birch-bark everything. Open year-round.

SARANAC LAKE

Adirondack Trading Company (518-891-6278; 48 Broadway). Gift shop with plenty to choose from, especially cards, picture frames, and tchochke with bear and moose themes. Open year-round.

Northwest Lakes

TUPPER LAKE

The Wild Supply Company at the Natural History Museum of the Adirondacks (the Wild Center) (518-359-7800; www.wildcenter.org; 45 Museum Drive). Decorative items for the home, jewelry, cards, Wild Center–themed gifts, and more. Open year-round.

Central and Southwestern Adirondacks

BLUE MOUNTAIN LAKE

Adirondack Museum Store (518-352-7311; www.adkmuseum.org; NY 30). Books, prints, clothing, jewelry, housewares. Shop online as well, 400+ items. Open Memorial Day Weekend through Columbus Day.

Northville
Adirondack Country Store (518-863-6056; www.adirondackcountrystore.com; 252 N. Main Street). Amish furniture and accessories, regional books, local crafts, food products, clothing. The soap opera *Guiding Light* outfitted a family cabin set with products from ACS. Open year-round.

Old Forge
Moose River Trading Company (315-369-6091; www.mooserivertrading.com; NY 28, Thendara). Pack baskets, canvas hats, Duluth packs, maps, compasses, bug dope, camp cookware, and blankets, Adirondack chairs, and Guide's Choice Coffee—what more could you need for an Adirondack expedition or for creating your own Great Camp room? Open year-round.

Wells
Mountain Memories (518-924-7778; www.mountainmems.com; NY 30). Rustic furniture, dishes, and other decorative items with pinecone, bear, and moose themes; posters, prints. Open year-round.

Antiques

While traveling along rural routes in the Northeast, we just expect to find barns full of milk-painted country furniture, salt-glazed crocks, and marvelous hand tools. But these artifacts don't always relate to the territory we're passing through. When you're antiquing in the Adirondacks, keep a thumbnail sketch of the region's past in your mind, and that will guide you to old things true to the countryside.

Expect to find artifacts from logging and farming days and good-quality mass-produced nineteenth-century furniture. Local pottery, except in the far southern part of the park, is rare; Redford glass, made in the Saranac River Valley during the early 1800s, is highly prized and hard to find. Vintage rustic furniture, which was discarded willy-nilly in the 1950s as camp owners modernized, is scarce, but Old Hickory pieces have the right look and feel and are widely available. If you're hunting for a pair of snowshoes or antlers to hang at home, you shouldn't have any trouble finding them here.

Many shops stock wood engravings and hand-tinted etchings of Adirondack scenes; these prints—many of them by Winslow Homer or Frederic Remington—which originally appeared in *Harper's Weekly, Every Saturday,* and other magazines, are affordable.

Stereoviews of the grand hotels, postcards from 1910–1930, and photographs by George Baldwin, H. M. Beach, "Adirondack" Fred Hodges, and others are charming and not too dear. For photographs of the lakes, mountains, and resorts by Seneca Ray Stoddard, a contemporary of William Henry Jackson and Matthew Brady (all three Adirondack-born), you can expect to pay more, but the images are exceptional. Another name on the list for ephemera fans is Verplanck Colvin: mountain panoramas, diagrams, and maps from his 1870–1890 surveys are meticulous curiosities.

Another aspect of the Adirondack past to keep in mind is that the area has been a tourist destination since the Civil War. There's a brisk trade in historic souvenirs and small things relating to bygone transportation networks: embossed-brass luggage tags from steamboat and stagecoach lines are one example. Beside items designed to catch a visitor's eye or track his or her property, you can find objects that summer folk brought with them from back home or around the world to decorate camps. These nineteenth-century part-time residents amassed an eclectic variety of knickknacks, musical instruments, rugs, silver, and china that has become part of the antique scene as modern families spurned the elephant-foot humidors, Japanese lanterns, and other peculiar things the Victorians adored.

South to Fulton County there are numerous shops in the Sacandaga and Mohawk basins. In Glens Falls there's **200 Glen Antique Marketplace** (518-792-0323; 200 Glen Street); in Queensbury there's **Glenwood Manor Antiques** (518-798-4747; 60 Glenwood Avenue).

The best fair is unquestionably the **Adirondack Antiques Show**, formerly at the Adirondack Museum, but now Indian Lake's Byron Park. (Contact the **Indian Lake Chamber of Commerce** at 518-648-5112 or www.indian-lake.com for details.) At press time there's talk of moving the premier dealers back to the Adirondack Museum, but countless booths will line Main Street in Indian Lake hamlet as in years past. There are occasional auctions of antiques within the Blue Line, though those listings will appear in regional newspapers.

A sampling of the antique shops you'll find in the Adirondack Park is described below. Most are open several days a week in July and August and on weekends in spring and fall; some are open year-round. Many dealers travel to shows, so always call ahead.

Lake George and Southeastern Adirondacks

BOLTON LANDING
Black Bass Antiques (Henry Caldwell and Kate Van Dyck; 518-644-2389; www.blackbassantiques.com; 4920 Lakeshore Drive). Books, antique fishing tackle, Lake George souvenirs and photographs, general Adirondack items. Open Thursday through Monday or by appointment.

CHESTERTOWN
Atateka Books & Collectibles (Mark Walp; 518-494-4652; 1329 Friends Lake Road, near NY 8). Paper ephemera, books, and smalls; call ahead.

LAKE GEORGE
Ralph Kylloe Antiques and Rustics Gallery (518-696-4100; www.ralphkylloe.com; 1796 NY 9N). Established in 1995, enormous shop with exceptional rustic furniture, quality smalls, and sporting antiques. Open year-round; worth a special trip.

SCHROON LAKE
Emporium (518-532-9900; 1063 Main Street). Large shop with antique furniture, clothes, glass, you name it. Open Friday through Monday; closed January through March.

    Dusty Roads Antiques (518-532-9555; 1454 Charley Hill Road). Buys, sells, and repairs antiques. Call ahead.

WARRENSBURG
Discoveries (518-623-4567; www.discoveriesusa.com; US 9 & NY 28, 1 mile north of town center). Real miscellany from kitchen to bath, glassware, sporting goods, and occasional gems in furniture. Open year-round.

    Riverside Gallery (Maclaren Richards; 518-623-2026; 2 Elm Street, 1 block West of US 9 & NY 28). Old prints, paintings, reproduction furniture, picture framing, and Adirondack gifts. Open daily, year-round.

Yesteryear and Main Street Books (Ed and Pearl Kreinheder; 518-623-2149; 3922 Main Street). Rare books; country furniture and accessories. Open year-round, Monday through Saturday. Call ahead.

Champlain Valley

ESSEX
Summer Shop (Colin Ducolon; 518-963-7921; NY 22). Painted furniture, early pressed glass, nineteenth-century textiles, coin silver. Open June through October.

TICONDEROGA
Lonergan's Red Barn Antiques (Craig Lonergan; 518-585-4477; NY 9N). Old barn packed to the roof beams with things you've been looking for—books, china, furniture, photos, prints, Lake Champlain souvenir plates, Fiesta ware, crocks, tinware, trunks, farm implements, horse-drawn equipment, guns—or, as the flyer says, "Useful Stuff for Man and Beast." Open daily Memorial Day through Columbus Day; weekends in spring and fall.

WILLSBORO
Ben Wever Farm (518-963-8372; 221 Mountain View Drive). Ten rooms of antiques in a beautifully restored farmhouse: pine, cherry, walnut, and mahogany furniture; fine china, porcelain, and silver; rugs; paintings; lamps; glass; Adirondackana, Americana, and Victoriana. Open daily late June through Labor Day; also Memorial Day weekend.

Brown House Antiques (Suzanne Medler; 518-963-7352; www.brownhouseantiques.com; Main Street). Six rooms of linens, prints, pine and mahogany furniture, china, books, Fiesta ware, toys and dolls, wicker, Adirondack collectibles. Open late June through August; Tuesday through Saturday, weekends in September by chance.

High Peaks and Northern Adirondacks

AU SABLE FORKS
Don's Antiques (Rick and Dawn Blaisdell; 518-647-8422; 25 North Main Street). Furniture, Depression and patterned glass, clocks and clock repair, stoneware, postcards, "ancestral paraphernalia." Open year-round by chance or appointment.

BLOOMINGDALE
Buyer's Paradise (518-891-4242; NY 3). Antiques, used furniture, horse-drawn equipment, and more inside and outside an old roadhouse. If you're fed up with precious prices and uptight dealers, go here for serious rummaging. Call for hours.

Germaine Miller (518-891-1306; NY 3). Country and small Adirondack furniture, painted cupboards, Majolica and Quimper, china, glass, silver. By chance or appointment; practically next door to Buyer's Paradise.

Sign of the Fish Studio & Gallery (Henry and Virginia Jakobe; 518-891-2510; NY 3 just north of town hall). Furniture, books, paintings and prints, glass, china from the nineteenth-century to the 1950s. Call for hours.

LAKE PLACID
Alan Pereske (518-891-3733; 2158 Saranac Avenue). Don't be deceived by the small road-side storefront; there are rooms and rooms to see. Quality oak, pine, and rustic furniture; paintings and prints of local interest; glass, toys; ephemera. Open weekends spring and fall; Monday through Saturday, summer.

Log Cabin Antiques (Greg Peacock; 518-523-3047; 86 Main Street). Furniture, prints, kitchenware, Adirondackana, some reproduction stuff mixed in. Open year-round.

Summer Antiques (Mark Wilcox; 518-523-1876; www.summerantiques.com; 111 Main Street). High-end paintings, Mission and country furniture, camp items, sporting antiques. Open year-round; call ahead in off-season. Recommended.

LOON LAKE
Arden Creek Designs (518-891-4518; www.ardencreek.com; 2433 County 60 Road). Excellent selection of antique baskets and rustic furnishings in vintage Adirondack camp. Call ahead.

SARANAC LAKE
The Emporium (518-891-9364; 29 Broadway). Rustic and vintage furniture, old toys and pottery. Open year-round.

Forest Home Furnishings (Gail Veto; 518-891-6692; 141 River Street). Rustic furnishings. Call ahead.

Ted Comstock (518-891-9009; Park Avenue). Adirondack books, prints, photographs; fine small items; paintings; antique guideboats, Rushton rowboats, and other small craft. By appointment only.

VERMONTVILLE
Forest Murmurs (518-891-6933; NY 3). General line plus new rustic furniture. Open daily in summer.

Northwest Lakes

TUPPER LAKE
Sorting Gap (Kathleen Bigrow; 518-359-3463; 123 Park Street). Named for a narrows on the Raquette River where logs were sorted according to the brands burned on their butt end. Rustic furniture, old books, glass, pottery, toys, games. Open daily in summer. Call for hours.

Wildwood Arts & Antiques (Jon Kopp; 518-359-2336; 85 Park Street). Adirondack postcards and other ephemera; glassware, china, crafts, paintings. Open year-round.

Central and Southwestern Adirondacks

INLET
Lakeview Antiques (Barb and Walt Wermuth; 315-357-4722; NY 28). Clocks and clock repair; house full of furniture, paper, postcards, china, Oriental rugs. More than three decades in the business. Open late June through Columbus Day.

LAKE PLEASANT
Airdville Antiques & Clock Repair (518-548-5390; NY 8). All sorts of antiques; clock sales and repair. Call ahead.

Long Lake
Wide River Antiques (Pat Benton; 518-624-4749; NY 30). The former post office is packed with furniture; call ahead. Closed Monday.

Minerva
Mountain Niche Antiques (John and Kathy Feiden; 518-251-2566; NY 28N, 2 miles north of Minerva post office). Excellent assortment of country furniture, textiles, books, prints, tools, pottery, glassware. Open most days year-round.

North Creek
Hudson River Trading Co. (518-251-4461; www.hudsonrivertradingco.com; 292 Main Street). Furniture, pottery, antique sporting goods, prints, and advertising art in a nicely restored livery stable. Open year-round.

Northville
The Red Barn (518-863-4828; 202 S. Main Street). Furniture, prints, collectibles, baskets, taxidermy animals in a mid-nineteenth-century livery stable. Open spring through fall, daily in summer, otherwise by chance or appointment.

Old Forge
Indian Summer Antiques (315-369-3899; NY 28 across from the old Bald Mountain trailhead). Camp furnishings, sporting antiques, prints, smalls in an old roadside tourist stop. Open June through September; call ahead.

Olmstedville
Board 'n' Batten Antiques (Floss and Bob Savarie; 518-251-2507; 1447 County 29). Furniture, country items, Adirondack postcards, buttons, steins; focus on quality glass and pottery. Open daily July through August; or by chance or appointment. Recommended.

Pottersville
Stagecoach (518-494-3192; US 9, across the street from the Wells House). Excellent assortment of country furniture, textiles, books, prints, tools, pottery, glassware. Open most days year-round.

Riparius
Clen's Collectibles (Donalda and Clennon Ellifritz; 518-251-2388; River Road). Large, bright shop across from the Riparius train station with a general line of antiques and smalls; vintage clothing; Adirondack postcards and prints. There's a barn full of furniture near the main shop—a treasure trove. You have to ask for the key. Open year-round by chance or appointment; daily in summer.

Art Galleries and Painters' Studios

The best nineteenth-century American painters came to the Adirondacks to interpret wild scenery on paper and canvas, and many artists still rely on the great outdoors for inspiration. Listed here you'll find local artists in residence as well as fine-arts galleries representing painters from different eras and regions.

Lake George and Southeastern Adirondacks

Bolton Landing

Lake Shore Gallery (518-644-9480; www.lakeshoregalleryboltonlanding.com; 4985 Lakeshore Drive). Paintings by regional artists. Open July through October; call for hours.

Vivian Simonson (518-644-3106; www.viviansimonson.com; 4580 Lakeshore Drive). Watercolor portraits and more. Call for an appointment.

Lake Luzerne

Lynn Benevento Gallery (518-696-5702; www.lynnbenevento.com; 4 Bridge Street, next to Rockwell Falls). Local landscapes, wildflowers, and town scenes available as original paintings or limited-edition prints. Open daily in summer.

Champlain Valley

Essex

Adirondack Art Association (518-963-8309; 2750 Essex Road). Fine art by regional artists. Call for hours.

Cupola House Gallery (518-963-7494; www.thecupolahouse.com; 2278 Main Street). Folk art: paintings, quilts, rugs, and antiques. Workshops available.

Keeseville

Water Edge Studio (Ann Pember; 518-834-7440; www.annpember.com; 14 Water Edge Road). Watercolor paintings of flowers and nature scenes. By appointment.

Westport

Atea Ring Gallery (Atea Ring; 518-962-8620; 236 Sam Spears Road). A modern professional fine-arts gallery like you'd expect to find in a major city, located instead in an out-of-the-way farmhouse. One-person and group exhibitions of paintings, quilts, prints. Past shows have included works by Harold Weston; realist Paul Matthews; primitive paintings by Edna West Teall (who was the Grandma Moses of Essex County); and Lake Champlain fish decoys. Open June through September.

Willsboro

Cornerstone (Kristen and Jim Hardman; 518-963-4900; www.cornerstonerusticgallery.com; NY 22 and Maple Street). Original paintings and crafts. Open seasonally.

East Side Studio (Patricia Reynolds; 518-963-8356; 828 Point Road). Watercolor and oil landscapes of Lake Champlain and the Adirondacks; lovely flower paintings from the artist's extensive perennial gardens; usually a hundred or so works on hand. Open by chance or appointment year-round.

High Peaks and Northern Adirondacks

Au Sable Forks

Sue Cassevaugh (518-647-8614; 87 Sheldrake Road). Fine flora and fauna watercolors. Call for an appointment.

Keene

Heritage Gallery (Bruce and Annette Mitchell; 518-576-2289; corner Spruce Hill and

Hurricane Roads). Oil and watercolor paintings of Adirondack and Vermont scenes; limited-edition wildlife, floral, and landscape prints. Call for hours.

KEENE VALLEY

Skylight Fine Art (Mary Buschman-Kelly; 518-576-9208; www.skylightfineart.com; 1767 NY 73). Nineteenth-century American landscape paintings by artists of the Hudson River School and works by contemporary landscape artists. Call for hours.

LAKE PLACID

511 Gallery (518-523-7163; www.511gallery.com; 2461 Main Street). Satellite branch of the Chelsea gallery of contemporary art, in New York City. Contemporary work and fine art from the nineteenth- to early- and mid-20th centuries. Call for hours.

    Capozio Gallery (518-523-4000; www.capoziogallery.com; Alpine Mall, 2527 Main Street Suite 1). Mixed media works by Joe Capozio; enamel plaques, jewelry, oils, and watercolors by Stevie Capozio; and photography by Jamison. Call for hours.

    Laura's Custom Signs & Artwork (518-523-4575; 45 Sentinel Road). Adirondack photos and prints; frame shop. Open year-round.

SARANAC LAKE

7444 Gallery (518-524-8207; www.7444gallery.us; 28 Depot Street). Work by regional, national, and international artists. Open year-round.

    Adirondack Artists Guild (518-891-2615; www.adirondackartistsguild.com; 52 Main Street). Gallery that features local artists of note, with changing exhibitions. Open year-round.

    Georganne Gaffney Fine Art Gallery (518-891-1856; 70 Main Street). Fine arts paintings. Hours by appointment or chance.

    Mark Kurtz Photography (518-891-2431; www.markkurtzphotography.com; 41 Broadway). Commerical, special occasions, and fine art. Open year-round.

    Matt Burnett (www.mattburnettpaintings.com). Adirondack paintings. E-mail Burnett through his Web site for an appointment.

    Small Fortune Studio (Timothy Fortune; 518-891-1139; www.fortunestudio.com; 76 Main Street). Realistic Adirondack landscapes by an internationally regarded artist; works range from tiny, charming scenes to massive triptychs. Open year-round.

Northwest Lakes

CRANBERRY LAKE

End of the Pier Studio (Jean Reynolds; 315-848-2900; NY 3, at The Emporium). Watercolor paintings of Cranberry Lake and Adirondack vistas; limited-edition prints. Open by chance or appointment.

GABRIELS

Point of View Studio (Diane Leifheit; 518-327-3473; 815 NY 86). Meticulous pen-and-ink drawings of noteworthy Adirondack buildings; pastel work of Adirondack landscapes and flowers; special commissions. Call ahead.

SOUTH COLTON

Snow Line Design (Suzanne Langelier Lebeda; 315-262-3150; www.snowlinedesign.com; 63 Bay Road). Watercolors and prints. Call for an appointment.

TUPPER LAKE

Casagrain Gallery (Gary Casagrain; gallery: 518-359-3805, studio: 518-359-2595; 68 Park Street). Fine art of the Adirondacks. Open year-round, Thursday through Saturday or by appointment; call ahead for hours.

Round Lake Studios (Burdette Parks; 518-359-9324; 680 Bartlett Carry Road). Photography and more. By appointment.

Central and Southwestern Adirondacks

BRANT LAKE

Wild Visions (Carl Heilman II; 518-494-3072; www.carlheilman.com; 6990 NY 8). Fine Adirondack photographs. Call for an appointment.

EDINBURG

The Dodge House Lakeside Gallery (Constance Dodge; 518-863-2201; 936 S. Shore Road). Oil paintings and mixed-media drawings; portraits from photographs. Open Tuesday through Sundays in summer or by appointment.

INDIAN LAKE

Abanakee Studios (Kathy Larkin and Jane Zilka; 518-648-5013; NY 28). Photographs, paintings, antiques, workshops, and readings. Occasional workshops in writing and painting. Open summers.

LAKE PLEASANT

Cabin in the Woods Adirondack Creations (315-826-3172; www.adirondackcabin creations.com; P.O. Box 790). Adirondack oil paintings and photographs. Call ahead.

NORTHVILLE

Stinky Dog (518-863-7051; www.stinkydog.com; 142 N Main Street). Paintings and other Stinky Dog—a white sock-puppet-like cartoon created by the owner—merchandise. Call for hours.

OLD FORGE

Gallery North (315-369-2218; 2999 NY 28). Limited-edition wildlife and Adirondack prints, posters, and woodcarvings; picture framing. Open year-round.

RIPARIUS

Scenic Outlook Studios (518-494-5367; www.scenicoutlookstudios.com; 440 Riverside Station Road). Hand-thrown pottery by Lisa Steres. Call for hours.

BOAT BUILDERS

The region's interconnected waterways led to the development of a specialized craft, the Adirondack guideboat. Traditional guideboats, which first appeared after the Civil War, are smooth-skinned rowboats with quarter-sawn cedar or pine planks, and have naturally curved spruce roots for ribs. These delicate looking vessels are fast on the water and easy to portage between ponds, lakes, and rivers. In the nineteenth-century, a handmade boat cost $30 or $40. (These days guideboats go for about $10,000.)

Besides guideboats, a number of local craftsmen have developed their own special designs, from ultralight pack canoes to cold-molded multipurpose sport boats. Listed below you'll find a variety of watercraft; call ahead for hours. Also, you may find that there's a waiting list of other prospective buyers. Beautiful things take time to create.

Lake George and Southeastern Adirondacks

SILVER BAY
The Hacker Boat Company (518-543-6666; www.hackerboat.com; 8 Delaware Avenue). Demonstrations and tours available at the company's Silver Bay marina and factory; additional factory in Ticonderoga.

High Peaks and Northern Adirondacks

LAKE PLACID
Placid Boatworks (Joe Moore and Charlie Wilson; 518-524-2949 or 518-523-9696; www.placidboats.com; 263 Station Street). Builders of top quality carbon/kevlar canoes. Test paddling on site.

SARANAC LAKE
Hathaway Boat Shop (Christopher Woodward; 518-891-3961; 9 Algonquin Avenue). A long line of boat builders has occupied this shop on the edge of town, including Willard Hanmer, whose boats are displayed at the Adirondack Museum. Chris learned the trade from Carl Hathaway, who was taught by Willard himself. Traditional wooden Adirondack guideboats; boat repairs. Traditional guideboats with oars and yoke.

    Spencer Boatworks (Spencer Jenkins; 518-891-5828; www.antiqueandclassicboats.com; 956 NY 3, Bloomingdale Road). Inboard wooden boats built along classic runabout lines with modern epoxy lay-up; models include cruisers and utility boats 18 to 26 feet long. Also wooden boat and inboard-motor repairs.

Northwest Lakes

LAKE CLEAR
Boathouse Woodworks (James Cameron; www.adkguideboat.com; 518-327-3470; P.O. Box 317). Traditional wooden Adirondack guideboats built to order. Seat caning; boat restoration.

TUPPER LAKE
Spruce Knee Boatbuilding (Rob Frenette; 518-359-3228; NY 30 near Moody Bridge). Rushton-design wooden canoes and rowboats, guideboats, and sailboats all built to order; wooden boat repairs; seat caning.

Central and Southwestern Adirondacks

BRANT LAKE
Gar Wood Custom Boats (Larry and Tom Turcotte; 518-494-2966; www.garwoodcustomboats.com; 20 Duell Hill Road). Construction and restoration of Gar Woods: Baby Gars, custom Runabouts, and Speedsters.

LONG LAKE
Adirondack Goodboat (Mason Smith; 518-624-6398; www.adirondackgoodboat.com;

HC01 Box 44). This craft, which won the "Great Versatility Race" at Mystic Seaport's annual small-boat gathering, is a car-toppable multipurpose (row, sail, or motor) wooden boat, built with modern materials for easy maintenance and strength without weight. Other models are the Lakesailer and the Chipmunk canoe; kits available.

Olmstedville

Hornbeck Boats (Peter Hornbeck; 518-251-2764; www.hornbeckboats.com; 131 Trout Brook Road). Nessmuk (George Washington Sears) pioneered the go-light outdoor movement in the 1880s, and Pete has brought his designs into the twenty-first century. Kevlar pack canoes in 9-, 10 1/2-, and 12-foot lengths, perfect for tripping into remote ponds, weigh only 12–19 pounds; Kevlar guideboats and ultralight sea kayaks (26 pounds) are available by special order.

Books

Within the Adirondack Park, there are about a dozen independently owned bookstores. Each place has its own personality: some highlight nature books; others offer art supplies and crafts, too.

Lake George and Southeastern Adirondacks

Bolton Landing

Trees (518-644-5756; Lakeshore Drive). Regional books. Closed January through April.

Lake George

Lake George Historical Association Museum and Bookstore (518-668-5044; www.lakegeorgehistorical.org; The Old Warren County Court House, 290 Canada Street). Books about the history and events of the Lake George region. Call for hours.

Warrensburg

Maren Dunn Bookstore & Coffee House (518-623-2236; www.marendunnbooks.com; 3933 Main Street). New bookstore, constantly expanding its inventory. Check Web site for book signings, live music, and other events. Open year-round.

Warrensburg Country Store (518-623-4000; 3898 Main Street). Regional books section among racks of gifts, homemade fudge, cards, and other Adirondackana. Call for hours.

Champlain Valley

Ticonderoga

Fort Ticonderoga (518-585-2821; www.fort-ticonderoga.org; off NY 74). In a huge log cabin at the entrance to the museum, if you go beyond the bins of souvenirs, you'll find books, prints, monographs, maps, and audiotapes pertinent to eighteenth-century military history. Open daily mid-May through mid-October.

Westport

Inn on the Library Lawn Book Store (518-962-8666; www.theinnonthelibrarylawn.com; 1234 Stevenson Road). Sweet little bookstore with thousands of titles; grab breakfast or lunch at the inn before you browse. Call for hours.

High Peaks and Northern Adirondacks

KEENE VALLEY

The Birch Store (518-576-4561; www.birchstore.com; 1778 Main Street). Regional titles. Open year-round.

The Mountaineer (518-576-2281; www.mountaineer.com; NY 73). Good selection of outdoor, international adventure travel, nature, and Adirondack titles; topo maps. Open year-round.

LAKE PLACID

The Bookstore Plus (518-523-2950; www.thebookstoreplus.com; 2491 Main Street). Racks of paperbacks; good how-to guides; contemporary fiction; regional histories and guidebooks; cookbooks; children's books; coffee-table books; art supplies; stationery and cards. Open year-round.

Eastern Mountain Sports (518-523-2505; www.ems.com; 2453 Main Street). Adirondack and outdoor guidebooks, camping cookbooks, and adventure travel tales; maps; gear and garb. Open year-round.

A New Leaf (518-523-1847; Hilton Plaza, 2408 Main Street). New Age and self-help books; cards and stationery; tea, coffee, and cappuccino. Open year-round.

With Pipe and Book (Julie and Breck Turner; 518-523-9096; 91 Main Street). Landmark shop with new and rare Adirondack books; a huge selection of used books; antique postcards, prints, and maps; pipe tobaccos and imported cigars. Worth a visit just to browse books from their lovely porch overlooking Mirror Lake. Open year-round; closed midweek in fall and winter. Recommended.

SARANAC LAKE

Books and Baskets (518-891-3665; 169 Olive Street). Used books and basket weaving supplies. Call for hours.

Fact & Fiction Bookshop (518-891-8067; 17 Broadway). Compact but well-stocked independent bookshop. Open year-round.

North Country Community College (518-891-2915 ext. 224; Connector Building between the Classroom and Science Building). College bookstore; general interest; magazines. Open fall through spring; call for hours.

Northwest Lakes

PAUL SMITHS

Paul Smith's College Bookstore (518-327-6314; www.paulsmiths.edu; NY 30, Paul Smith's College, below the snack bar). Regional guides and histories; forestry books; topo maps; magazines. Open year-round.

Fact & Fiction Book Shop, in downtown Saranac Lake, is compact and complete. James Swedberg

TUPPER LAKE

Off the Beaten Path Books and Stuff (518-359-2005; 28 Lake Street). Buys, sells, and trades books. Call for hours.

The Wild Supply Company at the Natural History Museum of the Adirondacks (the Wild Center) (518-359-7800; www.wildcenter.org; 45 Museum Drive). Extensive collection of regional titles. Open year-round.

Central and Southwestern Adirondacks

BLUE MOUNTAIN LAKE

Adirondack Museum Shop (518-352-7311; www.adkmuseum.org; NY 28/30). Complete assortment of Adirondack histories and guidebooks; books on antique boats and furniture; children's books; Adirondack folk music and storytelling on CD; prints, postcards, stationery, and gifts. 400+ products available online. Open daily late May through Columbus Day.

INLET

The Adirondack Reader (315-357-2665; 156 Main Street). Large selection of Adirondack books, *New York Times* best sellers, and kids' books. Open Memorial Day through Columbus Day.

LONG LAKE

Hoss's Country Corner (518-624-2481; www.hossscountrycorner.com; 247 Lake Street). Adirondack histories and guidebooks, Christian books and tapes, children's nature books, general store. In summer Hoss's sponsors Adirondack Authors Night, showcasing throngs of regional authors—worth a visit. Open year-round.

OLD FORGE

Old Forge Hardware (315-369-6100; www.oldforgehardware.com; 104 Fulton Street). Way in the back of this enormous emporium is a huge bookstore with Adirondack histories and guidebooks, cookbooks, nonfiction, children's books, paperbacks—constant new arrivals according to weekly *New York Times* best seller list—and art supplies. Books can be ordered online. Open year-round. Recommended.

SPECULATOR

Charlie Johns Store (518-548-7451; www.charliejohns.com; The Four Corners). Between fresh produce and the deli counter are aisles of regional books (more than 350 titles on the Adirondacks and outdoor life), maps, and posters. Open year-round.

Beyond the Blue Line

See Chapter 3 for news about the lively local book scene. Heading north to Plattsburgh, **Borders Books & Music** (518-566-7006; www.bordersstores.com), in the Champlain Centre Mall, is open daily.

Several regional publishers specialize in books of local interest and have online and mail-order catalogs: **North Country Books** (315-735-4877; www.northcountrybooks.com; 311 Turner Street, Utica NY 13501), **Syracuse University Press** (315-443-5534; www.syracuseuniversitypress.syr.edu; 621 Skytop Road, Suite 110, Syracuse NY 13244-5534), and **Purple Mountain Press** (1-800-325-2665; www.catskill.net/purple; P.O. Box 309, Fleischmanns NY 12430). The **Adirondack Center for Writing** (518-327-6278;

www.adirondackcenterforwriting.org; Paul Smith's College, Paul Smiths) is an excellent resource for lists of current regional books and where they can be purchased.

Clothing

Hunting for designer bargains in "shop till you drop" mode is best pursued outside the Adirondack Park. Here you'll find classic woolens, practical sportswear, and high-tech outer gear. Lake Placid's Main Street, which has a pleasant parade of storefronts and outlets, is described here; also listed below you'll find haberdasheries plus clothing designers.

Lake George and Southeastern Adirondacks

Bolton Landing

Adirondack Cotton Company (Janice & Jack Fox; 518-644-2813; www.adirondackcottonco.com; 4941 Lake Shore Drive). Clothing boutique featuring Lilly Pulitzer, Vineyard Vines, and Fresh Produce Clothing. Call for hours.

Bolton Bay Traders (518-644-2237; 4963 Lake Shore Drive). Quality sportswear for men and women, including Merrell and Nike hiking boots; Columbia, Big Dog, and Sierra Designs jackets, shirts, pants, and shorts; outdoor guidebooks. Open year-round.

Lake George

They call it the "Million Dollar Half Mile," and it's just a quick toss of the gold card from Lake George Village. Separate plazas on both sides of US 9 (near its intersection with NY 149) add up to outlet heaven (www.lakegeorgeshopping.com) for the dedicated shopper:

There's **Adirondack Outlet Mall** with Eddie Bauer, Swank Factory Store, Rue 21, and other stores; **Log Jam Outlet Center**, which has Carter's Childrenswear, Orvis, Brooks Brothers, and a couple of other shops; **French Mountain Commons Outlet Center**, where you can shop at Tommy Hilfiger, Nine West, Gap Outlet, Banana Republic, Jockey, Oshkosh B'gosh, and Lillian Vernon; and **Lake George Plaza Outlet Center** with Polo Ralph Lauren, Maidenform, Izod, Bass, and Lane Bryant, among others.

High Peaks and Northern Adirondacks

Bloomingdale

Two Horse Trade Co. (518-946-7709; 236 Plank Road). For all your buckskin needs.

Lake Placid

Most Lake Placid shops are open year-round.

Alpine Meadow (518-523-9300; www.alpinemeadow.net; 2489 Main Street). Hip jeans, Juicy Suits, Free People—brand clothes, and lots more, including belts, shoes, and jewelry.

Blu Jean Bar (518-523-8932; 2475 Main Street). Decidedly hip blue jeans and other accessories.

Body & Sole (518-523-9398; www.lakeplacidbodyandsole.com; 2439 Main Street). What to do if you arrive for a winter weekend in the Olympic village and forgot your flannel PJs? Or for that matter, left all your undies behind? This trendy shop has lingerie in the back, sweaters, coats, skirts, handbags, belts, and shoes up front.

Cinderella's (518-523-3666; 2527 Main Street). Quality women and children's clothing.

Eastern Mountain Sports (518-523-2505; 51 Main St.). Outdoor clothing and footgear by Woolrich, Patagonia, Merrell, Nike, and EMS.

Eliza Hugh Clothing & Gifts (518-523-2125; 2509 Main Street). Upscale clothing and gifts.

F. Matthews Company (904-206-1937; 2413 Main Street). Upscale clothing and gifts.

Fallen Arch (518-523-5310; www.thefallenarch.com; 2537 Main Street). All sorts of athletic shoes, including Nike, New Balance, Puma, Reebok, Saucony, the list goes on.

Far Mors Kids (518-523-3990; 2407 Main Street). "Far Mor" means grandmother in Swedish; picture an indulgent, tasteful granny and you've got a glimpse of this shop. Designer infant and children's clothes; educational toys and puzzles; quilts.

Gap Outlet (518-523-4651; 2457 Main Street). Cookie-cutter outfits for all ages in flannel, denim, fleece, and khaki; kids' clothes in basement, men's on first floor, and women's upstairs.

GH Bass (518-523-7229; www.bassshoes.com; 2466 Main Street). Fine shoes, of course, and clothing and accessories, too.

Karma: Fair Trade for the Conscious Consumer (518-523-3282; 2518 Main Street). Fair-trade clothing, accessories, and more from all over the world.

Maui North (518-523-7245; www.mauinorth.net; 2532 Main Street). Clothing and gear for snowboarding, skiing, and other outdoors pursuits.

A Placid Life (518-523-6487; 2439 Main Street). Life is Good apparel and accessories.

Ruthie's Run (518-523-3271; www.ruthiesrun.com; 2415 Main Street). Men's and women's clothing from Alpaca Imports, Obermeyer, Dale of Norway, and such.

Super Shoes (518-523-4452; www.supershoes.com; 2044 Saranac Avenue). Brand-name shoes such as Sketchers, Born, Dexter, and Timberland.

Where'd You Get That Hat? (518-523-3101; 2569 Main Street). The question friends back home are bound to ask. . . . Head gear of all descriptions; great selection of Converse high tops.

SARANAC LAKE

Bling (518-891-5800; 245 Lake Flower Avenue). Life is Good and Horny Toad clothing and accessories, Crocs, and lots more.

Cinderella's (518-891-4431; 44 Broadway). Handmade fashions for infants to teenagers; special-occasion dresses.

Major Plowshares (518-891-7214; 28 Broadway). A surplus store, yes, but also the outlet for Wild Oats locally made children's clothing in woodland prints, corduroys, and denim.

Pink (518-891-4042; 5 Broadway). Fun and funky women's clothes, accessories, and shoes.

T. F. Finnigan (518-891-1820; 78 Main Street). Men's clothing, including NorthFace, Nautica, B.D. Baggies; formal-wear rental and sales.

The Wear House (518-891-8135; 135 Broadway). Trendy and affordable women's apparel and accessories; juniors section, too.

In 2007 the **Saranac Lake Community Store**, New York State's first community-owned department store, is being developed. At press time, shares in the project are being sold, and a site for this future collection of shops has yet to be determined. For more information call 518-891-0197.

Central and Southwestern Adirondacks

BLUE MOUNTAIN LAKE

Blue Mountain Outfitters (518-352-7306; 144 Main Street). Columbia sportswear, Teva and Merrell shoes, outdoor wear of all kinds. Open year-round.

INLET

French Louie's Adirondack Sports Equipment & Clothing (315-357-2441; 156 NY 28). Apparel, footwear, and accessories for men and women including Pendleton shirts and sweaters. Call for hours.

OLD FORGE

Holly Woodworking (315-369-3757; www.hollywoodworkingoldforge.com; 3286 NY 28). Ladies and men's apparel, clogs, and other footwear. Call for hours.

Lady Jane (315-369-4440; 3018 NY 28). Nice ladies' wear shop. Great selection of summer linens and cotton dresses, beautiful sweaters. Closed winter.

Mountain Peddler (315-369-3428; www.themountainpeddler.com; 3049 Main Street). Clothing and jewelry. Call for hours.

Mountainman Outdoor Supply Company (315-369-6672; www.mountainman outdoors.com; 2855 NY 28). Life is Good apparel and accessories, Crocs, and more.

SPECULATOR

Speculator Department Store (518-548-6123; NY 8). Just past the intersection with NY 30 is this sixty-plus-year-old landmark selling Woolrich sweaters, Jantzen swimwear, and more Pendleton woolens than you can shake a spindle at. Open daily.

Beyond the Blue Line

In Plattsburgh, the north and south **Champlain Centres** (518-561-8660; www.champlaincentres.com) are close to the Northway and contain chains like Sears, the Gap, Old Navy, and J.C. Penney, plus dozens of other stores.

CRAFT SHOPS

Functional handmade items have always been part of Adirondack life; in the last few decades, the region has attracted contemporary craftspeople from outside, and encouraged local folks to rediscover old-time products. Part of this renaissance has been nurtured by the **Adirondack North Country Association** (ANCA), a nonprofit group that twenty years ago published the first "Craft Trails" map highlighting studios and stores. For a free copy of the map, write to ANCA (183 Broadway, Saranac Lake; www.adirondack.org).

Listed below you'll find craft shops showcasing a variety of media. Many of the studios are in private homes, so call ahead. Further on in this chapter you'll find fiber and fabric artists and basket makers; carvers of wood, plaster and other materials; and furniture makers.

Lake George and Southeastern Adirondacks

BOLTON LANDING

Trees (518-644-5756; Lakeshore Drive). Adirondack chairs; wooden toys, baskets, balsam items; regional books, prints, and photos. Closed January through April.

Champlain Valley

ELIZABETHTOWN

Adirondack Outdoor Company (518-873-6806; www.adirondackoutdoor.com; 8549 US 9). Locally made pack baskets, antler lamps, antler and birch-bark picture frames, camp signs, woodcarvings, and decorative snowshoes. Call for hours.

PERU

Yarborough Square (518-643-7057; 672 Bear Swamp Road). Works by 150+ North Country and Canadian artisans; open year-round.

PORT HENRY

Stillworks (518-546-3335; 4316 Main Street). Glass jewelry, stained glass, photography, birdhouses, and homemade glycerin soaps. Call for hours.

TICONDEROGA

Hancock House Gallery (518-585-7868; www.thehancockhouse.org; 6 Moses Circle). Works by local artists; historical souvenir items. Open year-round.

WESTPORT

Artifacts and Westport Trading Co. (Kip Trienens; 518-962-4801; 6511 Main Street). Bark and twig baskets, pottery, jewelry, contemporary furniture, stained glass, and eclectic crafts. Open year-round, most of the time.

The Pink Pig (518-962-8833; www. pinkpigwestport.com; 661 NY 22). Cottage country furniture, décor, and antiques, crafts by local artisans, linens and bedding. Store open May through December; year-round on-line.

High Peaks and Northern Adirondacks

KEENE

Keene Trading Post and North Country Taxidermy (518-576-9549; NY 73). You can't miss this place—there's usually a full-size stuffed creature out front. Bring a camera so the kids can pose next to the moose or mountain lion. If you'd like to buy a souvenir antler or two, there are boxes full of them, plus rustic furniture, birch bark items, etc. Bearskin rugs are a specialty. Open year-round.

LAKE PLACID

Adirondack Craft Center (518-523-2062; www.adirondackcraftcenter.com; 21114 Saranac Avenue). More than 250 upstate New York craftspeople are represented here. Jewelry made of silver, porcupine quills, semiprecious stones, and feathers; designer clothing for dolls, children, and adults; leather bags and backpacks; quilts; handmade paper; woodcarvings of fish, birds, folk figures; baskets; pottery; rustic and contemporary painted furniture; prints; photographs; stationery. Call for hours.

Caribou Trading Co. (518-523-1152; Hilton Plaza, Main Street). Pottery, jewelry, kites and mobiles, woodenware, handwovens. Open year-round.

SARANAC LAKE

Smith's Taxidermy (518-891-6289; 108 Lake Flower Avenue). Rustic furniture by Thomas Phillips and the Smith brothers; antler chandeliers, pottery, baskets. Open year-round.

Northwest Lakes

Childwold

Leather Artisan (Tom Amoroso; 518-359-3102; www.leatherartisan.com; NY 3). Classic leather handbags, wallets, belts, and backpacks made on the premises; quality crafts; Naot shoes and Minnetonka moccasins. If you want a gorgeous made-to-order leather golf bag, look no further. Open year-round; closed midweek in winter. Call ahead.

Paul Smiths

Train Brook Forge (David Woodward; 518-327-3747; www.trainbrookforge.com; 243 NY 86). Hand-forged ornamental elements and décor. Call for an appointment.

Central and Southwestern Adirondacks

Blue Mountain Lake

Blue Mountain Designs (518-352-7361; www.bluemountaindesigns.com; NY 30). Blue Mountain Lake's old-time schoolhouse is packed with contemporary jewelry, fine rustic and camp-style furniture, wrought iron, woodenware, pottery, handwovens, silk-screen prints, photographs, etchings, stationery, candles, toys, leather, and clothing. Also, custom-cast hardware for Adirondack guideboats. The problem of how to entertain the kids while parents do some serious shopping has been solved amusingly at Blue Mountain Designs: There's a big wooden sluiceway outside for gem mining. A sack of sand and assorted precious pebbles costs about five bucks and can avert a meltdown, especially when followed by an ice-cream bar or fresh-squeezed lemonade from the adjacent stand. Separate building for antiques on property. Open daily mid-May through mid-October; weekends before Christmas.

Indian Lake

Bear Paw Forge (Dan Crotty; 518-648-0155; NY 28). Blacksmith shop. Hooks of all shapes and sizes, letter openers, candle snuffers, fireplace tools, and more. By appointment.

Mayfield

Havlick Snowshoe Co. (Richard Havlick; 518-661-6447; www.havlicksnowshoe.com; NY 30). Handmade snowshoes and snowshoe furniture, Adirondack pack baskets, and outdoor gear. Open daily, year-round.

Northville

Adirondack Country Store (518-863-6056; www.adirondackcountrystore.com; 252 N. Main Street). Rambling old home filled with quality local crafts: hickory and oak rockers made by Amish woodworkers, quilts, handwovens, jewelry, hand-spun yarns, baskets, pottery, toys, decoys, Adirondack books. Call for hours.

Old Forge

The Artworks (315-369-2007; Main Street, NY 28). Cooperative gallery featuring North Country artisans. Ash-splint baskets, stained glass, hooked rugs, woodcarvings, patchwork quilts and pillows, toys, and jewelry. Open year-round.

    Holly Wood Working (315-369-3757; www.hollywoodworkinggoldforge.com; 3286 NY 28). Rustic furniture, gifts. Open year-round; call for hours.

    Mountain Peddler (315-369-3428; Main Street). Quilts, tinware, baskets, woodenware, gifts. Open year-round; daily Memorial Day through Columbus Day.

Childwold's The Leather Artisan features handmade wallets, backpacks, handbags, and other quality crafts.

Annie Stoltie

RAQUETTE LAKE

Sagamore Bookstore (315-354-9905; www.sagamore.org; at Sagamore Great Camp). Rustic furniture and miniatures; ash-splint baskets, stained glass, wrought iron, carved and painted shelf fungus, handmade paper. Available by special order are place settings of the Vanderbilts' woodsy china, reissued by Syracuse China in 1997. Open daily Memorial Day through Labor Day; spring and fall weekends.

FAIRS AND FLEA MARKETS

For a true shopping adventure, consider the outdoor extravaganzas: Many Adirondack communities sponsor craft fairs and flea markets. At one end of the spectrum are juried craft shows with high-quality items, while flea markets and town-wide garage sales escape succinct categorization as to just what you can expect to find. Many villages offer annual townwide sales that go the full range from jumbled castoffs to surprising finds. But that's the fun of those affairs—nosing past the velvet paintings and tube socks to discover a box of stereoviews of Ausable Chasm. Listed below, in chronological order, are some annual events arranged by region and date; check local newspapers for information about other festivals. The "Inside & Out" calendar of events in *Adirondack Life* magazine is another good source of information.

Lake George and Southeastern Adirondacks

Arts and Crafts Fair (518-532-7675; Town Park, Schroon Lake). fifty-plus craft booths, music, rustic-furniture building and other demonstrations, third Saturday in July. The Community Church Bake Sale and Luncheon (US 9), is also that day in Schroon Lake.

   Arts and Crafts Festival (518-623-2161; Warrensburg). Annual event held the first weekend in July.

   Riverview Arts & Crafts Festival (518-696-3423; Lakeside Park, Lake Luzerne). Craft fair, third Saturday in July.

   Quality Antique Show–Under the Big Top (518-644-3831; Bolton Central School Ballfield, Bolton Landing). Antique show with thirty-plus dealers, first weekend in August.

   World's Largest Garage Sale (518-623-2161; www.warrensburgchamber.com; throughout Warrensburg). The traffic backs up to Northway Exit 23 for this townwide blow-out, first weekend in October. More than 1,000 vendors, plus many local families offer a bewildering array of items for sale. Plan to walk once you get to town; there are shuttle buses from the parking lots.

   Christmas in Warrensburg (518-466-5497; townwide, Warrensburg). Special events, crafts sales, shops open extended hours, sleigh rides, lots more, first weekend in December.

Champlain Valley

Old-Time Folkcraft Fair (518-963-4478; Paine Memorial Library, Willsboro). Last Saturday in July.

   Champ Day (518-546-7212; Main Street, Port Henry). Craft-and-food fair with activities for children celebrating "Champ," Lake Champlain's legendary monster, first Saturday in August.

   Downtown Essex Day (518-963-7222; Main Street, Essex). Craft fair, games, and races, first Saturday in August.

Christmas in the Village (518-963-7222; Essex). Shops reopen for an early December weekend; music; food sales.

High Peaks and Northern Adirondacks

Craftfest (518-891-1489; The Lodge, Lake Clear). Juried craft show featuring furniture, pottery, baskets, jewelry, stained glass, and more, third weekend in July.

    Adirondack Antiques Show and Sale (518-891-1990; www.saranaclake.com; Harrietstown Town Hall, Main Street, Saranac Lake). A high-summer tradition and one of the best around, in late July.

    Artisans' Studio Tours (www.jaystudiotour.com). Craftspeople in the Jay-Wilmington —Upper Jay area open their studios to the public, in mid-August.

    High Peaks Arts and Antiques Show (518-576-4719; Marcy Airfield, Keene Valley). Large assortment of crafts and regional antiques, in late August.

    Sparkle Village Craft Show (518-891-1990; www.saranaclake.com; Harrietstown Town Hall). One of the biggest craft shows of the season, last weekend in November.

Northwest Lakes

Backwoods Craft Fair and Flea Market (315-848-2916; NY 3, Cranberry Lake). Dozens of local artisans selling their wares and demonstrating their skills plus flea market, third weekend in July.

    Masonic Flea Market (518-359-3328; www.tupperlakeinfo.com; Municipal Park, Tupper Lake). Hundreds of dealers—everything from Adirondack ephemera to used furniture and new footwear, plus fried dough, sausage-and-pepper sandwiches, and other delicious, artery-clogging carnival chow—third weekend in August.

Central and Southwestern Adirondacks

Neighbor Day (315-369-6411; www.artscenteroldforge.org; Arts Center, Old Forge). Craft fair with music, special exhibitions, chicken barbecue, and events for children, second Sunday in June.

    Central Adirondack Craft Fair (315-369-6411; www.artscenteroldforge.org; sponsored by the Arts Center, Old Forge). Craft fair with seventy-five-plus exhibitors, first weekend in July.

    Caroga Historical Museum Craft Fair (518-835-4400; www.carogamuseum.org; Caroga Historical Museum, London Bridge Road, Caroga Lake). Annual outdoor craft fair, second Saturday in July.

    Arts in the Park Craft Fair (866-464-6538; www.inletny.com; Arrowhead Park, Inlet). Outdoor craft fair, third weekend in July.

    Speculator Flea Market (518-548-4521; Ballfield, Speculator). Fifty-plus vendors, third Saturday in July.

    Piseco Craft Fair (518-548-8732; Piseco Community Hall, Piseco). Fifty-plus craft booths, last Saturday in July.

    Antique Show & Sale (315-369-6411; www.artscenteroldforge.org; Arts Center/Old Forge). Last weekend in July.

    Heart of the Park Craft Fair (518-624-3077; Mount Sabattis Park Pavilion, Long Lake). Craft fair "under the big top," July or August.

TWIGS **Arts and Crafts Show** (518-548-4521; NY 30, Speculator). Seventy-five-plus craftspeople, second Thursday in August.

Rustic Furniture Makers' Fair (518-352-7311; www.adkmuseum.org; Adirondack Museum, Blue Mountain Lake). Showcase of more than forty rustic furniture builders, early September. Museum admission required for fair visitors.

FIBER AND FABRIC; BASKETS AND BALSAM

Fiber arts encompass more than things made of thread and yarn; handmade paper relies on wood and other plant fibers, while traditional and modern baskets use wood splints, grasses, leaves, and ropes. The needle arts in the true Adirondack sense of the word include sweet-smelling embroidered or silk-screened pillows and sachets; balsam fir (*Abies balsamea*) needles are gathered, dried, and stuffed into calico fabric bags and pillows. Listed below you'll find quilters, basket makers, paper makers, spinners, weavers, and balsam crafters. (Check under "Clothing" in this chapter for handmade ready-to-wear items.) If you'd like to visit sheep, goat, and rabbit farms, there's the annual **Washington County Wool and Fiber Tour** held on the last weekend in April; Glens Falls newspapers usually publish a map of participating farms. If you'd like to experience an old-fashioned balsam bee—from chopping the needles to hand-stitching pillows—the **Big Moose Community Chapel** (315-357-5841; Big Moose Road) holds one in late July; the extra-fresh pillows are sold at its annual bazaar, held on the first Saturday in August.

North of the Adirondack Park border, on the St. Lawrence River, is Akwesasne, home of many Mohawk families, an excellent place to look for baskets woven of ash splints and sweetgrass. **The Akwesasne Cultural Center** (315-358-2240; 321 NY 37, Hogansburg) has a shop selling baskets, from tiny thimble cases to full-size pack baskets, plus moccasins decorated with beadwork and porcupine quills. Call for hours and directions.

Lake George and Southeastern Adirondacks

BOLTON LANDING
Running Ridge Studio (518-644-3166; www.runningridgestudio.com; 48 Church Hill Road). Hooked rugs and wall hanging gallery. Call for hours.

WARRENSBURG
Blue Heron Designs (Charlene Leary; 518-623-3189; Truesdale Hill Road). Fine handwovens and women's clothing from her fabrics. Call ahead.

Champlain Valley

ESSEX
Pioneer Weave (Mary Beth Correy; 518-963-8067; 2259 Lakeshore Road). Traditional finely woven cotton rag rugs in assorted sizes and made to order. Call ahead.

MERRILL
Lynne Taylor (518-425-6805; 5439 NY 374). Silk-painted scarves and other textiles. Call for an appointment.

WILLSBORO
Alice Wand and Dennis Kalma (518-963-4582; www.alicewand.com; 103 Spear Road). Handmade paper sculptures and wall pieces. Call ahead.

Northwest Lakes

HARRISVILLE
Heirlooms (Lis Barsuglia-Madsen; 315-543-2214; www.scandinavianweaveandknit.com; 12996 Kimballs Mill Road). Traditional Scandinavian rugs, wall hangings, and accessories. Online store. Call for hours.

High Peaks and Northern Adirondacks

LAKE PLACID
Adirondack Weaver (Annoel Krider; www.adirondackweaver.com; Box 163). Exceptional tapestries and naturally inspired rugs. Commissions by appointment.

JAY
The Alpaca Shoppe (518-946-7886; www.alpacashoppe.com; 13036 NY 9N). Apparel, accessories, blankets, and yarns made from alpacas. Call for hours.

Donna Foley, of Four Directions Weaving, in Vermontville, weaves items for the home from her Lincoln sheeps' wool. Courtesy of Kelly Kilgallon

Buttons Buttons (Barbara Smith; 518-946-7625; www.buttonsbuttons.com; John Fountain Road, across from the Jay Village Green). Pillows, belts, and handbags made from vintage fabrics, ribbon, and buttons. Call for hours.

SARANAC LAKE
Moody Tree Farm (Former Asplin Tree Farm property; 518-891-2468; www.adirondackbalsamwreaths.com; 60 County Rte 55). Balsam pillows and other products, wreaths, centerpieces, Christmas trees. Order online or call for hours.

NEWCOMB
Adirondackwoolery (Judy Blanchette and Pam McLoughlin; 518-582-2144; www.adirondackwoolery.com; 48 Pine Tree Road). Hand-spun yarns and creations by Pam from Judy's own sheep; hand-knit sweaters; spinning wheels; spinning lessons. By appointment only.

VERMONTVILLE
Four Directions Weaving (Donna Foley; www.fourdirectionsweaving.com; 215 Paye Road). Items woven for the home, made from eco-friendly and sustainably grown organic cottons, linens, natural dyes, and naturally raised Lincoln sheep. Call for hours.

Central and Southwestern Adirondacks

AMSTERDAM
Adirondack Blanket Works (Baker Studios; 1-888-844-2388; www.bigblankets.com; 4703 NY 30). Fleece and appliqué blankets and accessories; made from heavyweight recycled cotton yarns. Call for hours or visit online store.

BLEECKER
Judith Plotner (www.judithplotner.com). Fabric art. Contact the artist via her Web site to make an appointment.

INDIAN LAKE
Homemade Quilts and Crafts (Kathleen Herrick; 518-648-5360; NY 28). Tied quilts, patchwork pillows, dolls, baskets, balsam pillows. Open daily Memorial Day through Columbus Day; other times by chance or appointment.

LONG LAKE
Adirondack Basket Case (Patty Farrell; 518-624-2501; NY 28N). Ash-splint baskets of all sizes and styles. Call for an appointment.

FURNITURE

Regional woodworkers create furniture in a variety of styles, from Shaker-inspired designs, to rugged sculptural pieces, to the straightforward Adirondack chairs that now come in an infinite range of permutations. Several of the furniture makers listed below have online catalogs or brochures; if you're planning to visit an individual's shop, call ahead. Many studios are in private homes, so don't expect a large ready-made inventory. For a Web overview, check out www.adirondackwood.com. It includes sources for quality hardwood lumber if you wish to build your own furniture or install a rustic railing in your home. For furniture making classes, including rustic methods, the arts centers listed in Chapter 6 offer hands-on workshops.

Lake George and Southeastern Adirondacks

ADIRONDACK

Lean-2 Studio (John and Shirl Stacy; 518-494-5185; www.lean2.com; P.O. Box 222). Table lamps, hanging lamps, and beautiful hand-painted shades, some with leaves and pine needles embedded in vellum. By appointment.

BOLTON LANDING

Jason Henderson (518-321-4445; P.O. Box 496). Artistic rustic furniture. Call for an appointment.

   Thomas W. Brady, Furniture Maker (518-644-9801; P.O. Box 835). Elegant contemporary furniture in cherry, walnut, and figured maple: screens, bedsteads, desks, blanket chests, tables, and chairs, some with painted motifs or in Shaker designs. Color flier available; open year-round by appointment only.

CHESTERTOWN

Chester Creek Woodworks (Bob Walp; 518-494-0003; 1339 Friends Lake Road). Furniture and useful wooden ware. Open weekends or by appointment.

DIAMOND POINT

Pine Plank (Don Farleigh; 518-644-9420). Adirondack chairs. Call for an appointment.

   S. T. Siadak (518-644-9703; 75 Timlo Drive). Mission-style Adirondack lanterns for interior and exterior use. By appointment.

LAKE GEORGE

Ralph Kylloe Rustic Design (518-696-4100; www.ralphkylloe.com; P.O. Box 669). Huge old log cabin packed with antlers, twigs, bark, and leather in and on every kind of antique; worth a detour. Open year-round; call ahead.

QUEENSBURY

Sutton's Marketplace (518-798-1188; www.suttonsmarketplace.com; US 9). Some rustic frames and chairs; large selection of leather furniture. Open year-round.

SCHROON LAKE

Adirondack Rustics Gallery (Barry Gregson; ; 518-532-0020; www.adirondack rusticsgallery.com; US 9, a mile south of town). Gorgeous building with excellent selection of rustic tables, chairs, settees, beds, corner cupboards, and sideboards, made of burls, cedar, white-birch bark, and assorted woods. Clocks, frames, and selected items by area artisans. Open daily summers.

Champlain Valley

AUSABLE CHASM

Aloof Doors (Glenn Miller; 1-800-383-5423; www.aloofdoors.com; 37 Old State

Adirondack Rustics Gallery, in Schroon Lake, features the work of Barry Gregson and other masters. James Swedberg

Road). Beautifully carved custom doors in black walnut, red and white oak, cherry, pine, or mahogany. Call for hours.

CROWN POINT
Crispin Shakeshaft (518-597-3304; US 9). Rustic furniture and garden structures. Call ahead.

MINEVILLE
Essex Industries (518-942-6671; www.essexindustries.org; P.O. Box 374). Canoe and guideboat accessories: backrests, caned seats, yokes; folding canvas camp stools and shopping bags. Flier and price list available; year-round.

WILLSBORO
Old Adirondack (1-800-342-3373; www.oldadirondack.com; NY 22). Specializing in cedar furniture. Open year-round.

High Peaks and Northern Adirondacks

CADYVILLE
Wood Grain Furniture (518-293-6268; www.adirondackfurniture.com; 1976 NY 3). Unfinished chairs, tables, beds, outdoor furniture in Shaker, country French, and Adirondack styles. Open year-round.

JAY
Earth Works (David Douglas; 518-647-1279; www.artofdaviddouglas.com; P.O. Box 118). Mirrors, lamps, shelves, and more made from birch bark and twigs. By appointment.

Swallowtail Studio (Wayne Ignatuk; 518-946-7439; www.swallowtailstudio.com; 55 Trumbulls Corners Road). Award-winning sculptural furniture with fine dovetailing and mortise and tenon construction. Call ahead.

Twisted Tree Rustics (Spencer Reynolds; 518-647-5378; P.O. Box 141). End tables, coffee tables, lamps, and wall art. By appointment.

KEENE
Rusted Rock (Paul and Kim Bodean; 518-647-5475 or 518-576-9102; Main Street NY 73). Great source for birchbark frames, mirrors, etc.; buy the frame stock cut to your specifications. By appointment.

KEENE VALLEY
Bald Mountain Rustics (Steve Bowers; www.baldmountainrustics.com; 1884 NY 73). Chairs, benches, beds, cabinets, tables, frames, and other items for the home. Call for hours.

George Jaques Rustic Furniture (518-576-2214; www.georgejaques.com). Traditional Great Camp–style furniture. Call for an appointment.

LAKE PLACID
Twigs (518-523-5361; 121 Cascade Road). Big shop with antiques and rustic furniture by several makers; look for the giant chair. Open year-round.

RAY BROOK
The Ray Brook Frog (518-891-3333; www.raybrookfrog.com; NY 86). Rustic and fine furniture; decorating accessories. Open year-round.

SARANAC LAKE
Adirondack Antler Art (Charles Jessie; 518-891-5383; 664 McKenzie Pond Road). Chandeliers, lamps, and sconces made from moose and whitetail deer antlers. Call ahead.

Goody Goody's (518-891-9070; 9 Broadway). Upscale toys in nice independent shop.

VERMONTVILLE
Adirondack Rustic Creations (David Daby; 518-891-2557; 150 Keith Road). Handcrafted home furnishings, including coffee tables, beds, and vanities. Call ahead.

Northwest Lakes

LAKE CLEAR
Jay Major Dawson (518-891-5075; www.majorpieces.com; off NY 30). Need a rustic gate or archway over the entrance to your Great Camp? Jay's the guy. He'll also make custom railings, built-in furniture, and lawn pieces. By appointment.

PAUL SMITHS
Train Brook Forest (David Woodward; 518-327-3747; www.trainbrookforge.com; 243 NY 86). Travel trunks and document boxes made of wood and leather; wrought-iron fireplace screens with wildlife silhouette designs; fireplace accessories; iron lighting fixtures in Arts-and-Crafts designs. Open year-round; by appointment only.

TUPPER LAKE
Jean Armstrong (518-359-9983; Big Wolf Lake). Rustic boxes, frames, and furniture, fungus art. Summer only, by appointment.

Michael Trivieri (518-359-7151; Moody Road). Burl bowls and tables; woodcarvings; mantels; custom railings and rustic trim work done on site. By appointment.

Thomas Phillips Rustic Furniture (518-359-9648; 681 Bartlett Carry Road). Ash-splint baskets with sculptural branch handles; twig-style and birch-bark chairs, tables, benches, and beds; cedar outdoor furniture; rustic furniture restoration. Price list available; open by appointment only.

Central and Southwestern Adirondacks

INDIAN LAKE
Backwoods Furnishings (Ken Heitz; 518-251-3327; NY 28). A Paul Bunyan–size log chair arches over Ken's driveway, marking the home of one of the originators of the Adirondack rustic revival. Twig, birch-bark, and cedar beds, tables, sideboards, settees, rockers, and custom orders. Ken's furniture has been featured in *House Beautiful*, *House and Garden*, *Gourmet*, and many other publications. By appointment only.

LONG LAKE
Cold River Gallery & Woodwork (Jamie Sutliff; 518-624-3581; P.O. Box 606, Deerland Road). Painted arch-top trunks; carved furniture, mirrors and frames with wildlife designs; custom doors and signs. Open year-round by appointment only.

North Country Images and Accents (Brian Morris; 518-624-4811; PO Box 211). Rustic furniture and frames. Call for an appointment.

Mayfield

Sampson Bog Studio (Barney and Susan Bellinger; 518-661-6563; 171 Paradise Point Road). Twig mosaic and birch-bark tables, desks, wall shelves, benches with fine hand-painted details and graceful lines. Call ahead.

Northville

Peter Winter's Rustic Studio (518-863-6555; 132 Division Street). Rustic furniture and accessories, open daily in summer.

   Russ Gleaves and Bill Coffey's Fine Handcrafted Rustic Furniture (518-863-4602; 322 North Third Street). Armoires, vanities, cabinets, beds and more. Call ahead.

Old Forge

Shelter (315-369-5014; 3109 Main Street, next to the arcade). Rustic and contemporary Adirondack-style furniture. Call for hours.

Otter Lake

Otter Lake Rustics (315-369-6530; www.otterlakerustics.com; 13977 NY 28). Rustic furniture, carved doors, and other Adirondack-style décor. Open year-round.

Speculator

Jerry's Wood Shop (518-548-5041; www.jerryswoodshop.com; Box 116 NY 30). Adirondack chairs and settees that fold for storage; picnic tables; lawn furniture. Open daily year-round.

General Stores

In a town that shall remain nameless, there's an abandoned cobblestone building with a sign proclaiming that it's the "Shop of Three Wonders: Wonder Where It Came From, Wonder What It Costs, and Wonder How Long It's Been Here." Those kinds of intellectual exercises make an expedition to a real general store fun. Chances are you'll find odd things like nail pullers and chick-feeding troughs alongside the glass percolator tops and sugar shakers, an aisle over from the suspenders and boot socks, around the corner from the chips and salsa. Don't worry about the dust; don't be afraid to ask the price. If you can't find it here, you can probably live without it.

   Some general stores really take the word "general" to heart, so that you can pick out a nice graduation gift as well as the fixings for an afternoon picnic, including sunglasses, bug dope, and sustenance.

Lake George and Southeastern Adirondacks

Adirondack

Adirondack General Store (518-494-4408; www.adkgeneralstore.com; 899 East Shore Drive). There's a fine line between country-looking places that try too hard and end up cutesy and those authentic country stores that mix the antique and the modern—and turn out charming. This mercantile, which was the company store for a tannery dating back to the 1850s, hits the nail on the head. You can hang out by the woodstove when it's cold; read the paper on the porch when it's warm; buy a nice gift; or get milk, eggs, bread, and such for camping in Pharaoh Lake Wilderness Area. The deli is very good. Homemade soups are scrumptious, and if there are any pies left, grab one. They're the best around. Open year-round.

PARADOX
Paradox General Store (518-532-7462; www.paradoxgeneralstore.com; NY 74). Deli, gifts, camp necessities. Call for hours.

Champlain Valley

CROWN POINT
Champ's General Store (518-597-9779; 694 Bridge Road). Full-service convenient store, deli, and gift shop. Open year-round.

McCabe's General Store (Julie Budwick; 518-597-4475; Middle Road). Selection of food and other supplies. Call for hours.

High Peaks and Northern Adirondacks

BLOOMINGDALE
Norman's Wholesale Grocery (518-891-1890; NY 3). Norman's has been in the same family since it began in 1902, and display drawers still have ornate hardware and lettering declaring "Socks and Mittens" or "Silks and Laces." For retail customers, the stock is mainly convenience-store items, but the place still feels very much like the old times when the stagecoach stopped here. Open year-round.

McCabe's General Store has a little bit of everything for folks in Crown Point. Courtesy of Kelly Kilgallon

Northwest Lakes

Cranberry Lake

The Emporium (315-848-2140; NY 3). Tiny place crammed with souvenirs, maps, fishing tackle, announcements of coming attractions, canned goods, frozen treats, and T shirts, but there's even more—the Emporium is a marina with gas pumps, water taxi, and a big, long weathered wooden dock. This kind of place used to be common in the Adirondacks, and the Emporium is one of the few lakeside general stores that remains. Open daily year-round.

Lakeside General Store (315-848-2501; 7140 NY 3). Liquor store, laundromat, campground, gas pumps, plus just about any supplies you need, such as home-baked goods and medical supplies.

Central and Southwestern Adirondacks

Indian Lake

Pine's Country Store (518-648-5212; www.pinescs.com; 1 Main Street, NY 28). Clothing, garden equipment, extensive hardware and houseware selection. Also renting yard equipment, bikes, etc. Open year-round.

Long Lake

Hoss's Country Corner (Jules Pierce and Ali Hamden; 518-624-2481; www.hossscountrycorner.com; corner 247 Lake Street). Exemplary modern general store with aisles of groceries, fresh meats, and deli items; Woolrich clothing for men and women, camp furnishings; stuffed animals; quilts, rugs, and baskets galore; cold beer; topo maps; Adirondack, outdoor, children's, and Christian books; jewelry; soaps and candles; out-of-town newspapers; film . . . the list is nearly endless, as is the rambling frame building that goes up, down, and around. Open year-round.

Minerva

Murdie's General Store (518-251-2076; 1688 NY 28N). If you're on the Teddy Roosevelt Memorial Highway retracing his 1901 midnight ride to the presidency and find that you need gas, night crawlers, crusher hat, six-pack, transmission fluid, ice cream, spaghetti, or maps, well, look no further. Open year-round.

Old Forge

Old Forge Hardware (315-369-6100; www.oldforgehardware.com; 104 Fulton Street). A visit to Old Forge Hardware is to Adirondack shopping as a trip to the Adirondack Museum is to regional history. This coliseum-size landmark bills itself as the "Adirondacks' Most General Store," a title with which we can't argue. Need a pack basket? Bamboo steamer for your wok? Spar varnish? Snowshoes? Reflective dog collar to fit a Newfoundland? Authentic shade for your antique Aladdin lamp? Spiles for maple sugaring? Replacement handle for your peavey? Any sort of book? You can spend an entire day here. Open year-round. Recommended.

Raquette Lake

Raquette Lake Supply (Jim Dillon; 315-354-4301; Main Street). The Dillon family has owned Raquette Lake Supply in one manifestation or another for more than a century. The building is huge, with a bakery, laundromat, and the Tap Room on the ground floor and a cheap hotel upstairs; the store takes up most of the floor space facing the water. There's a soda fountain, excellent meat counter, dairy case, and groceries, plus toy tomahawks, vintage postcards, and fish poles. This is the only place in the park where you can get honest-to-gosh, cut-from-the-lake ice for your cooler; the huge bluish blocks come with a frosting of sawdust that a quick plunge in the lake rinses off. Open year-round. If you're around in February for the annual ice-cutting weekend, drop by for a glimpse of a time-honored process.

SABAEL
The Lake Store (Eris Thompson; 518-648-5222; NY 30). Toys, gifts, sports gear, souvenirs, moccasins, and clothing, plus a summertime soda fountain, year-round deli, and all the major food groups. Open year-round.

STILLWATER
Stillwater Shop (315-376-2110; 2590 Stillwater Road at the boat launch). A true wilderness outpost, with food, gear, boat rentals, gas, snowmobile rentals, and a seaplane base. Open year-round.

GLASS

A handful of glass workers ply their trade in the Adirondacks, making custom beveled or stained-glass windows. In Westport, visit **Westport Trading** (Kip Trienens; 518-962-4801; 6511 Main Street) for architectural stained-glass windows, panels, and mirrors in stock or made to order; repairs for antique stained glass. Kip's shop is open most of the time, year-round; drop-ins welcome. In Old Forge, for Tiffany-style shades and lamps, the venerable **Meyda Stained Glass Studio** (315-369-6636; Main Street) has a great selection, plus planters, jewelry boxes, and mirrors. Open daily Memorial Day through Labor Day. **Adirondack Stained Glass Works** (518-725-0387; www.adirondackstainedglassworks.com; 29 W. Fulton Street), in Gloversville, offers Tiffany-style lamps, windows and night-lights; open year-round.

JEWELRY AND GEM SHOPS

Many of the craft shops listed above carry silver, gold, or porcelain jewelry by local artisans; the jewelers and mineral shops described below specialize in contemporary designs or native gemstones.

Lake George and Southeastern Adirondacks

POTTERSVILLE
Natural Stone Bridge and Caves (518-494-2283; www.stonebridgeandcaves.com; 535 Stone Bridge Road). Extensive mineral shop plus sluiceway where the kids can pan for gems. Open daily in summer.

WARRENSBURG
Tamarack Shoppe (518-623-3384; www.tamarackjewelry.com; 3861 Main Street). Fine handmade gemstone jewelry. Year-round; call for hours.

CHAMPLAIN VALLEY

Bailey Forge (Shelle Bailey; 518-962-4039; www.baileyforge.com; P.O. Box 55). Silver pendants impressed with leaves and cedar branches, glass beads enveloped in silver peapods, silver nests with pearls, and bracelets and necklaces embedded with ammonite fossils, geodes, and polished rocks. Call for an appointment.

Northwest Lakes

CROGHAN

Silver Bench Jewelry (Lisa Norz, daughter of the Bramhalls, mentioned below; 315-346-6805; www.silverbenchjewelry.com; 8270 Soft Maple Road). Intricate silversmith work including pack baskets, earrings, bracelets, and handmade chains. Call for an appointment or order online.

Stonehouse Silversmiths (Butch and Pat Bramhall; 315-346-1205; 8174 Bush Road). Just outside of the Blue Line; absolutely gorgeous intricately woven silver and gold creations, such as pack baskets and nests. Call for hours. Recommended.

High Peaks and Northern Adirondacks

LAKE PLACID

Arthur Volmrich (518-523-2970; 2413 Main Street). Amusing earrings and necklaces mixing antique charms, buttons, and stones with modern components; turquoise bracelets and watchbands; custom rings; repairs and resettings. Open year-round.

Darrah Cooper Jewelers (518-523-2774; www.darrahcooperjewelers.com; 2416 Main Street, next to the Hilton). Delightful sterling silver and gold charms and earrings representing miniature North Country objects: pack baskets, canoe paddles, guideboats, oars, pine cones, and Adirondack chairs. Also rings, bracelets, and necklaces in precious stones, silver, and gold. Open year-round.

Spruce Mountain Designs (518-523-9212; www.spruce-mountain.com; Box 205). Adirondack wildflowers in sterling silver and gold. By appointment only.

WILMINGTON

Winona Studio (Jessica Mulvey; 518-946-2401; 44 Mulvey Road). Porcupine quill jewelry and pack baskets. Call for an appointment.

Central and Southwestern Adirondacks

LONG LAKE

Minerals Unlimited (518-624-5825; 965 NY 28/30). Geodes, crystals, fossils, silver jewelry with semiprecious stones made by Leslie Knoll. Open daily in spring, summer and fall weekends.

NORTH RIVER

Gore Mountain Mineral Shop (518-251-2706; www.garnetminestours.com; Barton Mines Road, 5 mi. off NY 28). Garnet jewelry; faceted gemstones; rocks and minerals from around the world; garnet mine tours; gem-cutting demonstrations. Open daily late June through Labor Day.

J and J Brown Garnet Studio (68 Casterline Road). Specializing in Adirondack garnet; will customize pieces.

Jasco Minerals (Jim Shaw; 518-251-3196; NY 28). Specializing in native garnet, plus fossils and semiprecious stones from around the world; custom jewelry orders. Call for hours.

OLD FORGE
Allen's (315-369-6660; 3017 Main Street). Fine jewelry; Adirondack charms; snowmobile earrings, pendants, and charms. Open daily year-round.

RAQUETTE LAKE
South Bay Jewelers (Mary Blanchard, 315-354-5481; www.southbayjewelry.com; P.O. Box 35). Fine silver jewelry. Mary gained fame a couple of years ago for creating a special piece for Neil Diamond, but anyone can make arrangements to see the production line, which includes necklaces, bracelets, and earrings in silver and gold. By appointment.

OUTDOOR GEAR

Many shops in the Adirondack Park offer sports equipment, outdoor clothing, and camping supplies; you'll find them listed in Chapter 7, under specific headings like Camping, Fishing, Rock and Ice Climbing, or Skiing.

POTTERY

Lake George and Southeastern Adirondacks

CHESTERTOWN
Fawn Ridge Pottery (David and Sharon Coleman; www.fawn-ridge-pottery.com; 518-494-4373; 34 Fawn Ridge Road). Pottery dinnerware, mugs, casseroles, and more, with Adirondack scenes and themes. Call for hours.

    Red Truck Clayworks (Bill Knoble; www.redtruckpottery.com; 518-494-2074; 11 Dennehy Road). Truly fine stoneware, from everyday dishes to paella pans, casseroles, salad bowls, ceramic buttons, and more. Call ahead to see the whole wood-fired operation. Call for hours; open daily in summer. Recommended.

High Peaks and Northern Adirondacks

JAY
Jay Crafts Center (Lee Kazanas and Cheri Cross; www.jaycraftcenter.com; 518-946-7824; NY 9N). Pottery lamps, bowls, vases, and dinnerware made by Lee and Cheri; wooden toys; ash-splint baskets; silver jewelry; prints; custom matting and framing. Call for hours.

    Youngs' Studio and Gallery (Sue and Terrance Young; www.adirondackpottery.com; 518-946-7301; 6588 NY 86). Wonderful pottery (raku and stoneware) made by Sue; limited-edition etchings of Adirondack landscapes by Terry; full range of other local crafts. Open year-round; call for hours. Recommended.

KEENE
Amsterlaw Clayworks (518-576-9535; www.amsterlaw.com; P.O. Box 183). Bowls and cookware. Call to make an appointment.

SCULPTURE

Architectural-design elements, folk-art figures, realistic wildlife, and modern concrete sculpture are just a few of the things shaped by Adirondack hands. Listed below you'll find a sampling of decorative items for indoors and out.

Lake George and Southeastern Adirondacks

HADLEY

Tom O'Brien (518-696-5997; www.obrien-fineart.com). Portrait sculpture in bronze, terra cotta, carbon steel, and stainless steel. By appointment.

WHITEHALL

Small Ponderings (John H. Sharp; 518-642-2408; County Route 12). Whimsical metal sculptures. Call for an appointment.

Champlain Valley

Bailey Forge (Russell B. & Shelle A. Bailey; 518-962-4039; www.baileyforge.com; P.O. Box 55, Essex). Blacksmith shop and art studio specializing in forged architectural ornamental ironwork, sculpture, silver jewelry, and fine art. Call for an appointment.

Crooked Brook Studios (Edward Cornell; 518-962-4386; www.crookedbrookstudios.com; 154 Sayre Road). Monumental sculptures, including installations of minimally processed found objects. Call for an appointment.

High Peaks and Northern Adirondacks

BLOOMINGDALE

Concrete Abstracts (Ralph Prata; 518-891-2417; www.ralphprata.com; West Main Street). Abstract concrete carvings: freestanding sculptures, wall reliefs, and framed limited-edition works. Brochure available; open by appointment only.

LAKE PLACID

PJ LaBarge (518-523-5353; www.pjlabarge.com). Bronze sculptures; life-size panthers and other wildlife. Call for an appointment.

Robert Scofield (518-572-8126; www.adirondackburlwoodsculpture; 20 Strathknoll Way). Adirondack burl wood sculpture and bowls. Call for an appointment.

RAINBOW LAKE

Peter Shrope Studio (518-327-5247; www.shrope.org; 473 County Route 60). Sculpture and mixed media. Call for an appointment.

UPPER JAY

Julia Gronski (518-946-7968; 20 Andrus Way). Fine ceramic work; by appointment only.

Northwest Lakes

TUPPER LAKE

Michael Trivieri (518-359-7151; Moody Road). Burl bowls and tables; bas-relief sculptures of Adirondack wildlife; commissions. Call ahead.

Central and Southwestern Adirondacks

WELLS

John Van Alstine (518-924-9204; www.johnvanalstine.com; P.O. Box 526). Granite, bronze, steel, and works on paper. The artist's eight-acre Adirondack River Sculpture Park showcases his work. Call for an appointment.

9

INFORMATION

Nuts, Bolts, and Free Advice

Consult this chapter to find the answers to questions about important community services and organizations, and for an array of miscellaneous facts and figures.

Checking the latest news in Chestertown.

Itsuzo Sumy photograph courtesy of the Town of Chester Museum of Local History

Ambulance, Fire, State and Local Police

There is no unified emergency-assistance system that operates throughout the Adirondack Park, although 911 service has been extended to Warren and Essex Counties. If you're traveling on I-87, the Northway, know that there are very few cell towers in remote areas, so there are stretches of highway that don't get cell phone service.

Clinton County, which covers the northeastern portion of the Adirondack Park, has enhanced 911 service; this means that when you call, your name and address pop up on a display screen at the safety center.

Elsewhere in the Adirondacks, you should dial 0 to reach the operator; stay on the line and you'll be connected to the appropriate agency. If you're lucky enough to have a telephone book nearby when you run into trouble, check the inside front cover for emergency listings for individual towns.

The New York State Police has offices throughout the Adirondacks. If no local officer is available, calls are forwarded to a twenty-four-hour central dispatcher. Numbers are:

Chestertown	518-494-3201
Elizabethtown	518-873-2111
Indian Lake	518-648-5757
Keeseville	518-834-9040
Moriah	518-546-7611
Old Forge	315-369-3322
Ray Brook	518-897-2000
Schroon Lake	518-532-7691
Ticonderoga	518-585-6200
Tupper Lake	518-359-7677
Westport	518-962-8235
Willsboro	518-963-7400

The national hotline for **Poison Control** is 1-800-222-1222.

Area Codes

The area code for the eastern two thirds of the Adirondacks, including Lake George, Warrensburg, Schroon Lake, Elizabethtown, Westport, Keene, Lake Placid, Saranac Lake, Tupper Lake, Long Lake, Blue Mountain Lake, Indian Lake, North Creek, Speculator, Wells, and Northville is 518. For communities in the northwestern and west-central Adirondacks, such as Cranberry Lake, Star Lake, Raquette Lake, Inlet, Eagle Bay, Big Moose, and Old Forge, the area code is 315.

BIBLIOGRAPHY

Diverse authors have been inspired by the Adirondacks, from Robert Louis Stevenson, who completed the *Master of Ballantrae* when he was a tuberculosis patient in Saranac Lake, to Nathanael West, who penned part of *Miss Lonelyhearts* during a sojourn in Warrensburg. Sylvia Plath chronicled her ski accident at Mount Pisgah in *The Bell Jar*. Keene resident Russell Banks is the leading light of Adirondack literature with *The Sweet Hereafter, Rule of the Bone, Cloudsplitter,* based on John Brown's life, and *The Reserve.* Ian Fleming's *The Spy Who Loved Me* is set in a dreary motor court near Lake George; L. Sprague DeCamp's horror-fantasy *The Purple Pterodactyls* has a definite Adirondack flavor. Mystery writer John D. MacDonald, of Travis McGee fame, even wrote a book about his cats spending their summers in Piseco.

Anthologies *The Adirondack Reader* (Adirondack Mountain Club, 1982), edited by Paul Jamieson, and *Rooted in Rock: New Adirondack Writing* (The Adirondack Museum, 2001), edited by Jim Gould, offer collections of regional essays.

The two lists that follow include recent books and out-of-print volumes that may be read at several local libraries. The latter books don't circulate; an appointment may be necessary to peruse a special collection. For a list of libraries with special sections of Adirondack literature, consult Chapter 6. For where to buy Adirondack books, check Chapter 8.

BOOKS YOU CAN BUY

LITERARY WORKS
Banks, Russell. *The Darling*. New York: Harper Perennial, 2005. 400 pp.
 —*The Reserve*. New York: Harper Collins, 2008. 287 pp.

Barrett, Andrea. *The Air We Breathe*. New York: W. W. Norton, 2007. 320 pp.

Cooper, James Fenimore. *The Last of the Mohicans*. Numerous paperback editions. New York: Bantam Classics, 1982. 384 pp.

Doctorow, E. L. *Loon Lake*. New York: Random House, 1980. 258 pp.

Dreiser, Theodore. *An American Tragedy*. Paperback editions available. New York: Signet Classics, 1964. 832 pp.

LaBastille, Anne. *Woodswoman*. New York: E.P. Dutton, 1976. 277 pp.

ARCHITECTURE AND DECORATIVE ARTS
Gilborn, Craig. *Adirondack Camps: Homes Away from Home*, 1850–1950. Blue Mountain Lake and Syracuse, NY: Adirondack Museum and Syracuse University Press, 2000. 367 pp., color and black-and-white photos, index.

Kaiser, Harvey. *Great Camps of the Adirondacks*. Boston: David Godine, 1986. 240 pp., color photos, maps, index.

Kylloe, Ralph. *Cabin in the Woods*. Layton, UT: Gibbs Smith, 2007. 176 pp., color photographs.

O'Leary, Ann Stillman. *Rustic Revisited*. New York: Watson-Guptill, 2006. 208 pp., color plates.

HISTORY

Bellico, Russell. *Chronicles of Lake Champlain*. Fleischmanns, NY: Purple Mountain Press, 1999. 415 pp., historic vignettes, photos, maps, drawings, index.

Bond, Hallie. *Boats of the Adirondacks*. Blue Mountain Lake, NY: Adirondack Museum, 1995. 334 pp.

Brown, Phil. *Bob Marshall in the Adirondacks: Writings of a Pioneering Peak Bagger*, Pond Hopper and Wilderness Preservationist. Saranac Lake, NY: Lost Pond Press, 2006. 308 pp., photographs and maps.

Brumley, Charles. *Guides of the Adirondacks*. Utica, NY: North Country Books, 1994. 320 pp., photos, list of guides, index.

Donaldson, Alfred L. *A History of the Adirondacks*. Two-volume set originally published in 1921; reprinted, Fleischmanns, New York: Purple Mountain Press, 1993. 766 pp.

Jerome, Christine. *An Adirondack Passage: The Cruise of the Canoe Sairy Gamp*. Lake George, New York: Adirondack Mountain Club, 1999. 246 pp., photos, maps, index.

MacKenzie, Mary. *The Plains of Abraham: A History of North Elba and Lake Placid*, Collected Writings of Mary MacKenzie. Utica, NY: Nicholas K. Burns Publishing, 2007. 397 pp.

McMartin, Barbara. *The Great Forest of the Adirondacks*. Utica, NY: North Country Books, 1994. 266 pp., photos, charts, index.

   —*The Privately Owned Adirondacks: Sporting and Family Clubs*, Private Parks and Preserves, Timberlands and Easements. Lake View Press, 2004. 304 pp.

Nelson, James L. *Benedict Arnold's Navy*. New York: McGraw Hill, 2006. 386 pp.

Prochnik, George. *Putnam Camp: Sigmund Freud, James Jackson Putnam, and the Purpose of American Psychology*. Other Press, 2006. 480 pp.

Schneider, Paul. *The Adirondacks*. New York: Henry Holt, 1997. 340 pp.

Starbuck, David. *Massacre at Fort William Henry*. Hanover, NH: University Press of New England, 2002. 152 pp., photos, sketches, diagrams.

Svenson, Sally. *Adirondack Churches*. Utica, NY: North Country Books, 2006. 256 pp. Black-and-white and color photographs.

Terrie, Philip G. *Contested Terrain*. Syracuse, NY: Syracuse University Press, 2008. 223 pp.

NATURAL HISTORY

North Country Books, in Utica, publishes a series of field guides on native birds, mammals, trees and shrubs, wildflowers, and mushrooms. All of the books are paperbacks with numerous color photos.

Bell, Allison W., and Slack, Nancy G. *Adirondack Alpine Summits: An Ecological Field Guide*. Adirondack Mountain Club, 2007. 80 pp., color photographs.

DiNunzio, Michael. *Adirondack Wildguide*. Elizabethtown, NY: Adirondack Conservancy/Adirondack Council, 1984. 160 pp., illus.

Jenkins, Jerry. *Adirondack Atlas: A Geographic Portrait of the Adirondacks*. Syracuse, NY: Syracuse University Press, 2004. 296 pp. 450 color figures, maps, and tables.

McMartin, Barbara. *The Adirondack Park: A Wildlands Quilt*. Syracuse, NY: Syracuse University Press, 1999. 94 pp., color photos, maps.

Stager, Curt. *Field Notes from the Northern Forest*. Syracuse, NY: Syracuse University Press, 1998. 272 pp., illus.

Terrie, Philip G. *Wildlife and Wilderness: A History of Adirondack Mammals*. Fleischmanns, NY: Purple Mountain Press, 1993. 176 pp., photos, index.

PHOTOGRAPHIC/PAINTING STUDIES

Bogdan, Robert. *Exposing the Wilderness: Early 20th Century Adirondack Postcard Photographers*. Syracuse, NY: Syracuse University Press, 1999. Photos, index.

Bowie, Mark. *Adirondack Waters: Spirit of the Waters*. Utica, NY: North Country Books, 2006. 144 pp., color photographs.

Heilman, Carl E., II. *The Adirondacks*. New York: Rizzoli Press, 2006. 224 pp., 160 color photos and panoramas.

Ringer, Michael C. *Adirondack Seasons: Old as Time*. Canton, NY: St. Lawrence Gallery, 2006. 144 pp., color photos of Ringer's paintings.

RECREATION

There are two main sources for Adirondack guidebooks for hiking, snowshoeing, and cross-country skiing: the Adirondack Mountain Club (ADK), based in Lake George, NY, and North Country Books, out of Utica. The Forest Preserve Series by various ADK authors covers seven different regions of the park, from the High Peaks to the Northville–Lake Placid Trail; these pocket-size paperbacks have plenty of detail and each comes with a separate topo map showing trails. North Country Books distributes the Discover the Adirondacks Series, written by the late historian/hiker Barbara McMartin and now updated and expanded by Bill Ingersoll. These are livelier to read, with notes on the human and natural history of a particular destination.

Three guidebooks covering hiking, canoeing, and backpacking by Barbara McMartin are intended for young readers to share with their parents and are available from North Country Books; another is *Kids on the Trail,* equal parts how-to and where-to, published by the Adirondack Mountain Club in 1998. If you can't decide on which region to trek, read Barbara McMartin's *Fifty Hikes in the Adirondacks: Short Walks, Day Trips, and Extended Hikes Throughout the Park,* from The Countryman Press, in Woodstock, VT.

Aprill, Dennis. *Good Fishing in the Adirondacks*. The Countryman Press, 1999. 224 pp., photos, maps.

———. *Paths Less Traveled*. Elizabethtown, NY: Pinto Press, 1998. 181 pp., maps, photos, with descriptions of good hikes on smaller mountains.

———. *Short Treks in the Adirondacks and Beyond*. Utica, NY: Nicholas K. Burns Publishing, 2005. 160 pp.

Goodwin, Tony. *Classic Adirondack Ski Tours*. Lake George, NY: Adirondack Mountain Club, 1996. 127 pp., maps, index.

Haas, Jeremy, and Lawyer, Jim. *Adirondack Rock*. Self-published, 2008 (www.adirondackrock.com).

Jamieson, Paul, and Morris, Donald. *Adirondack Canoe Waters: North Flow*. Lake George, NY: Adirondack Mountain Club, 1999. Includes new state acquisitions. 368 pp., maps, index.

Kick, Peter. *25 Mountain Bike Tours in the Adirondacks*. Woodstock, VT: The Countryman Press, 1999. 190 pp., photos, maps.

McKibben, Bill; Halpern, Sue; Lemmel, Barbara; and Hay, Mitchell. *25 Bike Rides in the Adirondacks: Bicycle Adventures in the East's Largest Wilderness*. Woodstock, VT: The Countryman Press, 1995. 174 pp.

Mellor, Don. *Climbing in the Adirondacks: A Guide to Rock & Ice Routes*. Lake George, NY: Adirondack Mountain Club, 1996. 318 pp., photos, maps, index.

Morrissey, Spencer. *The Other 54: a Hiker's Guide to the Lower 54 Peaks of the Adirondack 100 Highest*. Dacksdescents Publishing, 2007. 256 pp., black-and-white photos, color maps.

Travel

Folwell, Elizabeth, and Godine, Amy. *Adirondack Odysseys*. Lee, MA, and Blue Mountain Lake, NY: Berkshire House Publishers and the Adirondack Museum, 1997. 220 pp.

Stoddard, Seneca Ray. *The Adirondacks Illustrated*. Glens Falls, NY: Chapman Historical Museum, 1983. Reprint of 1874 guidebook. 204 pp., illus., index.

Books You Can Borrow

Barnett, Lincoln. *The Ancient Adirondacks*. New York: Time-Life Books, 1974. 184 pp., photos, index.

Colvin, Verplanck. *Report on a Topographical Survey of the Adirondack Wilderness of New York*. Albany, NY: 1873. Engravings and maps.

Deming, Philander. *Adirondack Stories*. Boston: 1880.

Murray, William H. H. *Adventures in the Wilderness*. Boston: 1869.

Climate and Weather Information

"Nine months of winter and three months of poor sledding" sums up an Adirondack year if you happen to ask a native in, say, mud season. A typical twelve months has about 190 days of subfreezing temperatures. The western Adirondacks, including Old Forge, Eagle Bay, Big Moose, Inlet, and north to Cranberry Lake and Star Lake, gets considerably more snow than the eastern Adirondacks, with about 10 feet falling in an average winter, much of it from lake-effect storms off Lake Ontario.

Spring in the Adirondacks can be elusive. March is winter, despite the date of the vernal equinox. April weather bounces between brief flashes of hot and dry, or sustained snow and cold, or mixtures of mild and moist. May tends to be reliably above freezing during the daytime, although in 1976, nearly 2 feet of snow fell on May 19. June temperatures can be sweltering, with plenty of bug activity.

July and August days are usually in the 70s and 80s, with occasional hotter spells, but evenings cool off pleasantly. Early September often brings the finest dry weather for outdoor activities, with highs in the 70s and lows in the 50s.

Fall can be brilliantly sunny, providing great leaf-peeping opportunities from about September 20 through October 15, depending on the elevation. Or autumn can be dismally rainy, with the only chance to see fall colors by looking in mud puddles. There's a toll-free hotline for fall foliage reports, 1-800-CALL-NYS.

Generalities about the weather are one thing; getting an accurate forecast is another. There is no nearby National Weather Service station. Predictions for Albany; Syracuse; or Burlington, Vermont, need temperatures to be adjusted downwards by 5 or 10 degrees, with a corresponding change for precipitation—40 degrees and rain in the Albany area usually means subfreezing temperatures and sleet or snow in the Adirondacks.

The Lake Placid radio station, WIRD (105.5 FM), has a weatherman on staff who provides good information for the area from Tupper Lake to Keene. If you're hiking anywhere near the High Peaks, call 518-523-3518 for the Adirondack Mountain Club's recorded weather forecast, plus a word or two about what to expect on mountaintops and the trails that lead there.

North Country Public Radio, WSLU-FM (see radio station section), broadcasting out of St. Lawrence University, in Canton, airs extensive forecasts that cover much of the Adirondacks. The "Eye on the Sky" weather update from Vermont Public Radio, WVPR (107.9 FM), tends to be fairly reliable for the eastern Adirondacks. The Albany television station, WRGB, also has a weather forecast at 518-476-WRGB, which covers the southern Adirondacks.

Although there are a couple of weather phone numbers you can call, the Internet has usurped this service. The Web site accuweather.com shows five-day forecasts for Lake George and Lake Placid. The Weather Channel (www.weather.com) and Weather Underground (www.wunderground.com) allow you to plug in a zip code and receive current conditions and a ten-day forecast, although it may not work for zips of smaller Adirondack towns.

North Country Public Radio's Web site, www.ncpr.org, has links to weather information by county, and Indian Lake meteorologist Darrin Harr maintains a site, www.ilsnow.com, that provides a central Adirondacks forecast, with powder particulars for snowmobilers. Workers at Whiteface and Gore Mountains rely on www.snocountry.com for powder reports.

HANDICAPPED SERVICES

For disabled New Yorkers, free passes to state-operated camping, swimming, golf facilities, and historic sites are available by applying to the **Office of Parks, Recreation and Historic Preservation**. Write to OPRHP at Agency Building 1, Empire State Plaza, Albany, NY 12238, or call 518-474-0456.

Some of the nature trails at the Adirondack Park Agency Visitor Interpretive Centers, at Paul Smiths and Newcomb, are designed for the mobility-impaired. The Adirondack Mountain Club (see "Bibliography," above) has appendices on appropriate trails for wheelchairs in some of its hiking guidebooks. The new **John Dillon Park** (518-524-6226 from May through September, and 518-327-6266 from October through April; www.johndillonpark.org) is open to anyone with a disability, his or her family, friends, and caregivers. You need a permit, which you can get for free, and the lean-tos and trails are designed for people with disabilities. The park, with Grampus Lake and Handsome Pond, has more than 2 miles of nice trails with good surfaces for wheelchairs. Also, the Department of Environmental Conservation's campground at **Scaroon Manor**, in Schroon Lake, has trails and campsites for those with mobility concerns (518-457-2500;

www.dec.ny.gov). Contact the Department of Environmental Conservation about the **universally accessible trails** for people with mobility impairments at Ausable Marsh, Lampson Falls, Francis Lake, Moss Lake, and Silver Lake Bog.

Cultural institutions, such as the Adirondack Museum or Lake Placid Center for the Arts, libraries, and theaters are generally accessible; some historic buildings are not. Chapter 6 provides more information. Restaurants that are accessible are described in Chapter 5; lodgings with handicapped facilities are listed in Chapter 4.

Health Centers and Hospitals

Most local health centers are open weekdays; Hudson Headwaters centers (www.hhhn.org) are open Saturdays as well. Many town health centers have answering services that can help with emergencies any time, day or night.

Lake George and Southeastern Adirondacks

Bolton Health Center, 518-644-9471; www.hhhn.org; 11 Cross Street, Bolton Landing

Chester Health Center, 518-494-2761; www.hhhn.org; 6223 US 9, Chestertown

Glens Falls Hospital, 518-926-6670; www.glensfallshospital.org; 102 Park Street, Glens Falls

Schroon Lake Health Center, 518-532-7120; www.hhhn.org; 24 Fairfield Avenue, Schroon Lake

Warrensburg Health Center, 518-623-2844; www.hhhn.org; Health Center Plaza, 3767 Main Street, Warrensburg

Champlain Valley

Champlain Valley Physicians Hospital Medical Center, 518-561-2000; www.cvph.org; 75 Beekman Street, Plattsburgh

Elizabethtown Community Hospital, 518-873-6377; www.ech.org; 75 Park Street, Elizabethtown

Moriah Health Center, 518-942-7123; www.hhhn.org; 27 Hospital Road, Mineville

Smith House Health Care Center, 518-963-4275; 39 Farrell Road, Willsboro

Ticonderoga Health Center, 518-585-6708; www.hhhn.org; 102 Racetrack Road, Ticonderoga

High Peaks and Northern Adirondacks

Adirondack Medical Center, 518-523-3311; www.amccares.org; 29 Church Street, Lake Placid

Adirondack Medical Center, 518-891-4141; www.amccares.org; 2233 NY 86, Saranac Lake

Mountain Health Center, 518-576-9771; www.amccares.org; NY 73, Keene

Newcomb Health Center, 518-582-2991; Winebrook Hills, Newcomb

Wilmington Health Center, 518-946-7080; www.amccares.org; 7 Community Center Circle, Wilmington

Northwest Lakes

Adirondack Health Center (formerly Mercy Health Care), 518-359-3355; 115 Wawbeek Avenue, Tupper Lake

Clifton-Fine Hospital, 315-848-3351; 1014 Oswegatchie Trail, Star Lake

Tupper Lake Health Center, 518-359-7000; www.amccares.org; 55 Church Street, Tupper Lake

Central and Southwestern Adirondacks

Central Adirondack Family Practice, 315-369-6619; South Shore Road, Old Forge

Indian Lake Health Center, 518-648-5707; www.hhhn.org; Main Street and Pelon Road, Indian Lake

Long Lake Medical Center, 518-624-2301; NY 28N, Long Lake

Nathan Littauer Hospital, 518-725-8621; www.nlh.org; 90 East State Street, Gloversville

North Creek Health Center, 518-251-2541; www.hhhn.org; Ski Bowl Road, North Creek

LATE NIGHT FOOD AND FUEL

Most towns with more than a few hundred people now have convenience stores open until 11 PM, offering gas, food, and personal-care essentials. From Lake George to Lake Placid to Old Forge, look for Nice n' Easy, Stewart's Shops, or Top's Express. Most of these spots have cash machines.

MAPS

A standard road-atlas page showing New York State shrinks the Adirondack Park down to a postage stamp and indicates maybe three highways. The **Adirondack North Country Association** (www.adirondack.org) publishes an excellent full-size road map that shows just the park and adjacent counties; send $2.00 (check or money order) and a stamped, self-addressed legal-size envelope to ANCA, 183 Broadway, Saranac Lake NY 12983, to receive one. JiMapco, in Round Lake, New York, publishes individual county maps that are widely available in grocery stores and bookshops. *The New York State Atlas and Gazetteer* ($19.95), published by De Lorme Mapping Co., Freeport, Maine, uses a topographical map format to show areas in still greater detail; these can be found in most area bookstores, and larger stores elsewhere. The most beautiful map is *Adirondack Life*'s 3' x 4' topographical map; the magazine also sells a raised relief map of the park. Both are available at 518-946-2191 or at www.adirondacklife.com.

MAGAZINES AND NEWSPAPERS

Adirondac (518-668-4447; www.adk.org; RD 3, Box 3055, Lake George, NY 12845). Bimonthly magazine. Published by the Adirondack Mountain Club, with articles on local history, outdoor recreation, and environmental issues.

Adirondack Life (518-946-2191; www.adirondacklife.com; Box 410, Jay, NY 12941). Award-winning bimonthly magazine, plus two special issues: *Annual Guide to the Great Outdoors* and *Collectors Issue*. Known for excellent color photography; publishes essays, short stories, columns, and features on history, outdoor recreation, architecture, culture, local life, regional products, politics, and environmental issues by nationally known writers.

Lake George and Southeastern Adirondacks

Glens Falls Post Star (518-792-3131; www.poststar.com; Lawrence and Cooper Streets, Glens Falls, NY 12801). Daily newspaper covering the Adirondacks from Lake George to Long Lake.

Lake George Mirror (518-644-2619; www.lakegeorgemirror.com; 4591 Lake Shore Drive, Lake George, NY 12845). Weekly newspaper covering events in and around Lake George.

Champlain Valley

Lake Champlain Weekly (518-563-1414; 4701 US 9, Plattsburgh, NY 12901). Weekly newspaper with arts and culture focus.

Plattsburgh Press-Republican (518-561-2300; www.pressrepublican.com; 170 Margaret Street, Plattsburgh, NY 12901). Daily paper covering Clinton, Franklin, and Essex Counties, with news bureaus in Lake Placid (518-523-1559) and Ticonderoga (518-585-4070).

Valley News (518-873-6368; www.denpubs.com; Denton Publishing Co., Elizabethtown, NY 12932). Weekly paper for Elizabethtown, Westport, Willsboro, Essex, Keene, Keene Valley, Jay, and Upper Jay.

High Peaks and Northern Adirondacks

Adirondack Daily Enterprise (518-891-2600; www.adirondackdailyenterprise.com; 54 Broadway, Saranac Lake, NY 12983). Daily paper for Lake Placid, Saranac Lake, Paul Smiths, and Tupper Lake area; the Friday *Weekender* insert has a good regional calendar of events plus local history features.

Adirondack Explorer (518-891-9352; www.adirondackexplorer.org; 36 Church Street, Saranac Lake, NY). Tabloid-size newspaper with paddle trips, hiking treks, and environmental issues.

Lake Placid News (518-523-4401; wwwlakeplacidnews.com; 6179 Sentinel Road, Lake Placid, NY 12946). Weekly paper for Lake Placid, Keene, Keene Valley, Wilmington, and Au Sable Forks.

Northwest Lakes

Tupper Lake Free Press (518-359-2166; 136 Park Street, Tupper Lake, NY 12986). Weekly paper covering Tupper Lake, Piercefield, Cranberry Lake, and Long Lake.

Watertown Daily Times (315-782-1000; www.watertowndailytimes.com; 260 Washington Street, Watertown, NY 13601). Daily paper covering Thousand Islands/Lake Ontario area, including the northwestern Adirondacks.

Central and Southwestern Adirondacks

Adirondack Express (315-369-2237; www.adirondackexpress.com; 3046 Main Street, Old Forge, NY 13420). Weekly newspaper with coverage from Blue Mountain Lake to Otter Lake.

Adirondack Weekly (315-369-9982; Main Street, Old Forge NY 13420). Weekly newspaper with coverage from Blue Mountain Lake to Otter Lake.

Hamilton County News (518-548-6898; NY 30, Speculator, NY 12164). Weekly newspaper for Long Lake, Blue Mountain Lake, Indian Lake, Speculator, Wells, Piseco, and Benson.

North Creek News (518-251-3012; www.denspubs.com; 288 Main Street, North Creek, NY 12853). Weekly paper for Johnsburg, Bakers Mills, Minerva, Olmstedville, North Creek, and North River.

Times Union of Albany (518-454-5694; www.timesunion.com; News Plaza, P.O. Box 15000, Albany, NY 122121) and *The Daily Gazette* (518-374-4141; www.dailygazette.com; P.O. Box 1090, Schenectady NY 12301). Frequently offer Adirondack features.

RADIO STATIONS

National Public Radio

Three NPR affiliates reach different parts of the Adirondacks:

WAMC-FM, 90.3; 518-465-5233; Albany NY; also translator WANC, 103.9 (Ticonderoga) and WCEL, 91.9 (Plattsburgh).

WSLU-FM, 89.5 (Canton), 91.3 (Blue Mountain Lake and Thousand Islands), 88.9 (Paul Smiths), 88.3 (Peru), 90.1 (Keene), 96.3 (Keene Valley), 93.5 (Lake George), 91.7 (Long Lake, Lake Placid, Tupper Lake), 88.1 (Lowville), 90.9 (Malone), 97.3 (Newcomb), 104.3 (North Creek), 88.7 (Old Forge), 90.5 (Saranac Lake), 95.3 (Schroon Lake), 97.5 (Speculator), 101.7 (St. Huberts); 315-229-5356; www.ncpr.org; Canton, NY. The best news and feature coverage for the entire Adirondack Park by any media outlet; maintains an excellent Adirondack News Bureau at Paul Smith's College.

WVPR, 107.9; 802-655-9451; Colchester, VT. News coverage for the eastern Adirondacks and relatively reliable weather forecasts.

Commercial Radio Stations

WLPW-FM, 105.5; 518-891-5186; www.theclassicrock105.com. Lake Placid. General. (Signal broadcasts through WRGR-FM, 102.3, Tupper Lake as well.) The radio show, the Pat McAvoy Experiment, on Saturdays from 10 AM to 7 PM, is a local favorite.

WNBZ-AM, 1240, 518-891-1544. Saranac Lake. General.

WSLK-FM, 106.3, 518-891-1544. Saranac Lake. Country.

TELEVISION STATIONS

There are no television stations broadcasting from within the Adirondack Park, and TV reception in areas not covered by cable or satellite service can be awful. The Plattsburgh NBC-affiliate, WPTZ, reports on news from Lake Placid, Saranac Lake, and elsewhere in the eastern Adirondacks during the *Today Show* and in evening slots. WCAX, the Burlington, VT, CBS-affiliate, has a reporter filing stories from the Adirondacks on a relatively regular basis.

REAL ESTATE

Because the population of the region has been fairly stable over the last century, there are often older farmsteads and village homes for sale, as families build new houses to meet their needs. If you're not afraid of the "handyman's special," the Adirondacks could provide some challenges and rewards for you, with perhaps some acreage to boot. Town houses and condominiums are popping up most places, and after intense initial speculation, prices have stabilized at a level that shouldn't be too shocking to a typical New England urbanite. Some lodgings, such as the new Whiteface Lodge (518-523-0534; www.thewhitefacelodge.com), in Lake Placid, are fractional-share resorts, in which you can own a suite and use it or rent it through the resort rental pool. Waterfront—on just about any lake, river, or pond inside the Blue Line—tends to be scarce and very pricey. Add a summer cottage, or a real winterized house plus a decent driveway, a boathouse, or a garage, and the figures start to escalate.

Even crossroads that don't have grocery stores have real-estate offices. Weekly newspapers usually have some real-estate listings, and many realtors publish bimonthly buyers' guides. *Adirondack Life* magazine has a large real-estate section in each issue. The Web offers yet another way to let buyers know about potential homes or land for sale—check out www.adirondackbyowner.com. An added bonus for the visitor: Most realtors offer private rentals of well-equipped lakefront homes and ski chalets.

Religious Services and Organizations

Churches throughout the Adirondacks anchor the communities and provide a network of help and social life along with spiritual guidance. Several local churches are interesting for their architecture and are listed on the National Register of Historic Places; a few seasonal chapels are located on lovely islands accessible only by boat. Some churches even put on great, inexpensive dinners (see Chapter 5, for advice on chicken barbecues and church suppers). Check the papers for listings of church services. Inside the park, Lake Placid has the only active synagogue; Temple Beth Joseph, in Tupper Lake, is open as a historic building and occasionally offers services.

Road Service

For AAA members, there are local offices in Glens Falls, 518-792-0088; Johnstown, 518-762-4619; and Plattsburgh, 518-563-3830. Local police and emergency services can help you find a tow truck.

Tourist Information

Taking care of visitors is the number-one industry in the Adirondacks, and communities have become quite skilled at educating the public about their unique offerings. Warren County (which encompasses Lake George and the southeastern Adirondacks) publishes a colorful guide with a calendar of events, lists of hiking trails, boat-launch sites, museums, libraries, attractions, campgrounds, and much more; call 518-761-6366 for a copy. Likewise, the Lake Placid/Essex County Visitors Bureau (518-523-2445; www.lakeplacid.com) has an extensive promotional packet.

Franklin County publishes a four-color booklet with general background information plus publications detailing services and outdoor recreation; these are available from the tourism office at 518-483-6788. Clinton County offers a magazine-size guide, available by calling 518-563-1000. Hamilton County has a series of pamphlets about hunting and fishing, snowmobiling, craft shops, dining, and lodging, plus a magazine-format booklet, available by calling 518-648-5239.

A selection of chambers of commerce and visitor information centers are listed below; check out www.adirondacks.com for links to these towns and areas.

Lake George and Southeastern Adirondacks
Bolton Landing: Box 368, NY 9N, Bolton Landing, NY 12814; 518-644-3831; www.boltonchamber.com

Chestertown–Brant Lake–Pottersville (Adirondack Regional Chambers of Commerce): P.O. Box 490, NY 8, Chestertown, NY 12817; 518-494-2722 or 1-888-404-2722; www.adirondackchamber.org

Hague Ticonderoga: NY 9N, Hague, NY 12836; 518-543-6239 (in summer only); www.hagueticonderoga.com

Lake George: P.O. Box 272, US 9, Lake George, NY 12845; 518-668-5755 or 1-800-705-0059; www.lakegeorgechamber.com

Lake Luzerne: Box 222, Lake Luzerne, NY 12846; 518-696-3500; www.lakeluzerne-chamber.org

Schroon Lake: P.O. Box 726, Main Street, Schroon Lake, NY 12870; 518-532-7675 or 1-888-724-7666; www.schroonlake.org

Stony Creek: Box 35, Stony Creek, NY 12878; 518-696-4563; www.stonycreekchamber.com

Warrensburg: 3847 Main Street, Warrensburg, NY 12885; 518-623-2161; www.warrensburgchamber.com

Champlain Valley

Essex County Visitors Information Center: Bridge Road, Crown Point, NY 12928; 518-597-4646; www.lakeplacid.com

Ticonderoga-Crown Point: Box 70, Ticonderoga, NY 12883; 518-585-6619

Westport: General Delivery, Westport, NY 12992; 518-962-8383; www.westportny.com

High Peaks and Northern Adirondacks

Lake Placid/Essex County Visitors Bureau: 2610 Main Street, Lake Placid, NY 12946; 518-523-2445; www.lakeplacid.com

Saranac Lake: 39 Main Street, Saranac Lake, NY 12983; 518-891-1990 or 1-800-347-1992; www.saranaclake.com

Whiteface Mountain Regional Visitors Bureau: NY 86, Wilmington, NY 12993; 518-946-2255 or 1-888-WHITEFACE; www.whitefaceregion.com

Northwest Lakes

Tupper Lake: 121 Park Street, Tupper Lake, NY 12986; 518-359-3328; www.tupperlakeinfo.com

Central and Southwestern Adirondacks

Blue Mountain Lake Association: NY 28, Blue Mountain Lake, NY 12812; 518-352-7659

Central Adirondack Association: P.O. Box 68, Old Forge, NY 13420; 315-369-6983; www.caany.com

Gore Mountain Region: Tannery Pond Community Center, NY 28 and Main Street, North Creek, NY 12853; 518-251-2612 or 1-800-880-GORE; www.goremtnregion.org

Indian Lake: Main Street, Indian Lake, NY 12842; 518-648-5112; www.indian-lake.com

Inlet: 160 NY 28, Inlet NY 13360; 315-357-5501; www.inletny.com

Long Lake/Raquette Lake: P.O. Box 496, NY 28N, Long Lake, NY 12847; 518-624-3077; www.longlake-ny.com or www.centraladirondacks.com

Speculator–Lake Pleasant–Piseco: NY 30 and 8, Speculator, NY 12164; 518-548-4521; www.adrkmts.com

Town of Webb: 3140 NY 28, Old Forge, NY; 315-369-6983; www.oldforgeny.com

10

IF TIME IS SHORT

A whirlwind tour to see the Adirondacks can mean an awful lot of time spent in the car rather than getting to know a few nice places. Maybe it's best to carefully consider your tastes and concentrate your energy within a 40-mile area.

If you're a history buff and want to stroll through attractive, well-preserved towns and old forts, then head for the Champlain Valley, especially Ticonderoga, Crown Point, Westport, and Essex. Great restaurants and lovely bed & breakfast accommodations in Essex and Westport offer an excellent counterpoint to more rustic experiences. If you crave sweeping mountain vistas, aim your sights at the High Peaks, highlighting Keene Valley, Keene, and Lake Placid. The view from downtown Lake Placid, with chains of craggy peaks marching around the village, is unlike any other town in the park. If you like clean, island-dotted lakes, use Upper Saranac, Cranberry, Long, Blue Mountain, Indian, Raquette, Piseco, or Lake Pleasant as a base. For a terrific overview—literally—charter a floatplane from Long Lake or Inlet or take flight above the High Peaks from Lake Placid.

The magnificent Water Witch *at the Adirondack Museum, in Blue Mountain Lake.*
Courtesy of the Adirondack Museum; photograph by Richard Walker

Recommended drives include NY 22 along Lake Champlain, NY 73 between Keene and Lake Placid, NY 30 between Long Lake and Lake Pleasant, and the Blue Ridge Road between Interstate 87 (the Northway) and Newcomb. Take a trip up the toll roads on Prospect or Whiteface Mountains; the views before you get to the summit are amazing, and accessible. Incidentally, the Northway offers quite possibly the most scenic high-speed road experience in the Northeast.

A FEW SUGGESTIONS FOR PLACES TO SEE OR STAY:

LODGING

The Hedges (518-352-7325; 11 Hedges Road, Blue Mountain Lake). Beautifully restored rustic architecture, good cooking, and wine list; a very private spot on the lake where families have vacationed since the 1920s.

The Lake Placid Lodge (518-523-2700; www.lakeplacidlodge.com; Whiteface Inn Road, Lake Placid). When this venerable resort reopens to the public in 2008 (a fire razed its main historic lodge in 2005), it will be great—a stylish rustic/Arts and Crafts—style lakeside structure with the same high standards for food and wine, rooms, and cabins.

Mirror Lake Inn Resort and Spa (518-523-2544; www.mirrorlakeinn.com; 77 Mirror Lake Drive, Lake Placid). It's right in town and a quick walk to the shops on Main Street, it's elegant, and it does everything well: lovely rooms, fine dining, a newly refurbished spa, a sweet little beach on Mirror Lake, and theme getaways, such as the Adirondack Food & Wine Weekend.

The Sagamore (518-644-9400; www.thesagamore.com; 110 Sagamore Road, Bolton Landing). A particularly beautiful spot on Lake George, this is a thoroughly luxurious modern resort with an exceptional eighteen-hole golf course, several gourmet restaurants, spa, huge indoor pool, and tennis. Do take a cruise on the *Morgan*, a handsome wooden tour boat that leaves from the Sagamore dock.

CULTURAL ATTRACTIONS

The Adirondack Museum (518-352-7311; wwww.adkmuseum.org; NY 28/30, Blue Mountain Lake). Generally open from late May through Columbus Day, and no visit to the Adirondack Park is complete without spending a whole day here. The scope of the exhibits ranges from classic watercraft to fine arts to indigenous crafts.

Adirondack Park Agency Visitor Interpretive Centers (518-327-3000; www.adkvic.org; NY 30, Paul Smiths and 518-582-2000, NY 28N, Newcomb). Exhibits on the park's natural history; interpretive trails for hiking, skiing, and snowshoeing; and numerous programs for adults and children from preschoolers to teens. Open year-round.

Fort Ticonderoga (518-585-2821; www.fort-ticonderoga.org; 30 Fort Ti Road, Ticonderoga). A handsomely restored fortress that played important roles in the French and Indian Wars and the American Revolution; it's in a beautiful promontory on Lake Champlain. Plan your visit on a nice day so you can enjoy the view. Open early May through late October.

The Natural History Museum of the Adirondacks (The Wild Center) (518-359-7800; www.wildcenter.org; 45 Museum Drive, Tupper Lake). A beautiful new state-of-the-art museum devoted to the natural history of the region. The live otters steal the show. Workshops, lectures, and events are scheduled throughout the year; the museum's Fourth of July Wild Fest event is a big hit, with nationally renowned music acts, booths, and demonstrations.

Sagamore Great Camp (315-354-5311; www.sagamore.org; Sagamore Road, 4 miles off NY 28, Raquette Lake). The real deal, a grand rustic estate in the heart of the wilderness. Guided tours are offered twice daily in summer; inquire about May through October schedule. Concerts, workshops, and other activities are offered on many weekends.

RESTAURANTS

Interlaken Inn (518-523-3180; www.theinterlakeninn.com; 39 Interlaken Avenue, Lake Placid). Lake Placid's hideaway hotel, with a lovely dining room, cozy bar, and fantastic food.

Owl at Twilight (518-251-4696; 1322 County Rte. 29, Olmstedville). New American/Latin—inspired dishes draw an incredibly loyal fan base. Olmstedville may seem a little out of the way, but a meal at this place with its serene atmosphere (and a screen porch for summer dining) is worth the drive. Open Friday, Saturday, and Sunday.

The *William West Durant* (315-354-5532; Pier One, Raquette Lake). A wonderful tour boat that presents a movable feast as it cruises Raquette Lake, the fourth largest lake in the Adirondacks. Open May through October.

If you don't see any critters in the wild, stop by the Natural History Museum of the Adirondacks, in Tupper Lake, and meet Squeeker, one of the resident otters. Courtesy of the Natural History Museum of the Adirondacks

THE ADIRONDACKS IN FIVE REGIONS

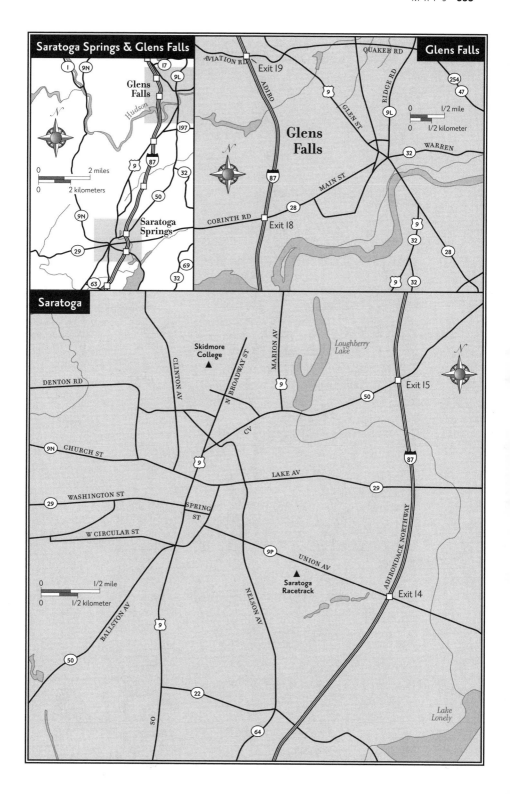

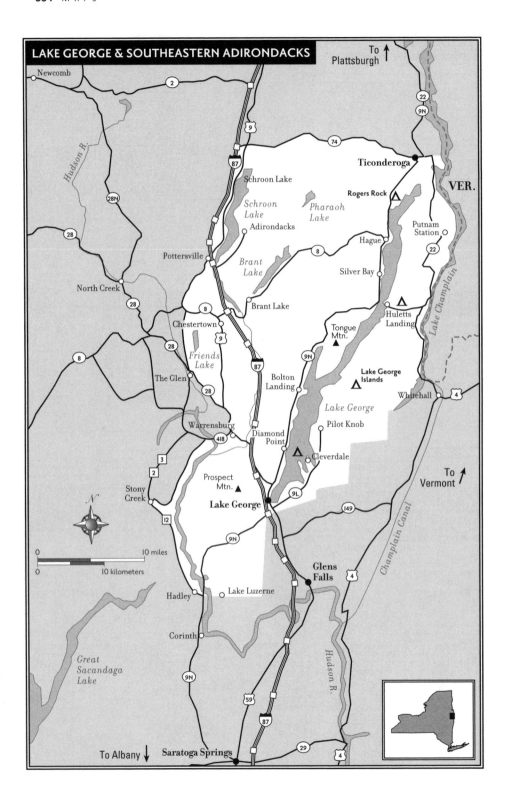

LAKE GEORGE & SOUTHEASTERN ADIRONDACKS

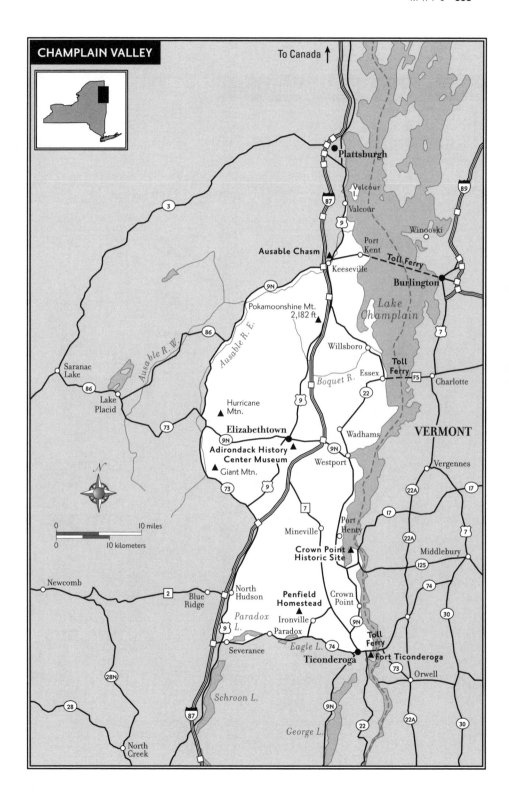

CHAMPLAIN VALLEY

To Canada ↑

Plattsburgh

Valcour I.

Valcour

Winooski

89

3

87

Ausable Chasm

9

Port Kent

Toll Ferry

Keeseville

Burlington

9N

Lake Champlain

Pokamoonshine Mt. 2,182 ft

Willsboro

7

Ausable R. W.

Ausable R. E.

86

Saranac Lake

Boquet R.

Essex

Toll Ferry F5

Charlotte

86

Lake Placid

22

9

Hurricane Mtn.

73

Elizabethtown

Wadhams

VERMONT

9N

Adirondack History Center Museum

9N

Westport

Vergennes

Giant Mtn.

73

9

22A

17

N

7

17

7

0   10 miles
0   10 kilometers

Mineville

Port Henry

22A

Middlebury

Crown Point Historic Site

125

Newcomb

2

Blue Ridge

North Hudson

Penfield Homestead

Crown Point

74

74

9

Paradox L.

Ironville

9N

30

Paradox

Eagle L.

74

Toll Ferry

Severance

Ticonderoga

Fort Ticonderoga

73

Orwell

28N

Schroon L.

28

87

9N

22

22A

30

North Creek

George L.

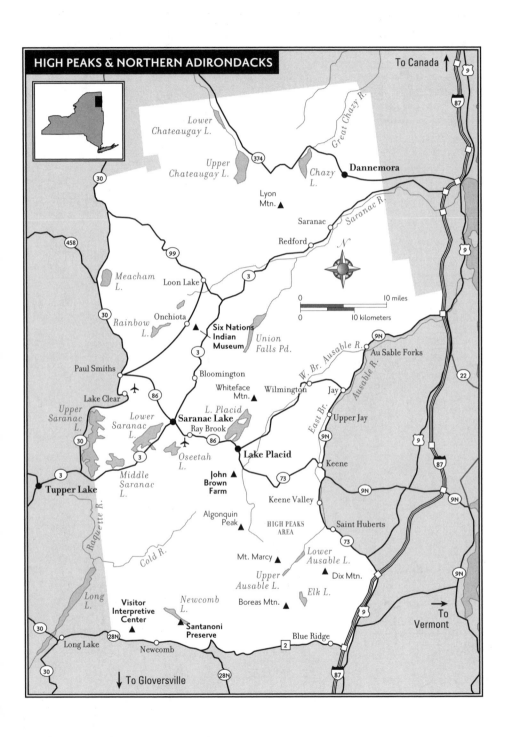

HIGH PEAKS & NORTHERN ADIRONDACKS

To Canada

Lower Chateaugay L.

Upper Chateaugay L.

Great Chazy R.

Dannemora

Chazy L.

Lyon Mtn.

Saranac

Redford

Saranac R.

Meacham L.

Loon Lake

Rainbow L.

Onchiota

Six Nations Indian Museum

Union Falls Pd.

W. Br. Ausable R.

Au Sable Forks

Paul Smiths

Bloomington

Lake Clear

Whiteface Mtn.

Wilmington

Jay

Ausable R.

Upper Jay

Upper Saranac L.

Lower Saranac L.

Saranac Lake

L. Placid

Ray Brook

East Br.

Tupper Lake

Middle Saranac L.

Oseetah L.

Lake Placid

Keene

John Brown Farm

Keene Valley

Algonquin Peak

HIGH PEAKS AREA

Saint Huberts

Cold R.

Mt. Marcy

Lower Ausable L.

Dix Mtn.

Raquette R.

Upper Ausable L.

Elk L.

Long L.

Visitor Interpretive Center

Newcomb L.

Boreas Mtn.

Santanoni Preserve

To Vermont

Long Lake

Newcomb

Blue Ridge

To Gloversville

0 10 miles
0 10 kilometers

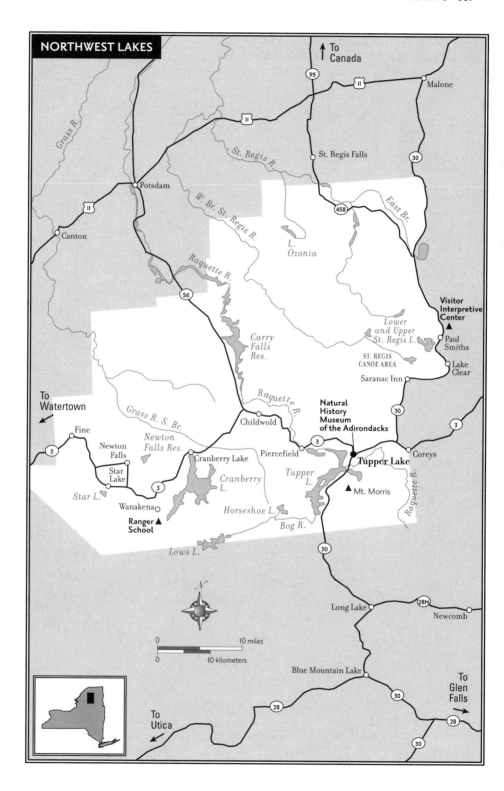

NORTHWEST LAKES

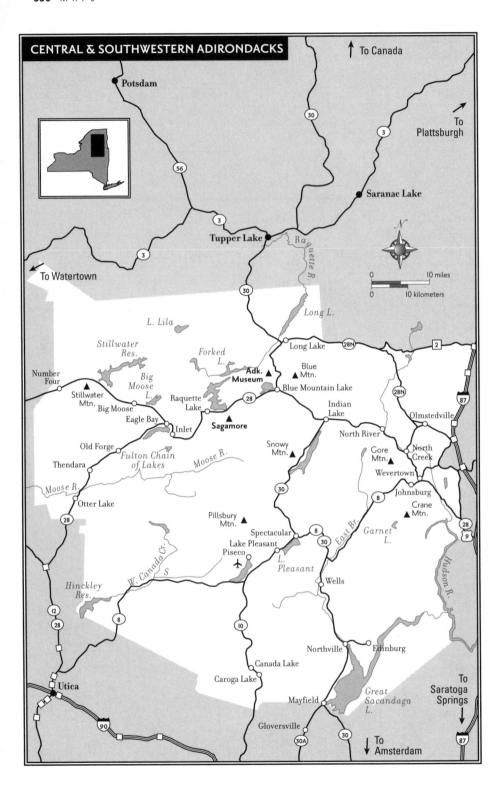

CENTRAL & SOUTHWESTERN ADIRONDACKS

General Index

Lodging by Price

Dining by Price

Dining by Cuisine